CONJURIS

FOR PLEASURE AND PROFIT

Cover design by Alex Sumner

Published by
Thoth Publications
64 Leopold Street, Loughborough, LE11 5DN
ISBN 978 1 913660 34 5
Web address: www.thoth.co.uk
email: enquiries@thoth.co.uk

CONJURING DEMONS

FOR PLEASURE AND PROFIT

AN ABRAMELIN MEMOIR,

By

ALEX SUMNER

Dedicated to Angel McAllister, with love.

Contents

Illustrations

Acknowledgements

Pictures

Cover artwork : Angel – https://www.maxpixel.net/Light-Angel-Mood-Magic-Spirituality-Moon-Fantasy-4806740 accessed 2022-02-22, licensed under Creative Commons Zero. Demon – https://static.wikia.nocookie.net/halfbreedbattles/images/1/12/Demons.jpg/revision/latest?cb=20191123193018 accessed 2022-02-22, licensed under the Creative Commons Attribution-Share Alike License 3.0 (Unported) [CC-BY-SA].

"Jacob's Ladder" picture of the Tree of Life : https://commons.wikimedia.org/wiki/File:Jacobs_ladder_config.png accessed 2022-02-11, licensed under the Creative Commons Attribution-ShareAlike 4.0 International License.

Thanks to :

My fiancée ; my family ; Tom Clarke ; Markus Katz ; Aaron Leitch ; M… my Holy Guardian Angel ; and GOD.

None of the organisations mentioned herein – Masonic, Martinist, Magical or Mystical – endorsed the writing of this book, and I do not claim to be a spokesman for any of them. However, many of their members gave me invaluable help and encouragement, for which I thank them all.

Introduction

And Jacob was left alone ; and there wrestled a man with him until the breaking of the day. And when he saw that he prevailed not against him, he touched the hollow of his thigh ; and the hollow of Jacob's thigh was out of joint, as he wrestled with him. And he said, Let me go, for the day breaketh. And he said, I will not let thee go, except thou bless me.[1]

*

The day of the interview I felt nervous as to whether I would get the job or not. The recession had hit the City, and I decided I needed a permanent job to provide the security that contract work could not offer. Hiding in the firm's toilets in advance of the meeting, I calmed myself by performing the Middle Pillar Ritual, pulling an abundance of white light into my aura, and visualising success for the encounter to come with crystal clarity.

I walked into the meeting room, and surprised myself by giving the best performance of my life. I found myself isolated outside my comfort zone, yet I functioned in that curious state experienced by soldiers who, in the moment of battle, exclude from their mind whether they have any fear or not. I said the exact things I needed to please the managers grilling me, and all of it being true : I had succeeded in presenting myself in the best possible manner.

I got the job alright : however it amounted to a Pyrrhic victory. Although it had the benefit of permanence, it represented a pay-cut compared to some of the more prestigious contracts I had had whilst in the city. I could only console myself by relying on the additional income from my book-sales. Nevertheless, for the first time in my life I had a pension, and the wherewithal to move into a new apartment.

Eleven years later, when the pandemic hit, the City became a ghost-town, new contract work evaporated, and those temping at the time found themselves furloughed. I, however, having a permanent contract, could not get furloughed myself, so my employers told me to work from home on full-pay instead. The little piece of magic which I had performed in their toilets many years previously had, in effect, given me the ability to fulfil a lifetime ambition : the Abramelin Operation.

*

---

[1] *Genesis* 32 : 24 – 26 (King James Version).

During the year 2020, the COVID-19 Pandemic affected people across the world in a number of different ways. Living under lockdown for a greater part of the year, they discovered ZOOM, working from home, reduced air-pollution, facemasks, furloughing, social distancing, and hand-sanitising. Panic-buying of lavatory paper and the Thursday-night Clap for Heroes came and went : paranoid conspiracies about first the virus itself and subsequently the attempts at creating a vaccine did not disappear so easily. Captain Tom became a hero in the UK, as well as a Knight, before his passing. For a great part of the year, *no news occurred* : since everyone remained at home, reporters could only find yet another angle to spin on the dreaded disease.

More serious, though, proved the varied ways that people trapped at home formulated to cope with day to day living. Some experienced a descent into a hell of mental health problems and domestic abuse. Others found an opportunity to become a star in their own living room, as they learnt that all manner of day-to-day interaction, from running a business, to leading a fitness class, hosting social events for clubs who up to now had only ever met in person, to even staging raves and rock concerts, could take place through video-conferencing software.

I personally chose to use the time to carry out a lengthy Magical Ritual to invoke an Angel and subsequently summon and bind all the Demons of Hell.

I can imagine that a sceptic reading this might wonder whether this itself provided an example of the mental health problems I mentioned above ? If so, the lockdown had not caused it : I had built up to it for almost the whole of the preceding twenty-five years.

I first became seriously interested in the *practice* of the Occult in the mid-nineties, although *Unexplained* Magazine, Usborne Books' *Mysterious Powers and Strange Forces*, Arthur C Clarke's *Mysterious World,* and latterly, *Call of Cthulhu* Role Playing Game, had all planted the seeds of my fascination in my childhood. When I renewed my interest as a college student, I read almost every book on the Occult with no discrimination whatsoever.

Soon, however, my beliefs began to crystalise, and I came to pay particular attention to the works of Dion Fortune. By using her books – especially *The Mystical Qabalah*[2] – as a starting off point, I started to explore the various influences to which she herself referred, and soon became acquainted with the Golden Dawn, and Aleister Crowley.

No-one can read Crowley without becoming aware of the great importance he attached to *"The Book of the Sacred Magic of Abramelin the Mage,"* a 15th century grimoire first translated into English by the founder of the Golden Dawn

---

[2] FORTUNE (1935)

(and one of Crowley's erstwhile mentors), Samuel Liddell MacGregor Mathers.[3] Crowley effused about it in his own "Autohagiography,"[4] and identified its fundamental concept, "Knowledge and Conversation of the Holy Guardian Angel," as nothing less than the central attainment of his own system of thought, Thelema, which he spent his life promulgating.

I have always hesitated to consider myself as a card-carrying Thelemite, as I do not care to emulate what I see as Crowley's personal failings. But I cannot deny that Crowley made himself probably the single-most influential occultist of the twentieth century, and maybe of any century, and that *Abramelin* remains an important occult text because of him.

Hence : not long after first reading about this grimoire, I came across it on sale in a (mainstream) bookshop on Charing Cross Road (Blackwell's – not there anymore, unfortunately). I bought it and devoured it : but otherwise, I felt content to let it sit on my shelf for the next quarter of a century. The main problem, as I saw it, consisted in the commitment it demanded, which involved having one's own place *and* remain off-work for at least six months. Living in the west, one cannot afford one's own place to live unless one works for it, and if one *does* work for it one can hardly take the time-off. Hence, short of coming into a large inheritance, or winning the lottery, modern life militates strongly against the Abramelin Operation : *unless a worldwide Pandemic forces one to stay off work, on full pay.*

Or so I had assumed before starting. After having completed it, I would revise my opinion. Nevertheless, before starting the Abramelin Operation proper, I had spent the intervening twenty-five years studying and practicing Ceremonial Magick, mainly in the context of the Golden Dawn and grimoires such as the Lesser Key of Solomon. I practiced lucid dreaming and astral projection : I meditated regularly and could often reach deep mystical states of consciousness. I not only became familiar with the Bornless Ritual, but I also chose to *memorise* it as an exercise one afternoon when I had nothing else to do. I even believed I had made contact with my Holy Guardian Angel itself, but via a method other than *Abramelin.*[5]

Hence, come Easter Monday 2020, I started my own *Abramelin* operation not as a complete newbie, but as an already experienced magician, and moreover with having an idea about how to recognise an authentic contact with my Holy Guardian Angel should one occur within the next six months. I cannot therefore

---

[3] MATHERS (1900).

[4] CROWLEY (1929)

[5] I talk about this in greater detail under Day 15 : *vide infra.*

claim complete objectivity when describing what happened during my Abramelin semester : I worked from a very definite set of preconceived notions.

One might argue that I didn't *need* to do the Abramelin operation, that my magical development did not render it strictly necessary : but I went ahead with it all the same for three especial reasons :

Firstly, although the book had lain on my bookshelf for a quarter of a century, yet I had resolved after first reading it that one day I would actually accomplish the Abramelin operation. Hence, with enforced lockdown caused by the Covid-19 pandemic, I realised I had an excellent opportunity to achieve a lifetime-ambition.

Secondly, precisely because it *does* have so much fame as a grimoire, and "knowledge and conversation of the Holy Guardian Angel" constitutes such an important topic in the occult world, I felt in all conscience that I could not contribute to any discussion on the matter without first having done it myself. If I could not speak from a position of experience, anything I did say would just increase the idle chatter, of which too much existed in the world already.

Thirdly, I did it for the Art. This book which you now read comprises my Work of Art. In Conceptual Art, the important moment takes place when the idea forms in the Artist's head, and what happens subsequently becomes the outward expression of that moment. So, whereas an artist like Lindsay Seers can create an installation devoted to a concept she has devised : yet it amounts to a staging post. The Art began in her mind (and maybe not even there), manifests as the installation : but in a sense the people attending the installation form part thereof, so that the Art does not stop there but continues onwards in the reactions of the audience. In the same way, for *my* Concept I decided that I should perform this magical operation, and then write a book about it : you, by reading this and reacting to what I write, become a participator in the artistic process. Because Conceptual Art does not reify as a discrete entity but consists in an ongoing interaction between the Artist, the work itself, and the audience, one might even say that Art spreads like a Virus. Which I suppose is rather an unfortunate analogy given the circumstances in which this book came to be written.

One could therefore describe this book as a "spiritual successor" to my 2013 novel *Taromancer*, in that I went through the magical operation described in that book as well : the main difference being that I wrote that up in the form of a fictional story : whereas as this current work is intended as autobiography.

Finally, I ought to make some apology for what some might see as "Unverified Personal Gnosis," a current buzzword on occult-related social media around about the time I wrote this. In this book I mention such terms as "Knowledge and Conversation of the Holy Guardian Angel," "Samadhi," "Angel contact,"

"Success," etc, without any sense of modesty or irony. Does this mean that I claim the status of Guru, or Master, or Ipsissimus ?

I *do* claim that Unverified Personal Gnosis only ever causes a problem if one uses it to assert one's authority *in opposition to other people*. However, without such opposition, no problem exists. I feel I ought to say this because UPG seems such a common experience of people on the path that only a fool would deny that it occurs. Strip away all the ego-issues, it becomes a valuable treasure, precious to each individual. Trying to invalidate other people's treasure – whether from a position of inferiority or supposed superiority – that's bad.

"Ye are Gods," as Jesus said to a crowd of angry people about to stone Him. If this book helps convince people "Knowledge and Conversation of the Holy Guardian Angel" of its reality and attainability, and that they would find it easier to achieve than many seem to think – and hence *drop their own stones* and take up the "Sacred Magic" themselves – I will have judged this book to have achieved its purpose.

What is Abramelin Magic ?

In 2016 the film-maker Liam Gavin wrote and directed the horror film *A Dark Song*, in which an occultist helps a woman perform a lengthy ritual, identified in the script as "the Abramelin Operation," in order to make contact with a Holy Guardian Angel. The film depicts the various ritualistic preparations ; the shenanigans up to which the pair get ; and an important plot-twist at the Mid-Point which threatens to derail the entire project.

This film, being the only movie to ever mention Abramelin in the history of cinema, has given *The Book of the Sacred Magic of Abramelin the Mage* its highest ever profile in popular culture outside the limited circle of occult enthusiasts. I therefore find myself obliged to make the following statement, which will prove crucial to understanding my own book, to wit :

The *real* Abramelin Operation is Nothing like that depicted in *A Dark Song.*

A Holy Guardian Angel does feature, as do many demons, but apart from that, Gavin has changed *every* detail about the procedure, apart from the name. Far from intending any disrespect towards Gavin's work, I understand why he did so : he wanted to come up with something deliberately dramatic.

I labour the point, because I have come into contact with people on the internet speaking confidently on the subject, but having no idea that *A Dark Song* is a work of fiction. Instead, I can summarise the real story of Abramelin as follows :

The manuscripts which refer to the Magic of Abramelin describe it as "the Sacred Magic" or "the Mystical Cabala of the Egyptians and Patriarchs," but

xvi   CONJURING DEMONS FOR PLEASURE AND PROFIT

ironically not as "Abramelin," until after the publication of the famous Mathers edition. Up to that point Abramelin amounted to no more than a character in the story told by Abraham the Jew - in one manuscript the title page makes Abraham, not Abramelin, the eponymous hero.

I, however, shall refer to it as "Abramelin" as the name most familiar to modern occultists. Abramelin magic comprises three parts :

- An initial operation lasting six months – or eighteen months, depending on which source you read – known as the notorious "Abramelin Operation" ;
- A seven-day ritual, to which I shall refer as "the Culmination Ritual" as it completes the preceding Abramelin Operation, and to which the Operation has been leading all this time ; and
- The follow-up work, or the actual day-to-day practice of the Sacred Magic.

The "Abramelin Operation" consists of a number of daily rituals, at the beginning of the rite at dawn and in the evening, every day for the period of the operation : each ritual involving a theurgical rite of self-reflection, leading to a kind of spiritual purification. In the first third, the operand concentrates on confessing his or her sins, and hence purifying the Moral side of their character. In the second third, one continues the confession, but adds in making a daily study of Holy Scripture as well. In the final third of the period, one adds an extra ritual at noon as well, and the operand updates his or her aspiration to specifically invoke the good angels. The operand must also perform certain other duties and make certain lifestyle changes (e.g., following a vegetarian diet, etc).

The "Culmination Ritual" consists of, after one day devoted to preparation, attaining what has become a much-abused term in modern occultism, "Knowledge and Conversation of the Holy Guardian Angel," over the next three days ; and binding all the various spirits over the last three days. At least : a literal reading of the source-texts gives this impression, but as I later realised, the first glimmerings of Angelic-contact begin months before, during the term of the Abramelin Operation itself. Full Knowledge & Conversation is really just the *end* of the process.

The follow-up work consists mainly of : firstly, at least once a week on the sabbath (or on the Holy day of your particular religion) to commune with one's Holy Guardian Angel ; secondly, spending time with one's Holy Guardian Angel to resolve the finer points of how to make the Sacred Magic work ; and thirdly, the actual practice of Sacred Magic, typically through the use of "word squares," which derive their power from the spirits that one has bound during the Culmination Ritual. Most of the word squares listed concern fantastical thaumaturgical phenomena which seem irrelevant over five hundred years after the book's supposed date of authorship : although I found some exceptions, which I discuss towards the end of this narrative. However, in one detail the original book gives an assurance that one's Holy Guardian Angel will teach you *more than is written in the book*. Abraham the Jew states that one can learn more word squares than the book contains :[6] and indeed more spirits exist with which to work than are listed.[7] This, to my mind, gives hope that through an ongoing interaction with one's Angel, one can develop one's own Sacred Magic, which will have relevance to oneself.

(Here, incidentally, lies another reason why Liam Gavin could never have realistically depicted the Abramelin Operation in *A Dark Song*. In ideal circumstances one performs the Operation ; everything goes according to plan ; one completes the Operation successfully ; and one lives happily ever after. Although the operand will be convinced that he or she has achieved something of tremendous importance, from the point of view of someone writing a horror film, this would prove incredibly *boring*. Hence, the only way to turn the Abramelin Operation into a movie plot would consist of having something *go wrong* – and hence *"causing all hell to break loose."*)

Most importantly: one should remember that the whole point of the Abramelin Operation – attaining Knowledge and Conversation of the Holy Guardian Angel – constitutes not an End, but a Beginning. I interpret the clear message of the book as that one can start to become a Ceremonial Magician only *after* attaining Knowledge & Conversation. In my case this amounted to rather a pious sentiment, as I had actually practiced ceremonial magic for a quarter of a century before attempting the Abramelin Operation. So now I have become just a neophyte in a new course of magic. Indeed, on the spiritual path, without any false humility I could say one is always a neophyte, because one will always have something new to learn. If I were to become a veritable Ipsissimus and reach the top of my current ladder, finding the bottom rung of a new ladder, leading to even greater mysteries of which at this moment I cannot conceive, would not surprise me in the very least.

(Another sense exists in which one always has the status of a Neophyte in that only then one learns the greatest lessons in the Occult – experiences one retains and uses throughout one's life. If one were to forget being a Neophyte, one would forget one's spiritual basis : true progression does not mean moving out of one phase and into the next, but adding continually to what one already possesses. I am a Neophyte : I am also everything that has come after, as well.)

I mention this because schools of thought exist – promulgated by people who have never gone through Abramelin, but have only read about it, in some cases

---

[6] MATHERS (1900), book 2, chapter 20.

[7] Ibid. chapter 19.

second- or even third-hand – who believe that Knowledge & Conversation of the Holy Guardian Angel amounts to the "Ultimate Attainment," reached only at the very End of the Path, and hence unattainable for most mortals. Consequently, they disempower their followers by giving them unrealistic expectations. Abraham the Jew predicted that only two or three out of every hundred who attempt the Abramelin Operation will attain :[8] but many more people who have heard of the phrase "Holy Guardian Angel" do not even know about the Abramelin Operation, nor that a book exists which sets out the true context of the origin of their supposed beliefs.

In the context of Abramelin, however, I could summarise it by saying : one does not do Magick to attain "Knowledge and Conversation of the Holy Guardian Angel," but the other way round : one attains the latter in order to do the former. It refers to the completion of the first and most important task of a Magician, but only the first. This would explain, for example, why "777" attributes "Vision of the Holy Guardian Angel" to Malkuth on the Qabalistic Tree of Life, because, like Malkuth, it provides the first step on the path of return.[9] It is, quite literally, a true Initiation.

---

[8] Ibid., chapter 20 again.
[9] CROWLEY (1909), Column XLV, row 10.

PHASE ONE

Day 1

13 April 2020

My oratory consisted of a room in the house in which I then resided, which doubled as an office. For the purposes of ritual, I cleared all the furniture to the walls to make a space in the centre of the room, but even so, I had hardly more than one square metre to use as my working area, two at most.

The room had an "Oriel Window" in its Eastern wall. The space enclosed by the Oriel, whilst technically inside, nevertheless lay outside the natural line of the wall of the room : it struck me that I could therefore adapt it for use as a stylised "terrace" where the spirits would congregate during the final days of the working.

In a departure from The Book, I did almost all of the operations "sky-clad" i.e., naked. Given that no-one either inside or outside the house ever saw my comings and goings at the time, privacy concerns never became an issue. Only two exceptions occurred, the one being the final seven days of the ritual, which I did wearing actual robes ; the other being one day during the final phase when the weather had begun to turn autumnal. To save myself from grabbing a dressing gown on future occasions I made sure the heating came on early every morning for the rest of the operation.

For my "magical diary," I used OneNote for Windows 10, which had the advantage of cloud storage on OneDrive. I typed my first entry as follows :

"Sunrise 6 :05am (British Summer Time).

"Up half an hour before - prepare with LL Ritual.[10] Then :

"LBRP.

"Bornless Ritual.

"Swear Oath. Confess sins.

"Licence to Depart.

"LBRP.

"Total time = 15 minutes."

By "The Bornless Ritual," otherwise known as "the Preliminary invocation of the Goetia," I refer to the same ritual that Crowley used in his own Abramelin semester. Originally a Gnostic-influenced rite of exorcism from the Greek Magical Papyri,[11] the Golden Dawn re-wrote it in the 19th century as an "extremely powerful invocation for daily use," and circulated it amongst its members for their interest. Crowley took this without acknowledging its source –

---

[10] "LL Ritual" = my usual was of abbreviating the title of the famous "Middle Pillar Ritual" i.e. because "LL" is the "Middle" of "Pillar."

[11] BETZ (1992), p103.

as he did so many other Golden Dawn documents – and incorporated it into his edition of the Goetia:[12] he later re-wrote it again as *Liber Samekh.*[13] I would return to my thoughts about the Bornless Ritual throughout my own Abramelin Operation.[14]

Looking back at it now, "15 minutes" seems absurdly short : I think the reason lay in me only really starting to incorporate meditation into the "confession" stage of my morning ritual from several days after the operation began. Even so, I plotted graphically how the duration of my morning ritual changed over the course of my Abramelin Operation : (see below).

The graph has a clear upward trend over the course of the sixth months. When I first started incorporating meditation into my morning rituals, I averaged around forty minutes. At the end of the six months, I averaged between eighty and ninety minutes – over twice as long.

I can identify three main reasons for this : firstly, going "by the book" required me to alter the nature of my morning ritual over time, by adding in extra elements in Phases Two and Three. Secondly : as I felt my own understanding of the Abramelin operation grow, I chose to add in extra elements when I felt it appropriate to do so (e.g., by incorporating the Lesser Banishing Ritual of the Hexagram, whereas previously I had only performed the Pentagram Ritual).

Thirdly, and most importantly : I developed the habit of putting more effort into performing the ceremonial, so that I would perceive the various rituals and meditations as continuously improving in quality. I suppose a desire for novelty and to avoid boredom actuated me, because otherwise I would have not looked forward to doing the exact same ritual two hundred days in a row.

---

[12] See: MATHERS (1995).

[13] "THE MASTER THERION" (1929), Appendix IV.

[14] See, e.g., day 20, *infra,* and numerous instances *passim.*

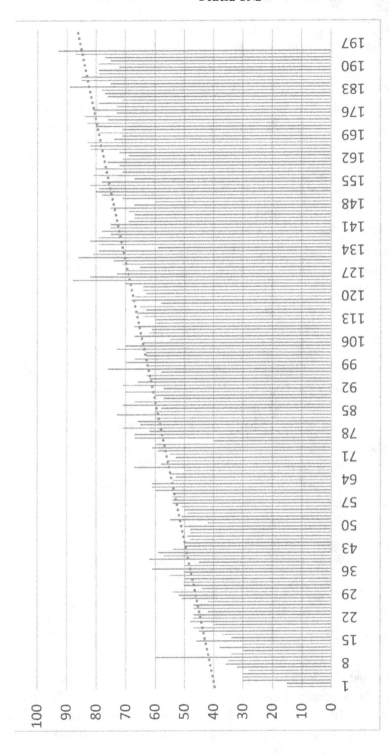

Figure 1 Graph showing how the length of my morning ritual changed over time during the Abramelin Operation : note the clear upward trend.

My diary entry for Day 1 continued :

"The combined effect of the LL Ritual and Bornless Ritual is peaceful, powerful. Had been sleepless prior to this, wondering what would happen.

"Afterwards I returned to bed : my fiancée said my energy was 'different' - radiating outwards like ripples on a pond, even to infinity itself. Afterwards, sleep - dreams of seeing her in light (my real fiancée was sitting in bed next to me reading Blavatsky)."

The Oath

The Oath I swore consisted of this :

"I will complete the Abramelin operation upon the same terms as did Ramsey Dukes. I will only have sex with 'A.' I will use my efforts to raise £10,000 for charity, in lieu of donating ten golden florins for the reception of the Sacred Magic. So mote it be !"

"Ramsey Dukes" (the pen-name of Lionel Snell, born 1945) is a writer and Chaos Magician who undertook the Abramelin Operation himself in 1977. The particular Oath he swore at the outset of his attempt ran like this :

"I vow that, subject to the conditions mentioned below, I will endeavour to keep to the Abramelin operation for six months starting on Easter Monday. As stated in the book, severe illness will be recognised as a God-sent hindrance. However, in the case of great danger to my immediate family, who have been such a support, I would also consider suspending the operation. Also, if I am the victim of bureaucratic intervention, and can find no way of delaying or buying time, then I will be forced to step down. In all such cases, or in any unforeseen mishap, I will consider very carefully and calmly and make my decision in the light of advice from the I Ching."

"I cannot see how I can obtain and use a child as instructed in the text, so I plan to do without – unless a suitable child conveniently makes himself known to me in time for training for the part.

Signed,
Lionel Snell." [15]

I included the line "I will only have sex with 'A.'" (i.e., my fiancée) as my token to chastity. This amounted to a bit of a cheat as I never dreamed of having sex with anyone else anyway : besides which, the black-and-white text of The Book allowed the Operator to have relations with his wife during the first year of their marriage, which (after the traditional Jewish manner) it considered an auspicious time to do so. I turned a blind-eye to the question of whether this still

[15] DUKES (2018).

counts if one only does the six-month instead of eighteen-month version of the Operation. To her credit, she insisted on me conserving my Odic force during the final culminating rituals, much to my chagrin.

Day 2

14 April 2020

From my magical diary :

> *Sunrise 6.03am. Get up with only 3 minutes to spare – nb : must sort out alarm.*

As it happened, later that day I found an app for my Android smartphone that would tell me the precise times for sunrise and sunset – and which also promised to sound an alarm half an hour before the break of day.

"How fortunate I am," I thought, *"to be living in a time when such things as smartphones and the Internet make it easier for one to perform the Abramelin operation !"*

Indeed, I later reflected just on how much the Magical practices of an age reflect the social trends of the times. E.g.

"A Brief History of Grimoire Magic Through the Ages"

In the times when magicians first started writing Grimoires, illiteracy affected a widespread swathe of the population. Only people who had a formal education could read. Hence, the potential readership of any particular grimoire would have included only either : the male children of royals and noblemen ; or those who had had a clerical education (e.g., monks).

Consequently, Grimoires tend to make assumptions about their readership, e.g., the Lesser Key of Solomon contains spells for raising armies and for destroying cities. Does this mean, as some modern magicians have tended to think, that the reader ought to take these metaphorically ? No ! The grimoire intended one to take them *literally* – these being the everyday concerns of its actual readership, i.e., Kings interested in waging war, and noblemen wanting to foment revolution.

Conversely – the central magical operation of The Sworn Book of Honorius exactly mirrors the lifestyle of a monk – the daily structure of the invocations reflecting that of the prayers laid down by the Benedictine Rule. Might not one explain this most plausibly by saying that *Honorius,* as a monk, wrote his book for other monks ? Again, the *Heptameron* slips in the instruction that one must consecrate the magical robe by saying a "Mass of the Holy Ghost" over it – difficult for a lay-man, but quite easy for someone already a priest.

Females, whether high- or low-born, tended not to receive a formal education, and hence not learn how to read, it being assumed that they would not have to use such a skill. Consequently, they would have had to resort to occult practices which did not rely on grimoires, such as folk magic or oral traditions.

Unfortunately, this explains why history stayed silent for the most part about the achievements of female magical practitioners : because they did not have access to Academia, Academia ignored them – except to record unfavourable details – such as allegations of Witchcraft.

From the Renaissance onwards, Grimoire magic started to extend to the Middle Classes. Magicians such as Dr John Dee provide the most famous early examples of this trend. As the son of a civil servant, Dee benefitted from a "public school" and University education. Anyone with a sufficiently rich enough family, noble or otherwise, could afford an education, which saw a lot of "commoners" now get involved in the occult (still only men – as far as History recorded). However : because the Upper classes still had the most wealth and power vested in them, royalty and nobility could still exert their influence over the development of the occult through the patronage system.

Truly inclusive education did not begin to take on anything like a modern form until the early 19th century, with women at last gaining access to Academia – and consequently, academic recognition. By almost certainly no coincidence, History started to record the exploits of women in the occult in favourable terms around this time, instead of dismissing them as Witches. Consequently, the writers of occult literature adopted the viewpoint that women would comprise a large part if not the majority of their readership, whilst occult orders experienced a great movement towards egalitarianism, most famously, in the Golden Dawn.

However, the reality of occultism in the 19th century indicated that male-female equality only really found favour with young, urban, sophisticates – the Victorian equivalent of *hipsters*. The incredulity at treating a female as an equal in the occult increased in direct proportion to the distance from the metropolis. Moreover, education at the time, although becoming more egalitarian with regard to the sexes, still had a bias in favour of the Middle Class, even though it had grown in proportion in the previous few centuries.

The Ceremonial Magic of the time tended to assume that given that the Victorians perceived *lacunae* in their understanding of old grimoires, then-current magical technology such as practices derived from Theosophy and spiritualism could fill these perceived-gaps and turn these old tomes into workable occult systems. This, for the time, constituted Modernism in magic. Had its practitioners said "…and in the future, people will be entitled to use the technology of the future as well," they might have made the jump to *Post Modernism*, but alas, this was not to be.

In the 20th century, three main trends arose which affected grimoire magic. Firstly traditional magical orders experienced a Decline. Secondly, the Occult became Commodified to an extent which had not previously existed. Thirdly, marked social changes occurred throughout the era, including those which arose as a consequence of World War Two, and the rise of Feminism.

The Decline of traditional orders such as the Golden Dawn on the one hand, combined with the lure of the almighty dollar on the other, led to the phenomena of the "Occult Manual." More than just a grimoire, these books described *whole magical systems* in detail – for example, Regardie's "The Golden Dawn," and the works of Franz Bardon and Aleister Crowley. This sparked a new wave of "Amateur" (in the pure sense of the word) occultism, such as the increased prominence of solo practitioners, and new occult orders to take the place of the old ones.

Meanwhile, at exactly the same time as the Decline of traditional occult orders, old-school grimoires drew greater attention than ever before. Orders tend to go into decline when they fail to uphold their own high-standards, or they admit people with insufferable personalities as members, or both. By coincidence – and a supreme irony – the same person caused both the downfall of the Golden Dawn, and the publication of new editions of Abramelin, the Goetia, and the Key of Solomon, i.e., MacGregor Mathers.

Hence, not only did interest in grimoires and related scholarship increase, but so did the number of occultists who wanted to explore these old grimoires, i.e., because they did not want to associate themselves with old-fashioned occult orders.

Meanwhile, society was changing. In Britain, at any rate, improved education came about as a consequence of the 1945 Labour Government, which undoubtedly owed its election to the combined effects of the Second World and the economic mess created by the *1935* Conservative government. This led to a breakdown in division between social classes, as it now meant that anyone of any social background could enjoy an education of the standard only enjoyed before then by the upper and middle classes.

At the same time, Feminism – the rise of which orders like the Golden Dawn in the late 19th century anticipated – came to prominence in a big-way throughout the 20th century. This combined with the breakdown of class structures ensured that the new occultism which arose in the 20th century incorporated all genders and all social classes, whereas previously it had remained the preserve of privileged men.

Hence, we saw a new vibrancy in Grimoire magic. For the first time the Publisher, not the Occult order, became a key person of influence. Unfortunately, this led to a Commodification of the Occult on a scale not heretofore experienced, but on the plus side this Commodification *did* drive many of the positive changes that the Occult in general and grimoire magic in particular experienced *(See illustration)*.

Now, in the first quarter of the 21st century (as I write), the rise of the Internet has caused the biggest change in the field of Grimoire magic. Notably, people like Joseph H Peterson and the late Benjamin Rowe converted many public-domain grimoires into electronic form and published them online, *for free*. I myself have benefitted directly from this development, as I used such resources to prepare for my own Abramelin operation (although I had also gone the old-fashioned route and bought a physical copy of Mathers' translation of Abramelin some twenty-years ago).

Moreover : for the first time in Grimoire magic history, a sense of *Community* exists. Grimoire magic practitioners from across the world can communicate with one another in relative safety, sharing ideas and best practices. Before the internet, no easy way existed for them to do so, hence each Grimoire magician developed his / her craft as best he / she could in isolation.

Unfortunately, I have noticed that the rise of social media has changed the manner in which public discourse on Grimoire Magic occurs on the Internet. I am old enough to remember when Social Media did not exist : my generation only had Usenet. An unmoderated group like *alt.magick* provided the venue of some interesting and enlightening discourse, but if some naïve person came along spouting anything resembling bullshit, the regulars would tell them to *fuck off* without mercy and in no short order. A minority of people – like myself – found this a refreshing tonic to the problem of ego-inflation, and welcomed the high-standard of intellectual debate this encouraged. The majority, however, those told to fuck off (or in the jargon of *alt.magick,* caught by the "idiot-filter"), found that Social Media allowed them to retreat to moderated online communities whereby if anyone said anything nasty, the moderators could block or expel them. Unsurprisingly, *alt.magick* declined at the exact same time that Social Media became prominent.

Discourse on Grimoire Magic still takes place on Social Media, but moderation in groups can lead to "echo-chambers" – the only voices heard reflect ones' own sentiments, as opposing points of view become excluded. "Woke Culture" increasingly means that nastiness causes blocking or expulsion, increasing political incorrectness.

The internet has also facilitated the increase of "less reputable grimoires," now published in ebook form. As we move from an "Internet-of-Computers" via an "Internet of Things" to an "Internet of Everything" I find it likely that Smart technology will change the way people appreciate Grimoires. I myself have already experienced this. I have performed magick whereby I found a Spirit's sigil (from the Lesser Key of Solomon) from the internet on my smartphone, as well as the "Enn" needed to invoke it, and manifested magical effects almost immediately. I consider it important that long before I attempted to do so, I had evoked the spirit in question by conventional means on a previous occasion – i.e., the old-fashioned route – although I wonder how many magicians will attempt this without that level of preparation.

I believe that the COVID19 pandemic of 2020-21 will not fail to enter the history books as one of the defining events of the 21st century. I already know at least one small way that this has affected Grimoire Magic : I felt motivated to knuckle-down to the Abramelin Operation directly as a result of being locked down, throughout the Spring and Summer of 2020. Not only did it provide something with which to take up my time whilst I remained under quarantine, but it also served as a substitute for the meetings of the Golden Dawn which had we had to abandon during the same time-period.

One wonders whether one will see if this reflects a wider trend in the occult community.

*

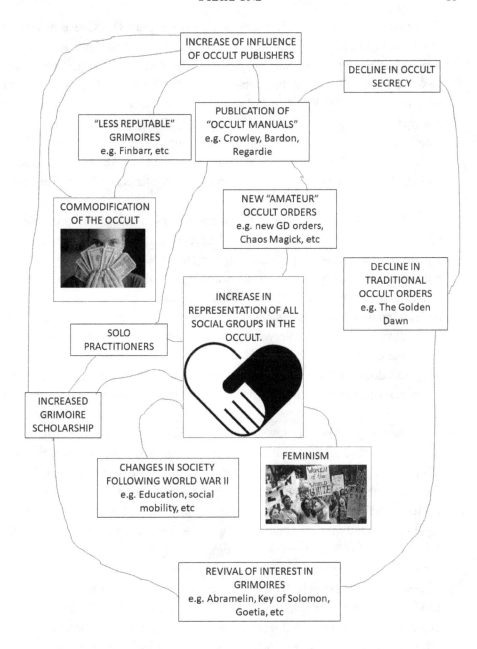

Figure 2 Mind map summarising the state of grimoire magic in the 20th Century

Back to my record of my daily Abramelin activities. I saw Day One as merely an introduction to the whole thing : Day Two became the first day I got into the serious business of "confessing my sins." So, for example, after performing the Lesser Banishing Ritual of the Pentagram and the Bornless Ritual (and, on this occasion, the Middle Pillar Ritual), I settled down into a period of "contemplating sins and my asking mercy for them" : on this day and on subsequent days I made a note of all the sins I recalled in my magical journal.

The prime result of all this confession throughout the Abramelin Operation consisted in provoking a serious contemplation of the nature of Sin, as well as the Miracle of Grace.

I did not understand the reason for confessing one's sins as due to the dogma of any religion, but for a very practical Ceremonial Magic consideration. The Abramelin operation ends with one conjuring the most fearsome demons of Hell who, one is led to believe, will do everything in their power to prevent the Magician imposing his Will on them. Hence the sins of the Magician become the demons' ammunition. The demons, in the face of this exorcism, I presume would say "Why should we listen to you, since you're a sinner ? You're not worthy to command us ! If you want *our* help, you'll have to do what *we* say !" And if the Magician does not have a credible answer for the demons, his whole magical operation will come to a stuttering halt if he does not want to make a full transition to *The Dark Side*.

On the first day that I confessed my sins in the proper manner (i.e., day 2), the ones that shocked me the most to remember them proved the very first to come to me. I could think of perhaps three incidents in my life when I felt appalled at the consequences of my actions, leaving me wondering whether any moral justification for them could. None of these incidents added up to "crimes" in any legal sense of the word, but this did not give me spiritual comfort. As I reflected : *Laws are created by Lawyers, not by Spiritual People.*

I remember using black magic to prevent a crime taking place. I told the spirit : "*Let no innocent person be harmed.*" As an unintended side-effect a person – the one committing the crime - did indeed suffer harm. The victim of the crime expressed both delight that I had succeeded beyond all expectations, and astonishment at my awesome magical powers. The incident, however, terrified me : I tried to console myself by thinking "*Oh well, the guy can't have been innocent, then.*" But even so, I had no idea that Goetic spirits really possessed that much power, and I had felt a mighty temptation to go ahead and choose to become a mighty sorcerer – the shocking result becoming a massive boost to my ego.

That I chose not to do so I attribute to my strong moral sense which I in turn attribute to my upbringing and my parents.

For a long time, I had terrible anguish over the situation. I had reduced myself to the status of the lowest, most despicable creature of which I could conceive – a thoroughly disgusting wretch with no more rectitude of character than that of a dumb animal – but then I realised :

I had done nothing more than become an American.

"This must be what Americans experience every time they shoot an intruder who breaks into their home," I thought. As an Englishman, my education had conditioned me to consider the idea of exacting vigilante justice against criminals as repugnant : yet I supposed that this ought not to afflict my conscience any more than it would to that of a US Citizen, with his or her Second Amendment rights, who deliberately keeps ordnance at home with the intent of defending themselves. The only difference being that instead of carrying a firearm, I had just attempted to use a magic spell : and even then, harming the target had not been the purpose thereof.

For me it presented a great moral dilemma : had I sinned, even though I had done it accidentally ? Even though I did not intend it ? Even though the target of my magick actually deserved it ? Cases where the moral issues are black and white are never troublesome, it's the grey areas which cause me sleepless nights !

On the day that I contemplated all this *again* as part of my Abramelin operation, I noted down that *"the greater sin is to take pleasure in having done it - of even letting it be a boost to my ego at all."*

I recalled other occasions of which I felt ashamed : when I thought I had hurt or offended people who said that they forgave me : yet I wondered : *"do they feel, or did they feel underlying resentment ?"*

The seriousness of my past misdeeds overwhelmed me. Surely, I must go to Hell for everything I had done ! Or if not go to Hell, then perhaps wait until my next incarnation to resolve my outstanding karma, for the burden of it weighed too heavily for me to discharge it in one lifetime. But then, if karma is real, then so must Destiny : in which case I had incurred a curse by being born into a life, only to ruin it by my failings. *"Just why* did *I incarnate in this body ?"* I reflected, as it appeared to me that even before I had begun to find out my life's true purpose, I had already beggared my quest by fucking it all up.

In short, I had to wrestle with the question : "How is it possible to have one's sins forgiven ?" What right do I have to claim that my sins are forgiven ? Not just out of concern over whether or not I will go to Heaven, but because it has relevance to the success of this Abramelin Operation, which I had resolved to complete ? That is to say, for an overtly selfish motive, as opposed to one only covertly so ?

At this point that I realised : I *cannot* forgive myself. But God *can*. Therefore, I could do absolutely nothing, except abandon all pretence of pride and ego, and humiliate myself before God, relying solely upon His Mercy.

I had in effect re-discovered the significance of the Christian teaching of Grace, i.e.

> *"For by grace you have been saved through faith, and that not of yourselves ; it is the gift of God, not of works, lest anyone should boast."*[16]

I often think that for over two-thousand years Christians have wrangled needlessly over the concept of "Salvation by Grace," when I perceive it as a very simple and understandable message. To state that one can achieve Salvation solely by Grace means recognising that God alone, being infinite, knows who is and who is not worthy of being saved. No finite being such as a human can speculate as to whether someone will go to Heaven or Hell after their demise : to attempt to second-guess *God* would seem to imply that someone in the Universe knows better than the Almighty ! Which would be blasphemous if it were not a complete absurdity.

When one says that one can only achieve Salvation through Grace, one admits that no-one has *entitlement* to being saved : and if it happens at all, it means we should ever thank God on account of His mercy. "Grace" indeed literally means "thanks," as in the Latin *Gratia,* Italian *Grazie*, Spanish *Gracias,* and the English "gratitude" ; whilst the Greek Χαρις serves the same purpose.

Hence : I cannot *hope* that God forgives my sins : so, if it turns out that He does so notwithstanding, I would owe exclusive *thanks* - i.e. Grace - to Him, for I have no entitlement in any way.

I think it ironic that undertaking an operation of Ceremonial Magic, out of self-interest, can lead me back to God : in that in order to perform it authentically, one learns one must divest oneself of any self-interest. This reminds me of an anecdote told by Crowley, of a magician of his acquaintance who took up black magic out of "sheer hatred of God and Christ" (Crowley never revealed whether he meant *himself* in the third person). The said black magician realised that in order to command the various devils he had to learn to identify with God, which lead him back to Divine Union in a manner not dissimilar to, amongst others, Miguel de Molinos (a Christian mystic, unfairly branded as a heretic).[17] I therefore find myself much in sympathy with Crowley's black magician, because like him I may have set out with an unworthy motive, but I nevertheless arrive at a Worthy one in spite of myself.

---

[16] *Ephesians* 2 :8-9 (KJV)

[17] See : CROWLEY, A, *"My Crapulous Contemporaries, no. IV : Wisdom While You Waite,"* in "The Equinox," Volume 1, book 5, March 1911.

Day 3

15 April 2020

As the days progressed, I continued to contemplate the nature of "sin," i.e., what exactly I ought to confess.

On Day Three, having confessed all the most serious things of which I could think, I felt myself at a loss. I experienced a *great* deal of shame over *small* number of incidents. Hence if I confessed everything all at once, I would quickly run out of sins to confess for the next two hundred days.

So after preparing with the Middle Pillar Ritual, and opening with the Lesser Banishing Ritual of the Pentagram and the Bornless Ritual, I had to dredge my memory for the "Confession" part of the morning ritual. As I wrote in my journal afterwards :

"Asking the Lord to be worthy enough to attain KCHGA, [18] and for forgiveness for those things identified yesterday. It occurred to me I should be as merciful to others as I have had mercy shown to me."

I then wracked my brains and decided :

"Also beginning to plead forgiveness for all my past lives as well."

I had departed from strict Christian theology, but I figured that whatever the Science of Reincarnation, by treating past-life memories *as if* real, positively helped me deal with the issues arising therefrom. In effect I identified "sin" as "Karma" – although the literalist would dispute my conflation of the concepts.

I doubted that Abramelin himself had meant past-life memories, but – it made sense *to me.*

I had not, in fact, ever made any serious study about the nature and extent of my past lives, as I had long abided by some advice from the occultist Franz Bardon :

" [I]t is without a doubt possible to investigate the previous incarnations as well. But the magician is warned against doing so, because any investigation of the future as well as of the former life, in his own case or that of another person, is a sort of meddling in the affairs of Divine Providence, and such a curiosity would cause dangerous consequences ... the magician is entirely responsible for all the blunders committed in his former lives. The only advantage would be that he would become conscious of the experiences in his former life, a fact that would never compensate for the disadvantages." [19]

---

[18] "Knowledge and Conversation of the Holy Guardian Angel." I had picked up the acronym from the internet at least as far back as the days of Usenet.

[19] BARDON (1971), Step IX, Magic Mental Training, section 14, "The Magic Mirror for Investigation of the Past, Present & Future."

Unfortunately, I now decided that undertaking something as momentous as the Abramelin Operation constituted a sufficiently important moment to become "entirely responsible for all the blunders committed in [my] former lives."

Besides which, on several occasions my curiosity had made me its bitch. I recall several years previously I had, on a whim, tried to incubate a dream about "The Corridor of Many Doors," a visualisation which has become so hackneyed amongst past-life therapists and their clients that I feel certain it must now have some sort of objective existence on the astral plane. On opening the door which I supposed would correspond to the previous incarnation which at the time held most importance to me, I looked in and I saw... the Freemason, mystic and writer, *Walter Leslie Wilmshurst*. I did not attach too much importance to this revelation at the time. Granted, I am both a Freemason and much influenced by Wilmshurst's writings in my conscious life. Hence, I supposed, if my Individuality had indeed occupied Wilmshurst's persona, that would perfectly explain how my present incarnation has turned out. However, precisely because it had provided a perfect explanation, it had vitiated itself as evidence towards a Scientific explanation of the reality of Reincarnation : a sceptic could dispute that I hadn't really had a past-life memory, claiming that my present life had informed the content of my dream instead, and I would have no position to say otherwise. In any case, it added nothing to my knowledge of myself : *or so I thought at the time...*

Some while after recovering this supposed past-life memory, I learnt something about Wilmshurst's life that I had not known at the time : to wit, following World War I Wilmshurst had become permanently estranged from his son, which became his biggest regret in life. With a shock I realised that the pain he must have felt over his estranged son *reflected my own pain at never becoming a father myself*. Hence, even if I had *not* incarnated as Wilmshurst in a former life, I could nevertheless resolve my own issues by taking Wilmshurst's pain – that is, the karma he would have incurred over the incident – as my own. The coincidence between myself and Wilmshurst's life struck me as downright spooky.

But I managed not to feel overwhelmed by the existential futility of it all. I had previously some familiarity with Kriya Yoga meditation, so by identifying each "sin" I ought to confess as an item of karma, I conceived of a plan of action consisting of raising each sin up from where I imagined they were stored (figuratively speaking) at the base of my spine, up my *Sushumna*, like Kundalini being raised to my *Sahasrara Chakra*. Or, in the language of the Golden Dawn, up from my "evil persona" via the Middle Pillar of the Tree of Life to my Higher Self.

Incidentally, when I refer to "Kriya Yoga" in this book, I use it as shorthand to mean a process *similar* to Kriya Yoga, or at least what I imagined as it. Paramhansa Yogananda, whilst writing about it extensively in his book nevertheless omitted revealing the precise details of his technique, on the basis that one could only give it to someone via a ceremony of initiation.[20] Needless to say, however, like all good occult secrets this has now become the subject of an exposé, or so at least one source has claimed.[21] Rather like Colonel Sanders' recipe for *Kentucky Fried Chicken*, anyone who has received the true secret in a legitimate manner remains tight-lipped, neither confirming nor denying anything. The author of the exposé which I read himself claimed that initiates told him that even if he actually knew the secret, it would prove useless to him if he had not received it from a proper teacher.[22]

By meditating in this way, I noted from my journal :

"This, plus the combined effects of the Middle Pillar and Bornless Rituals, is a calming, soothing experience."

Hence on that day, whether God *had* forgiven my sins or not, at least I felt better.

*

As I mentioned in the introduction, although I only now for the first time attempted to perform the Abramelin Operation, I believed that I had actually made contact with my Holy Guardian Angel over twenty years previously by other methods. Hence not only did I go into this operation with an idea of what an authentic experience of KCHGA would feel like should it occur, I believed that I had already enjoyed the benefits thereof these past two decades.

In my journal for day three, I noted :

"A strange coincidence. By strange chance, I discovered that I can now order items on the Amazon Vine programme. I thought I had been excluded from it, but apparently now not so."

In other words, during the day, after my ritual for the morning, I went on to the internet and on a whim I decided to visit the link to the Amazon Vine programme, which Rationality would have told me ought not to have worked. *It worked.* This had provided a source of a stream free items, many of which proved quite valuable : the deal being that by leaving a review for the product, I got to keep it

---

[20] YOGANANDA (1946), chapter 26.

[21] NIMIS (2018)

[22] Ibid.

afterwards. I thought Amazon had terminated my participation in the programme, but here, for some reason, I discovered otherwise.

The coincidence lay in that the first time Amazon invited me to join the Vine program when I invoked my Holy Guardian Angel on New Year's Day 2009, instead of making New Year's Resolutions in the conventional manner. I thus believe it the most successful piece of "manifesting" that I had pulled-off, and all because of my Holy Guardian Angel. That I now somehow found myself re-admitted to it again I took as a good omen for my current Abramelin Operation.

Day 4

16 April 2020

Although I tried to stick as close to "the Book" as possible, doubtless nit-pickers will point out that I did not succeed one hundred per cent. I can admit my fault in this, at least to an extent, especially as at the beginning I rushed with enthusiasm into starting the Abramelin Operation with the intent of only learning about how to do so later.

So, for example, The Book has an injunction against performing any other type of magic during the currency of the operation, but on numerous occasions during the six-months I performed examples of Golden-Dawn style rituals, such as the LBRP and the Middle Pillar Ritual, outside the scope of the operation. Ironically, my operation consisted of me adapting several Golden Dawn techniques for use in an Abramelin-style … such as the LBRP and the Middle Pillar Ritual.

The fact is that I am a Golden Dawn magician, and have identified as such for at least a quarter of a century : I actively performed Golden Dawn magic even before I became initiated in a formal order. I have such a complete immersion in the Golden Dawn that I use its techniques and teachings on a day-to-day basis, so to choose to refrain from doing so for any reason would have struck me as unnatural. *(The Golden Dawn itself was not meeting at the time in Britain, due to the COVID-19 restrictions then in place).*

When I first took up the Golden Dawn, I came almost immediately to the Meditation of the Neophyte Grade, i.e., to meditate upon a point, "as defined in Mathematics." (I have since come to suspect that Mathers got the idea for this and other meditations in the Golden Dawn from Lenain's *Science of the Kabbalah[23]*). I attempted to carry this meditation out by visualising a point in the form of a dot, holding the image before my mind's eye, and trying to maintain unbroken awareness thereon. This I found incredibly difficult, and I *almost* gave the whole thing up as impossible…

… Until I reasoned that although the Neophyte knowledge lecture had told me on *what* to meditate, the *how* proved considerably looser in definition, which led me to conclude that I should try to find the method most convenient to myself to arrive at the desired destination. Thus, in a spirit of experimentation, I soon found that the whole business of meditation upon a point became a great deal easier for me if I made an effort to deliberately relax my body and mind before attempting to do so. As it happened, I found that performing the Middle Pillar Ritual itself served to induce just the right state of relaxation.

---

[23] LENAIN (1823).

As an aside, although this made meditation easier, it did not make it *easy*. I often found that to meditate for *one minute* on a point or any other given subject took approximately *half-an-hour* – i.e., the first twenty-nine minutes attempting to meditate, and only in the last minute coming close to success.

Hence, twenty-five years later, when performing my morning Abramelin invocation, I got into the habit of preparing for the main invocation with the Middle Pillar Ritual, to get myself in the right frame of spirit. This entailed me getting up considerably earlier than the *"fifteen minutes before dawn"* specified in The Book, and performing a short magical rite which a critic might argue as being beyond the pale as regards Abramelin. Alternatively, one could counter-argue that the same Book gives the operator latitude as to the exact form that one's own invocations should take. Thus if one took the Book literally in every particular, it would lead to the paradox that one could acceptably incorporate one rite (such as the Middle Pillar Ritual) *within* one's Abramelin regime, but the exact same rite practiced apart therefrom would become anathema to it.

(This, incidentally, happened on at least one occasion during my Operation. On day seven - April 19th – I did this over ZOOM with some fratres and sorores, as a type of Healing Ritual.) The Reader will therefore appreciate that I believed (and still do) that one cannot take the Book one-completely literally, the more-so because Abraham the Jew wrote it in the fifteenth century : although one should always act as authentically as possible. I therefore carried on with my peculiar method of adapting my Abramelin practice, and not paying too much attention to the problem of not practicing other magical systems, unless they appeared to have a stark variance with the spirit of the Operation. E.g. on day four I noted in my journal that in addition to my Abramelin exertions I also performed the LBRP and Rose cross ritual, followed by "magick" *(i.e. sex)*.

Modernism did however prove to have a plus side. Thanks to the internet one can now find the *exact* date of sunrise and sunset on any given day. However, when I came to perform my Operation, I wanted an app that would function as a Sunrise-alarm automatically – but I could not find one (I had an Android smart-phone). I therefore got into the habit of looking up the time for sunrise and setting the alarm manually to thirty minutes prior thereto the night before, throughout the whole course of my operation.

Day 5

17 April 2020

By the fifth day, the structure of my morning ritual had evolved into this :
  *Sunrise : 5.56am. Up in good time to prepare with LL Ritual (good).
  Then :*

- *LBRP ;*
- *Bornless Ritual ;*
- *Entreaty to God that I may be worthy of attaining KCHGA ;*
- *Meditating on confessing my sins ;*
- *Licence to Depart ;*
- *LBRP.*

The entry *"(good)"* reflected my economy with words which I habitually employed when journaling. Had I found it unremarkable, I would not have mentioned it all, so I must assume that if I bothered to say it was "(good)" then at the time I would have experienced as mind-blowingly awesome.

Following on from my reflections about the nature of sin and Grace I had had two days previously, I noted :

  *"Have run out of sins for this life so am now meditating on resolving the
  Karma I incurred in previous lives as well."*

"Run out of sins !" And in less than five days as well ! I amended my point of view to something more modest as time-progressed, but I felt certain that I had recalled all of my most memorable sins in a very short-time – my life so far had indeed been *that* unexciting. Moreover, I figured that if God were to pardon my transgressions at all, I only needed to ask Him once : hence I did not feel inclined to keep confessing the same sin over and over again. I planned, after all, to remain here for some two hundred days, so unless I had seriously more sins to confess than of which I had awareness, *the confessing must serve some other purpose as well.* I thus began to pay even closer attention to the nature of my past-lives. I could not say that I had actual past-life memories, but instead I contemplated them in a theoretical sense, like a series of thought-experiments. E.g. If I did have one or more past-lives, what would they be like ? What implications would they pose ?

Hence, for me at any rate, forming my ideas about Reincarnation, Karma and past-lives became not so much a Spiritual exercise as rather one of Philosophy – albeit one with Spiritual implications. For example : I noted

  *"Thought : I inherited my talents for meditation, lucid dreaming and
  ceremonial magic from someone so I had better take ownership for their
  Karma as well."*

At least – I *assume* I inherited them. I mean that, given I have developed those talents somehow, saying they came from a past-life amounted to a case of *Post Hoc, Propter Hoc*. But if it *were* true then the point about taking ownership for Karma would stand. As it happened, in the absence of knowledge of actual Karma from those past-lives, I ended up assuming that that Karma existed all the same, and acted accordingly. In effect I took responsibility for *imaginary Karma*, although without either denying its reality, or implying its futility.

Again, I noted :

"Thought #2 : if one of my previous incarnations was as a guru, then that means I have to take responsibility for the chelas' *Karma as well."*

This might seem overly careful, but I could have only definitively ruled it out by having *complete* knowledge of my past-lives. In the absence of some or any past-life memories, I had to take the precaution, just in case.

In effect, I took responsibility for not just *my* imaginary Karma, but *other people's* as well.

*

After the ritual that day, I experienced some hypnogogic imagery whilst lying in bed : *"A Master Mason's apron with Hebrew writing all over it."* Being heavily involved in both Qabalah and Freemasonry, this could have quite easily arisen from my mind by chance, rather than revealing a major a key to my psyche : however, at the time I took it as indicative of a deeper meaning of which I had not yet thought. This became more significant as my Abramelin operation progressed.

Other imagery I experienced included *"A man in a red shirt."* "Why red ?" I asked myself. Perhaps it symbolised Death and Sacrifice, i.e., that of my Ego. Or in other words, my Holy Guardian Angel saw fit to communicate with me in the language of *Star Trek*.

More seriously, later that day I had a falling out with my fiancée. I had started the Abramelin operation whilst still in the process of moving in with her, a big step for both of us : however, that day, she suddenly got cold feet about the matter, and left me suddenly at our new place, announcing she would drive back to her old flat.

I however felt certain that she would not want to walk out just like that, so I sent her re-assuring messages that everything would turn out alright, she had no need to leave, and that she should come back immediately. I even phrased my words as if it were a done-deal that she would come back (admittedly, an old law-of-attraction technique for creating assertive communication). My hunch proved itself accurate : she could not bring herself to go through with driving away forever – she had in fact only driven as far as the nearest off-licence to find something with which to calm her nerves. She pitched up back to our front-door after no more than an hour.

Although the incident passed, ending happily that night, I noted that others who have gone through the Abramelin reported their relationships went through turbulence because of the operation – for example, Aaron Leitch :

"This very thing happened to me. My girlfriend stood loyally by my side throughout my Abramelin work. ... And for all her trouble, we broke up spectacularly just a few months after the operation was complete."

However, Leitch *did* go on to say :

"The upside ? During our time apart we each did some serious growing – in ways we could not have done together. Several months later we met back up and started seeing each other again. Before you knew it, we were together again – and we are still together and have a beautiful little girl to show for it."[24]

So, *they* survived, but did tonight's incident portend an omen of things to come for my fiancée and I ?

---

[24] LEITCH (2012)

Days 6,7,8

18 – 20th April 2020

From Day six onwards I would note down dreams which occurred to me during the night if they struck me as memorable. I recorded them mainly to stimulate my lucid dreaming faculty : I did not expect them to *all* have deep spiritual significance, but a number of them would surprise me, nevertheless.

Every day of my operation I tried to write something more than just "*operation adhered to,*"[25] although often this might only amount to a sentence at a time. Spending some two hundred days performing the same limited rituals every day caused me to contemplate each one with ever-increasing depth. On day six, for example, I wrote of my daily Pentagram ritual and of the Bornless ritual, "*I imagine when I vibrate each 'barbarous name' I'm manifesting a divine power into the material universe.*" Thoughts of a Qabalistic nature would also occur to me whilst performing the Middle Pillar Ritual prior to the main invocation, e.g. :

"*Thought : 'YHVH Elohim.' The creator of each plane of existence is a manifestation of the Eternal God - which, when reflected microcosmically, means the Creator of each level of my existence is an Elohim which is a manifestation of the Eternal God.*"

I had, of course, spoken prematurely in saying that I had confessed *all* of the sins of my current incarnation – I also had to deal with the sins which arose from day to day, as well as the notional sins of my previous lives. Moreover, in attempting to confess something each day, *new methods of recalling my sins* would occur to me during my meditations, hence giving me more food for confessions. For example, I noted :

"*How many times have I been guilty of the crimes of which I accuse others ? Hence I should examine what I criticise to get a better idea of what I should confess.*"

And on the next day :

"*It occurs to me that as a guru to others I would take responsibility for the passage of my chelas' would from one body to the next. I ought therefore to take responsibility, when confessing my sins, for how I have managed the incarnation of my own soul : has it always been appropriate for solving the karmic issues I have had at any one time ?*"

It seemed the more I confessed, the more willingly sinful memories sprung up from my subconscious. On day seven, I recalled incidents from my childhood of which I felt ashamed. Not just acts, but sinful thoughts I recalled having. "*[M]y*

---

[25] Cf : BLOOM (1976)

so-called 'sins' are a manifestation of 'The Imp of the Perverse,' " I wrote at the time, recalling the short-story by Poe, although I late realised this amounted to gilding the lily : after all, Poe's protagonist went on to confess to a murder, whereas the same Imp only got as far as making me *think* about evil which I never committed.

The more I thought about the philosophical implications of past-lives and Reincarnation, the more I realised that the potential Karma could prove *infinite*. For example : if I truly owned *all* my Karma, then I reasoned, I ought to take responsibility for the act of Incarnating itself. Not just as "Alex Sumner," but also as each of my past lives, stretching back into the past *ad infinitum*. I came to this conclusion on the basis that the Real Me was neither "Alex Sumner," "W L Wilmshurst," nor any of the incarnations the names of whom I did not know : rather, it is that which exists in Eternity, and which only incarnates periodically from time to time as a human being. Or, to use the vocabulary of Zen Buddhism, it is the owner of *my Original Face which I had before my parents were born.*

Moreover : I had heard about one theory of reincarnation that a Soul returns to dwell amongst the companions of his former toil, on the basis that their karma involves one another, and each member of the group inevitably assists the other members thereof to achieve their destiny jointly and severally. If this had any truth to it, I reasoned - if I manifest the people and circumstances in my life to fulfil my karma, I must take responsibility for the karma of causing *them* to incarnate as well.

Perhaps my traditional Roman Catholic upbringing influenced my awareness of Sin and the need for confession – it certainly informed much of my theological speculation on the point. I had seen others, who I presume must have had stronger faith than my own, paralysed with terror about eternal damnation. I remember even talking to one friend who, going through a deep depression, cited the fact of the Sinful nature of Suicide as the only reason he did not take his own life. (He did not harm himself, as it happened : when I met him again a few years later, he had recovered his good-humour and enthusiasm for living. His depression had lifted, it appears, very soon after he walked out on his long-term girlfriend.) This may sound like an extreme case, but I do believe it indicates the attitude of a great many people who buy into this whole hellfire-and-brimstone superstition.

But when it came to confessing my own sins for the purpose of the Abramelin Operation, I had a curious equanimity about it. I remember learning the literal meaning of "sin," once. The English term for it comes from the Latin *sine*, meaning "without," though more proximately it came from Medieval Archery to refer to arrows which lay "without" the bullseye. Any occasion when one *misses the target* set by God qualifies as a literal "sin."

However : God is Infinite, and therefore He sets an Infinitely high standard.

On this basis (I reasoned), everything must constitute a "sin" to a greater or lesser extent, if for no other reason than it falls short of the Perfection of God. In other words, the mere fact of me not being God inevitably means that I am a Sinner, even if I haven't done anything particularly wicked. So, for example, if on any day when I tried to meditate I could not do so properly the first time – I would have to regard that as a sin, because it fell outside God's target.

Ironically, this realisation filled me with hope. If everything technically was a Sin, but not everything was demonstrably evil, then it occurred to me that Sin by itself was not necessarily evil. Hence my confession did not entail me owning up to my status as a great villain, but just acknowledging my finite nature as a Human being aspiring to union with God.

The seeming pre-occupation with Sin, and the need to submit to God for forgiveness, has led many people of my acquaintance to abandon Christianity. However, from my point of view, instead of shying away from the subject after superficial examination, by persisting in what I had thought was an unpalatable subject day after day, I had succeeded in making it palatable. I had, in effect, removed the stigma I associated with Sin in my mind, and achieved a new, more mature appreciation of it.

The confession phase held some similarity to psychotherapy – abreacting each repressed memory as if I were psychoanalysing myself. In resolving my Karma by imagining drawing each "sin" up my spine, the resulting Kundalini manifested like Orgone as described by Wilhelm Reich, liberating itself from each neurosis. I noted this as a calming process. But why do it at all ? I figured that by confessing all these sins and taking karmic responsibility for them, I would pre-empt the *"Dweller on the Threshold."* I had long suspected that one of the immediate effects of undergoing a powerful initiatory experience meeting this entity – figuratively if not literally – and what was the Abramelin Operation but a course of self-initiation *par excellence.* Owing to its very nature, trying to explore one's past lives would inevitably trigger a "Dweller on the Threshold" (hereinafter : "DOTT") Incident. As I myself had written in 2012 :

> *"The [DOTT] ... is a nasty beasty that you will meet when trying to uncover your past-lives. It is so terrifying that it is likely to put you off attempting to discover your past lives if you don't realise what it really is. The DOTT was first described Bulwher ('It was a dark and stormy night...') Lytton in his book* Zanoni, *and seems to have been adopted as gospel by Blavatsky, so that it was repeated in hushed tones by the likes of Dion Fortune, Rudolf Steiner, etc.*
>
> *"The DOTT looks different for every person who encounters it : it might appear astrally as a thing, an entity, or a disturbing situation ; or instead of appearing astrally it might manifest in your life as something disturbing or challenging. It is described in Theosophical texts as an astral double which*

each person leaves hanging about on the astral plane from the last time they incarnated.

"It is this which gives the key to understanding its true nature : the DOTT is in fact an astral representation of all the Karma you have accrued from previous lives, *and a DOTT-experience amounts to suddenly having to deal with all your Karma all at once. The Dweller on the Threshold is, thus,* you.*"*
26

However, although this might very well put off the faint hearted, it need not deter the serious spiritual seeker.

"By not losing one's nerve and by carefully interrogating it, the DOTT successively reveals the Karmic lessons which the individual must learn, and the tasks that the individual must perform in order to free him/herself from his/her Karmic burdens."[27]

Ultimately,

"... there are at least two positive outcomes which will arise from the whole business of going up against the DOTT. The first is in the realisation that the DOTT is not the Shadow, because it represents all of ones Karma both good and bad. Hence, although the DOTT might appear off-putting to some, to those who have led saintly lives so-far or at least not terribly bad ones, the DOTT may well prove far less traumatic than one might have first feared.

"Secondly, the authorities all predict an optimistic outcome for those that go through with the ordeal of confronting the DOTT and rising to the challenges that it sets. Rudolf Steiner, for one, says that as one resolves each Karmic issue that one has, the DOTT appears less and less like a horrible monster and more and more like an Angel of Light, so that eventually it becomes not a barrier but a Spirit-Guide. Most importantly however, it leaves the Initiate with an idea that Death is not the End, and that the terrors of the grave are purely illusory."[28]

Hence, by confessing all possible sins, and thus resolving my Karma, *before* facing the DOTT, I attempted to make that inevitable confrontation as free from trauma as possible : whilst in aspiring to attain practical magical powers, I did so not for any base or frivolous reason, but to acquire the actual tools I would use to resolve the Karmic issues that the Dweller would present to me.

(A curious sidenote, not necessarily related to the above : around this time, I found an Archangel coin or medallion. It lay in an old drawer of bits and pieces which had belonged to my parents, which I effectively "inherited." Both of them

---

[26] SUMNER (2012)

[27] Ibid.

[28] Ibid.

had always held conventional Christian beliefs and would have run a mile from anything occult : I presume that they had picked it up as some trinket from a Christian gift-shop on some pilgrimage or other. I noticed, however, that the names of the Archangels lay inscribed around the rim of the medallion in the same order as in the Pentagram ritual, which struck me as unusual. A sign, perhaps ?)

Day 9

21 April 2020

During the night I had an example of a strange dream which turned out to prove more meaningful than I first suspected. Superficially it concerned a Golden Dawn meeting. No-one in the dream looked like a member of the GD whom I knew – a fact which should have triggered my lucidity for a start. I did notice, though, some stranger acting in a pompous manner, and trying to order us about : so I laid down the law to him.

Then, when it got to my morning ritual, I came to the part where I confessed my sins, and I realised : the memory of the dream, and of the figure who struck me as a pompous so-and-so, caused me to think of all the times that *I* had been pompous and full of pride myself. *The dream had thus served a useful purpose in directing my meditations for that day.* One could even say that the figure in the dream whom I did not like represented an aspect of myself.

Here I would like to make a digression. I believe that when MacGregor Mathers formulated the teachings of the Golden Dawn, he quite blatantly drew inspiration from the grimoires, the translation of which made him famous. The method of evocation in the Golden Dawn's "magic of light" formulae, for example, shows a clear resemblance to *The Key of Solomon*, in that one evokes a spirit by first consecrating a talisman or seal intended to attract the presence of the entity.

The *Book of the Sacred Magic of Abramelin The Mage* itself influences the way the Golden Dawn views the Qabalistic parts of the Soul, and the Adept's particular responsibility to equilibrate them. Essentially, one has a Higher Soul (Hebrew : *Neshamah),* a Conscious Soul *(Ruach),* and a Sub-Conscious Soul *(Nephesh).* Although the Higher Soul refers to the *Neshamah* in general, in particular it comprises three parts attributed to the Supernal Sephiroth in the microcosm : the Divine Spark, the Life-force, and Higher Intuitive Mind, i.e., *Yechidah* (Kether) ; *Chiah* (Chokmah) ; and the *Neshamah* itself (Binah).

The Higher Soul remains a thing unknown to people who never take an interest in Spirituality. For those who *do* walk The Path, however, the aim of life (according to the Golden Dawn) comprises the ability to aspire with full consciousness to the Higher Soul, or in other words, to establish regular communication between the *Ruach* and *Neshamah,* and beyond that, all the other parts of the Higher Soul as well.

However : therein lies only half the story. One must also get the *Nephesh* working properly. The Golden Dawn translates this as "animal consciousness" : the Bible uses it to denote "a living being." In other words, *Nephesh* denotes the type of consciousness that all living beings possess. I tried explaining the *Nephesh* to a friend once, relying on them being an animal-lover to illustrate my point.

"Every dog-owner knows that dogs have a kind of intelligence," I said, "And that if you train them whilst at the same time treating them properly with love and respect, they are no mere dumb-animals but faithful members of the family.

"In the same way, the *Nephesh* can be trained so that it can be like a faithful guard-dog, and a source of great strength to the initiate. But left untrained and unloved, it will become feral and all-over the place."

Here the analogy with a family pet breaks down, because the method of training the *Nephesh* envisaged by the GD involves purifying it of all its "evil" impulses, and make sure that it works under the direction of the *Neshamah* and *Ruach*. When all three work together like a well-oiled machine, then the *real* magic happens : great flashes of Numenosity which prove both ecstatic (often literally) and always life-changing.

Most importantly one should consider that the Golden Dawn does not simply exterminate or "banish" the evil impulses which infest the *Nephesh*, but consigns them to a place below the personality, and over which the *Nephesh* has a firm control. The GD refers to this as the "Evil Persona," symbolised in the Neophyte Ceremony as the Devouring monster standing ready to dispatch the souls of those not found worthy in the Judgement Hall of Osiris. This "Evil Persona" is trod down, but *not* banished, to signify that the true initiate rules over it, and not be ruled *by* it. The Golden Dawn had anticipated Jung's concept of "The Shadow" by at least twenty years.

However, Mathers, in an inner-order paper, went one step further.

"The evil persona can be rendered as a great and strong, yet trained, animal whereupon the man rideth, and it then becometh a strength unto his physical base of action. This Mystery shalt thou keep from the knowledge of the First Order, and still more from that of the Outer World, that is as a formula, seeing that it is a dangerous secret."[29]

Something so secret that the adept must keep it from the public ? Allowing the Evil Persona to become powerful so that one can become oneself a stronger magician sounds suspiciously like an apology for Black Magic – something repugnant to the prudish Victorians, and not completely unscandalous in the second decade of the twenty-first century. *And yet, this summarises the very rationale envisaged by the Sacred Magic of Abramelin the Mage.*

I have seen people who do not understand the concepts of "metaphor" and "Analogy" claim that "Knowledge and Conversation of the Holy Guardian Angel" has nothing to do with the Golden Dawn. I would only point out that :

---

[29] "Tasks Undertaken by the Adeptus Minor," quoted in REGARDIE (1989), Book I

- MacGregor Mathers did not refer to the "Higher Self" literally as the "Holy Guardian Angel," but he *did* refer to it as one's "Angelic Nature";[30]

- The state of superconsciousness that one experiences when in conscious contact with the *Neshamah* or Higher Self has a similarity to that which one experiences when possessing consciousness of one's Holy Guardian Angel, so that one may only distinguish them subjectively with difficulty – *as I shall explain hereafter*;

- One may take the effort necessary for the Adept to purify and exalt his or her nature as equivalent to the effort required for the Abramelin operation ; and

- The constraining and controlling of one's Evil Persona, to the intent of using it as a source of power for magical works, has its equivalence in constraining the King and Princes of Hell and their attendant demons for much the same purposes.

Which leads me back to ritual I undertook that morning, and the dream I had in the night which informed its contents. Although this dream had reminded me of my pride, causing me to argue and be assertive – the same Pride also formed part of my Evil Persona, and hence a source of strength ! Therefore, although I confessed this Deadly Sin, I also willed that I could sublimate it unto the good.

---

[30] Ibid.

Day 10

22 April 2020

Because one has to start in the Spring (specifically : Easter Monday) and carry on for six-months, one inevitably performs the Abramelin Operation during the warmest part of the year. However, because one has to get up in time for dawn, one also has to get up increasingly earlier every day, at least for the first few months. (Towards the latter part of my operation, heading into Autumn, I had to modify this so that I had to get up several hours before sunrise – *vide infra*).

Throughout my Operation I could jump out of bed immediately my alarm went off, but that rarely meant I liked doing so. "*Very sleepy, difficult to concentrate,*" I wrote on day ten. "*Then do morning rituals as before : concentration improves with Bornless Ritual.*"

I got to the point in my ritual where I confessed my sins. "*My past life who practiced yoga - that's someone for whom I should take responsibility,*" I thought. "*All people who incarnated because of my need to fulfil my karma - I need to take responsibility for them as well.*"

A sudden realisation made me shudder. I had had a brother whom I never knew. He died of childhood leukaemia before I ever came into this world. It had occurred to me in the past, although my parents had never said so in so many words, that had not my elder brother passed away at a young age, they might not have wanted to have any more children.

Hence : did "I" in fact bear responsibility for my brother's death ?

On the one hand of course I could not, because I had a complete alibi, to wit : I was not alive at the time.

On the other hand, though, if this Original Face of Me existed in eternity, it must have decided when and how to incarnate as a human being. If I accepted the reality of this whole idea of Karma and Reincarnation, then I presume I incarnated when I did because it was karmically right for me to do so : when, in fact, the Original Face of Me discerned that the right time had come.

Looking back now, my familiarity with Astrology clearly influenced my train of thought, because I equated "being born with the right tools to resolve my Karma" with "being born with the right planetary and astrological influences." My natal horoscope provided, therefore, a snapshot of the Karma which caused me to incarnate, and hence pointed out my destiny for this present incarnation.

But if that were the case, did the Original Face of Me noticed the stars and planets in right position if I incarnated there and then, and say "*What a jolly coincidence !*" Or did it say, years in advance, "*Perhaps I should give one boy cancer to make sure another boy gets born at the right time and place ? You know, nudge things along a bit ?"*

The thought disturbed me, but as a matter of pure logic, disbelieving it just because I found it distasteful would have presented a fallacy. Rather, I should resign myself to the idea that even if "I" did not technically cause my brother's death, I should at least take responsibility for his karma in addition to my own.

But if that were true, why stop at considering just my own brother's death ? After all, I was born in England, a country that has won every war in which it has ever got involved. Should I feel responsible for all the Germans that died in World War Two so that my parents might live and grow up in a free country ? And what of the deaths of those that died in previous wars so that my more distant ancestors might themselves survive ?

Do the French therefore have the least Karma in the world, because they keep surrendering so quickly ?

As I pondered this, it occurred to me that :

- Ultimately, everyone has responsibility for *everyone's* karma ;
- No human could possibly handle the guilt associated with their karma, because the *total* karma which affects them is potentially Infinite ;
- Although no human could, God can ;
- Hence why relying upon the Grace of God, having humility, and thanking Him for his forgiveness holds so much importance ;
- Perhaps, instead of looking at all the negatives, I could more productively look at all the positive and beneficial reasons why people in general, and myself in particular, happen to (re-) incarnate ?

In regard to this last point, I had flattered my ego to think that if I traced my desire to keep incarnating back to the root of my being, all of these people who incarnated just so that I could fulfil my karma – they did so out of a desire to bring enlightenment to humanity - hence an act of compassion. Looking back on this sentiment now, I can see how this desire to qualify as some sort of Hegelian World Soul for whom all of History up to this point has solely existed, could come across as massively hubristic – were it not for three important factors : firstly, I saw it as a coping mechanism for coming to terms with the full implications of karma ; secondly, I fully expected History to ultimately lose me in anonymity, thereby rendering any hubris as folly ; and thirdly and most importantly, if what I believed about everyone being responsible for everyone's karma was true, then the World Soul would not comprise me the individual but *everyone collectively.* Or to put it more succinctly :

"I am the most important person in the entire Universe – and so is everyone else."

*

Perhaps my cogitations that morning had some effect, as I recorded going back to bed for a little sleep afterwards, and having a lucid dream about doing the Qabalistic Cross.

Later, that day, I gave some serious thought as to how I would go about fulfilling the terms of the Oath I had sworn at the start of my Abramelin Operation. I therefore decided to set up a "JustGiving" page as a practical step towards raising the money which I had vowed to donate to charity, and I published a blog-post about doing so. Given that the original point of donating money in Abramelin was to give it to poor people, and given also that the world was then in the midst of the dreaded Covid-19 Pandemic, it made sense to arbitrarily select a charity which helped poor and vulnerable families affected by the current crisis.

This actually marked the first time I mentioned publicly undertaking the Abramelin Operation. As a result of me doing so, I received messages from a number of occultists across the internet all over the world, who said that they themselves were taking the opportunity of the lockdown caused by the COVID 19 hysteria to attempt the Abramelin Operation. Others wished that they had but could not do so for some practical reason or another. As I wrote in my journal :

"I foresee that there will be a new level of spiritual maturity in the world arising because of this - a new community of all those adepts who went through this together."

Day 11

23 April 2020

The battle which I had between my tiredness and my need to get out of bed seemed to resolve itself in favour of the latter today : *"Feeling better than I was at this time yesterday,"* I wrote in my journal. *"Vibrating divine names out loud or at least physically as opposed to mentally is better at keeping me on track."*

My rendition of the Bornless Ritual particularly pleased me that day. I wrote :

"In the end it's as if I can really feel as if my Body of Light is transforming into the Bornless One. As if I can consciously operate whilst maintaining the state of 'I Am-ness' which I experienced when I attained nirvikalpa samadhi *nine years ago."*

This requires some explanation – although I call it "nirvikalpa samadhi" I've no idea whether I use the terminology accurately in either a technical or literal sense. I shall therefore try to explain :

I had studied Yoga, both Raja and Hatha, since around 1996, after reading BKS Iyengar's "Light on Yoga" and "Light on the Yoga Sutras of Patanjali." Sometime later, I read Paramhansa Yogananda's "Autobiography of a Yogi" as well. From these three books (as well as a few others) I drew the following conclusions :

- Many types of *Samadhi*, the eighth of the limbs of Raja Yoga, exist – categorised in a sort of ladder based on difficulty. At the bottom of the ladder lies yer basic *Samadhi*, which is what one experiences when one first gets good at meditation. At the top of the ladder one finds *Kaivalya* or final Liberation.

- I felt certain that I had several times attained yer basic *Samadhi* (so to speak) as momentary peak-experiences whilst meditating. However : *Kaivalya* remained so far removed from anything of which I could conceive, I felt that it must exist only in legend : in any event, I felt confident that I would never attain it in reality.

- *"Nirvikalpa Samadhi"* consisted, as far as I could tell, of a kind of Samadhi which, once you attain it, you never go back... I could only translate this into anything my mind could understand by assuming that it really meant a form of Samadhi which completely and permanently transformed one's consciousness, so that one would never experience reality the same way again. Here, however, I got conflicting interpretations : on the one hand some sources seemed into imply that it meant one experienced "God-Consciousness" 24/7, whilst others described it as a specific state one attained when meditating. Either way, I figured that on the ladder of attainability it occupied a rung near to *Kaivalya*, i.e., impossible for all practical intents and purposes.

Over time, however, my views began to change. I read Ken Wilber's *One Taste*, in which he casually mentioned that he had attained *Nirvikalpa Samadhi*.[31] Upon investigating further, Wilber admitted the heavy influence of Ramana Maharshi (1879-1950) upon him, so for Wilber, *Nirvikalpa Samadhi* meant perfecting the kind of *Jnana Yoga* which Maharshi advocated during the twentieth century.

The essence of the technique consists of abiding in The Witness. When one enquires "who am I ?" one realises that if one can say, "I *have* this or that," then clearly one cannot identify as the thing possessed, but the one possessing. E.g., If I say, "I have a body," that implies "I am *not* the body, I merely own it." In which case, who or what is the "I" that possesses the body ?

Thus, by a process called "Neti Neti," (a Sanskrit phrase meaning "Nasal cleaner, nasal cleaner"), one flushes away all possibilities of the true nature of the "I," until one realises it could only be some kind of observing awareness without any defining characteristics whatsoever – i.e. The Witness.

I attempted this kind of *Jnana Yoga* several times, and although I experienced some very deep states of meditation, I could not claim it struck me as anything revolutionary at first. I also attempted to dream lucidly of abiding in the Witness, which although I thought I achieved, it did not strike me as any great shakes. Yet the idea of the achievability of *Nirvikalpa Samadhi,* and that some person claimed to have achieved it, intrigued me greatly, and stayed on my mind for some time.

Quite separately I studied the history of Neo-Platonism, and the story of Plotinus in particular, of whom his biographer Porphyry stated he had united with God four times – at least during the time that he knew him.[32] According to the modern writer David Godwin :

"*The way to achieve these states was by contemplation. One recommended technique was to visualize the universe and then mentally abolish its limitations.*"[33]

Meanwhile, in around 2009 I was initiated into a tradition which recommends as one of it practices, a particular method of lucid dreaming in which the object is to dissolve *all* of the contents of one's dream into light : the idea being that when one has dissolved as much as possible, that which remains no longer comes from the personal mind but from the Astral Plane itself.

---

[31] WILBER (2000).

[32] "Porphyry : On the Life of Plotinus and the Arrangement of his Work" from PLOTINUS (250).

[33] GODWIN (1992), p146.

Unfortunately, I ended up doing it wrong. Instead of dissolving the contents of my mind, I ended up dissolving *everything* – including the Astral Plane.

In one fell swoop, therefore, I had realised the equivalence of dreaming about abiding in the Witness (what Wilber described as a "pellucid dream") and Plotinus' method of achieving *Henosis*. Floating disembodied in a void of pure white light, without thinking I dissolved the one thing left : *The Dissolver.*

What happened next, I can only describe with exceeding difficulty. *Nothing* is perhaps the best word in the English language. Not "nothing in particular," which is how colloquial usage often employs the word, but Nothing-as-in-Actual-Nothing. It was certainly Nothing describable : and if asked for a simile for it, I would not be lying if I said it was "like Nothing."

And yet I would not be telling the whole Truth either, because it was patently *Something*, save that it had absolutely No characteristics whatsoever based upon any kind of ideation.

Eternity, too, is a possible descriptor – not in the sense of lasting forever, but in that of complete Time-less-ness. Einstein had said that the rate at which Time flows is relative to the Inertial-frame in which one is travelling. But if no physical objects exist either to travel or remain at rest (i.e., travel with zero-velocity), then no Inertial-frame exists either, and hence there is no Time. And indeed, all physical objects had disappeared, as had any sense of duration whatsoever : so too had any way of telling how long the experience lasted, whether a few minutes, a hundred years, or forever. And yet – not only had all physical objects disappeared, so had all boredom and emotions associated with the passing of Time, so that there only remained an Eternal *Now*.

But by far the most astounding part of the experience was that *I* ceased to exist. Presumably *Something* must have existed, because it retained a memory of the experience – albeit a Memory of Nothing. But *I* did not exist : *Non Cogito, Ergo Non Sum*. The Awareness which did exist rested *perfectly still*. Hence, no possibility existed of saying where the I or anything else had gone, because any attempt to discover this would have caused a new thought, which would have disturbed the *perfect stillness*.

The fact that I can write this now, however, came about because after an Eternity dwelling in this state of non-being, the Awareness started to notice a thought. Just a little movement, but it was enough to make clear to the Awareness that if there is something *in* the Void, it is a technical Void no longer. In relatively quick succession, *Cogito Ergo Sum* occurred : I realised I was thinking, and from it I realised that *I* existed, and very soon I realised *I* had Reincarnated.

I eventually opened my eyes and felt astonished to find myself in the same body, and lying in the same place, as I had been before ceasing to exist. I had made no note of the time, so I have no idea how long I had existed in Eternity –

it *felt* like forever, of course, but I don't know if that meant half an hour, or an hour, or what. It was certainly the same day as I had ceased to exist.

I got up feeling invigorated and full of energy – and raging libido. Most immediately, I reacted to the experience with an entirely positive outlook : after all, everything unpleasant had ceased to exist. Technically everything *else* had ceased to exist as well, but as I consider myself a glass-half-full kind of guy, I interpreted this only as a good-thing.

Eventually I felt able to collect my thoughts and reflect on what had happened – and what I had done.

"This must be an inter-carnatory state," I thought. *"This must be what souls experience whilst they are between bodies, waiting to reincarnate."* I had experienced Death – and moreover – *I had killed myself.* I noted that when I decided to "dissolve the dissolver," I had tellingly not thought about the implications of what I did – and a good thing to, because if I had thought about it in any depth or at all, my mind would have revolted against the idea in the same way that a sane man or woman feels dissonance at the thought of suicide. I had destroyed myself by the power of my own mind, *and had had no idea beforehand that I would survive the process*. If I had had any idea, it might have prejudiced my experience on the one hand, or caused me to unconsciously resist doing so on the other.

Subsequently, I tried to consult the works of mystical writers to attempt to get a handle on what had happened to me. I tried to work out where exactly this placed me on the Qabalistic Tree of Life, by referring to Crowley's *One Star In Sight*[34] – but I became convinced in this instance the Great Beast didn't know what he was talking about, or if he did, he expressed himself in an egregiously bad manner. Besides which, it struck me as completely absurd to invite one to confer a title of superiority on oneself for achieving such a uniquely personal experience. I felt as if Crowley expected me to inflate the very Ego which I had taken so much trouble to cause to disappear (at least temporarily). I abandoned this line of enquiry.

More promisingly, however, on one hand, I perceived how this coincided with the process of attaining *Henosis*, so I felt confident I had experienced something of what Plotinus himself had done. I did not consider myself as an equal to Plotinus, because after all he remained four to my one – assuming Porphyry had kept score correctly.

On the other hand, I had also been attempting to attain *Nirvikalpa Samadhi,* and I had succeeded in attaining a Samadhi-like experience, but one of a higher and far-superior order than I had ever attained in yoga meditation up to that point.

---

[34] "The Master Therion" (1929), Appendix II.

Moreover, the experience proved so profound that it permanently changed my ideas of what is and what it not possible with mystical states, and it resolved the conflict that I felt over whether it entailed God-consciousness 24/7, or whether it was a specific state one attained when meditating. *It was both.* Although I did not live every moment of my life in the ecstasy I had experienced in the peak of my peak experience, I knew that it was there and that it existed as an intellectual certainty, and I could tune into the meditative state of mind more easily because it had made such a vivid impression upon my memory.

Thus, it came about in 2020, whilst performing the Abramelin Operation, I found myself able to use my experience of *Nirvikalpa Samadhi* (assuming that describes it correctly) to inform how I interpreted performing the Bornless Ritual : not only could I compare the two, but I actively Willed that the Ritual invoke that sort of meditative awareness. I must assume that this approach did me some good that day, because of the meditation I did on confessing my sins, I wrote in my journal :

> "*Great peace - on previous occasions I have observed that this is evidence of Angels at work indeed, it is the Angels.[35] I express gratitude to God, my HGA, and all other Angels under their command.*"

(I spent the rest of the day relaxing, playing music on my Yamaha WX5.)

---

[35] This remark should also be read in the light of what I have written under Day 15 – *vide infra.*

Day 12

24 April 2020

On day three I had written about having used the "Corridor of Many Doors" technique several years ago to explore past-life memories : it now occurred to me I could put the same exercise to use in my current Abramelin Operation. I wrote in my journal :

"Theoretically, the sum total of all possible sins that both I and my previous incarnations either did or could have committed can be symbolically represented as Sin-entities (energies) which, by the power of my Holy Guardian Angel, are abstracted out of the Many Doors and then are sublimated up my sushumna to be resolved like Kundalini rising."

Hence, I came up with the idea, when it came to the part of my morning ritual where I confessed my sins, of entering a trance state and visualising myself entering the Corridor of Many Doors. However instead of entering any of the doors to find my sins, I remained in the corridor and bade the sins come to me, imagining them as "Sin-Entities," or types of elementals, coming through all of the doors and into the corridor. There, as they amassed in that narrow space, I acknowledged them and called upon God to forgive me for them.

Lest I be thought of creating this method as a cheat or cop-out, I will state here that it was the opposite. As each Sin-Entity came through its door, I became consciously aware of the Sin which it represented. I therefore had to will that they not come through all at once, so that they did not overwhelm me.

One session proved not enough to abstract all possible Sin-Entities this way. Hence, I repeated the same exercise several days running. I did however note that this seemed an effective manner of working, as I recorded afterwards that it led to *"great peace."*

Day 13

25 April 2020

When I first started the Abramelin Operation, the Government had completely locked-down England due to fears about COVID-19, i.e. the first time that it had ordered such a measure. My fiancée, being a temporary worker, found herself "furloughed," which caused her great distress at first, although she later discovered that the terms of her furlough were more generous than she had first realised. I, however, had a permanent job – working in a School. My employers reacted to the first lockdown by telling of all of its staff – myself included – to work from home. Ironically, the nature of my job was such that it could not be performed at home, but I went home anyway. I thus found myself in the luxurious position of being paid to do absolutely nothing.

This proved an auspicious time for me. Not only did I start the Abramelin Operation during this period, but the enforced holiday gave my fiancée and I the opportunity to move out of our respective flats and move in together, for the first time. It thus became the equivalent of our "first year of marriage."

However, as with all good things the inevitable happened. About a month after the lockdown started, my employers decided they couldn't carry on like this, and that they needed a skeleton crew to come in to the work-place two days a week to perform a bare minimum of tasks which could not otherwise get done. I therefore got the call that my unexpected holiday would soon end, which I could hardly turn-down as technically I was a "key-worker."

This led me to seriously consider : how *does* one reconcile having to work full time with doing the Abramelin Operation ?

According to The Book :

"...[T]he best counsel which I can give is that a man should go into retirement in some desert or solitude... nevertheless now this is hardly possible... and being unable to carry it out in one way, we should endeavour to do so in another ; and attach ourselves only unto divine things."[36]

So what about potential aspirants who have worldly occupations – i.e. like myself ? Abraham the Jew gave limited options as to what job an aspirant could pursue :

"We may then exercise the profession of medicine, and all arts connected with the same ; and we may perform all operations which tend unto charity and mercy towards our neighbour purely and simply."[37]

---

[36] MATHERS (1900), book II chapter 10.
[37] Ibid.

That's it. In an earlier chapter he recommended that if one were one's own master, one should free oneself from all business altogether.

Clearly I was not involved with the profession of medicine : however, as a key-worker I *did* help people albeit indirectly during the COVID-19 crisis, which one could also construe as an act of charity or mercy. However, although a generous reading of The Book might excuse me, I still had a major practical problem :

No amount of moral laxity could blind me to the central thrust of Abraham the Jew's intended meaning, namely that one's circumstances in life should disturb the performance of the Operation as little as possible. Virtuous action is here assumed not to be a disturbance, because works of a wholesome moral character such as saving people's lives, being charitable and merciful, etc, are the will of the Lord and serve to strengthen the attraction of the blessed Angels to oneself.

However : if one had the opportunity to perform the Operation properly, and one tried to get out of doing so due to a sketchy interpretation of the original instructions, this would amount to *taking the piss.* Hence (I reasoned) I ought to perform all of the required orations and ceremonies as much as possible.

I figured that as the requisite ceremonies for phases one and two of the Operation were early in the morning and late at night, I would have enough time in the middle of the day to continue to hold down a nine-to-five job. However : during phase three, the Book would require me to add in another ceremony, during the middle of the day as well. Immediately I saw potential difficulty.

As for the conclusion of the Operation, this required an epic series of rituals for me to perform over seven consecutive days : one day to consecrate all of the items involved in the final ceremonies : three days to commune with my Holy Guardian Angel itself ; and three days to conjure all of the Kings of Hell and their respective servants. I did not see how this could be done whilst holding down a job *at all.*

The need for retirement from worldly affairs during some or all of the Abramelin Operation must be the principal reason it has been performed so very little : I certainly used this as my own excuse for not performing it for twenty years after I first read about it. Inspired by my unexpected holiday, I foolhardily began the operation, only to be completely shafted by finding out I would not be spending the entire time off work after all. And yet I had a steely determination to finish the Operation, convinced that to pull out of doing so would heap down immense shame and bad luck upon me. My challenge was therefore how to cope, notwithstanding.

Hence : the final weekend of my unexpected holiday, I went into my Oratory that morning as usual. I did not actually concern myself with the problem of holding down a job : instead, I just concentrated on performing the ceremonies. I noted that the Bornless Ritual went well that morning : *"... can feel my solar body energised. I contemplate references to 'I' and 'me' as being to my Higher Self."*[38]

With regards to the confessing of sins, I noted that this ought to include everything which might hold me back from attaining KCHGA. I also recalled the story in Dion Fortune's Psychic Self Defence about how Theodore Moriarty "Absorbed" an evil spirit (he had succeeded, but it knocked him out cold for three days).[39] When I first read this, I compared this to the sacrifice of Jesus Christ on behalf of the whole world, when He died upon the Cross – He effectively "Absorbed" the Sins of the world. It occurred to me that this absorption of sins lay not too far removed from what I aspired to do with *my own sins* in the Abramelin Operation. However the interconnectedness of Karma compounded my own situation, as I had noted previously, so in effect, I didn't just do it for myself : I represented humanity, and hence bore responsibility - at least in part - for all sins committed collectively by humanity, ultimately throughout all epochs of history. It wasn't just a *similarity* to what Christ did, I felt the Abramelin Operation obliging me to become *literally* Christ-like. I noted :

"It would almost be unthinkable, unless God really is all-merciful and the redemption of mankind a reality. In not caring about the world's ills, people don't appreciate just how important God is."

But despite the fact that that day's ritual seriously threatened to give me a Messiah Complex, it nevertheless did some good and must have unlocked some doors in my mind. Afterwards, I wrote in my journal :

"... I have a brilliant idea about finishing the Abramelin Operation. It is meant to culminate in an epic six-day ritual [sic – see below] - three days to actually attain KCHGA, and three to conjure all the spirits of Hell. Interpreting 'six months' literally would take me to October 13th : however, by extending the operation for just a few weeks, I could make the six-day culmination coincide with the October half-term. Then it would be easy to get time off work to devote exclusively to the ceremony !"

(NB I should have said "seven-day ritual," i.e. including the day of consecration which preceded the final six-days. This turned-out to be academic, as in the end I was able to fit the day of consecration into the October half-term holidays as well.)

Hence, ironically, my solution to the problem of performing the Abramelin Operation as authentically as possible entailed taking a liberty with the literal instructions in the original book – the very thing I had wanted to avoid doing. On day two, I had noted that the *"Magical practices of an age reflect the social trends*

---

[38] For a fuller explanation of "solar body," see Day 15, *infra*.
[39] FORTUNE (1930), chapter V, pp60-61.

of the times"[40] : now it appeared to me that the modern necessity of life in the twentieth century necessitated observing the *Spirit* rather than the *Letter* of the old grimoires.

---

[40] *Vide supra.*

Day 14

26 April 2020

As I noted on day four, apparently The Book has an injunction against performing any other kind of magic : in fact the exact wording runs like this –

As for what concerneth the liberal arts ye may interest yourselves in astronomy, etc., but flee all arts and operations which have the least tincture of magic and sorcery, seeing that we must not confound together God and Belial *: God wisheth to be alone ; unto him pertain all honour and glory.*[41]
(Emphasis added).

I take "Belial" as a metaphor – any other Demon or entity would be just as good – but the point appears clear to me. One should not shun other kinds of magic just for the sake of it, but because there might be a danger of mixing up God with something which is inimical to the integrity of what is, after all, meant to be *Sacred* Magic.

Whilst the principle is sound, I could not help but think that the sentiment betrays just how old-fashioned it really is. In the five hundred years since The Book was first written, Ceremonial Magic has moved on – mainly thanks to the efforts of people like MacGregor Mathers, the translator of *Abramelin*. Back in the fifteenth century, people ignorantly making pacts with evil beings might have been a real problem, and hence The Book's injunction would have been very necessary. When it came to the Golden Dawn, however, Mathers and his colleagues deliberately structured its magical practices so that if done properly, such a confounding together of God and Belial would not actually take place. One can speculate that this represented another lesson which Mathers had learnt from *Abramelin* itself.

Perhaps (I thought to myself) most importantly this rule serves to keep one's mind fixed solely upon God. Perhaps, even, this meant that shunning other types of magic and sorcery would do you no good whatsoever if one did not maintain this steadfastness of devotion !

Anyway : the guilty secret to which the above forms the preface was that in addition to my association with the Golden Dawn, I am a member of "Builders of the Adytum," and I took part in BOTA activities during my Operation.

I first became a BOTA member after I induced my fiancée to join Co-Masonry : by way of revenge, she subscribed me to the weekly BOTA correspondence lessons without telling me. It would never have occurred to me join BOTA on my own volition, but after I found out what my fiancée had done,

---

[41] MATHERS (1900), book II chapter 10.

I thought : "Why not ? I'll suppose I'll give it a go." Hence I managed to frustrate my fiancée's machinations when, instead of losing my temper, I reacted with good humour and a certain amount of curiosity about the whole escapade.

BOTA does not practice either magic or sorcery – certainly not in the same way as envisaged by *Abramelin*. I cannot speak for the "BOTA Chapter" meetings, and I have deliberately not enquired about what goes on there, as I understand that the first and second rules about the BOTA Chapter correspond to those of *Fight Club*.

Instead, BOTA encourages self-development and self-improvement through meditation, reflection, and a number of exercises which stimulate the development of one's intuitive and psychic faculties. It does almost all of this through Tarot Cards, hence : after being introduced to the basic concepts of practical occultism, one learns about the twenty-two tarot trumps. And then one learns about the twenty-two tarot trumps at a deeper level. And then one learns about the twenty-two tarot trumps at *an even deeper* level. And *then…* etc etc etc.

Although most of the work in BOTA is done by each member individually working through their own lessons at home, the organisation does provide support in the form of Study Groups, and units referred to as Pronaoi,[42] in which group ritual work takes place (apparently different from Chapter meetings) – this in addition to occasional international gatherings.

In order to bring it into line with every other organisation – esoteric, occult, masonic or otherwise – the international headquarters of BOTA ordered all its various manifestations to suspend meetings whilst COVID-19 still raged like a foul pestilence across the face of the planet. However : just a couple of weeks after the lock-down began, BOTA headquarters instructed the various BOTA groups worldwide that they were now allowed to use ZOOM, although for conducting Study Group meetings only.

Thus it came about that on day fourteen, the completion of the first two weeks of the Operation, I took part in an BOTA Study Group meeting via ZOOM – the second such meeting since lockdown began.

The day began with the by-now usual ritual at sunrise. "*Up at 5.08am. Feeling sleepy and hungover,*" I had begun my journal entry that day. However, afterwards I wrote : "*I end the morning ritual feeling energised : certainly more awake and feeling better than when I started it.*"

Later that morning, I occupied my time doing some BOTA work unconnected with the subject of that day's study group – i.e., I was colouring-in Key 16, "The Tower," in accordance with my then current BOTA lesson. "*Destruction of the old to make way for the new,*" I noted : coincidentally, a convenient metaphor for

---

[42] Singular : "Pronaos."

the self-transformation which occurs when one undertakes something like, well, the Abramelin Operation.

The colouring-in forms a key part of the "Tarot Fundamentals" course, which a BOTA member encounters early on – it being the third discrete course of lessons. Each BOTA member receives a Tarot deck as part of the materials they are sent – consisting of 78 black & white line-drawings. The twenty-two Major Arcana focussed on almost immediately : the fifty-six Minor Arcana not forming part of the curriculum until several years into one's membership.

Whilst receiving teachings about what Paul Foster Case believed constitutes the meaning of each Tarot key, the student also receives instruction on how to colour each key, which he or she does by coloured pencils. BOTA leaves no detail of the colour-scheme to chance, instead prescribing *everything*. However, I myself interpreted this as a rather clever way of impressing the importance of the symbolism on the student. By hand-colouring each key, not only does the student think more deeply about the detail of each card, but it leverages one's child-like fascination with colouring something in to make the Keys personal to oneself. This process thus transforms the Tarot Keys from someone else's cards into *one's own*, a thing you have made yourself, despite the fact that they will inevitably be identical in every other important respect to the set belonging to every other member.

The online BOTA study group took place that afternoon : they were due to talk about Key 15, "The Devil," a key which I had coloured-in just two weeks ago.

What happens at a BOTA study group is this : first of all, everyone recites the *"Pattern on the Trestleboard."* This short piece, which BOTA publish in their publicly available material, consists of a summary of the Qabalistic Tree of Life in symbolic language. BOTA expects every member to memorise the Pattern by-heart : by thus reciting it before every significant exercise, the student briefly aligns him- or herself with both the Tree of Life and the organisation's egregore.

Secondly, the group reviews of the known-data regarding the selected Tarot Key : the gematria of the letter (in this case, Aayin), the gematria of the letter's spelling (Aayin – Yod – Nun), its correspondences in Astrology, the *Sepher Yetzirah,* the Cube of Space, the Book of Tokens, and also Paul Foster Case' and Anne Davies' other writings. A brief period of silent reflection ensues.

There *then* follows the real 'meat' of the study group session, which consists of ten questions, each intended to stimulate discussion. When I first attended a BOTA study group meeting, I could not help but find myself shocked by these questions' *banality*. BOTA HQ obliged the Study Group to ask them, I presume so that aspirants the world over could gain a standardised experience. I have since had it intimated to me that more advanced sets of questions exist, but the organisers have kept them in reserve for as long as I can remember, as BOTA aims to include *everybody* in the potential discussion, and let no-one feel left out.

Thus far the usual Study Group format, but the London study group had for a couple of years spiced up the regular meeting by adding to the agenda a meditation, composed by Ann Davies. Davies (1912-75) succeeded Paul Foster Case as the head of BOTA : notably she is the only other person apart from Case credited with authoring the order's lessons. Of what I have seen, Case's lessons deal with the "hard-facts" of occultism, whilst Davies' deal with the psychic and intuitive development. In any event, quite apart from her lessons, she also recorded a large number of meditations at BOTA's Sunday Services – church-like gatherings held in Los Angeles. In modern times, BOTA have made these recordings increasingly available to its members.

Unfortunately, because these recordings date from, on average, forty years ago or more – and do not sound as if recorded professionally at the time – the sound quality proved not great, a fact exacerbated by the difficult of playing sound files over the internet in a ZOOM call. Nevertheless, although this meditation did not hold direct relevance to my Abramelin Operation *per se*, Davies' manner of describing the guided visualisations – such as her instruction regarding placing my consciousness into the various spheres of the Tree of Life when in my astral body – did inspire me with ways that I could improve my own meditations during my subsequent rituals. For example …

Day 15

27 April 2020

Today I mainly concerned myself with my "Solar Body," by which I mean how my astral body will turn out after I have transmuted it from Philosophical Silver to Philosophical Gold. I do not claim to have fully realised my Solar Body – if I had, I would have realised the *penultimate* stage of spiritual development in the great Hermetic scheme of things. I did, however, find that it a useful mental exercise to imagine what my Solar Body would look and feel like if I *did* realise it – the speculation helped make my meditations more lively.[43]

So, for example, as I wrote in my journal :

"Up at 5.06am. Preparation with Middle Pillar Ritual. Kether is four feet above my head, Malkuth is four feet below. I imagine I am in my astral body, placing my consciousness in each sephirah down the Middle Pillar."

(This shows the influence of the Ann Davies meditation to which I had listened on the previous day).

"I imagine that whilst residing in my Golden Body (solar body), I am in touch with my Nephesh. The experience is empowering - particularly the idea of uniting my Solar Body with my Nephesh."

My concern with my Nephesh probably derived from reading BOTA material as well, which refers to superconsciousness, self-consciousness, and sub-consciousness : I identified it with the latter of these three, whilst I associated *Neshamah* and *Ruach* with the first two. BOTA teaches early on that one should establish a healthy and co-operative relationship with one's subconsciousness, which I interpreted to mean I should consciously speak to my Nephesh in appropriate language to show how much I appreciate it.

"Sunrise 5.36am. Working on this principle [i.e. that of uniting my Solar Body with my Nephesh] *I perform the Lesser Banishing Ritual of the Pentagram and Bornless Ritual - both very powerful. I can feel my Solar Body being energised."*

I then contemplated confessing my sins, although I seemed to be going over things which I had confessed on previous days. I was running out of new ideas. Then :

"At the end, I thank my Nephesh (as is my custom), and spontaneously thank my Solar Body as well. This is unexpectedly inspiring - by treating both my

---

[43] In my own mind I also conflated the "Solar Body" with the "Resurrection body" of exoteric Christianity, and the "Body of Glory" of Gnosticism. For more background on these terms, see MEAD (1919).

Nephesh and my Solar Body as separate bodies yet aspiring to become one with them is empowering. Concentrating on this, I pass into a state of contemplation even deeper than before."

*

This made me consider an important question : how would I actually *know* that I had attained KCHGA if and when I had done so ?

Unfortunately I had not gone into this Abramelin Operation with an open mind : instead, I had a set of pre-conceived notions about what does and what does not constitute an Angelic presence, going back almost twenty-five years. I had based them upon an experience which I now recognise as one of the most remarkable of my entire life, which I had in the late Nineties – it went something like this :

Right from the start of my involvement with the Occult, I had been a keen lucid dreamer. So much so, that if I decided to have a lucid dream about any particular thing, I felt confident that I could achieve it. Moreover, I particularly remember Dion Fortune claiming that astral projection was *like* lucid dreaming,[44] and that one of the methods Ophiel mentioned in his book on the subject entails projection from within a lucid dream.[45] Hence, I thought to myself : why don't I use my talent for lucid dreaming for those tasks for which others use astral projection ?

Thus by day I would read about, study and practice magick and the Qabalah to the best of my ability, whilst at night I would use my lucid dreams perform rituals like those of the Pentagram and Hexagram, and the Middle Pillar, as well as rising on the planes, assumption of god-forms, and diverse other types of astral working.

One of the books I read was Crowley's "Autohagiography,"[46] which I found invaluable as a contemporary account of one who went through the Golden Dawn system (it has also proved useful as a reference in regard to my Abramelin operation for a similar reason). At one point, I became convinced that I had read a remark in that book to the effect that a certain method existed of vibrating *Adonai Ha-Aretz* which invoked one's Holy Guardian Angel. Later I tried to go back to the book to find the reference, but it had disappeared, as if I had travelled across time, and the version I remembered existed in an alternate timeline ! A far more boring explanation would involve me having read a remark about a method of vibrating *Adonai Ha-Aretz* which brightened one's aura : I had separately read

---

[44] "These astral journeys are really lucid dreams in which one retains all one's faculties of choice, will-power and judgement." - Op. cit., chapter XIV

[45] I.e., section 2, "Dream Method" – OPHIEL (1974)

[46] i.e., CROWLEY (1929), op. cit.

a remark about the same Divine Name being the name of the "Holy Guardian Angel"; my mind had somehow concatenated the ideas together.

Why is the divine name of Malkuth associated with the Holy Guardian Angel? The book "777" lists a number of spiritual experiences, (usually) one for each Sephirah of the Tree of Life: against Malkuth, it gives "Vision of the Holy Guardian Angel."[47] Confusion arises because, as Crowley also said that attaining "knowledge and conversation of the Holy Guardian Angel" forms the work of an Adeptus Minor of the A∴A∴, this has led some to infer that the HGA is somehow associated with Tiphereth.[48] To my mind, however, the Malkuth association retains perfect plausibility, given that it equates to the *first step* on the Path of Return, whilst the wording of *Abramelin* implies that KCHGA forms the *first step* in becoming a fully-fledged ceremonial magician.

I thus found myself one night becoming lucid in a dream, and I decided rather much on a whim to put the occasion to good use to attempt to find the method of vibrating *Adonai Ha-Aretz* which I had assumed would invoke my Holy Guardian Angel. I therefore went through the "vibratory formula of the Middle Pillar": visualising the divine name in glowing white Hebrew letters, I imagined drawing it as a force down through the top of my head, through my *Kether*-point, to my heart-centre (my *Tiphereth*-point), where I momentarily contemplated it, whilst visualising an Angelic figure standing before me. I then sent the force down my middle-pillar, down to my *Malkuth*-centre: quickly assuming the God-form of Horus, I drew the force back up again and projected it towards the Angelic figure with the Sign of the Enterer, whilst vibrating the Name aloud. I then just as quickly assumed the God-form of Harpocrates, and made the Sign of Silence.

The result astounded me. I experienced, quite unexpectedly, the phenomena I usually associated with *samadhi*, in particular, a sudden Kundalini awakening. This one incident completely altered my outlook on life. I believed that I had discovered, if not *the* method of vibrating *Adonai Ha-Aretz* properly, then certainly *a* method – and one which had validly caused me to experience the Vision of the Holy Guardian Angel itself. It further opened my mind to the possibility that the spiritual experiences listed in "777" were in fact all types of *samadhi*: I imagined the Vision of the Holy Guardian Angel as equivalent to one of the more basic types, and hence perfectly compatible with association with *Malkuth*, rather than *Kaivalya*, which I associated with "Divine Union," the experience of *Kether*.

Moreover: from that point on, I came to believe in the essential reality of Angels, and in the likelihood that many of the saints and mystics of the past who

---

[47] CROWLEY (1909) – Column XLV, row 10.
[48] Discussed further *infra*.

had claimed to have beheld Angels must have experienced something of what I had done. Furthermore, I had received an invaluable key for telling whether a future Angel-contact would be genuine or not : if I experienced the same or similar feelings of ecstasy whilst in the presence of an Angelic-being, then it was likely to be *mint*.

This signalled a huge turning point for me, as previously I had only been *faking* magic, but now I was really *making* it. Previously, I had tried to kid myself that magic only *might* be real and somehow based on the psychological model – an infamous intrigue between Jung and Reich. Now, however, I abandoned the psychological model immediately, realising what great adepts of the past have always claimed – that if you treat these things as real, then the Universe itself behaves as if they are real. In short, for the first time, I had become a *real* Magician.

In the months and years after this event, I repeated this method of invocation, and became convinced that the Angelic figure which had appeared before me was my actual Holy Guardian Angel – a being with whom I communed on many occasions through meditation. I would always remember to invoke Him when performing ceremonial magic. If at any time I suffered insomnia, I would get up in the middle of the night using his Name as a mantra. I entered into a full relationship with Him. I came to suspect that this must be what Knowledge and Conversation of the Holy Guardian Angel was like, even though I had not at this point gone through the Abramelin operation.

Meanwhile, the more I contemplated my experiences, I pondered : "*what if,*" I thought to myself, "*the Angel does not just cause samadhi, the angel* is *the samadhi ?*" In other words, what if the Angel is both a genuine Angel, and the feeling one experiences when in an exalted state of spiritual consciousness ?

I therefore began to suspect that if I experienced *samadhi* on any occasion, I might be able to infer that it was an Angel. Likewise, this would imply that Kundalini awakening is the evidence of Angelic presence – it *is* the Angelic presence. Hence, all the Kriya Yoga that I was doing as I contemplated confessing my sins, and the flowing Kundalini and transpersonal states which I experienced as I did the Abramelin operation, was in fact the actual HGA manifesting.

Thus, I surmised that I would be able to judge whether I attained KCHGA on completing this operation by the state of meditative awareness which resulted therefrom.

Some magicians claim that spirits appear to visible appearance, and even claim that if it doesn't, then one hasn't performed a genuine evocation. But I have long suspected that as Sight is only one sense, then (to use the vocabulary of neurolinguistic programming), people are more suited to clairvoyance, clairaudience or clairsentience depending on whether they prefer the Visual,

Auditory or Kinaesthetic Modalities. Judging a spirit not on how if appears (if it appears at all) but on what kind of state of spiritual awareness it produces admirably suits those who are more comfortable with clairsentience than clairvoyance.

*

I noted in my magical journey that day that the operation had taken significantly longer than usual – which I attributed to the extra deep meditation that day.

Later, I added the following note :

"... [D]uring day I go to work – the first time in six weeks. Technically speaking, Abramelin does not lay down an absolute prohibition on going to work during the six month operation, but strongly advises against it. After today, I can appreciate why ! Getting up before dawn to do ritual, and doing a full-day's work is exhausting. I compensate during the evening by deliberately getting an early night."

Day 16

28 April 2020

Iperformed the Middle Pillar Ritual this morning whilst incorporating the ideas regarding my *Nephesh* and Golden body which I had formulated yesterday : I noted that this felt very good.

On a whim, I had the idea to perform the Bornless Ritual with an Attitude of Gratitude towards all the "barbarous names" – on the basis that each one is the name of a pagan god whom I am invoking. As it happened, I realised that I had *not* run out of sins to confess in my morning ritual. I wrote in my journal :

> *"It is presumptuous to think that I have already run out and need to go on to the karma of previous lifetimes. Arrogance, lack of compassion. I ought to mentally prepare myself to be ready at any time to go back to the beginning, out of humility, and if necessary to rise afresh from trauma. May I be brave enough to face down the Dweller on the Threshold !"*

*

Later that day, I got into a discussion with my fiancée about Abramelin. She did not understand it : i.e., she knew what The Book said well enough, but she felt bemused by it and found it hard to have sympathy towards me for doing it. At least she did not want to interfere with my exploits. I thought : *"Perhaps this is one of the difficulties that other occultists have flagged up as the sort of thing one has to face when doing the Abramelin ?"*

In any event, the question "how would I explain the point of the Abramelin Operation to someone unfamiliar with it," has led me to collect my thoughts on how I would go about explaining what the Holy Guardian Angel is to begin with. So, I came up with a survey of what other people have said :

What is the Holy Guardian Angel ?

Historical references to Guardian Angels

The earliest reference to "Guardian Angel"-like beings lies in the *Arda Fravas* of Zoroastrianism. Although this has roots going back to 2000BC, the oldest surviving written records date from only as recently (!) as the 9th - 10th centuries AD.

The first biblical reference occurs in Psalm 91, speculated to have been written about 979 BC or earlier :

"For He shall give his angels charge over thee, to keep thee in all thy ways. They shall bear thee up in their hands, lest thou dash thy foot against a stone."[49]

Whilst in the New Testament examples abound that Jesus and His Apostles at least believed in the concept, e.g., Matthew 18 :10 ; Hebrews 1 :14 ; etc.

In between the writing dates of the Old and New Testaments, ca 375 BC, Plato developed the concept of the "Genius" or "Dæmon." He makes the point that the allocation of Genius to the person does not occur in a random or arbitrary manner, but through one's own soul attracting the Genius to oneself, thereby determining one's own destiny.

About six-hundred years later, the Neo-Platonist Iamblichus mentions Guardian Dæmons whose essence *"is effective of purposes, bringing to maturity the natures about the world, and exercising guardianship individually over those coming into existence."*[50] Meanwhile, the Greek Magical Papyri composed between the 2nd Century BC to the 5th Century AD contained numerous examples of spells to acquire "magical assistants," although one can debate to what extent anyone of them can be called a "Holy Guardian Angel." (Coincidentally the Bornless Ritual derives from the Greek Magical Papyri, though it originally described a rite of exorcism, not of acquiring a magical assistant *per se).*[51]

The earliest example of Jewish belief in Guardian Angels comes from the sage Rashi (died 1105), some 350 years before supposed authorship of "Abramelin."[52] In the same century, Honorius of Atun became the first Christian theologian to specifically mention Guardian Angels.

"Abramelin" supposedly dates from the fifteenth century, though purportedly describing a system of magick already existing in the late fourteenth century. NB the earliest known Abramelin manuscript dates from the early 17th century.

The Franciscan Order first instituted a "Feast of the Guardian Angels," in 1500, which the Catholic Church adopted in 1607. Meanwhile in Protestantism, Martin Luther included prayers to the Guardian Angel in his Small Catechism in 1529.

Catholics still celebrate The Feast of the Guardian Angels on October 2nd each year. This proved especially important to Josemaria Escrivà, the founder of *Opus Dei*, who believed that angels had inspired his own his order. This would make

---

[49] *Psalm 91* :11-12 (KJV).

[50] IAMBLICHUS (1911) chapter 5.

[51] BETZ (1992).

[52] See commentary on Daniel 10 :7 -
https ://www.chabad.org/library/bible_cdo/aid/16493/showrashi/true accessed 2021-12-16.

Escrivà the *second* person in the twentieth century to found a prominent religious movement inspired by his Holy Guardian Angel.

"Holy Guardian Angel" as an actual Angel

The first occultist in modern times to attempt the Abramelin Operation, Aleister Crowley, came to believe his Holy Guardian Angel was an objectively-existing being – an actual Angel. He also insisted that it was definitely *not* the same as the "higher self." Crowley wrote this in 1943, over thirty years after he first claimed to make contact with his Angel : the chapter in which he made this statement makes clear that he had spent the time earnestly contemplating his Angel to investigate its nature.[53]

William Bloom, author of *Sacred Magician,* started his own Abramelin Operation with an equivocal view of the actual nature of the Holy Guardian Angel : on the one hand he suspected that it might have a psychological explanation, but on the other it might come from a world of "*spiritual realities normally unperceived by our five senses.*"[54]

However, at its conclusion and with the benefit of several years' hindsight, he was more definite :

"I had also fully opened the doors of my perception on to the angelic realm. I could now openly perceive and enter into telepathic rapport with this whole parallel dimension."[55]

The contemporary occultist, Aaron Leitch, argues :

"Abraham of Worms was NOT writing about the Nativity Angel or any of his servient angels. He was writing about the one Agrippa called 'the Holy Angel' who 'comes only from God' meaning it is not part of a hierarchy like most angels, but is the direct Holy Spirit and presence of God Itself."[56]

Of this Holy Angel who comes only from God, Agrippa himself elaborated :

"This [i.e. the Holy Angel] doth direct the life of the soul, & doth alwaies put good thoughts into the minde, being alwaies active in illuminating us, although we do not alwaies take notice of it ; but when we are purified, and live peaceably, then it is perceived by us, then it doth as it were speak with us, and communicates its voyce [voice] to us, being before silent, and studyeth daily to bring us to a sacred perfection."[57]

---

[53]CROWLEY (1954), "Chapter XLIII : The Holy Guardian Angel is not the "Higher Self" but an Objective Individual."

[54] BLOOM (1992), p2.

[55] Ibid., p160.

[56] LEITCH (2020)

[57] AGRIPPA (1533), book 3 chapter 22.

Leitch continues :

"... [The Holy Angel] comes from above the created realm - and thus has no relationship whatsoever to your birth chart. In fact, Agrippa says you can work with the Holy Angel to overcome your birth chart. Abraham stresses again and again that astrology - while it has its uses here in the created realm - has no part whatsoever in the Holy Guardian Angel or the Sacred Magick."[58]

A Synonym for the Higher Self

Regardie described it as the *"... Holy Guardian Angel, the Augoeides, that nobler part of [the Magician's] consciousness which is real, permanent, and the bountiful, undying source of inspiration and spiritual sustenance."*[59] Hence, Regardie appears to conflate the Holy Guardian Angel not just with the Higher Self, but also with the *Augoeides* which properly speaking translates to the "shining body" or transmuted astral body.

The Builders of the Adytum explicitly associate the Holy Guardian Angel with the Higher Self, and often use the terms interchangeably.[60] In fact, some of BOTA's teachings imply that there exists only *one* Holy Guardian Angel – and hence Higher Self - for all humanity, which is the Archangel Michael, Archangel of the Sun.[61]

Lon Milo Duquette has at times seemed to conflate the Holy Guardian Angel with the Higher Self,[62] but has elsewhere implied that *one's consciousness* of the HGA is the Higher Self, leaving of what the HGA actually consists ambiguous. He tends to follow the Crowley line that KCHGA is a state of consciousness associated with Tiphereth.[63] He admitted that he has never undertaken the Abramelin operation *per se.*[64]

Third Option

As part of the teachings of the Golden Dawn, MacGregor Mathers referred to the Higher Genius as *"an Angel Mighty and Terrible."* From the context of the quote, Mathers appears to mean that the same Higher Genius is somehow above and beyond the Yechidah or part of the Soul corresponding to Kether, which as the

---

[58] LEITCH, op. cit.

[59] REGARDIE (2004), ch12.

[60] See, e.g., DAVIES, A, *"Esoteric Extension of Tarot to Develop Supersensory Powers,"* lesson 38.

[61] Ibid., lesson 39.

[62] DUQUETTE (1997) p163.

[63] DUQUETTE (1999) p158

[64] KATZ (2011), Introduction.

"Lower Genius" is its viceroy. This would imply that although the Higher Genius / Angel *transcends* the individual in one sense (i.e., is a separate being), yet in another sense there remains a definite connection with it. Mathers never actually out and out says that the Higher Genius / Angel is identical with the "Holy Guardian Angel" of *Abramelin*.[65]

What appears to have happened is that Mathers meant the Higher Genius / "Angel Mighty & Terrible" to be *higher-than-the-Higher-Self*: however, whereas Regardie interpreted it as *the Higher Self*. If – for the sake of argument – one were to postulate that the "Angel Mighty & Terrible" is indeed the "Holy Guardian Angel," then by interpreting Mathers' definition of the "Higher Genius" very strictly creates a route to reconcile the viewpoints of those who claim the HGA is a separate being.

My own feeling based on experiences I've had for over twenty years or so is that the Holy Guardian Angel *looks* like an Angel, *feels* like an Angel, and if you treat it like an Angel, the universe responds as if it *is* an Angel. Hence, notwithstanding the science of the thing, this forms a philosophically valid argument for postulating that it is indeed an actual Angel.

---

[65] REGARDIE (1989), book 1, "The Microcosm – Man."

Days 17, 18

29th to 30th April 2020

The idea of checking in with both my Nephesh and my Solar Body, as well as incorporating gratitude into my rituals, proved fruitful. I wrote :

"The idea of being 'thankful' helped greatly. Besides the desirability of being thankful anyway, it helped centre my mind on the ritual at that moment, making e.g. The LBRP and Bornless Ritual particularly effective.

I began to record evidence that the act of confessing one's sins in the ritualised setting of Abramelin had some practical effect. I wrote in my journal :

"Resentment, holding grudges - remembering past arguments, not letting go of them. Not having compassion for people who don't fully understand me. Allowing memories of past arguments to interfere with my current ritual - all 'sins.'

"Thankfully, however, meditation upon confessing them like this helps calm my mind down and helps me to release my consciousness from dwelling on them."

Likewise I wrote again :

"I seek forgiveness for ... [an argument which I ought to have avoided] yesterday, and reflect - as it happened, I manifested the means to correct my faults in the course of the day. This cannot be a coincidence ! I believe it is my Holy Guardian Angel at work. By confessing with a true heart, my Holy Guardian Angel can manifest the means to correct not just those faults but potentially all of them, including the ones for which I ought to take responsibility, such as those of past lives."

In other words, in the act of Confession one does not debase and humiliate oneself just for the sake of it : instead, one performs a practical method of self-healing. If one has hang-ups about religion and guilt complexes from childhood, one might never realise this before one starts : but I discerned it as one of the hidden properties of the whole Abramelin procedure.

I had feared that by undertaking this procedure I might see evidence of the Dweller on the Threshold manifesting. However, it appeared to me that by keeping my nerve and sticking to the procedure, the same confessing which might bring up the Dweller also became the method whereby to alleviate its worst effects.

Quite separately, it occurred to me that I would sin if I did not complete the literal terms of my original vow : hence I ought to devise some method to carry it out more effectively.

(During the day : more relaxation with music, this time recording a duet with my fiancé, me on my WX5, she on her clarinet.)

Day 19

01 May 2020

Only after almost three weeks of doing the ritual did it occur to me that perhaps I should read The Book to get a more in-depth understanding of what the whole operation involved. One could label this as the magical equivalent of only consulting the instruction leaflet *after* turning the new gadget on – "*typical man behaviour*" as my fiancée might say – but I prefer to think of it as a Punk Rock approach to Abramelin, i.e., not letting the fact that one has not fully informed oneself about the operation prevent one from starting it.

Nevertheless, the diary entries of this and subsequent days had a general theme, that after I had had a really good look at The Book in detail, I now began to adapt my practices in line with my research. I also made an effort to track down books which others had written about the Abramelin operation, such as Bloom's *Sacred Magician*[66] and Newcomb's *21st Century Mage.*[67]

So, for example, after I did my preparation with the Middle Pillar Ritual as on preceding days, and opening up with the LBRP and Bornless ritual, I added afterwards an impromptu conjuration that any spirits that might be present harm not me nor anyone connected with me or with this place. After I included such a conjuration for the first time today, it subsequently became a standard feature of my daily rituals.

The precise wording of the conjuration evolved over time not only in line with my understanding of the source text, but also because of the insights I would receive from my daily practice.

However, I had another reason for adapting my ritual in such a manner: I wanted to make sure nothing went wrong, especially in the light of what happened to Crowley the first time he attempted the operation at Boleskine. E.g., take the following passage written by John Symonds:

> "*Even the butcher down in the village came in for his quota of bad luck through Crowley's casually jotting down on one of his bills the names of two demons, viz. Elerion and Mabakiel, which mean respectively laughter and lamentation. Conjointly these two words signify 'unlooked for sorrow suddenly descending upon happiness.' In the butcher's case, alas, it was only too true, for while cutting up a joint for a customer he accidentally severed the femoral artery and promptly died.*"[68]

---

[66] Op. cit.

[67] NEWCOMB (2002)

[68] Although this was originally from SYMONDS (1951), I had never read that particular work, and instead remembered it quoted in WILSON (1987), the first book I had ever read about the Great Beast.

The same Symonds alleged that the Abramelin demons started to congregate around Crowley's oratory *before* the completion of the Operation. Hence – following my intention not to make the same mistakes that Crowley did – I reasoned that I ought to not wait until the conjuration of the princes of Hell and their servants during the final six days : I ought to start taking precautions *now,* right at the outset.

It so happened that later that day I scanned, ocr'd and edited a list of all of the spirits named in the Book of Abramelin, with a view to incorporating them into the conjurations I planned to type out. Probably because I remembered the incident with the unfortunate butcher, I earnestly desired not dying in a freak, *Omen*-like accident at my computer. However, I am pleased to report, in retrospect, that no such incident befell me either that day or during (and, so far, after) my Abramelin Operation. So my caution well re-paid my foresight, and my idea proved a good one !

More generally : I had recorded in my journal the previous day :

" *[R]eading the* Book of Abramelin *to get a better handle on what the conjurations of the final six days will be. I intend to compose and type up appropriate conjurations for each day, based on the text of the book, so that I will have written* aide-memoires *when the time comes.*"

Thus, when it came to confessing my sins that day,

"*Inspired by my studies of the Book of Abramelin yesterday, I imagine what demons might try to taunt me with. The fact is that there are things I regret but which I thought at the time I was following my conscience, and which I thought might be sins but turned out not to be. There are also things I regret but which were not under my control.*"

I believed my Holy Guardian Angel actively helped me in my relations with my fiancée. At the time she had her own magical work to get on with – and it caused her much angst. "*She has a phobia about her work being judged by others,*" I recorded in my journal. "*My efforts to reassure her do not go down well.*"

However, whilst meditating during the "confession" part of my ritual, I came to believe that my HGA gave me advice – specifically, I had not showed her the right amount of compassion. "*I am karmically bound to* [her]," I wrote in my journal. "[T]*herefore I should be more forgiving and merciful towards her. If* [she] *argues with me it is karmically my fault, even if I am right !*"

I wrote the above with no trace of irony : I really did believe in the karmic connection between myself and my fiancée, hence I assumed the karma for all the arguments into which we got as the unfortunate but logical implication of this line of reasoning. Nevertheless, this approach seemed to work, for as I recorded later that day :

"Tensions with [my fiancée], *but following advice I received from HGA this morning they seem to resolve. By the evening she is laughing at it all."*

In fact she seemed so good humoured, that she later requested us doing some magic together, including a guided meditation from *A Garden of Pomegranates,*[69] as well as a horizontal invocation of Kether, with the appropriate divine and angelic names. As I recorded during the following day's ritual :

"I spend a lot of time thanking my HGA, because the guidance I received yesterday worked, and confirmed what I had been told on Day 18,"

i.e., that the act of confessing causes to manifest the means to rectify the thing confessed.[70]

.

---

[69] REGARDIE (2002) – the meditation actually came from the material written by Chic & Tabatha Cicero.

[70] *Vide supra.*

Day 20

02 May 2020

Daily repetition of the Bornless Ritual inevitably got me thinking about the meaning of the barbarous names which I invoked as a part thereof. I would "vibrate" each foreign sounding word individually, which naturally gave me time to contemplate the corresponding force.

For example -

"*'Osorronophris' - I get the impression that I'm invoking the egregore of a cult from ancient Egypt that ventured astrally into the underworld to commune with Osiris. No living man hath seen him at any time - hence the only ones who have are the Dead, and those who have learnt to transcend the boundaries of life and death.*

"*In fact, all these barbarous names of evocation are the names of God as worshipped by various cults throughout the ancient world. E.g. 'Aeeiouo' is that of the ancient Greek mysteries.*"

I had long ago memorised the whole Bornless Ritual, after I decided it would be a productive way to pass a wet weekend. As a young man, before I found a regular job, my time alternated between a succession of temporary positions and periods of unemployment. I used a lot of these periods to work on my magical studies. Hence, I managed to accumulate a large fund of erudition, but I also felt dissuaded from attempting the Abramelin Operation during that time : because I had such a precarious employment position, I had no settled home-life, and I often did not know what I would be doing from one week to the next.

Memorising the Bornless Ritual proved easy for me : I had it down in a couple of hours or less. It helped that it had a structure and repetition, so that the only real difficulty lay in learning the barbarous names of evocation. I often like to memorise large chunks of ritual, especially the most important conjurations, because I find that not having to read a script frees up brain-power to give me the luxury of being able to think about what I am saying.

The Bornless Ritual itself I would describe it as one of the most powerful conjurations ever, only comparable to the Enochian Keys. Incidentally, I *always* call it "The Bornless Ritual" and not the so-called "headless rite," because, being a student of language, I recognise that in ancient Greek, Hebrew, as well as in many languages of antiquity, the word for "head" was also a synonym for "beginning."[71] Hence it is good colloquial Greek to translate *Akephalon* not as "headless" but as "he who is without a beginning" – or "Bornless," just as the

---

[71] E.g., Genesis 1 :1 literally translated would be "In the *head*, formed the Gods the heavens and the earth."

original translator did. I despair of so-called magicians who insist on calling it the "headless rite," as it marks them as people whose knowledge of Greek extends no further than *Google Translate*.

I formed much of my opinion about the Bornless Ritual after I decided to investigate each barbarous word numerologically, the results of which I wrote in an article for the *Journal of the Western Mystery Tradition*.[72] Nevertheless, after more than sixteen years of constant use of this invocation, I still get fresh insights from time to time – as I did during this Abramelin Operation itself.

For example – jumping ahead to day 112 for a moment, I wrote :

> *"THOUGHT : 'Eben' in the Eastern section - is the* Lapis Philosophorum, *i.e. the Hebrew word for 'Stone,' the Father conjoined with the Son,[73] etc. It should not surprise me that Hebrew words should creep into the conjurations of the Bornless Ritual (after all it already features 'Sabaot,' 'Adonai,' etc). But - apart from the idea that one of the things I am invoking in the ritual is the Philosophers' Stone - perhaps this means I ought to be able to find greater meaning by analysing the barbarous words from a Hebrew point of view (up to now I had only really been considering Greek)."*

The point being that as I had these ideas about the meaning of the Ritual, it helped improve how I felt about the energies it summoned. Again, from day 183 :

> *"I am working on a theory that the 'Bornless One' is actually a manifestation of, or a god-form associated with, Kether. (NB there is precedent for this. I can remember seeing references to the Bornless One ['Akephalon'] in the Greek magical papyri and it was clear that it was synonymous with Ptah, himself a godform attributed in 777 to Kether.[74]) Therefore when I perform this ritual this morning, I imagine that when I invoke the Bornless One I am in fact invoking Kether : this proves quite effective."*

Thus far the main examples of insights into *meanings of words* : I also had many other insights of a more psychic nature. Most of these had to do with continually refining the ideal state on consciousness in which to perform the ritual in order to derive maximum benefit therefrom. In any event, never a day went by without me feeling *some* power from invoking the Bornless Ritual. As I noted on day five, I would employ vast understatement when recording the results in my journal : I had become so habituated to it power as a conjuration that often I would not remark upon the fact.

---

[72] SUMNER (2004)

[73] I.e., "אב" (Father) and "בן" (Son) when run together make "אבן" (Stone). For a fuller discussion on this point see CASE (2006).

[74] CROWLEY (1909) – See Column XIX, row 19.

*

My fiancée, who practiced knitting as a hobby, had made me a new scarf. A bit redundant for the time being, as it was the beginning of May. Nevertheless, she thought of me as a mighty wizard, so of course she had to knit me a Gryffindor scarf from *Harry Potter*.

More seriously, apart from my usual ritual that day, we practiced some Golden Dawn magic together. As I wrote in my journal :

"Later : at [my fiancée's] *request, we spend the afternoon invoking the Earth spirits, as suggested in the GD grade materials. Spend some time looking for* [my fiancée's] *Wand of Double Power. I use my pendulum to discern that it is in the garage somewhere. We improvise with a substitute - otherwise it goes well."*

As mentioned on day 4, this amounted to another example of me performing a magic ritual technically outside the scope of the Abramelin Operation. I suppose I should have regarded this as a big no-no, although the prohibition was against magic contrary to the *spirit* of the Operation. Besides, I had an excuse on this occasion, namely that I did not really do it myself : I merely assisted my fiancée, an initiate of the GD in her own right.

Day 21

03 May 2020

Today started out as a day much like any other, except that it marked a turning point the significance of which I only appreciated in retrospect. I began my journal entry for that day : "*Up at 4.55am for preparation with LL Ritual. Good,*" which probably meant rather splendid. I then began the actual ritual of the morning at sunrise, 5.25am, although in my panic to begin precisely on time I spent what seemed like an agonising aeon faffing around with the candle (it can't have exceeded a minute).

After performing the LBRP, I continued :

"**Bornless Ritual.** *I feel my mind calming down, so that by the end I can feel my subtle body being transformed by the barbarous names of evocation as I intone them.*

"**Confession of sins.** *Imagining what demons might throw at me : trafficking with demons ? But then I can throw the absurdity of accusing me of trafficking with them back at them !*

"*In a sense I have created the Universe to resolve my Karma, so all that is wrong with the Universe is my fault. But on the upside, all that is wrong with the Universe can be resolved and abreacted through me !*"

I apologise if the preceding seems trite, but this demonstrates exactly the kind of stream-of-consciousness type musings which often occurred to me during such moments alone with my own mind. I can only suppose that the actual subjective experience of the above held more importance than my attempts at describing it can express, on account of what happened next :

"*I pass into a deep state of meditation - which I recognise as the presence of an Angel - my Holy Guardian Angel.*[75] *Can my samadhi be manifest outside my body ? In any case, I experience a very profound stillness -* samadhi *- my Angel manifesting. Very encouraging.*"

This marked the first time I experienced Samadhi during the Abramelin operation. After I finished the Operation, and started reviewing my journal, I realised : *the quality of my daily rituals improved noticeably from this point on.*

Also, henceforth the duration of my daily rituals rarely dropped below 45 minutes and sometimes took even longer, because I spent so much time meditating.

On a different subject entirely : today I introduced an innovation which became a permanent fixture of my future behaviour. I amended the "Licence to Depart" at the end so that I did it in the names "YHVH," "Tzebaoth" and "Adonai."

---

[75] See : day 15 – *vide supra.*

These, according to Dehn, are the only three divine names used in the Abramelin operation, although the Book gives this instruction in the context of the conjuration of the first of the final six days.[76] I started performing the Licence to depart in this way because I decided that day to take my precedents from The Book, as opposed to just making it up which is what I had done up until then. By "making it up" I of course mean "relying on my experience as a Golden Dawn magician."

---

[76] VON WORMS *et al* (2006), p109.

Day 22

04 May 2020

By the beginning of the fourth week I felt myself *dredging* my mind for even more sins. "*It occurs to me that being negligent or reckless - given that it is an example of falling below the ideal standard - is itself technically a 'sin,'*" I wrote in my journal. "*I therefore spend time thinking about how I have been reckless in my life?*"

I probably did not help myself by having a legal background – I had studied law at University. Hence I could use my expertise as to what constituted *mens rea* to prosecute myself before the Court of Hell itself.

I had not, of course, ever committed anything which one could remotely consider a *crime* of Recklessness, although some people from my past to whom I bore animadversion had accused me years ago of behaving recklessly anyway, despite my belief in my innocence. "*Maybe my accusers were correct,*" I pondered. – "*In which case I try to contemplate seeking forgiveness from those I have wronged, and sending them real healing.*"

After the exalted heights to which I had ascended in the previous day's meditation, today proved a let-down by comparison. "*Not as deep a meditative state as yesterday,*" I wrote. "*I believe it is because in reaching one plateau, I have only succeeded in unlocking another layer which I now have to abreact and sublimate (with the help of my Holy Guardian Angel).*" This, incidentally, indicated a phenomena I had encountered often on the spiritual path, i.e., that as soon as I had come to what I thought was the top of one ladder, I only found myself at the bottom of another. In other words, Success in one task only signalled time to start something new and more difficult.

This had occurred so often that I had become used to it. I looked upon it as the norm of spiritual progress : so much so, that I have become completely disenchanted with talk of supposed "final attainments." Even if I ever became an "Ipsissimus" (I thought), it ought not to surprise me if it turns out as just the beginning of an Even-Greater Mystery, the nature of which I cannot yet surmise. Hence again why associating "knowledge and conversation of the Holy Guardian Angel" with Malkuth seemed perfectly reasonable to me.

Day 23

05 May 2020

I wrote in my journal : *"Up at 4.51am for preparation with LL Ritual."* Despite the fact that it happened in advance of the main event, it nonetheless became a fertile source of inspiration in its own right.

"Thinking about The Kybalion - *in amongst the spuriousness is the idea that just as Charles Dickens' spirit was inside all the characters he created in his novels, so the spirit of God is in all beings in Creation[77] - so indeed is my own spirit within all thought-forms I create in my own consciousness.*

"However : Papus - in one of his lectures on Martinism, says that the Universe - i.e. The physical Universe - is itself a living being, because the universal cosmic forces display the characteristics of life. Applying therefore the bona fide *Hermetic principle that the world of matter reflects the world of spirit, this would imply there is a Spirit within the Universe also. The astrological forces are one manifestation of this universal Spiritual Body, but there must be higher planes to it as well. Each wave of creation of the Universe is a macrocosmic reflection of the wave of creation of the individual (was this what Blavatsky was trying to say ?).*"

This rather abstruse point nevertheless perfect sense to me at the time, albeit in an intuitive way almost entirely divorced from conventional logic. I think the easiest way of explaining it would go like this :

The twelve signs of the Zodiac obviously refer to actual constellations in the physical universe *(macrocosm)*, but also in a symbolic sense to twelve parts of the human body *(microcosm)* as well – thus providing the basis of Medical Astrology, a well-known topic amongst conventional astrologers.

Hence, the Microcosmic Zodiac does not comprise twelve separate constellations, but a Unity of twelve connected parts, i.e. because it is all one body.

However – and here my line of thought started to seriously diverge from reality into originality – given that the famous Hermetic principle says, "As above, so below," this would also imply the converse : "As below, so above." Therefore, whereas Hermeticists have previously claimed events taking place in the macrocosm indicate processes in the microcosm, surely this also means that the Hermeticist may also speculate that processes taking place in the microcosm reflect those in the macrocosm ?

Hence, if we say that the Microcosmic Zodiac is a Unity comprising twelve parts, we also ought to be able to say that the Macrocosmic Zodiac, far from

---

[77] "THREE INITIATES" (1908), chapter VII.

comprising twelve separate constellations in space, instead makes up twelve connected parts in one Macrocosmic Body. I interpret this as the point that Papus attempted to make when he said that the Physical Universe was itself a living being.

And yet we can go further than this, by also saying that if we accept the Universe as a living being, then it should also possess macrocosmic versions of the other characteristics which we impute to living beings as well. For example, if we say that a human has an Etheric body, an Astral body, a Mental body, a Causal body (etc), then so too must the Universe itself. Moreover, by the same reasoning we could claim that Macrocosmic version of the true Ego must exist – and that the Universe itself undergoes reincarnation, as humans themselves do.

To rephrase this very simply : when the astrologer talks about the influence of one particular sign of the Zodiac, he or she actually refers to an energy that has its origin in one of the subtle, non-physical, bodies of the Universe.

However, I really bowled myself over when I speculated what would happen if I tried to hold both this concept in my mind as well as that principle mentioned in The Kybalion ? I.e. if us microcosms are characters in a drama written by a Macrocosmic author, the spirit of whom animates *us*, then *whose spirit animates the Macrocosmic author ?* This question I regard not so much as one that has a sensible answer, but more like a *Koan*, in that the act of attempting to consider it leads one, like the Zen Buddhist, into a state of enlightenment. In other words, that if one could somehow hold the concept of oneself as a reflection of the Macrocosmic Body, itself animated by the Spirit of Something-Even-Greater, and that one could perceive of what that Something-Even-Greater actually consisted, one would come to know God.

> *"Hence, the I AM-ness which is the real 'I' is a reflection of a 'Cosmic I AM-ness' which is above and beyond the Universe.*
>
> *"I say all this because centring my attention on my own 'I AM-ness' and contemplating the connection between that and its macrocosmic counterpart, and realising that my own spirit is ensouled in the concepts I conjure signified by the Names I vibrate - helps me much during the LL Ritual, and throughout this morning's ceremony."*

*

The reader might guess from my reference to *The Kybalion* as containing "spuriousness" that I do not necessarily include it in my list of favourite books, but that would do me an injustice. *The Kybalion* splendidly exemplifies early 20th century "New Thought" literature – the passage to which I refer in my journal entry quoted above being the best part thereof. However : despite the beauty of that particular piece of writing, it is not, as it claims, authentic Hermetic philosophy – one can quite easily find modern translations of the actual *Corpus Hermeticum* with which to compare it.

Had "the Three Initiates" not claimed for it a status it did not warrant, then *The Kybalion* would stand above criticism. Indeed, as shown above, I myself used ideas from it in order to help shape my own thought. However, the very large number of people who consider *The Kybalion* as literally traditional ancient Hermeticism worries me. The Builders of the Adytum treat it like a studied-text, and not surprisingly BOTA members in general assume "the Three Initiates" included their very own Paul Foster Case. However, I surprised myself some years ago when I discovered that its influence was wider than I had suspected :

Once upon a time, the influential French masonic writer Jean-Marie Ragon (1781 to 1862) claimed to be in possession of the fabled *Arcana Arcanorum* and had written it into the highest degrees of Memphis-Misraim. However, when Ragon passed to the Grand Orient Eternal, no mention of what the *Arcana Arcanorum* consisted turned up in his papers, so it remained a mystery.

This did not prevent a lot of people speculating, and – more to the point – hinting that they possessed the *Arcana Arcanorum,* in an effort to entice people to their own version of Memphis-Misraim and to one-up their rivals. For example, I heard one allegation that rituals deriving from the Bedarrides brothers (who would have been Ragon's contemporaries) contained the precious knowledge.

I tried to pursue this line of research, and found French documents purporting to be these rituals. These I translated myself and found, to my amazement, that the so-called *Arcana Arcanorum* consisted of nothing more than the seven so-called Hermetic Principles lifted straight out of *The Kybalion.*

Needless to say, I immediately assumed that the French documents which I had translated were hoaxes, and had nothing to do with either Ragon or the Bedarrides in the first place. I actually thought it was rather funny – someone's idea of a practical joke to play on someone more gullible than myself. (With hindsight and more evidence, I believe the hoax consisted of stealing a sincerely-written modern ritual and falsely passing it off as ancient.)

Incidentally, I have heard other theories about the *true* nature of the *Arcana Arcanorum*, some spoken of in Hushed Tones of Dread Importance – until I realised that Crowley had already summarised it explicitly in one of his most famous books.[78]

But I digress. The beneficial influence of the state of "I AM-ness" which I experienced in the Middle Pillar Ritual carried over into the main ceremony :

   "Sunrise at 5.21 am.

---

[78] "THE MASTER THERION" (1929), chapter XVIII.

"LBRP.

"Bornless Ritual.

"Prayer to YHVH, Tzebaoth and Adonai that I may attain KCHGA, and that all spirits be conjured and bound not to hurt me nor anyone connected with this place, etc."

Inspired by the thought I first had on day 19, I had composed this conjuration by drawing upon the specific wording of The Book. I would refer back to The Book again during the course of my Operation when I felt the need to update this conjuration.

*"**Confession of sins**. I call to mind the thoughts about my recklessness and negligence that I had yesterday, but this time realised that by surrounding it with an aura of love, I can - through the grace of God and my HGA - absorb it and transmute it."*

I had already written about how Dion Fortune described Theodore Moriarty absorbing a spirit.[79] It *now* occurred to me – what would happen if I tried to do the negative energies cropping up in my own psyche what Moriarty did to that vampiric entity ?

"Monkey-brain, being below the ideal standard, is a sin - I conjure and bind it.

"Can feel my I AM-ness present in the whole absorbing process. I realise the presence, albeit briefly, of my HGA in that for one brief moment I am able to attain a deep state of meditative awareness."

So it would appear that whereas I had previously thought of this "Absorption" as a general metaphor for the redemption of sins, I now had evidence that I could use it as a practical technique in my Abramelin practice. However, unlike Moriarty, who absorbed an external entity, I was using the practice to absorb *myself.*

*

From my magical journal, of that same day :

"Later : Thinking about the logistics of performing the final six-day ritual. When conjuring the Daemons, I will need the word squares laid out so they can empower them and 'seal the pact' as it were. Hence, I need each word square on a separate page, and neatly tabulated so I can find the appropriate squares in the course of the day - and file them away again when necessary.

---

[79] Day 13 – *vide supra.*

"Hence that particular day will consist of several ceremonies, one after the other. Get one set of word squares out - ceremony - put that set away and get next set out - ceremony - etc etc etc.

"Unfortunately, however, the supposedly corrected versions in The Book of Abramelin are not printed out in a convenient format (or at all), and there is no easy way to convert them into Word format without a lot of faffing around and data input ...

"It occurs to me that instead of trying to compose them using MS Word, it would be just as easy (difficult) to write them all out by hand. Counting up the word squares, there are 255 in total. Therefore, I print out 255 sheets of squared paper, which I intend to compile into my own working Abramelin Grimoire, i.e., collated in a lever-arch file which I will paginate and tab as appropriate.

"Today I begin by transcribing the word squares of the first chapter of Book 4, which are to discover all manner of hidden things which are not contrary to the Will of God. These, as it happens, are under the presidency of the Holy Guardian Angel. It occurs to me that I should only write out the squares which are under the presidency of the various demons in a consecrated space, with appropriate conjurations and safeguards, so I do not evoke a demon by accident. This is probably where Aleister Crowley went wrong when he first tried to do the Abramelin at Boleskine - he was writing out the names of demons and bad things started happening to people around him."

And so it came to pass. Some people judge the quality of their grimoires by how nice they look, whether it looks all pretty, or bound in leather, or gothicy / witchy / decadent etc. I on the other hand judge a grimoire on the basis of whether I can use it in the middle of a ritual. I therefore find that if one does not mind sacrificing aesthetic charm for utility, then one can create a perfectly good *working grimoire* from items easily purchased from any decent stationer.

I do indeed use a large lever-arch file as my Abramelin Grimoire, even as I described it above. By making it hand-written, instead of printing it out, it became more personal to me. Although this makes it large and quite bulky, I did it this way so that I could put all the details (or at least – all the important details) relevant to each square on each page. Moreover, I foresaw that it would be useful to have space on each page to which to add notes, as I predicted that my understanding of each word-square might evolve as I used it in practice.

I generally tried to write out all the squares relating to one chapter of The Book each day (this did not work out exactly, as I shall explain hereafter). I did not write them out in numerical order, but instead following a particular scheme : firstly, all the chapters relating to the squares which the Holy Guardian Angel alone gives – this on the "invoke the highest first" principle. Secondly, all those given partly by the Holy Guardian Angel, and partly by the Spirits – which one may only use with the Angel's permission. Thirdly and finally : those by the Spirits alone.

In each case I would not begin to work on the squares relating to *any* chapter without invoking protection upon myself, and formulating a conjuration in the names of YHVH, Tzebaoth, and Adonai, to keep me safe etc. Likewise, I would dismiss any spirits lurking invisibly in the vicinity when I had finished working on my grimoire for the time-being.

*

Later that day : more music. Instead of a classical piece, I transcribed the theme tune for "Citizen Smith" from memory so that we could perform it together, it being my fiancée's favourite comedy series when she was growing up.

Days 24, 25

6th – 7th May 2020

My explorations of Life, the Universe and Everything the previous day turned out to have a more profound effect than I realised. For a start, if affected the way I performed the Middle Pillar Ritual :

"Up at 4.51am. Preparation with LL Ritual. I make it less about multiple vibrations and more about contemplating the properties of the Sephiroth which I'm invoking - bearing in mind the principles which I mentioned yesterday. I end up spending as much time on it this way as I would by vibrating each divine name six times.

"I AM in the thought - as God is in The Universe."

Likewise, when I came to performing the Bornless Ritual that morning :

"By maintaining the awareness mentioned above, the barbarous names of evocation raise me to a level of magical consciousness. I AM in these thoughts, but also at the same time they link me to their macrocosmic counterparts - God as "He" is or has been worshipped in various ways across time and space."

When it came to confessing my sins, I again thought of "Absorbing" them in the manner I had previously mentioned. It also got me thinking about whether I could really call all these sins "evil" *per se.*

"Trying to absorb everything. Some sins while having questionable morality are also manifestations of (e.g.) craft, cunning, etc and hence useful qualities. Sublimation !"

As a result of all this, I passed into a very deep state of meditation. "*I experience Samadhi,"* I wrote. "*I AM in the Samadhi. Deep. Still."*

Only two days had passed since I had experienced such an orgasm of the spirit for the first time in my Abramelin Operation. Having "broken my duck" this state would on future days come more frequently. For example, on the following day, I could recall it precisely because the experience stayed so fresh in my mind. "*I AM in this Samadhi - and the Spirit of God is in Me"* I affirmed to myself, and found I could centre myself in this "I AM consciousness" as I performed my ritual of the morning. This proved so potent that when it came to meditating that morning, I experienced a samadhi-like state of consciousness for *the second-day in succession.*

But I did not let my guard-down : it occurred to me that if I kept experiencing this, it might set off another Dweller on the Threshold incident.

"Thought : if that which is below is a reflection of that which is above, does that mean that God is working out His own Karma (Tikkun) ? Perhaps even from previous emanations of the Universe ? Maybe there is a Macrocosmic Dweller on the Threshold *?"*

*

Over these two days I wrote out the word squares of Chapters 3 and 4 of Book 4 of Abramelin (i.e. the Dehn version). I had deliberately missed out chapter 2 for the time being as I kept to my rule of concentrating on those chapters given by the Holy Guardian Angel first.

Day 26

08 May 2020 *(75th Anniversary of VE Day)*

Georg Dehn's translation of *The Book of Abramelin* only rates as a superior translation of that work in the minds of people who have never completed the Abramelin Operation – or have ever tried to use it as a working grimoire. Everyone who has praised it, in effect, treated it like a mere coffee-table book. None of them have investigated the data it contains with the kind of nerdish attention to detail for which someone performing the Operation holds supreme importance. I reached this conclusion because in the course of my semester doing the Operation, *I became that nerd.*

I first began to suspect something amiss when I attempted to transcribe the word squares from chapter five of Book IV of the *Book of Abramelin* – *"To obtain servant spirits – either free or sealed – and how to send them away."* I did not feel particularly elated that morning : I had gone to bed late the previous evening and had awoken at 4.46am feeling tired. Consequently, when I performed my morning ritual, I noted : *"A meditative state, not as deep as yesterday, but palpable, nonetheless. Evidence that the Angel is present, if on this particular day I can perceive it but dimly (probably due to lack of sleep, noted above)."* Nevertheless, trying to maintain the sense of "I AM-ness" which I had been cultivating the past two days obviously did me some good, as I recorded : *"At the end I at least am feeling better than when I began."*

After a snooze to recover, I got stuck into the work of writing out the squares for today's chapter. Dehn's translation does *not* draw pictures of what the word squares should look like – instead, it lists the letters supposed to go in the square. I ought not to have found this a problem, as I only had to write them out in a square grid, row by row. Easy, right ?

Wrong. I got stuck when I came to the last word square, to make servant spirits appear in the form of a monkey or Ape. It consisted of six words, but instead of each having six letters as one would expect if they fitted into a square, *two of them only had five letters.*

At first, this only annoyed me. None of the squares from chapters one, three, and four had presented a problem, so perhaps (I thought) I had just encountered a one-off typo. I decided to check in with a Facebook group full of ceremonial magicians, to find out how *they* had solved the problem of the correct lettering for this square – only to discover that none of them had noticed the discrepancy. *And this in a group which included alleged Abramelin alumni !*

I did, however, receive a tip-off that several different Abramelin manuscripts, to which Dehn had referred in his bibliography, had – since the publication of the 2006 volume – been scanned and put online. I later realised that Joseph H

Peterson, the webmaster of "Esoteric Archives," had already indexed and provided links to almost all of the manuscripts then available on the internet.[80] (Months after I finished the Operation, I myself found another one which Peterson had missed – *vide infra*).

The Abramelin manuscripts, in the order in which I became acquainted with them, consisted of :

"The Leipzig Manuscript" – from the University of Leipzig. Circa 1750 ;

"The Dresden Manuscript" – from the State and University Library of Dresden. Circa 1700 ;

"The Bibliothèque de l'Arsenal Manuscript" – i.e. the same one which MacGregor Mathers used for his own edition – also circa 1750 ; and

"The Hammer Edition" – from the Humboldt University of Berlin, a scan of the 1850 printed version, which itself purports to be a facsimile of a printed version from 1725 – i.e., the one I discovered only afterwards.

Other Abramelin Manuscripts exist, but as far as I know, at the time of writing one cannot access them via the internet : instead, one would have to physically inspect them at the respective institutions which hold them.[81]

Hence, I found myself that morning faced with the Leipzig version. Searching through the manuscript, I came to a word square which at first glance looked like the one I sought – although I noticed several differences in spelling, e.g., "CEHHER" instead of "Cephir" in both Dehn' and Mathers' version.

Figure 3 The word square as it appears in the Leipzig Manuscript. The first letter of the fourth line appears to be an "E" overwritten by an "H," i.e. to make "HARRAH."

---

[80] See : http ://esotericarchives.com/abramelin/abramelin.htm accessed 2021-03-03
[81] This remark was written in March 2021, it may be edited in either the second edition of this book, or just the second printing, depending on how well it sells !

On looking closer it became apparent that the order and attributions in the manuscript differed to both Dehn and Mathers. For example, the 10th, 11th and 12th squares in the Leipzig version were :

KELEP in the form of a dog
CEHHER in the form of a lion
KOBHA in the form of an ape.

Whereas Dehn gave :

KELEF in the form of a lion
KOBHA in the form of a dog
CEPHIR in the form of an ape.

I had not yet found any other Abramelin manuscripts, but I immediately guessed some existed, for how otherwise could Dehn have made such a basic error unless he had access to sources more accurate than the Leipzig manuscript ? This started me on my quest to find as many original Abramelin source documents as possible, i.e., the Dresden Manuscript, the Bibliothèque de l'Arsenal version, and the Hammer edition. For the time-being, however, I resolved the issue by sticking with Dehn's arrangement as best I could. I figured that if I had started using his versions, I should at least remain consistent for now, and if I needed to change any squares, I would sort them out with my Holy Guardian Angel after the final seven-day ritual.

Later, I looked at the versions in the Dresden manuscript and concluded that not only did it contain full versions which were lacking in Dehn's book but had them in a different order again : hence leading me to revise not only the word-square which had given me a head-ache, but the whole chapter.

I might have quickly dismissed the affair of the Dog, Lion and Ape as a mere triviality – had I not later discovered that the discrepancy I discovered in chapter five of Book IV *was not an isolated incident.*

On Day 32, when attempting to transcribe the word-squares of chapter eleven ("to obtain lost books, hidden manuscripts and such,") Dehn gave a version of one square with letters which did not fit – and then he gave a different version of the same square with words that *did* on the very next page. I went with the latter, though I was left puzzled why he had not explained the difference when it lay right there on the page.

The next day, I ran into difficulties with the squares of chapter sixteen ("To recover treasures") : I recall having to take some liberties to attempt to create correct versions. The day after that I found problems with chapter eighteen ("Healing sicknesses") and decided to use the Dresden versions of three squares, whilst a fourth I had to judge the version I wanted to use based on those of both Dresden and Leipzig.

The following day, in chapter twenty-five ("moving around under water,") I found out-and-out *spelling mistakes.* By comparing Dehn's version to the Dresden version, I became convinced that he had confused the letter "f" and an old fashioned "s" in the middle of a word - which one must admit does look like a modern "f." *"But this is someone who's supposed to be* au fait *with ancient manuscripts,"* I thought.

For chapter twenty-eight ("to have as many coins as you need"), the Dresden manuscript had one extra word-square compared to Dehn, whilst it numbered two other word-squares differently. I began to think to the utility of publishing a book which collated all the word-square versions from the available manuscripts and put them side-by-side so that other magicians could see the variations for themselves and judge for themselves which the correct version.

It got to the point where I would resort to the Dresden and Leipzig manuscripts as a matter of course, as I did not feel comfortable with Dehn's book. On more than one occasion, comparison with other manuscripts provided little help. I recall having the most grief with those of chapter nineteen ("to achieve all sorts of friendships") which I found particularly hard going. Although I felt certain that mistakes and ambiguities existed in that chapter of Dehn's book, I found that none of the available manuscripts agreed with one another or spoke unequivocally. I reflected that I was worrying about a chapter which only concerned me for completeness' sake, not because I would make much use of what amounted to "love spells," which I found ethically repugnant. In my obsession for correctness, I had become a contributor to my own frustration.

As it happened, I borrowed an idea from Abramelin alumnus Aaron Leitch, and came up with arbitrary designations for the squares of this chapter by trying to decipher what the various words meant in Hebrew.[82] By the time I had done this I just wanted to put it away and have done with it.

Hence, although to begin with I thought that I could write out the squares of one chapter per day, the more I progressed, the more I realised I might need several days to investigate what the various manuscripts said, and then make an executive decision as to the version I felt comfortable using. In the end I spent

---

[82] The arrangement with which I came up consisted of: CALLAH - A Bride; CATAN - A Bridegroom; RAIAK - Courting DODIM - ones Relatives ("Dodim" is either Uncles or Aunts depending on the pointing); SICOFET (should be SI OFET) - a Judge; IALDAG - a Boy; ELEM - a particular youth; MAGID - a Priest ("Magid" means a Preacher); SALOM - Peace; AHIB - Friendship in general; BETULAH - a Virgin; IEDIDAH - Friendship in general ("Iedidah" is literally friendship); SAGAL - Affairs ("Sagal" literally means concubine); GEBHIR - to be beloved of a PRINCE (i.e. A powerful man); SARAH - a particular woman; TAAFAH - To be wanted / attractive (a pure guess this one); and EFEHA - Elopements ("Efeha" is literally "She flew away").

over seventy days performing a task which, had I had impeccable word-squares to begin with, I should have completed in less than half the time.

What really infuriated me, though, lay in the fact that in the midst of all these discrepancies – e.g., the rows of a word-square having an unequal number of letters, missing letters unaccounted for, things which ought to have been noticed straightaway in the proof-reading stage – Dehn provided no explanation for them. Indeed, although he listed the Abramelin manuscripts of which he knew, he did not explain precisely how they related to the final version of his own edition. Perhaps if he had devoted less space to autobiographical information, he would have more opportunity to explain how he used the various sources to compile his final product.

The whole wretched affair of trying to figure out the finer details of the various word-squares, led me to ask myself a very serious question : **how do I know that any of the available Abramelin sources are *better* than any of the others ?** For some time, a lot of people in the online occult community had lauded *The Book of Abramelin,* and thrown shade on Mathers' version, simply because the former seemed somehow more complete. But, as I discovered through my own researches, *The Book of Abramelin* had faults of its own. I must assume that they amounted to "mistakes" for the editor offered no explanation for why the discrepancies existed.

The Mathers version, on the other hand, one could at least describe as a competent translation of the manuscript from the Bibliothèque de l'Arsenal : the digitised scans of this manuscript made this easy to verify. I had noticed a lot of people, I presume repeating hearsay, state that Mathers had done a poor translation. He did nothing of the sort : any shortcomings in his version come from the manuscript alone – Mathers himself had worked in both a scholarly *and* magical fashion, to the highest standard.

I therefore started to entertain the idea : the version in the Bibliothèque de l'Arsenal has its faults, but then so does every other version – **hence one cannot differentiate between them qualitatively by examining the text alone.** For all I knew, this might apply to other differences between the sources, e.g., whether the operation should take six months or eighteen months. As far as concerned me, versions which said 'eighteen' certainly *differed* from those which said 'six,' but they provided absolutely no evidence to account them *better*. After all, one might explain the differences by the fact that an actual magician wrote down a particular version who found that that variation happened to work for him : so it would deserve respect at least to that extent.

I wrote in my journal at the time : "*[t]he word squares in chapter five are supposedly under the presidency of the Holy Guardian Angel. So ultimately, the only way we can be sure is after attaining Knowledge and Conversation, and thrashing out the problem with the HGA itself."* As it happened, I came to conclude that this would inevitably occur with regard to *all* of the word-squares in *all* of the chapters : that before using them, one would have to confirm the suitability of each for use with the aid of the Holy Guardian Angel, and the spirit or spirits associated with each square in particular.

More worryingly however, I came to regard people who praised *The Book of Abramelin* as being better than Mathers' version in the following manner : *"These people – including Lon Milo Duquette (who wrote the introduction), Ramsey Dukes, and all the rest of them – haven't gone through the text of this book in as much detail as I have. However, a real magician, in order to perform the operation, would have had to go into this much detail. Hence the people who say they prefer* The Book of Abramelin *must be speaking from a position of ignorance !"* I felt bad, as many of these people I otherwise enjoyed their writing. Besides which, because so many people respected a lot of these writers, I could foresee they would experience serious cognitive dissonance if I came out and pointed at their errors, which would manifest in animus towards me.

*

It being VE day, we took a walk in the local park, where the nearest war memorial lay situated. Despite being a sunny spring day, people had almost deserted the place : at that time the Government only allowed them out of their homes once a day to take exercise – whilst everyone stayed fearfully away from one another.

On a day when the nation would have come together, social distancing ensured that it remained apart. On television a military band played a patriotic tune in a public square, but each member thereof stood precisely two meters away from each other. And no members of the public stood around to provide an audience.

I had never believed in such a thing as "the end times," but I could well sympathise with people who felt demoralised. The Blitz had united neighbours in solidarity with one another : in that sense a virus had achieved far more than the Luftwaffe had ever done.

Day 27

09 May 2020

Tarot dominated my dreams during the night : although the subject in general interests me, the proximate cause on this occasion would come from me working through the "Tarot Fundamentals" course for BOTA.

"During night : Dreams about 22 powers being related to Abramelin, which I did not understand."

Although this had the potential for deep mystical significance, I would bet this happened merely due to my subconscious mixing up the two most pressing concerns I had at the time.

"Also about trying (unsuccessfully) to get a tarot card reading."

Consciously I thought I only held mild curiosity about what would happen to me after completing the Abramelin Operation : however, I suppose my Subconscious treated it as a bigger deal than I realised, and it got frustrated that I had no conscious idea.

With the benefit of hindsight this prompted me to express my thoughts and feelings in the form of verse :

> When I started *Abramelin,*
> I asked my genius, "What will I be ?
> Will I be powerful, mighty and rich ?"
> "You'll have to wait and see.
> *K-C-H-G-A !*
> The future's not yours to see,
> Except with chapter one, square three !
> *K-C-H-G-A !"*

Although this amused me, it did not create a literary sensation, as apparently the intersection between Abramelin devotees and people who appreciate bad poetry comprises a null set. Which I found ironic, as this never seemed to stop Crowley.

When it came to the ritual proper, today's attempt did not impress me as much as the two previous days, which had left me with a definite high. Throughout the operation I experimented with trying to get the right 'feel' for how I performed my rituals – at least on this day I managed to perceive where I might have gone wrong. From my journal :

"Confession of sins. Lack of compassion is a recurring worry. I must take ownership of everything that goes wrong with my life, otherwise I don't deserve to take credit when anything goes right. On the positive side, however, perceiving a fault is receiving an opportunity to learn.

"Some sense of the mystical as on previous days, but I allow a sense of being rushed to curtail the experience (not just a 'sin' but as it turned out a factual error on my part as well)."

Day 28

10 May 2020

I AM-ness – the peculiar state of mind deriving from *jnana yoga* – figured much in my ritual work during this time. *"Up at 4.42am for preparation with LL Ritual,"* I wrote in my journal. *"Attempting to combine contemplation of past few days* [i.e. the cultivation of I AM-ness] *with vibrating each divine name six times."*

When one asks oneself the question *"who am I ?"* and goes through the Neti-Neti process of *jnana yoga*, one finds oneself in the ironic situation that the closer one comes to an answer, the more one realises that *no* answer exists. Certainly not one which the seeker can express in language. The answer to "who am I ?" and the means of expressing that answer comprise not one thing but two, so in order to experience the pure unmixed I AM-ness one must give up the idea of trying to articulate it. In this sense it rather resembles the sentiment expressed in the opening line of the *Tao Te Ching*.

To cut a long story – made even longer by the fact that however many words used to express it will number too many – short, I find that contemplating I AM-ness in this way, one of my most effective means of bringing my mind to a complete stand-still in a short space of time.

Hence, I performed my morning ritual as usual this day, and when it came to confessing my sins, I recorded :

"Contemplating sublimating all my past karma by raising the fire of kundalini.

"Concentrating on the I AM awareness. Momentary deep state of meditation (i.e. Discerning the presence of my Holy Guardian Angel).

"THOUGHT : 'I AM' in the discernment of the presence of the Angel..."

The unfortunate side-effect of experiencing ineffable states of consciousness manifests in the fact that trying to "eff" them inevitably results in gibberish. Suffice to say that one can only really appreciate a statement like "I AM in the discernment of the presence of the Angel" by means of sympathy, when one might begin to appreciate how important it appeared from my own point of view.

More prosaically, incidents like this began to convince me that one does not just get "Knowledge and Conversation of the Holy Guardian Angel" at the end of the six-months, but it starts to germinate and grow throughout the term of the Operation. The Culmination ritual represents the final seal on the process.

*

I spent most of the rest of the day preparing for and then taking part in a Golden Dawn meeting. This, like other meetings during that time of lockdown, had to take place via ZOOM. I was damned if everything became samey-samey, and hence boring, during our monthly meetings, so I challenged myself to learn more about both ZOOM and all the other technology I had at my disposal in order to liven things up. On this particular occasion I created a PowerPoint presentation which I screen-shared to illustrate a guided meditation I delivered. Many of the images within the PowerPoint I had cobbled together with Photoshop.

During this time, I still worked on the assumption that COVID-19 would suffer defeat in a few months, and the country in general, and the Golden Dawn in particular, would go "back to normal" by September, some six-months after the lockdown started. I had particularly set my hopes on September 2020, because I thought our members would find it nice to restart with the new Equinox. The Equinox Ceremony of the Golden Dawn refreshes and revives the egregore of the order. In my mind I associated it with the Second Law of Thermodynamics, i.e., that the Golden Dawn system would "run down" unless it received new energy at regular intervals – so clearly (to me) the Equinox ceremony ideally suited for this purpose. Hence (I reasoned), if the GD did not renew itself at the September Equinox, entropy would start to creep in : this I regarded not as some nebulous metaphysical concept but rather as a metaphor for genuine phenomena such as lethargy, disinterest, and lack of motivation to take part in magick anymore.

Needless to say, as I would later find out, September 2020 came and went : and so I found myself plunged into even more vigorous efforts to keep our monthly meetings lively, even after the end of my Operation and subsequently into the new year as well. I started to learn more software packages, such as using (ahem) "vintage" software packages to create animations. My Holy Guardian Angel was not just transforming me into an Abramelin-Magician, I was fast becoming a Graphic Designer *as well*.

Day 29

11 May 2020

Repeating the Bornless Ritual day after day gave me the opportunity to ponder upon not only the meaning of the Barbarous Names themselves,[83] but also on the best way to invoke them from a magical or psychic point of view. "*I try to imagine that every barbarous name of evocation I invoke is a massive force streaming down into me - infinite, the size of the universe,*" I wrote in my journal that day. "*I try to simplify my thought processes by simply imagining that every such name is an objective force - a god or manifestation of God - ultimately that I can let go and let it transform me.*"

In fact, throughout the Operation I would try out different methods of invoking – partly in the hope of finding the right one, but also I suppose because I used novelty as my prime method in the fight against ennui. So, for example, at various times I tried performing the Bornless Ritual physically, and whilst astrally projecting – and even both at the same time. Likewise, I speculated whether I could lever the *Solar Body* (i.e. my transmuted astral body) into service in the ritual.

I experimented with whether, when calling on the names, I should direct my attention outwards towards the edges of the universe, or inwards to the very depths of my soul. Or both.

I would attempt to incorporate ideas which occurred to me as I read the work of other occultists. In this regard, I experimented with both Western and Eastern influences. Sometimes, original ideas came to me, which I then decided to investigate further. On at least one occasion I must have moved diagonally through time, as the source I remembered for an idea turned out to differ from the source I could verify with reference to available documents.[84]

I would see if whether doing it as briskly as possible, or as slowly as possible, proved better. I could see the relative merits of both – too slow and boredom would distract me, too fast and I would miss out vital experience in the rush. Finding the right pace meant everything !

I would try combining different approaches, to see if I could do them at the same time. Very occasionally, I would conclude that a particular approach only succeeded in making it all too complicated for myself, so I dropped it.

The most effective practice I adopted consisted of imagining that every Barbarous Name represented a God-form, which I "assumed" as I invoked it. To my mind this had the benefit of plausibility, as many of the barbarous words

---

[83] See : day 20, *supra.*

[84] Cf how I came up with my idea regarding "Adonai Ha-Aretz," discussed on day 15, *supra.*

consisted of demonstrable deity names anyway, so in effect I merely took the concept to its logical conclusion.

I would imagine that in each of the six-directions – East, South, West, North, Down, and Up – there stood a magical doorway or portal out of which would materialise each God-form in succession, and that its astral form would merge with mine as I vibrated its name. Inevitably I would pause briefly to contemplate the God-form, before moving on to the next one.

The Golden Dawn goes into great detail about what god-forms look like, so that building up and assuming one become a sophisticated magical ritual. Unfortunately, with the god-forms of the Bornless Ritual, I had no idea as to their supposed appearance, so I tended to view each one as a generic giant-figure glowing with white light. (I had a few exceptions : e.g. the well-known likeness of "Abraxas.")

Nevertheless, despite the vagueness of my visualisations, the fact that I contemplated the invoked forces in this manner *at all* had a profound effect – "something" indeed proved better than "nothing." Performing the Bornless Ritual in this manner invariably caused – and still does cause – the whole ceremony to put me in a deeply aware state of magical consciousness. Inevitably, however, it also caused me to take much longer to perform the ritual than I had done so previously : although I believed that the benefits of doing it in this manner far outweighed any disadvantages, so it quickly became perfectly natural for me. This added to the reasons why the comparatively short length of my conjurations at the beginning of my operation seemed so unthinkable in retrospect.

*

When it came to the Confession of sins in my morning ritual, I wrote in my journal :

> *"Not being able to fulfil my vow or keep my standards is a constant niggle - I must resolve to do something about this."*

My mind turned to the idea of *using magic against people.* I had never used magic offensively – to deliberately attack people. However, I saw defending myself – and those who asked for my protection – as another matter entirely. I had already philosophised over using magic trying to prevent a crime taking place,[85] but now a new memory occurred to me –

I have a character failing. I believe the politically correct manner of stating it is that I experience sensitivity to toxic people or those with negative energy –

---

[85] Day 2 – *vide supra.*

although the old-fashioned way of describing the same malady is that I don't suffer fools gladly.

Actually, technically speaking, I don't suffer "fools" *at all*. I do however have enough generosity to realise that someone whose ignorance is purely innocent is no fool – in which case I have infinite patience for them.

Nevertheless, I do come across people who, when I say, "that's alright, you'll know better next time," fail to recognise this as me Making Them An Offer They Can't Refuse. Or at least, I do so in my imagination. In fact, instead of serving them a horse's head in their bed the next morning, I tend to sit on the matter for as long as possible, hoping that the problem will solve itself of its own accord. When I can't stand it anymore, I start wondering if magic might provide a solution.

Immediately I find myself faced with the plain wrongness of using offensive magic. So : what to do ? The idea occurred to me once : *"Instead of doing something to the other person, I ought to protect myself from them. For example : by insulating myself from them with an appropriate Banishing ritual."*

When I first thought of this, I immediately saw the merits. After all, the other people didn't cause me the trouble : *me worrying about them* did. Instead of taking ownership of the source of my problems, I had allowed them to prey on my mind like an "obsession."

I remembered one guy whom I shall call D. I would describe him as a loudmouth of the old school : he had a singular gift for infuriating just about everyone he ever met. He also behaved in a paranoid manner, believing himself under constant attack from both spiritual entities, and from people he accused of owing him money. Hence, our paths crossed : I believed him quite eager to learn the occult arts, as he wanted to become a mighty ceremonial magician just so that he could defend himself from supernatural beings – and influence the many lawsuits he had instigated, *as plaintiff,* in his favour.

He proved incredibly inept at learning ceremonial magic. Neither did he take it kindly when I pointed out that many of his alleged grievances weren't, in fact, legally actionable. In hindsight I should have realised that only the thought of one day winning one of his lawsuits gave his life meaning, so I should not have attempted to rob him of his hope.

Perhaps one could most generously say about him that his mistaken belief in his ability as a humorous joke-teller actually engendered a certain degree of pathos, which convinced a minority of people who knew him that he must have some redeeming feature.

So, one evening (many years ago), after a day of having a tough time with this guy, in the privacy of my home I imagined myself expelling the thought of him from my aura with the "sign of the enterer," sealing my aura with the "sign of silence," and then performing the Lesser Banishing Ritual of the Pentagram. As I did so, I imagined the thought-form of D. I had created disintegrating behind the protective ring formed by the Archangels, and dissipating into the universe. Feeling a whole lot better – no more thought of this person on my mind – I managed to go to bed and sleep peacefully.

Soon afterwards, this same D. disappeared not just from my mind but from my life as well. His various legal actions suddenly took up more of his time, and he used it as an excuse to break off contact with myself and most of the people I knew.

I would take credit for all this except that I believed him the sort of person who could and did bring it all on himself. So much so, in fact, that I almost felt tempted to dismiss it all as a coincidence, were it not for a twist in the tail –

The one mutual acquaintance with whom D. had not fallen out received a message from him saying that he believed myself and another guy had been "casting black magic" at him. "No I have not !" I replied. "Besides which, the LBRP isn't black magic !"

The last I heard of D., he defied everyone's expectations and finally won one of his many lawsuits – only to keel over and die from an unrelated illness not long afterwards.

Although I *had* found D. irritating, I do not consider him the most unpleasant guy I have ever come across. There exists a class of people on the fringe of both occult and masonic orders in Britain who like to *go round telling everyone* that they have *secret* access to the Security Services and their respective files. Yes, I appreciated the irony, but these people clearly did not. One particular shifty individual who tried to join the Golden Dawn even boasted that he had read the police record of our former Cancellarius. Despite the fact that the members of the temple could have done with a good laugh, our informant failed to pass the initial interview and we never admitted him.

I had more problems, however, with a gentleman whom I shall call H., who was an even bigger loudmouth than D. He deluded himself into believing he was a master-spy, with intelligence gathering-skills second to none. In fact, his attempts to wheedle information out of people proved so painfully transparent that he fooled no-one except himself. After pentagramming him away, a mutual acquaintance received a text-message from H. threatening to go to the press with the secret file which MI5 kept on "that bloke I met the other day…" by which I guessed he could only mean me. Needless to say, the exposé never materialised.

I have not got a criminal or police record, nor have I ever done anything in my life which ought to merit the attention of MI5, MI6, Special Branch, GCHQ or anyone else for that matter. I rather think that those who believe that people like John Dee and Crowley were spies suffer from cognitive dissonance, because they cannot process the idea that the occult could genuinely interest an individual : neither can they comprehend that modern day occultists might simply want to follow in their footsteps.

I suspect that the Golden Dawn, and probably other occult orders as well, do have genuine "spooks" trying to infiltrate them from time to time. I can only guess this by the number of people who quickly leave the GD after being first initiated, when they realise it does not provide a cover for a group of terrorists or foreign spies, but is in fact a genuine magical order. The idea of using something like a secretive masonic organisation as a means to disguise espionage has a sort of romantic appeal, but an occult order is meant to be more even more secret than that, and hence, using that as a cover, it would actually defeat the object. E.g.

Immigration official : "Can you tell me for what reason you have chosen to fly over to the USA, and are flying out again the day after tomorrow, Mr Sumner ?"

Me : *(Thinks) "I can't tell him I'm here to take part in a bizarre occult ritual. What the hell do I say ?"* (Out loud) *"*Oh, I'm here to pick up the blueprints to a nuclear reactor from a mate of mine who said he couldn't send them in the post. Something about them being classified … uh… does that sound right ?"

Fast forward back to the present. When I banished these people out of my life, I had not had any bad conscience about doing so at the time. But now, going through this Abramelin Operation, I had to ask myself – did I *sin* against these people ? To divine the answer to this question, I had to meditate long and hard. I came to two conclusions.

Firstly : I realised that not only did I not have bad conscience at the time, but I also still didn't have any now. I honestly believed I had done the right thing. I protected not only myself but people under my care, and used the least forceful method of doing so – a classic case of proportionality.

Secondly, and more worryingly, I realised that I couldn't really feel desperately contrite for my actions : as they provided a source of strength for my "*Evil Persona.*" As I noted previously, in the Golden Dawn milieu one neither condemns nor banishes the "Evil Persona," but instead one constrains and even cultivates it.[86] I found myself in a quandary which presented no easy solution : I could potentially count the ego-boost at having successfully committed such an act as a sin, but I could also use the fact of having committed the same act as also a source of power – a foundation upon which to build. I would obviously have to take care in striking the right balance between them.

---

[86] Day 9 : *vide supra.*

Day 30

12 May 2020

At first I thought my morning ritual would proceed as usual. All went well : when it came to the "Confession of Sins" I mentally listed all the possible faults of which I could think of at that moment : "Holding on to past resentments," "Allowing myself to be distracted," and even "Spiritual pride." I marked the last one with a query. I could not think of any examples of spiritual pride *per se*, I simply feared becoming one of those megalomaniacs who unfortunately litter the occult scene.

Then, a new sin occurred to me : "*Choosing to incarnate in a finite body in the first place,*" I recorded, "*thus handicapping my ability to live as an infinite being !*"

Logically, I thought, if one's higher self really does determine how one reincarnates, at some point one ought to realise that the only thing still trapping oneself in the cycle of death and re-birth is oneself. But then, if "sin" means to miss the mark set by God, reincarnation would amount to deliberately choosing to live in a situation where one cannot but help miss the mark, even if purely innocently.

Hence, even if I had never done anything particularly sinful, the mere fact of living as a "finite" human would constitute something to confess. *This transmutes the whole nature of confessing of sins.* Far from dwelling upon guilt over wrongdoing, with all the associated hang-ups that implies, and which has poisoned the idea of religion in the minds of many of its adherents – *it becomes being awe-struck in wonder as one realises the infinity of God.* The "poison" becomes transmuted into veritable "elixir."

Realising this unlocked doors in my mind. The most proximate effect manifested in the rest of my meditation that morning improving from that point on. As I wrote in my journal :

"*I had been mentally restless before this, but by concentrating on the pure concept of I AMness I come, by turns, into a deep state of meditation - i.e., Evidence of the presence of the Angel.*"

Focussing on the I AM-ness which is in the stillness had been having a profound effect on my meditation for several days now. Abiding in that "deep state" I aspired that it would magnetise the corresponding forces in the macrocosm. I realised : ultimately I aspired that, by attaining KCHGA myself, the whole universe would do so as well.

*

During this time, my studies with BOTA influenced the thoughts that occurred to me as part of my Abramelin operation. Today, I applied myself to my Tarot card of the week : Key 17, "The Star," which I dutifully coloured-in in the prescribed manner.

(Incidentally : I have noticed that BOTA members have a peculiar habit, that when they refer to the Tarot trumps they always say, e.g. "Key 17," instead of "The Star," or "Key 1" instead of "The Magician." Or if they do give the name of the trump, they only tend to do so as an afterthought. For me, as a Golden Dawn magician first and foremost, I tend to think of the name of the trump first, its astrological or qabalistic association next, the Hebrew letter after that ; the numeric value of the Hebrew letter *after that* ; etc. I rarely used to think of the number of the trump *per se* at all, and had to accustom myself to doing so as I went through the BOTA lessons. I think the main reason BOTA does it in this way is that Paul Foster Case attached great importance to the numbers of the keys, which one doesn't really get in the Golden Dawn.)

Hence, thinking about the nature of the meditation in my Abramelin Operation, the following occurred to me :

> *"THOUGHT : In contemplating 'The Star,' Case said that the revelation comes to one from an outside source - no mortal has ever unveiled Isis, because Isis only unveils Herself. Hence one can only ultimately attain Samadhi if one gives up the idea of doing it oneself and realises that the Samadhi alone does it - the sacrifice of the Ego."*

Or in other words : one should treat the Holy Guardian Angel as a separate being, external to oneself – or at least, external to what one believes constitutes one's identity. If I tried to surrender to something which I considered part of me – that wouldn't work, because I wouldn't really surrender to anything. Surrendering to an external source, however, takes on an entirely different character : something edgy – difficult – outside my comfort zone – a true challenge – and hence a true achievement assuming I managed it.

*

That evening : my fiancée wanted me to invoke all four elements with her, as it comprised part of her own magical studies. With it being "her magic," and not mine, I felt satisfied that it would not entail going against the spirit of the Abramelin operation. Trying to think what would constitute an appropriate way of working, I hastily cobbled together a ritual. It consisted of a pattern laid down by Israel Regardie in "Ceremonial Magic," i.e. : first, perform the Watchtower ceremony ; secondly make ones Statement of intent, in this case 'With divine permission we will invoke the four elements, that we may meditate on them.'

Then perform the ritualistic actions necessary to give effect to that particular intention ; and finally the Closing by Watchtower.

For the medial point, I created an extended version of the Supreme Invoking Ritual of the Pentagram, in that after each set of Pentagrams in the appropriate quarters, we recited the Prayer of the Elemental Spirits of that quarter - before moving on to the next one : apart from that it followed the conventional pattern. I also added in a Lesser Invoking Ritual of the Pentagram, with the innovation that we directed the pentagrams at the symbols of the Elements upon the Altar. After meditating, we consumed the elements, like the Mystic Repast of the Golden Dawn.

At least that's how I planned it. It almost came undone during the opening by Watchtower as, being a bit rusty, my mind momentarily went blank at one point. Instinctively I stopped dead still : I had heard that sometimes stress causes memory loss, so I thought I should deliberately pause long enough to calm myself down.

As I stated previously, I try to memorise large chunks of ritual and avoid using a script as much as possible.[87] The Watchtower Ritual provided an example of one such ritual – however, unlike the Bornless Ritual, which I practiced every day, I had not performed it in a while. Hence, I relied on recalling it from memory in the middle of a ritual, without having rehearsed it first.

Fortunately, though, as I felt myself relaxing, the line upon which I had stumbled suddenly flooded back into my brain, to my great relief. I carried on with the ritual, ignoring my fiancée's quizzical looks. After we finished, she surprised me by expressing consternation that she couldn't improvise rituals like that herself ; but I eventually placated her : she asked me to type the ritual out for her so we could do it again the following week.

---

[87] See : day 20, *vide supra.*

Day 31

13 May 2020

Today I appear to have woken up in an experimental mood. From my magical journal :

   "Up at 4.38 am for preparation with LL Ritual.

"Sunrise at 5.08am

*"**LBRP**. As I vibrate each divine name, I momentarily place my consciousness out of my body and in the pentagram where I experience that particular expression of Divinity."*

I can't recall why in particular I did this : I presume I did so out of curiosity, to see what happened. As it turned out, after several days practising like this I satisfied myself that projecting one's consciousness like this whilst performing the LBRP can indeed enhance one's appreciation of this ritual *(vide infra)*.

   *"**Bornless Ritual** : astrally, whilst sitting in padmasana."*

I call the method for performing the Bornless Ritual in this manner "Bilocation," which I define as a kind of astral projection where one doesn't lose consciousness of one's physical body whilst moving around in one's astral vehicle. At least not completely : in order to do it effectively I have to maintain a trance-like level of concentration on my astral body. However, even so, I have the weird sensation of existing in two bodies at once : in this case, one sitting in the lotus position, and the other moving around my ritual space, performing the ritual with the accompanying motions as if physically.

   Amazingly, when I first tried to bilocate, I found that by practising carefully enough I could get to the point where I could invoke magical energy with my astral body and *feel* it – rather like if I had astrally projected in a more conventional manner. Except in this instance, I did not have an immersive out-of-body-experience, but instead maintained awareness of my physical body at the same time as my astral.

   I have met plenty of others who can astrally project in this manner : I don't claim uniqueness or to have invented the practice. More worryingly, though, I have also met others who believe they know all there is to know about astral projection, and refuse to believe me when I tell them of my experiences, staying convinced of bilocation's impossibility. "Well, I got started by just believing that it *was* possible," I say, "And I kept practising until I proved myself right."

   *"**Conjuration**.*

   *"**Confession of Sins**. I had a dream during the night that I wasn't respecting social distancing in my rush to catch a train. Perhaps this is a metaphor for being inconsiderate to others, especially whilst I am on my spiritual journey ?*

"If, potentially, I have the energy of every person who ever was, is or will be, within me, then ultimately I also have their karma as well !"

BOTA's "Pattern on the Trestleboard" appears to have inspired this last thought. The affirmation for Zero reads "All the power that ever was or will be is here now" –a clear reference to the Veils of negative existence, in the same way that the affirmations for the numbers one to ten relate to the Sephiroth of the Tree of Life.

This would imply that if this means literally *"All* the power," it must mean both in its positive and negative aspects – i.e., including the karma of everyone in the universe as well, both for good and ill.

"Able to momentarily achieve a state of I AM consciousness.

*"**Licence to depart**.*

*"**LBRP** as before.*

"Total time not including preparation : 44 minutes."

Day 32

14 May 2020

In my muggle life, my fiancée and I continued to adjust to our move into a new house. Whilst I got rid of psychic rubbish from my inner self whilst in my Oratory, the rest of my day I spent getting rid of actual rubbish from the garage into a skip. Meanwhile of course, the country remained in total lockdown. On the plus side, this meant traffic had vanished from normally busy roads as we moved our furniture out of our former homes. On the minus, it meant the rigmarole of long, socially-distanced queues outside supermarkets ill-stocked to cope with pandemic conditions.

That morning, I recorded in my journal :

"During night : brief lucid dream about encountering 'Gremory' and binding him to do my will. (NB : on reflection it may not have been Gremory - looked more like Glasya-Labolas, a winged dog)."

I had not started grimoire-magick with *Abramelin* by a long-chalk. I would rank the *Goetia* of the Lesser Key of Solomon as my favourite other grimoire. After some perfunctory experiments with it, I decided to make a serious study of it – by evoking each of the seventy-two spirits at least once, just so that I could get a feel for each of them. That, and the fact that I had a nagging suspicion that one cannot get the full potential out of a grimoire unless one immerses oneself in it seriously. As it happened, although none of the evocations proved disastrous, not all of the evocations struck me as particularly impressive.

A sizeable number of them, however, *did* – which led me to believe that certain spirits proved more suited to working with me – and I with them – than others. But the fact that I already had experience in ceremonial magic gave me transferable skills, or so I hoped, to use in my Abramelin Operation. More immediately it probably explained the contents of my lucid dream that morning.

Regarding the rest of my morning ritual, I wrote :

"Up at 4.36am for preparation with LL Ritual. Right from the start I have a sense of 'I AM-ness' which I formulate as an Energy which I direct into each of the Sephiroth and each of the divine names which I invoke. Very good.

"Sunrise at 5.06am

*"**LBRP**. Retaining this sense of 'I AM-ness' throughout this ritual and these rituals. When I come to project the divine name, I briefly astrally project through the pentagram itself to experience the Divine Name as a force external to myself. Powerful.*

*"**Bornless Ritual** in padmasana, as yesterday.*

*"**Conjuration.** As I am buoyed by a sense of exaltation carried over from the Bornless Ritual, and still retaining this sense of 'I AM-ness,' this short piece of ritual feels unusually potent.*

*"**Confession of sins.** THOUGHT : is Gremory (? Glasya-Labolas ?) from my dream a sign about what I should confess ?"*

NB : The office of Gremory (sometimes spelled "Gemory" although I remember her name with the extra "r") is

"to tell of all Things past present & to come, and of Treasure hidden and what it layeth in, & procureth ye love of women, both young & old, he[88] governeth 26 Legions of spirits ...."[89]

Meanwhile, Glasya-Labolas is described thus :

"... he teacheth all arts in an Instant, and is an author of Blood shed & Manslaughter, he telleth all Things past & to come, if desired, & causeth love of friends and foes ; he can make a Man goe Invisible ... "[90]

Apart from when I evoked them as part of my scheme to evoke all seventy-two spirits at least once, I do not recall ever having need to conjure either Gremory or Glasya-Labolas. I do recall that the experience of evoking each, though, as pleasant enough : after conjuring Gremory, I settled down to rest, and had a vivid lucid dream in which I both descended into Hell to illuminate it, and ascended to Heaven, rising on the planes, dissolving everything as I did so. Meanwhile, whilst resting after Glasya-Labolas' ceremony, I experienced several OOBEs, wherein I contemplated the spirit : again I dissolved the imagery of my visions into light.

I must therefore conclude that the demonic figure in my dream represented therefore a symbol or metaphor, not the actual demon itself. But what did it symbolise ? I remembered Glasya-Labolas' description as an author of bloodshed, and yet I had also remembered the curiously ecstatic feelings I had experienced after first encountering him. Several weeks previously I had worried about causing people's death inadvertently – perhaps I had remembered that and it prompted my current dream. But what then of the more pleasant side of Glasya-Labolas ? Did the fact that I dreamed of binding it to do my will mean that I had reached closure on the issue ? I did not find the answer to any of this obvious.

Nevertheless, the act of attempting to contemplate this appeared to put me in a strong position. I wrote further :

---

[88] Sic – Gremory is referred to using masculine pronouns even though the spirit is described as having the form of a beautiful woman.

[89] See : http ://www.esotericarchives.com/solomon/goetia.htm#gemory accessed 2021-04-01

[90] See : http ://www.esotericarchives.com/solomon/goetia.htm#glasyalabolas accessed 2021-04-01

"THOUGHT #2 : I direct the 'I AM-ness' energy up my spine as if it is Kundalini energy. The Kundalini does not just cause the Samadhi, the Samadhi energy is the Kundalini. Curiously powerful.

"Trying to focus on intuiting the presence of my HGA.

"Licence to Depart.

"LBRP, *as above.*

"Total time 1hr 1minute. The idea of cultivating 'I AM-ness' i.e. My spirit is in the Samadhi - and directing it as if it is an energy, which manifests that which I invoke, seems to be a definite step forward in my practice."

I later recalled the events of this day in terms of the highest Numenosity. As if the Universe wanted to respond with a sign of me doing well, I received news that someone anonymous had made, *à propos* of nothing, a donation of £100 to my JustGiving page.

Day 33

15 May 2020

Just how important a place does diet hold in the Abramelin Operation? During phase one, The Book says : *"Eat and drink little – avoid farmer's feasts and big, elaborate meals."* [91] During phase two, the advice is repeated.[92] However in phase three the advice changes to :

> *"In drink and food you should copy Daniel the prophet, and live on vegetables and water. Also fast on the eve of the Sabbath."*[93]

I had not been living as a vegetarian up to this point, figuring that the book only called upon me to literally do so during the final phase of the Operation. Today however I reconsidered :

> *"Up at 4.36am for preparation with LL Ritual. Feeling bloated since yesterday - must reform diet."*

My fiancée and I had ordered in pizza the previous evening. We had ordered large ones because she had some sort of meal-deal, although she did not consider the fact that she does not by nature have a large appetite and often cannot finish what food she does have. I therefore found myself faced with more pizza than one person would normally eat, in addition to garlic bread - and a lifelong animadversion to letting food go to waste, what with starving children in Africa and what-not.

The discomfort coming from my intestines that morning effectively demonstrated that *Abramelin* forbids "big, elaborate meals" as purely a practical consideration. Nothing one eats should distract one from the rituals one performs. Having learnt the hard way how big a Big and Elaborate Meal actually was, I fortunately managed to avoid eating to excess for the remainder of my operation.

But that simple lesson did not end my discomfort : I found the bloatedness causing me unusual consternation, such that I needed the LBRP to banish it.

> *"This helps : I place my consciousness in each of the pentagrams as I vibrate the divine names ; also in each of the Archangels and invoking them, as I invoke them, as it were. The feeling of being surrounded by Angelic protection alleviates my worries."*

Clearly something more going on than the after-effects of almost-indigestible food. I recalled :

> *"Perhaps, after the spiritual ecstasy of yesterday, comes the inevitable Dweller on the Threshold?"*

---

[91] DEHN (2006), p93.
[92] Ibid., p95.
[93] Ibid., p96

This sentiment coloured the rest of that morning's ritual. For example, when I came to confessing my sins, I thought :

"Repressed hatred. I imagine myself saying to it : 'When I said, "I conjure all demons," I was talking to you !'

"Also eating meat - the karma of dead animals is upon me (as it is on all mankind).

"The one sin is personal, the other general. I imagine my HGA guiding me so that I can transmute these aspects of my evil persona such that there strength is directed to achieving spiritual aims : e.g. Strength to accomplish my will ; the ability to derive spiritual nourishment, etc."

I actually believed that at the time I received a genuine message : that my Holy Guardian Angel wanted to use the incident with the pizza to stir my conscience to action.

I spent the day discovering and poring over one of the old Abramelin manuscripts which had been digitised and put on-line. In the evening, over a modest meal (this time), I told my fiancée what I had decided : I would become a Vegetarian, by degrees. In other words, I asked her that, after all the food we then had in stock had run out, she would only buy vegetarian food for me. Hence it took a week or so to become a full vegetarian. By doing it this way the decision would not take my fiancée by surprise.

She actually really got on board with the idea. She saw it as an opportunity to try out a large number of vegetarian recipes, filled with exotic herbs and spices. She also came up with many more vegetarian equivalents of meat dishes. It so happened that she had previously been an avid subscriber of "Hello Fresh" and "Gousto," so she had a stockpile of ideas upon which to draw for inspiration.

Yet again, it struck me just how easy one can fulfil the requirements of the *Abramelin* operation now, in the 21st century – compared to the book's first writing hundreds of years ago. The quality of vegetarian food has improved drastically in my own lifetime. Twenty or thirty years ago, "Quorn" existed only as a rarity, but nowadays, as I discovered, it seemed prevalent, and of such quality that I could quite easily forget that I had ever eaten meat. Likewise with other plant-based products. Or some of them at any rate. In my local supermarket I found some plant-based Cumberland Sausages which I considered even better than the real thing. Unfortunately, I also found Tofu Sausages *which I did not.* But I suppose that becoming vegetarian will always involve a learning curve.

Also : the original Book came from the fifteenth century when one could only eat plain fare. Nowadays one can find ingredients from across the world readily available : likewise the knowledge of cuisine from far off countries. Therefore if Abramelin originally intended that by limiting my diet I should live austerely, I failed, because during this time I had the wonderful opportunity to experience tastes normally associated with places such as Morocco, Spain, Italy, India, China, Indonesia, Thailand, Malaysia, South America, Mexico, etc.

A worldwide consciousness of vegetarianism as the right thing to do both drives demand and causes know-how to become more readily available. However, as a side-effect it also makes the conditions in which to do the Abramelin operation easier, such that I predict increasing numbers of people will attempt this in the future.

Day 34

16 May 2020

T oday I contemplated the ambiguous nature of good and evil. Specifically, when it came to confessing my sins that morning, I realised "good karma" and "bad karma" do not exist *per se*. Karma manifests in one form – which has both good and bad sides to it, as well as infinite shades of grey. Often a single instance of Karma has both good *and* evil to it at the same time – depending on one's point of view. I.e. :

"I realise that the reason I have powers of meditation, ceremonial magick, lucid dreaming, etc, is that I have past lives as dark yogis, black magicians, lucid dreamers who used their powers for less-than-perfect ends. That is both the source of the strength of my Evil Persona, and the karma I must resolve - by turning it all to good making it subject to my HGA."

After thanking my Holy Guardian Angel for enabling me to resolve my issues as they arise, I intuited something of the seductive power of the Dark Side.

"Whilst contemplating sublimating the full sordid details of my Evil Persona to the service of my HGA, I feel a fuzzy warm feeling, which is probably hellfire - being put to use !"

Actually, I think the more probable explanation would point to *not* hellfire, but Kundalini. *Or would it ?* Kundalini's symbolism includes both "fire" and "a serpent." Now in the west, one can often find the imagery of the "Serpent" and "Dragon" conflated – the more so especially when one involves Fire. Moreover, Christians have historically referred to the Devil as "the old Serpent,," or "the Great Dragon."

Hence, I could describe that my occult practice as "Satanism,," because I rouse the Devil *(Kundalini)* up from Hell *(the muladhara chakra)* and draw the Hell-fire upwards where it becomes sublimated when it reaches Heaven *(sahasrara chakra)*. Or I could describe myself as something else entirely, as on other days I could identify my sense of "I AM-ness" itself as a source of energy and draw it up the spine like Kundalini, leading to equally remarkable effects.

In short, I do *not* identify as a Satanist, literally or otherwise, nor do I accuse Kundalini practitioners of consorting with the Devil. However, I have long suspected that black magic (remember : I treat the terms "black" and "white" magic with suspicion) in general and goetic (in the general sense) evocation could form the basis of an actual philosophy of yoga.

Days 35, 36

17th – 18th May 2020

From my magical journal :

> *"During night : Interesting dream about tarot decks - one called '666' which on closer inspection is called 'Crowley Relax' (an inferior, dumbed down version of Crowley Thoth using some of its artwork). I groan - some pretty girls who are Thelemites sympathise and want to meet up with me. Further exploration of this dream is interrupted by my alarm."*

Not entirely sure of the meaning of this. Crowley, as one of the main authorities on the Abramelin experience, would naturally have occupied mind around this time. Alternatively, my contemplations of the previous day might also have inspired the dream, as might have me seeing, in waking-life, modern "interpretations" of the Crowley-Thoth deck : although one could not fairly describe them as either "inferior" or "dumbed down."

Unless, of course, my Unconscious meant to give me a metaphor not about tarot, but the state of Thelema in the modern day. I have never held membership in the OTO, so the only information I have about it has come in the form of war-stories from disgruntled ex-members : of whom I tend to run into *a lot*. What with the amount of both invective and contradictions I've heard, I must wonder : what did the elephant do to piss off so many blind men ?

In any event, I got up and made ready for my morning ritual. I noted my preparations with the Middle Pillar Ritual as *"Good - at least, better than yesterday,"* although I can't recall what precisely went wrong with the previous day's version.

When it came to the LBRP, I noted :

> *"I retain some of the 'I AM-ness' awareness - projecting myself through the pentagrams to experience the Divinity I invoke there. When I get to the Angels, I place my consciousness in each of them. I am not just surrounded by them, they collectively form part of my higher self. My Kether is their Tiphereth (following an idea from David Goddard). Whole thing satisfying."*

The idea in question came from the *first edition* of "Sacred Magic of the Angels,," by David Goddard. [94] I had originally got hold of a copy because Madeline Montalban's system of angelic invocation, of which I had favourable reports, intrigued me ; and this book apparently featured it within its pages. The same book also described a form of invocation [95] in the following terms :

---

[94] GODDARD (1996).
[95] Ibid. pp167-172

"You will feel the gentle, probing mind-touch of the angelic as it seeks your permission, your cooperation, to meld together. ....

*"The experience of entering into an angel's 'body' is highly subjective and, to the inexperienced, slightly disorientating. It is like being enfolded by living light that is ensouled -by a consciousness that is super-conscious by human standards. The physical faculties become quiescent, but the psychic faculties are awakened and expanded. To help stabilize what is, after all, an awesome melding, **renew your focus upon your crown-centre, gradually letting it merge or coincide with the heart-centre of the angel**. This will make the mind-touch and telepathic rapport clearer. "[96]*

(My emphasis).

To my mind I could only conceive of my "crown-centre" (Kether) merging with the Angel's "heart-centre" (Tiphereth) by imagining the Middle Pillar of Z'ev Ben Shimon Halevi's version of the Tree of Life – which comprises a concatenation of four Trees (one for each Qabalistic world) into one. The Middle Pillar of one Tree overlaps with that in the Higher World (and indeed with that in Lower world as well). Hence, if I took my Middle Pillar as that of Assiah and the Angel's as that of Yetzirah, then my Kether would indeed become the Tiphereth of the Angel, in the manner described. *"When I assimilate the Angelic presences into my life,"* I noted, *"my middle pillar doesn't stop at the top of my head, but becomes part of theirs as well."*

---

[96] Ibid. p170.

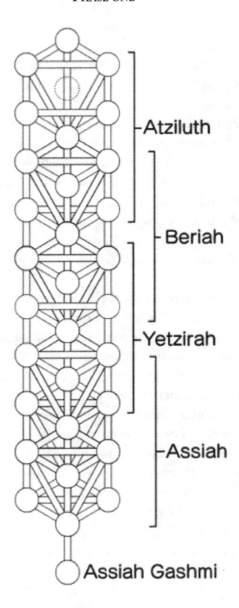

Figure 4 The "Jacob's Ladder," version of the Tree of Life.

I doubt that either Goddard or Halevi ever intended that one should use this method of Angelic invocation with the LBRP, but it appeared to work for me, and seemed to improve the whole quality of my morning ceremony in general, and indeed all my rituals over the next few days. I found the Bornless Ritual and the deep states of meditation I reached especially good. I willed that although I might well attribute this feeling to the presence of my Holy Guardian Angel, I ought to establish a reliable method of communication with it. As I wrote in my journal for the remainder of that day :

> *"I speak to my sense of I AM ness as if it is the manifestation of the presence of my HGA, imagining that it be unto me as did the Angels in the pentagram ritual, i.e. My Kether becomes its Tiphereth, etc. Together we sublimate all the karma identified yesterday. Perhaps there is even more power in my Evil Persona than I realised ? All the demons of Hell, for a start."*

It later occurred to me to think : if my crown-centre is the Angel's heart-centre, of what does the Angel's own crown-centre consist ? The heart centre of God ? What if God, my Holy Guardian Angel, me and my Evil Persona all linked themselves together by one big middle pillar, as in the "Jacob's Ladder" diagram above ? *"I am God's 'Evil Persona,'"* I concluded, *"the source of His strength and power ! I.e. I stand in relation to God as my own Evil Persona stands unto me."*

Of the LBRP which I used to close the ritual, I wrote :

> *"... as before, even feeling better than before, because I have inherited the benefits of meditating during the confession of sins phase."*

On a more sobering note, the effectiveness of the invocation helped to serve me the unpleasant realisation of where I had gone wrong in my life – in this instance, by getting into arguments with my fiancée :

> *"MacGregor Mathers once said that to tell someone a truth for which they are not ready is as bad as lying to them. Now I realise that I have caused an argument, and indeed, arguments with* [my fiancée] *by persisting in telling what I consider to be the truth without appreciating whether or not she is ready for it. I.e. by doing something as bad as lying ! I will that my HGA teach me how to correct this, and that in the future I may be able to discern what is and what is not appropriate."*

This, of course, assumes that one can ever speak the Truth about what are mostly metaphysical concepts anyway. But the point remained : whether it was the actual Truth or just what I believed to be so, I should still have regard to the other person's feelings.

The problem of my argumentative tendency vexed me. *"Getting into arguments = me not willing to forgive others for the fact that they are on their own path,"* I noted. *"But forgiveness, to be truly unselfish, is to accept that they have not done anything wrong in the first place."*

Hence the down side of invoking an Angel effectively, as I discovered, appears that it manifests itself whether one likes it or not – a case of *"be careful what you wish for,"* in other words.

Day 37

19 May 2020

I recalled having a strange dream during the night: about getting on a bus with a load of Golden Dawn Adepts, all on their way to take Exam B, because each had a Lotus Wand with them. "Exam B" refers to the examination in which a 5=6 consecrates his or her magical weapons. In the Golden Dawn, the Adeptus Minor uses the Lotus Wand as his or her prime implement, mainly for invoking zodiacal forces. More generally, in Egyptian art one can often see it in the hands of gods and goddesses – implying that an adept assumes a god-form when he or she comes to wield it.

When I did the Middle Pillar ritual that morning, by way of experiment I invoked each divine name only once, but made up for it by spending a lot of time contemplating the levels of meaning of each Sephirah.

The Bornless Ritual proved especially good this morning: I noted that it generated "good vibes" which carried over to the subsequent parts of the ceremony.

When it came to the Confession of Sins, I noted:

"Recklessness, carelessness - always a danger. So is spiritual pride.

"Yesterday I lost my temper - albeit in the nicest possible way - with [my fiancée], as I honestly thought her behaviour was so unreasonable that I could not indulge it any longer. I felt better afterwards. Perhaps although being nasty is a sin, I was sinning against myself by not speaking out about it? Geburah is also a divine Sephirah as well, so one has to be a little bit severe every now and again to maintain equilibrium."

I seem to have resolved that issue, for I subsequently passed into a deep state of meditation, which I took as indicative of the presence of my HGA.

*

Later at my fiancée's instigation I joined in with her in following a Maya Fiennes workout session: Kundalini yoga, aimed specifically at opening my *muladhara chakra*. I didn't note afterwards any signs that it worked, but then again I didn't note any signs that it *didn't* work. Apparently the author of this tradition, Yogi Bhajan, first introduced this type of yoga to the west in 1969 in order to help heroin addicts living in Los Angeles. Theoretically it contains techniques to open up all the chakras eventually, although it all seemed rather too strenuous for my tastes.

Magically, in my continuing efforts to write out every Abramelin square, I had moved on to annotating each one with the names of the demon prince or princes who preside over it. Still mindful of the incident involving Crowley's butcher, I aspired to complete my transcribing in sacred space, so that demons would not disturb me or my household.

Day 38

20 May 2020

From my magical journal :

> *"Up at 4.28am for preparation with LL Ritual. Inspired by reading something by Adam Forrest yesterday, about aspiring to the Holy Guardian Angel with every Sephirah of the Middle Pillar.*[97]

> *"Sunrise at 4.58am*

> **"LBRP.**

> **"Bornless Ritual.**

> **"Conjuration.**

> **"Confession of Sins**. *Spiritual pride, anger, impurity of motives. Allowing myself to be distracted by random thoughts and memories.*

> *"Meditating - deep ...*

> **"Licence to depart.**

> **"LBRP**.

> *"Total time 50 minutes."*

Later that morning in the course of conversation with my fiancée I had an argument with her which I noted at the time as "terrible" although thankfully short-lived.

> – *"[She] has read an article by Gareth Knight[98] and picked out all the bits which appear critical of the Golden Dawn. Later I read the article for myself : it is not really critical of the Golden Dawn at all, and is quite a reasonable article full of good ideas. It occurs to me how much subjectivity is involved in all this - we both read the same article but each through our own individual perceptual filters, thus getting different things from it.*

> *"Actually, one idea that Gareth Knight introduced - as a side remark, actually - was the concept of the Holy Grail, and the point that Parsifal is meant to ask the classic questions 'What is it ? Whom does it serve ? Who serves it ?' when he sees it, otherwise the Grail Castle and all its inhabitants disappear. Likewise, when one encounters something which is a metaphorical Holy Grail one should ask similar questions - hence avoiding spiritual pride. Perhaps this is where I have been going wrong - not taking time to ask, 'Whom does this serve ?' whenever I have experienced something spiritually enlightening ?*

---

[97] It was an article by him featured in CICERO, CICERO *et al.* (1995).

[98] From the same volume as the Forrest article – CICERO, CICERO *et al.* (1995).

"Despite the fact that I allow [my fiancée] to wind me up - I should be thankful as through her agency I have come into contact with this article in the first place !"

Luckily for me she did not hold a grudge long – especially when perceiving that I looked sick that evening aroused her compassion. As I wrote in my journal :

"Feeling ill, and exhausted, and a little dehydrated. I suspect it might be lack of sleep, combined with the hot weather. My fiancée wondered if the Abramelin operation was having some effect on me ? I hope she is not afraid it is something sinister ! I betake myself to bed early in an attempt to recuperate."

Day 39

21 May 2020

I woke up at 4.26am that morning feeling a lot better than I had when I went to bed. Evidently my problems had *not*, on this occasion, been caused by demons : sleep and plenty of water had proved just the tonic.

As I performed the Middle Pillar Ritual, I kept thinking all the while, "*Whom does this serve ?*" after the "Holy Grail" thought I had yesterday inspired me.

Whilst performing the LBRP, I suddenly thought : "*what if the* Shekinah *is the 'Nephesh' of God ?*" My thoughts about "Jacob's Ladder" from three days previously inspired me, in that I tried to use it as a model to work out just how my own Nephesh stood in relation to my own conscious personality (i.e. Ruach).

Through the Shekinah or Divine Presence, God manifests in Nature : the traditional Kabbalah also refers to it as the Divine Feminine. The Shekinah dwelled in the Holy of Holies of King Solomon's Temple, to show God's presence there : when the Shekinah rested on an individual person, the Lord blessed him or her with the gift of prophecy.

Some New Agey type people seem to consider the Shekinah as a Goddess in Her own right, although I do not think that corresponds to the traditional Qabalistic viewpoint : rather, She makes up the Feminine *side* of God, related to the Masculine like Heads to Tails of the one coin. This would enable both a Divine Feminine and Divine Masculine to exist within the Qabalah whilst still allowing it to remain monotheistic, as opposed to polytheistic.

However, I believe that allowing the Polytheistic view of the Shekinah to persist has caused Her to seem more mysterious and inaccessible than She actually is. Arthur Edward Waite, for all his talk Christian Mysticism, probably offended the most, in the way he featured Her as the Big Reveal to which his Fellowship of the Rosy Cross led. In the Bible, however, Qabalists tended to look upon the Shekinah as inseparable from God, so much so that if the good book described God as anywhere in particular, that implied *ipso facto* that the Shekinah rested there also.

In fact, here is a simple little exercise which you can do in five minutes to experience the Shekinah for yourself :

Meditate on the Tetragrammaton – Yod Heh Vav Heh – until you have some evidence of Yod Heh Vav Heh manifesting.

The fact that you can perceive Yod Heh Vav Heh manifesting *is* the Shekinah, the Feminine Side of God.

In other words, by saying that God manifests in Nature through the Shekinah, we effectively say God manifests to our senses through Her, or to our intuition or psychic awareness : hence the reason Qabalists associate Her with the gift of prophecy.

This got me wondering, however : it's all very well to call the Shekinah the Feminine side of God, but how exactly does She relate thereto ? And : is there one great Being with parts that Macrocosmically reflect the arrangement of the Microcosmic soul, and if so, where does the Shekinah fit into this arrangement ?

Anyhow, all this speculation gave me an idea of how to refine my performance of the Pentagram ritual : i.e., as I invoke each divine name I should attempt to perceive its manifestation and hence imagine that expression of Divinity united with the Shekinah. Thus I would automatically get to contemplate the Divine Feminine whilst going about my usual Qabalistic rituals.

Actually, my ideas about the Holy Grail on one hand and the Shekinah on the other – both powerful Feminine symbols – served to enrich my entire experience that morning. For example, when I performed the Bornless Ritual, a thought suddenly occurred to me.

"Previously I had been directing my attention outwards to the four quarters and to the Height & Depth. However : what if I have been doing it wrong ? What if instead I should be directing my attention inwards ? So for example, all these barbarous names of evocation I have been vibrating - they are forces within me. Real forces which exist objectively, but within me as opposed to out there. So that I am really invoking them. So that, indeed, when I say, 'Hear me, and make all spirits subject unto me,' I am speaking to forces within me - that I can feel within me ?

"Actually attempting to do this feels powerful. It also makes me feel humble and thankful - i.e. Humble that I recognise what I have been doing wrong so far, and thankful that I now have stumbled upon the right answer and have an opportunity to improve my practice.

"Taking a moment to think : 'Whom does this inner power serve ?'"

Likewise, when it came to the Conjuration :

"Inspired by experience during the Bornless Ritual, which I invoke YHVH, Tzebaoth and Adonai I imagine I am speaking to forces within me (all united with the Shekinah !). Powerful."

When I got to confessing my sins, my thoughts turned to illness I had experienced the previous evening :

"Not taking care of myself is sinning against myself. But then falling ill is the punishment, and deliberately taking steps to recuperate is me working off that punishment. In this I feel thankful for the opportunity afforded by God and my HGA for atoning for my sins in real time.

"I reflect that all that I am able to identify as a potential sin has already contained within it its own punishment. For example - following on from that

Holy Grail thought - each time I experience some form of spiritual ecstasy and not then ask myself 'Whom does this serve?' I find myself running up against the Dweller on the Threshold, or experiencing a low, or going for a long time without experiencing a comparable feeling. Hence : that was the punishment for my spiritual pride each time.

"Which sort of implies that because I have already been punished, I need not be punished again.

"Trying to concentrate on a deep state of meditation - whom does this serve? The simple answer is 'God,' but it occurs to me also that God must have a plan which it serves in particular - i.e. If everyone were to attain KCHGA, humanity itself would be transformed and the world would be a better place."

I ended the morning's ritual with the Licence to Depart, and then performed the LBRP again. I noted :

"...directing energy of divine names first inwards - so that I project an inner reality out into the cosmos, where it is united with the Shekinah. That is why I say, 'In the column shines the six-rayed star,' because it is the Shekinah itself - as in the old Jewish prayer upon which the LBRP is based - at work."

Overall, the experience of the morning ritual buoyed me greatly. I made a specific note that I spent the rest of the day going over magical exercises such as the LBRP (coincidentally) and a Chesed pathworking for my fiancée, and generally having an enjoyable evening with the warm Spring weather.

Day 40

22 May 2020

Yesterday – being filled with so much rich spiritual experience - proved a "high," after which only one direction remained to go. Actually, anything not as impressive as yesterday would inevitably have seemed disappointing by comparison. I recorded the following thoughts regarding confessing my sins :

"Worried that I have become overloaded with thoughts following yesterday's experiences. In which case - the sin is allowing myself to become distracted hence potentially spoiling my practice.

"As it happens, I have to spend extra-long in meditation to get anything close to a deep state.

"Arrogance - or more spiritual pride - in thinking that just because I accomplished something yesterday, that I had accomplished anything. The reality is that it is just a beginning, which needs to be worked on - a long hard slog."

In hindsight I believe this recurs as a feature of spiritual progress – of one day hitting a peak, only to subsequently experience a trough, and only getting back to a better state through a lot of hard-work. I remain a continual Beginner – sometimes I experience "beginner's luck," only to undergo the learning process that beginners have to go through. If I have any sense, I ought to expect this to happen : if it does not take me by surprise, I would limit my initial euphoria, but also mitigate my disappointment thereafter.

*

Later that day an argument arose between my fiancée and I about the 31st path of Tree of Life – i.e., the path of Shin, the Perpetual Intelligence, associated with Fire and most significantly the tarot key "Judgement." The Golden Dawn and Builders Of The Adytum have different teachings about this, specifically about which Angel features in the tarot key.

The GD says one thing for one reason, i.e. that the key depicts Michael, the Archangel of Fire.

BOTA however, says Gabriel for another reason entirely. Despite Gabriel's admitted association with Water, Paul Foster Case came up with a series of explanations why it was most appropriate to have him on this Tarot card : for one thing, it points to the Watery nature of the "secret fire" in Alchemy. It also enables Case to claim that each of the four Archangels appear in four different Tarot keys – with Michael as the angelic figure depicted in "Temperance."

However, the argument arose due to the third reason which Case gave for it being Gabriel – because as supposedly everyone knows, Gabriel blows the trumpet during the last judgement – hence it must be him.

I suppose I must have a nerdish obsession with exploding misconceptions. Therefore, in all innocence I pointed out that the evidence does not support this. In the Book of Revelation, *seven* Angels blow *seven* trumpets – with all of them remaining anonymous. Hence, the Bible gives no precedent to say that either GD or BOTA are right or wrong. The Angel featured in "Judgement" *could* be Michael, or it *could* be Gabriel, or it could be another Angel entirely. The only *wrong* teaching, in my opinion, would consist in saying that it *must* be one particular Angel and not any other, because nothing exists to back up such an assertion in the Bible, which provides the only source we have to claim that anyone blows any trumpets at the end of days at all.

In effect I characterise both the Golden Dawn's and BOTA's teachings on the matter as opinion only. Not that I see anything wrong with that : scholarly debate could not take place if one did not accept that people do have differing opinions on such things. Although I feel accustomed to thinking of the said angel as Michael, I ultimately recognise it as a type of prejudice on my part, as I bought into the Golden Dawn's teachings long before I became exposed to BOTA's point of view. To me it makes sense that that key depicts Michael as the angel, not because it is *true* in any absolute sense, but because it has subjective *comfort.* Gabriel on the other hand seems counter-intuitive at first, but the mere act of trying to hold the idea in my mind long enough to assess whether it has any merit *challenges* me and hence makes me contemplate the subject more than I would normally. The idea of investigating the Watery nature of the secret Fire genuinely intrigues me : the argument about four of the tarot keys representing four archangels sounds like bashing a lot of square pegs into round holes ; whilst the whole trumpet thing, because of its triviality, ought not to occupy my serious attention at all.

However, people do exist who believe that the teachings of their respective organisations – whether BOTA, the Golden Dawn, or any other school of thought – have the status of Holy Writ and hence not open to debate. I suppose that if I myself had such a deeply held belief, I might feel the same way if someone tried to challenge it. However, what seems like a "deeply held belief" to me, may not seem obvious to other people, and likewise other people's "deeply held beliefs" do not seem obvious. If one conducted a debate sensitively, in a true rational or philosophical manner, this would go a long way to assuaging the delicate natures of those involved. I suppose that Parliament describes its proceedings as "debates" not because they live up to what I would call proper debates, but as a euphemism for their real nature – the slanging back and forth between viewpoints held for political reasons, not rational ones.

(Euphemisms get used a lot in Parliament, such as calling an MP "tired and emotional" instead of four-sheets-to-the-wind, or saying they have used a "terminological inexactitude" when they really mean "an outright lie." I presume the House of Commons, out of custom, attempts to use language to soften the impact of just how awful politicians and the political process really are. Well I say "attempt" – it obviously has not succeeded.)

Anywho, to cut a long story short, I spent a lot of the day trying to convince my fiancée that just because I disagreed with her over a point of BOTA's teachings didn't mean that I wanted to have a go at her personally, or indeed thought any the less of her. I personally think that for practical purposes, one should best stick with one attribution the whole time one works with one particular system – so as to avoid confusion, as well as to make full use of that system's egregore.

Perhaps the real problem lay in me coming across as too forthright. In any event, I put a lot of effort into reassuring her, and that she would make me all too happy being strong independent magician in her own right. She almost thought I wanted to deny the importance of sexual polarity - but I tried to convince her that I meant I didn't want her to have any disempowering beliefs about herself.

Day 41

23 May 2020

With the days lengthening as the year fast approached Summer, I found myself getting up before 4.30am in order to start my morning ritual at the correct time. I prepared with the Middle Pillar Ritual. After yesterday's "downer" experience I applied the KISS principle : it felt relaxing.

The LBRP, Bornless Ritual, and Conjuration went smoothly. However, when it came to the Confession of Sins, the silence of my mind became overwhelmed with negative thoughts – very frightening to experience. I realised why – I remembered the arguments I had had with my fiancée the previous day, and figured I must have allowed them to have more effect on my subconscious than I realised. I wrote down my thoughts, stream-of-consciousness style : reading them back I felt as if I *excreted* the contents of my mind onto the page :

"I am conscious of resentment towards [my fiancée] - my sin is twofold, firstly in having it at all and secondly in allowing it to distract me.

"Hatred towards [my fiancée] because of the resentment she causes in me. Because she seems to succumb to an inferiority complex without realising how that hurts my self-esteem. Hatred towards myself, for not being able to find someone better. Hatred towards my mother. Hatred towards women, for forcing men to need them. Hatred towards God, for forcing mankind to depend on Him.

*"**All of these forms of hatred are ILLUSIONS.** Yet here they all are - manifestations of my Shadow, or Evil Persona. I allow them to distract me, and worse still to colour my judgement. I own them, because I have given them life. I must take responsibility for them, even if I did not consciously will them.*

"Does this mean that the things I love (e.g. Myself) are also illusions which I have created ? In which case that must mean that Illusions by themself are neither good nor bad, but it depends what I do with them.

"I will that my Holy Guardian Angel sublimate all these Illusions - put them under divine control - so that they work for me, not against me.

"I realise that when full realisation of KCHGA comes upon me, the dissolution of all these Illusions will be cathartic : humbling - leading to a better life, but traumatic in the extreme, liable to leave me feeling broken.

"I try concentrating on the stillness - the presence of my HGA. Fleeting. I thought I had come so far, but I have still a long way to go. It was foolish to think I had attained already, seeing as I am still in the first quarter of my sojourn."

Needless to say, I felt thoroughly ashamed at the negativity I experienced : yet I did not want to edit it, for the sake of brutal honesty, and to make the point this arises as a typical consequence of the self-examination that one encounters whilst going through an operation of this nature.

Not surprisingly, when my fiancée came upon me later that day, she noted that I looked more melancholic than usual. She even expressed concern that this Abramelin Operation might prove harmful for me.

I had to allay her worries. I explained in general terms that the Abramelin Operation had to do with becoming aware of and resolving my karma. "The operation is like a course of spiritual development that would otherwise take several years, but compressed into six months," I told her.

I could tell by the way she stared at me that she worried I might open up a hell-mouth and fall right into it – but she did not press the point for the moment.

That afternoon: we took part in a Golden Dawn study group via ZOOM. Astrology formed the general theme of the meeting: however, instead of just sticking to the curriculum, we had previously decided that by talking *around* the subject, it would help stimulate the participants' interest in Astrology in general, and indirectly in the astrological teachings of the Golden Dawn in particular.

Hence for this particular meeting, a Soror who had the muggle-life identity of a professional astrologer of long-standing, presented a talk on "chart shapes" – a theory first formulated by Marc Edward Jones (1888 – 1980) which asserts that the overall *shape* that the planets make in one's natal horoscope can itself provide insight into how one ought to interpret the chart. To demonstrate, she took the birth-charts of those who had volunteered their details and proceeded to analyse them in terms of the shapes she identified.

To the amazement of the individuals concerned – and the good-hearted amusement of everyone else – her analysis proved uncannily accurate.

Although I had intended the meeting to stimulate the members' interest in Astrology – I originally assumed this would mainly benefit for the younger members who needed help with their exams. Now, however, I began to realise an unintended consequence. It occurred to me that the "low" of yesterday, followed by the arguments, and the subsequent negativity I had experienced this morning, all happened at the same time approximately. So what if they comprised the same event – *for which there existed an astrological explanation?*

I had not kept track of the recent movement of the planets on a day to day basis, so when this thought occurred to me it came fresh and new in my mind. In fact, when it did appear in my mind, I realised with delight that I might have stumbled on a way to resolve my problems more effectively.

One might, if one did not know any better, assume that because one can calculate the movement of the planets with mathematical accuracy, and because astrologers claim these heavenly bodies have a consistent, predictable influence on us, that Astrology must therefore imply *determinism* – that it must deny the possibility of Free Will. However, once one embraces the Hermetic philosophy – upon which, after all, the Golden Dawn bases itself – one comes to an entirely different conclusion.

In ancient times, pagans did not believe the planets were named after the Gods – they believed they *were* the Gods (or more accurately, the planets ensouled them). Hence, a horoscope constituted a diagram which explained how the Gods interacted with one another and influenced the Earth at any given moment.

However, Hermeticism goes further than this. For example, the *Corpus Hermeticum* says :

"Nay more, if we must boldly speak the truth, the true 'man' is e'en higher than the gods, or at the [very] least the gods and men are very whit in power each with the other equal.

"For no one of the gods in heaven shall come down to the earth, o'er-stepping heaven's limit ; whereas man doth mount up to heaven and measure it ; he knows what things of it are high, what things are low, and learns precisely all things else besides. And greater thing than all ; without e'en quitting earth, he doth ascend above. So vast a sweep doth he possess of ecstasy."[99]

In other words, Hermeticism predicts the possibility for a human to ascend in consciousness "higher than the gods" – i.e. higher than the influence of the planets. Hence, in Hermeticism, a horoscope does not deny free will at all, but merely points out the obstacles one must learn to surpass in order to fully achieve it. This being so, if astrology had caused my current predicament, I ought to have the ability to transcend it, by applying basic Hermetic principles. The unintended consequence of that day's talk, in other words, helped *me* as well.

---

[99] Book X, "The Key" – MEAD (1906), volume 2 p157.

Day 42

24 May 2020

Working on the basis that I could solve the problems which assailed me by thinking in terms of Hermeticism, I engaged with this new morning's ritual with confidence.

"Up at 4.23am for preparation with LL Ritual. Focussing on getting in touch with my Nephesh *- together we arrange to be in the best possible state - i.e. The simplest and most straightforward - which is conducive to achieving effective ritual."*

I.e., by doing this I deliberately attempted to develop my theories of cultivating a relationship with my Nephesh, originally based on my BOTA studies. Throughout the rest of the morning's ritual I felt inspired to a greater extent than on any other days : so much so, that I shall quote magical record *in extenso* :

"LBRP. *THOUGHT : 'Adonai' - Aleph Daleth Nun Yod. The 'Aleph' stands for the 'Eheieh' consciousness, the Yod for 'YHVH.' Hence 'Adonai' represents the I AM ness united with the Eternal God.*

"However : within the calligraphy of the letter Aleph is Yod-Vav-Yod i.e. 26, the number of the Tetragrammaton. Therefore it is not a case of simply joining the Aleph to the Yod, but the Aleph transforms into the Yod, i.e. The I AM ness resolves itself into YHVH, like a flower germinating from a plant.

"I am a complex being surrounded by Angels, Pentagrams which are the manifestations of Deity, and the six-rayed star of the Macrocosm. Together we go on to perform the ...

"Bornless Ritual. *KISS. The barbarous names invoke power into me from the six directions.*

*"***Conjuration***. The divine principles which the names represent manifest within me - I really am 'invoking' them.*

*"***Confession*** *of sins. The realisation that many of my troubles could well have an astrological basis has a liberating effect. Whilst I allow myself to be circumscribed by the stars and planets I am prey to their influences, but only when I am outside - and hence united with the real God - do I get to transcend them and hence attain free will. Hence the real sin was in allowing myself to forget my divine nature, and my basic Hermetic principles - and hence being the author of my own misfortune.*

"Hence, by contemplating each negative aspect which I identified yesterday as one of the problematic features of my natal horoscope I was able - by aspiring to rise above the stars and planets - abreact them, and break their spell over me. After all, the so-called problematic features also have positive

sides to them, so by concentrating on them I can mitigate the trouble they seem to cause.

"Buoyed by this, I am able to attain a deep state of meditative stillness - the presence of my HGA - far more satisfying than I yesterday.

"I reflect : yesterday I had asked my HGA for help, and the same day there manifested this help in the form of me receiving the timely advice. So my HGA came through for me again ! I should place greater reliance on my HGA actually being able to help me in such circumstances. I thank my HGA for all this.

*"**Licence to Depart**

*"**LBRP**

"Total time not including preparation : 59 minutes. Feeling a lot more positive this morning than I was at the same time yesterday."

*

The strawberry plant had begun to flower. Only one so far – a simple little flower with light pink petals and yellow carpels – but to see it at all surprised me. I had never concerned myself with horticulture before, so to discover evidence of new life on a day like today seemed all the more remarkable. Only afterwards did I realise – before seeing it at all – that I had written "*The I AM ness resolves itself into YHVH, like a flower germinating from a plant*" in my magical journal that morning.

Living in social isolation, my fiancée and I had, amongst other things, got new plants and flowers for the garden to make our domestic life more interesting. Indeed, the mood pervaded the country at the time, due to the enforced lockdown, of developing a greater respect for nature. Not only die more people discover gardening, but evidence arose that air pollution had lessened due to the reduced amount of traffic on the roads – and from the closure of large numbers of factories and industrial plants. People begun to have a genuine optimism that the COVID-19 pandemic would have a surprise advantage, in allowing Gaia to finally push the reset-button after decades of abuse done to her.

My fiancée for her part had also used the time in lockdown to spend more time on her hobbies. She had knitted herself a cardigan in the two months whilst on furlough, and also re-started her collection of precious rocks and minerals, which she prized mainly for the meditation.

As it happened, I found I could devote time during the day to qabalistic study, which allowed me to compose some thoughts on the name "Shaddai El Chai," which assisted me in my subsequent meditations. I quote :

The Magickal Formula of "Shaddai El Chai."

*"This came about because I was thinking about 'Shaddai El Chai' on 24th /
25th May and decided my ruminations decided an entry on their own right. The
rationale behind all this is to penetrate into the deeper meaning of 'Shaddai
El Chai' by treating it as a NOTARIQON and building a "Chain of Atziluthic
correspondences" i.e. to imagine what each letter would stand for on the plane
of Atziluth (divinity). Analysing 'Shaddai El Chai' in this way helped me and
informed my invocation of the same subsequently, e.g. when performing the
Middle Pillar Ritual.*

*"NB I had also used this Atziluthic Notariqon principle for other divine
words, such as my analysis of "Adonai," which during the Pentagram ritual
(see above). 'Shaddai El Chai' - spelled in Hebrew*

שדי אל לחי

SHIN	Stands for 'Shekinah'
DALETH	Venus, i.e. Love ;
YOD	YHVH
ALEPH	Eheieh, consciousness of the One, etc ;
LAMED	Hebrew for 'To / for,' – as in 'Le-chaim !'
	(Or 'Le-Olam,' i.e. 'forever,' as in AGLA.)
CHETH	Chiah, Divine Life
YOD	YHVH

*"Hence, 'Shaddai' means that the Shekinah is united to the Eternal
Ineffable God (YHVH) through the power of Love.*

"It is not merely 'united,' it is transformed into it.

*"This takes on greater significance when one understands that it is the
Shekinah descending on a human that grants that human the power of
prophecy, then the Shaddai formula implies that it is possible to unite with the
Infinite God through contemplation of the psychic faculty.*

*"It takes on even greater significance when one realises that this is the same
God-force that rules over the sephirah Yesod, representing the unconscious.
Also : that Shaddai is equivalent to 'Metatron' by Gematria, an Angel who
was a man translated into the supernal realms (Enoch) - also the only Angel
who beholds God face to face. Hence, "Shaddai" suggests that a human can
become Angelic through linking in with the Infinite God via the psychic faculty.*

*" 'Shaddai' more prosaically means 'Almighty,' but the Qabalistic sense is
that 'Almighty' has the deeper connotation referred to above.*

"'El' – 'the God' - the 'I Am' consciousness linked to the Dative case of language [full mysteries to be worked out later – WIP]. Alternative explanation : '"El' – 'the God' - the 'I Am' consciousness is transformed or realises its identity with the concept of forever (Le-Olam).

"'Chai' - Life itself linked to YHVH the Eternal God - hence, 'Everliving' - which is curiously apt as 'Chai' is mundanely translated as 'Everliving' anyway."

Day 43

25 May 2020

Everyone is a Neophyte – and not just because one always has something new to learn, wherever one finds oneself upon the path. In the scheme of the Golden Dawn, initiatory experiences *cumulate* : hence when one takes e.g., the 1=10 advancement, one does not stop being a 0=0 – instead, one *adds* the experience of Zelator to that of Neophyte which one already has. Likewise, the 2=9 adds Theoricus to Zelator + Neophyte ; 3=8 adds Practicus to Theoricus + Zelator + Neophyte ; etc.

I once met someone beset by physical ailments, believing them resulting from the magical work she currently did. "Oh when will I get out of the Earth grade ?" she wailed in despair.

It felt heart-breaking to see her predicament, but I kept silent, to avoid insensitivity over pointing out the unfortunate truth. One *never* leaves the Earth grade – or any other grade for that matter – once one has become initiated into it. It must be so, because the magical rituals of the inner order presuppose that one can call upon the energies one has experienced in the grades through which one has already gone. Hence : how could one do that, if one did not still possess those energies ?

The two basic magical techniques that the adept uses, almost more than any other, in fact consist of those taught to him or her in the Neophyte grade itself – the Signs of the Enterer and of Silence. When a temple conducts a Neophyte ceremony properly, the teaching of those signs constitutes not just information but a conferral of power to make use of them for practical purposes. In other words, one never uses them as mere gestures but to respectively project and seal off power. They express magical experience – ultimately, one's own. The Lesser Banishing Ritual of the Pentagram too, the most important banishing ritual of them all, which an adept performs every time before any ceremony he or she performs – itself originates as a Neophyte teaching. Hence the adept more than anyone ought to realise how fortunate he or she is in being a Neophyte.

That said, however, although everyone remains a Neophyte, not everyone is a complete beginner, despite the vital importance of approaching every situation in magic – and in life itself – with "beginner's mind." At the time I started the Abramelin Operation the Book had lain on my shelf for over twenty years before I got round to putting it into practice. However, I had not spent that quarter-century doing nothing, but in gaining experience in other forms of ceremonial magic, and other forms of initiatory and spiritual activity.

I therefore wondered to myself : "Would I appreciate the Abramelin Operation as much as I do now, if I had started it twenty years ago ?" I believe I ought to have answered "no," because all my experience in the intervening time must colour my perception of what happened now. A simple example would lie in the fact that although I didn't particularly fancy conjuring all the demons of Hell, I *had* had experience of conjuring demons before, when working with other grimoires (mostly the Goetia of the Lesser Key of Solomon), hence I did not go into it cold. More to the point, although I had not achieved Knowledge & Conversation of the Holy Guardian Angel via the Abramelin method, I believed I *had* had experience of my HGA through entirely different methods.

Hence, I cannot claim that this account of my Abramelin Operation represents a typical endeavour. Indeed I do not believe a "typical" experience can exist for anyone. After I finished the operation I began reading other people's accounts of their own attempts, and I found that my experiences did indeed coincide with some – but not others.

However, one peculiar detail which I can claim consists of an initiatory experience I went through a couple of years ago. I can't say too much about it as I don't want to disturb the privacy of my initiator nor of the other people involved, but – to cut a long story short – I had conferred upon me the power to, amongst other things, seek spiritual guidance by means of a certain mantra. In that sense it is did not differ from the claims made by movements such as Transcendental Meditation, who say that in order to make use of TM one must first receive initiation into the use of one's personal mantra (nb : my particular mantra was *not* TM). Perhaps it works because the ceremony of initiation which makes it effective. Perhaps the ceremony forges a spiritual connection to the lineage claimed by the initiator. Perhaps both.

Anywho, that morning I prepared with Middle Pillar Ritual, as I did normally, and almost as an afterthought, I called upon this mantra to invoke its power. It helped me attain a state of relaxation conducive to good ritual. So all went well from my point of view, but I reflected : I could not have done that twenty-years ago. And because other people had not gone through what I had done, they could not necessarily use the same technique for themselves.

My morning ritual proceeded in a conventional way. When I performed the Bornless Ritual, I could feel the potency of the invocation of powers from the six directions.

The astrological and Hermetic thoughts I had been having the past few days continued to influence my thinking when it came to the Confession of Sins, e.g. :

> "It has occurred to me that some of the 'sins' or aspects of my evil persona have an astrological explanation. But what if I take this to its logical conclusion and posit that all of my potential sins can be explained astrologically ?

"So for example, Moon In Scorpio has a dark side, but potentially all of the planets, where they are placed, have dark sides, hence each is a potential sin or source of sin ; and hence also, each is a facet of my evil persona.

"By aspiring to the Hermetic ideal of rising above the influence of the stars and planets, I am thus able to rise above my evil persona, and sublimate it to my true will.

"Communing with HGA leads to a deep state of meditation."

*

A curious synchronicity happened later that day which impressed me so much that I had to write it down. Whilst scrolling through my social media feed, I noticed someone had posted one of those ubiquitous motivational-meme things which talked about "Pray without ceasing, pray with the heart." The accompanying text mentioned that this referred to some Russian story. *I did not click the "See more..." link,* but instead continued scrolling.

Nevertheless, this gave me pause for thought, as Abramelin, in particular the final phase – contains the injunction to "enflame thyself with prayer." I could see the parallel – that the one could use it as the means of achieving the other – so I tried thinking this through. What does "Pray without ceasing, pray with the heart" actually mean ? How can one do it literally ?

Then I realised : "*Make the* heartbeat *itself the actual prayer ! For by definition, that will not cease as long as one is living.*" In other words, one imagines that the constant *b-boom... b-boom...* in the middle of one's chest as an actual prayer, with all of the sentiment that that implies. After all, why assume that, just because most prayers consist of words, that *all* prayers must consist of conventional *language ?* The Spiritual Exercises of Ignatius of Loyola consist essentially of prayers in the form of visual images. Perhaps abstract ideation could also count as a prayer, for example prayer of emotions – or prayer of non-verbal body-sounds (especially ones which one associates with prayerful emotions).

Hence, by re-purposing one's pulse as a form of prayer, one prays automatically when one becomes mindful of one's own heartbeat. Taken to its logical conclusion one could get to the point where one prays unconsciously, just by living.

Despite my fascination with the idea, I did not at first feel inclined to pursue the matter any further, and would have forgotten about the Russian story which originally mentioned this altogether …

… Until that afternoon, when I happened to go to Amazon, and noticed that this same Russian tale had now showed up in my list of recommended books. Now normally I would have put this down to Amazon tracking my browsing history, reading cookies in my browser and so-forth. Except that *no* browsing history ought to have existed. I had merely seen somebody's post which I saw but I did not interact with it in any manner whatsoever. I certainly didn't do anything obvious like searching for the story online after I saw it. Either Facebook logs *everything* one looks at without clicking, perhaps noting when one is scrolling at a constant speed and when one momentarily slows down – *or :* greater forces were at work. Perhaps it might even have resulted from invoking that mantra earlier in the day, although I did not even begin to consider that possibility until much later.

Incidentally, the book in question, *The Way of A Pilgrim*, reached a different conclusion which I had altogether : although it *did* fascinate me to read of a central character engaged in a spiritual regimen of comparable intensity to that of my own *Abramelin* operation. [100]

---

[100] See : SAVIN (2001).

Days 44, 45

26th – 27th May 2020

That night I dreamt about being inside the Rosicrucian Vault. Most proximately my familiarity with the Golden Dawn would have inspired it, but looking back I wonder if I had experienced another after-effect of the same mantra which I suspected had caused the previous day's synchronicity ? Actually the Golden Dawn and its symbolism cropped up in my conscious awareness a great deal over the next couple of days : although, given the extent I immerse myself in it, it would have surprised me more if it had not.

So, for example, I noted down that I read in particular The Golden Dawn Journal volume 2 (on Alchemy),[101] as well as a tarot-based ritual created by Tabatha Cicero.[102] In addition, that evening my fiancée and I had cause for celebration, as today marked the anniversary of our first kiss. We got together after a Golden Dawn talk on Alchemy, as it happened. Anyway, this evening, she suggested that I read the guided visualization into the path of Resh from "A Garden of Pomegranates"[103] for her. In her romantic view of things she saw the children on the Tarot key of "The Sun" as representing us,[104] although the pathworking itself has little to do with the Tarot and more about discovering one's true name in the Temple of the Sun.

Quite aside from this, during this time I also tried to keep up with my weekly BOTA lessons (this week : The Star), and wondered whether I could use magic to help raise the money I had vowed to donate to charity.

Regarding my daily rituals themselves : over these two days I took the opportunity to review my magical journal so far. Apart from observing the gradual change in my meditations over time, I noted the importance of Gratitude, and made a renewed effort to incorporate this into my rituals on a regular basis. E.g. I would incorporate gratitude into invoking the various Divine (& Angelic) names in the Pentagram, and Bornless Rituals – by feeling *thankful* to the entities as I called upon them. (This had the effect of later causing me to start dreaming about the Bornless Ritual at night).

When I "confessed my sins," I recalled being nasty and horrible to people online twenty years ago : I can't recall specific incidents but I remember it as a time of "flame wars" when a whole load of keyboard warriors with massive egos

---

[101] CICERO / CICERO *et al.*, (1995)

[102] See : CICERO / CICERO (2012)

[103] REGARDIE *et al* (2002)

[104] NB : the Golden Dawn, BOTA, and Crowley Thoth decks all show two children on Key 19, unlike the Rider-Waite which only has one.

and poor social skills fancied themselves as occultists and did battle in cyberspace, in unmoderated forums such as *alt.magick* on Usenet.

The online Golden Dawn community found itself particularly damaged by a notorious law suit when an alliance of independent GD orders took another order to court over claims of trademark infringement. This led to supporters of both sides of the law-suit taking to the internet to slander one another to an extent which ought not to have manifested amongst true seekers of light and wisdom. An old friend suggested that I, as a veteran of the Golden Dawn Flame Wars, ought to write its definitive history, but I politely declined to do so. If the story were ever told in the form of a fictional novel, the reader might think that I had filled the book with unredeemable scoundrels.

Nevertheless, revisiting the trauma of two decades previous helped me to abreact it. By the second day, I noted down the results thus :

"I surround everything with love and try to absorb it.

"If my vices are Demons, does that mean my virtues are Angels ?

"Focussing on the I AM ness, I achieve a very deep state of meditation - Samadhi - the presence of my Holy Guardian Angel. The lesson of "Adonai" - out of the I AM-ness comes YHVH the Eternal God.

"Thankful."

Day 46

28 May 2020

During the night, I remembered that I had missed performing the money-spell of which I had thought to use to raise cash for charity. As the spell's instructions specified that one should to do it once a day for eleven days consecutively, I would appear to have frustrated its action. I wondered whether I could catch up with the invocation I had missed by performing it in "the active imagination," i.e. without the bother of getting out of bed. I would later attempt it two more times, before abandoning the venture altogether, the Abramelin Operation proving too much for this particular type of ritual. Besides which, I later came to the conclusion that this spell would too much resemble doing *other magic* during the currency of my Abramelin Operation, so I dropped the idea for the time-being.

When I did get to sleep, I had a peculiar nocturnal adventure which I thought at the time worth noting :

> *"Dreaming about Glastonbury - a man in danger of being assimilated by the Borg. I go into a tarot shop and snog two young girls, one black and one white."*

I have visited Glastonbury – the village, not the rock music festival – often. It provides the real-life inspiration for "Godric's Hollow." The high street has the largest concentration of occult supply shops and bookstores anywhere where I have visited, and evidence of the magical influence crops up all over the town. All the local businesses play up to its mythical reputation – once, on the outskirts of the village I passed a car repair workshop named "Avalon Motors."

Starry-eyed occultists dream of retiring to the sort of place like Glastonbury, although one who did once warned me against trying to do this in real-life : one would soon appreciate the difference going somewhere on holiday and actually living there. Suffice to say, I found it rather difficult to figure out what this dream meant. I have never snogged any girls of any ethnicity in any tarot shop in Glastonbury in real-life, or indeed anyone apart from my fiancée since I had her met two years previously.

The Borg reference may be due to me being a Star Trek fan : or at least I remained so until the end of *Voyager*. I sort of lost interest half-way through the first season of *Enterprise*, and the less said of *Discovery, Picard,* and the J J Abrams movies the better.

I feel the record of my magical ritual that morning worth quoting in full :

> *"Up at 4.19am for preparation with Middle Pillar ritual. I "Assume" each Divine name, as I invoke it. An idea ...*
> *"Sunrise at 4.49am*

"LBRP.

"Bornless Ritual. The idea I had of assuming each Divine name, i.e. Imagining each Barbarous name to be a god-form which I assume, is a powerful one. At the end of the Bornless Ritual I am 'enthused' so much that it enhances my appreciation of each of the subsequent ceremonies.

"Conjuration

"Confession of sins. THOUGHT : I remember, of all people, Dave Mustaine speaking with regret about how he fell out with the other members of Metallica. Mustaine, who had in recent years become a born again Christian, was in effect making a confession - and the key to his regret was his realisation that he loved the people that he had offended (or most of them, at any rate).

"Hence : it is not enough for me to call to mind everyone I have sinned against and feel sorry, but I have to genuinely love those people. This could be hard ...

"Concentrating on the presence of my HGA again leads to a very deep state of meditation."

The deepness of the meditation at this point reminded me of the Holy Grail, i.e. :

"It's all well to ask, 'Whom does it serve ?' (It serves God, duh !) but I feel a more enlightening question for this Parzifal to answer would be why it serves God, i.e. What is the particular reason for it ? Part of the Divine plan for the transformation of humanity ?

"Licence to depart

"LBRP.

"Total time not including preparation : 48 minutes."

*

The rest of the day I spent reading about the Qabalah in an article from the *Golden Dawn Journal,* whilst in the evening I ate what I assumed at the time amounted to not an overly-large meal.

Day 47

29 May 2020

Bowel movements – how I hated the way they interfered with my spiritual quest ! I had by now made the transition to full vegetarianism, as a consequence of which my digestive system had to learn to cope with a diet to which it only gradually became accustomed. Today this became an issue when I tried to perform the Middle Pillar Ritual after just getting up, but felt the urgent need to eliminate, which caused me to cut-it short and go for a much-needed toilet-break, before beginning my main ritual. "*On the plus side,*" I noted later, "*this would only have distracted me if it had not occurred.*"

I apologise for the tone to which this memoir appears to have descended, but I believe that bowel movements are a Fundamental Issue. Firstly – because a ceremonial magician in general, and an Abramelin practitioner needs to have the best possible state physically to perform a ritual. Secondly, a neophyte vegetarian would need to deal with this all the same.

It proved important enough to influence the content of my contemplations during my morning ceremony. I started off conventionally, although I incorporated the idea of "Assuming" each Divine Name as I invoked it, as I had done the previous day. After performing the LBRP, Bornless Ritual, and Conjuration in this manner, I got to the "Confession of Sins" :

"*Am I overdoing it with vegetarianism ? If I am causing my body to distract me from the Great Work, that is a sin, even if I am following the literal instructions of Abramelin ! Overindulgence is the real problem.*"

I then, however, came up with an idea which would go on to prove influential throughout the rest of my subsequent operation :

"*Distracting thoughts can be a problem to meditating. But then, an idea occurs to me :*

"*The 'Qlippoth' are shells. Bad when considered alone, but when they are aligned with the Divine and Angelic forces set above them in their hierarchies, the 'shells' become the outer protective husks thereof.*

"*Hence the work of the Greater Adept (I presume) is to conjure and bind the Qlippoth so that instead of working against oneself / the divine plan, they are protecting and preserving oneself against the negative qualities associated with a given Sephirah (etc).*

"*Let us then assume that a sin is either a Qlippah or a 'mini-Qlippah.' The key then is to ask – 'of what is it the outer husk which it is trying to protect ?' Hence by analysing it in this way one discovers a good intention behind it - or within it. E.g. A distracting thought arises from a desire to protect the ego from the trauma of undergoing dissolution. Hence the good intention is one of protection. Thus - one ought to re-purpose this 'mini-Qlippah' so that it protects the ego from uncontrolled or un-Willed dissolution, whilst allowing safe dissolution which is in accordance with the higher self.*

"This reminds me of a blog post I wrote called '666 step reframing' in which Goetic evocation is seen as a species of NLP - the reframing is possible because despite the Spirit appearing to be evil, it nevertheless has a good intention which makes reframing its purpose possible.

The sentiment of viewing the evil Qlippoth as the protective husks of Divine or Angelic forces comes from Lurianic Kabbalah,[105] as opposed to the more usual Hermetic Qabalah that seems to get pedalled in ceremonial magick nowadays. Assuming that this applies to the microcosm as to the macrocosm by analogy, it would imply a recognition that a good intention (a microcosmic Divine / Angelic force) lies at the heart of almost everything which is "evil" (i.e. one's own sin – a microcosmic Qlippah). Very rarely does there exist "pure evil" – evil done for its own sake. Most supposedly evil deeds really start out as good- or at least non-evil intentions reified badly. Sometimes very badly.

One might ask : *"Ah, but what about Hitler ? Or child molesters ? Etc ?"* I classify such people as psychopaths : they manage to commit monstrosities because they have re-defined their idea of "good" in their own minds to an extent which can one can only describe as delusional. Hence from their own point of view they give effect to a "good" intention, it's just that what they mean by "good" is shared by no-one else in the worlds, apart perhaps from other psychopaths. So, for example, Hitler might have believed he did what he did for the good of humanity : unfortunately, he excluded Jews, Gypsies, Homosexuals, Communists, Freemasons, non-whites, non-Germans, non-Aryans, and those who disagreed with him from his definition of "human."

I don't mean this as any kind of excuse for their behaviour – I myself would only too willingly to throw away the key on these people – but I do believe it explains why some humans have the capacity to commit unspeakable barbarity.

Let us suppose, however, that one is not a psychopath at all, but a regular guy who happens to perform actions sometimes of which he is not proud. E.g. a bloke who worries about not performing the Abramelin Operation as well as he could.

---

[105] "In Jewish Kabbalistic cosmology of Isaac Luria, the qlippoth are metaphorical "shells" surrounding holiness. They are spiritual obstacles receiving their existence from God only in an external, rather than internal manner. Divinity in Judaism connotes revelation of God's true unity, while the shells conceal holiness, as a peel conceals the fruit within. ... In this they also have beneficial properties, as peel protects the fruit, restraining the Divine flow from being dissipated..." *"Qlippoth : In Jewish Kabbalah,"* https ://en.wikipedia.org/wiki/Qliphoth#In_Jewish_Kabbalah accessed 2021-04-19.

I allow my digestive system to distract me – that technically qualifies a sin. However, if I trace the origin of this sin back along the chain of causation, I might analyse it as follows : "The state of my digestive system was caused by me eating a meal which was heavier than it ought to have been. The reason I ate the meal was to gratify my senses and to satiate my hunger. The reason I did *that* was (a) self-love or self-care ; and (b) self-preservation. Hence although it was a sin, it arose from me trying to satisfy two intentions both legitimate in themselves, except that I carried it out inefficiently."

Hence the "distracting thought" became the outer-husk around the juicy-kernel of goodness – a sincere desire to care for myself. *One deals with such "sins" by not condemning them as absolutely evil, but by acknowledging the goodness, and finding an alternative way of fulfilling this which does not have such unfortunate consequences.*

In this manner, one can acknowledge that one has sins, but not get hung up on being *sinful*, with all the guilt-complexes that implies, because one can console oneself that at least it came from a good place. The recognition that a "sin" is not necessarily completely bad is thus a first step in healing from it. It amounts to, what Neurolinguistic Programming calls, a "re-frame" – the same basis as I had for previously writing an article that one could re-frame Goetic spirits as potential forces for good.

(Incidentally, I found this article later that day and re-blogged it. It got an unusually large number of likes on social media, probably due to the Goetia's association with Crowley.)

Back to my ritual of that morning, I recorded that I experienced some appreciation of the presence of my HGA, although what I took as a tension headache rather spoiled the effect.

*

That evening I had a meal which the following morning turned out heavier than I ought to have eaten. Quite separately, an argument arose between my fiancée and I, about the general nature of the Adeptus Minor ceremony, and the Inner Order of the Golden Dawn in general.

I have found the Adeptus Minor ceremony spectacular, the most impressive dramatic ritual in all occultism. The thought of it, however, terrified my fiancée : having heard that it had something to do with crucifixion, she had a phobia about her "ego" being crucified and destroyed. I responded by trying to give her plenty of re-assurance, by saying that it wasn't as bad as all that. The initiatory path never just concerns destruction on its own, but *Destruction and Creation* – i.e. Death and Re-birth. Really, this metaphor represents what yogis term *samadhi*, where the sense of identity "disappears" when the mind becomes perfectly still, and re-appears when it starts to move again.

This has a curious effect, which comes as a complete surprise to anyone who has never experienced it before. For one thing, there results a sudden sensation of "ecstasy," often literally : another word used in yoga for it is *Ananda* – i.e. "bliss." I have experienced a sudden burst of *kundalini* when it happens, which feels highly sexual in nature. However, early on I recognised these as the symptoms of awakening, not the awakening itself. If one were to pursue enlightenment just to indulge these blissful or erotic sensations, one would become no better than a spiritual drug-addict, with all the unpleasant connotations that addiction implies.

The most important aspect of *Samadhi* is the quality of perfect mental stillness. I realised that if the Ego disappears while the mind itself remains perfectly still, then the Ego – or more accurately, what I had assumed to be the Ego – cannot equate to the real Self. Hence, one discovers the real secret of the Death and Re-birth scenario : although the Ego appears to die, *the Self does not.*

The Adeptus Minor ritual mainly concerns establishing "Christ-consciousness," which really equates to *samadhi* – which is reflected in the symbolism of crucifixion and throughout the Vault of the Adepti.

Needless to say, this did not reassure my fiancée one iota. "Does this mean that everyone in the inner order is enlightened ?" she asked.

"It means that everyone in the inner order has been *given the keys* to achieve enlightenment," I replied. "Whether they actually do so, it would be too presumptuous of me to say."

I did not like the direction of the conversation. I perceived her as quite dismissive towards the Adepti in this country : she felt I placed undue pressure on her to finish her portal thesis successfully so as to advance to the Adeptus Minor grade. For my part I thought she had actually *wanted* to become an Adeptus Minor, so my "pressure" consisted of nothing more than using language like "*when* you become a 5=6," rather than "*if* you become a 5=6."

At one point I realised the fruitlessness of any further discussion, so I removed my own ego from the situation by shutting-up and letting her have the last-word.

Day 48

30 May 2020

The next morning I got up as usual to prepare for my devotions with the Middle Pillar and with meditation. Last night's argument weighed heavily on my mind, whilst last night's meal weighed heavily on my colon. *"NOTE TO SELF,"* I recorded. *"Must do something about digestion / elimination ..."*

When I got to the Confession of Sins, I realised that without thinking, I had repeated a mistake which I had first identified two weeks previously, that of *"telling the truth to someone who is not ready to receive it."*[106] As I noted in my journal :

> *"On this basis, it is* my *fault that I got into an argument with my fiancée last night, because I told her what I thought was the truth, but I failed to do it in a way that she would find palatable. It didn't help that I took no account of her feeling ratty and irritable through having recently given up smoking. The inner good-intention of this 'sin' is a desire for Truth generally. I therefore summon up this sin before me and reframe it so that I shall speak Truth to the benefit of all beings only (Satya).*
>
> *"Likewise : it is* my *fault for not being tactful about her 5=6 - even though I chose to feel offended by her lack of fraternity to the other members of the temple. The inner good-intention is that because I love her, I want to share with her something which I find important and is a large part of my life - I would not want to share it with her if I didn't love her."*

I added : *"Raphael is turning this temple into one of excellence ..."* Because Mathers had once effectively confirmed the secret chief of the Golden Dawn's identity as an angel referred to as "R+," this had led to a theory in the GD community that this stood for the Archangel Raphael. It had the benefit of plausibility, after all : the very name "Golden Dawn" points to the importance of *Tiphereth*, of which Raphael is the archangel. I therefore interpreted the news that our temple's fortunes were turning for the better to indicate our Secret Chief doing great things for us, the more so because we had evoked Raphael for this reason some time previously.

*

Later that day, whilst compiling more of the word squares for my own grimoire, I had an idea for a future novel – a supernatural thriller based on some of the

---

[106] Days 35, 36 – *vide supra.*

magical effects that Abramelin purports can manifest. We also had a rare visit from the outside world, as we hosted a barbeque for my fiancée's ex (and his wife), to thank them for their help when we moved house just recently. Very tenuously could we include them as part of our "bubble," as my fiancée's son spent time at their household as well. But the event went well, no diseases were communicated. The only unfortunate thing that happened consisted of me realising that the vegetarian burgers I had bought did not really lend themselves to the occasion.

Day 49

31 May 2020

From my magical journal of that day :

"Up at 4.16am for preparation with LL Ritual.

"Sunrise at 4.46am

"LBRP

"Bornless Ritual - assuming every barbarous name like a godform. Powerful.

"Conjuration - good.

"Confession of sins. I thank my HGA for its continuing ability to help me Rectify what I Identify.

"I remember a theory - I think proposed by the author of Inner Guide Meditation *- that the horoscope for one's 'shadow' is the same as one's own horoscope but with the Ascendant rotated 180°."*

NB : the actual quote I remembered was this :

"The horoscope of your Shadow side is your horoscope upside-down. *The Descendant of your horoscope (the cusp of beginning of the seventh house) is your Shadow's Ascendant or rising sing. The Shadow contains all the astrological energies that the ego represses and thinks it does not possess, both positive and negative."*[107]

My train of thought continued thus :

"If, therefore, my 'sins' have an astrological basis, what does thinking about my 'shadow' in this way reveal about my sins ?

"It makes me think of a number of things which could be true of me and of which I am not proud - ingratitude for other people's generosity towards me, emotional distance towards my family. It also suggests, however, that any psychic ability I have is a feature of my 'Shadow' self - because its Moon would be in Scorpio in the ninth house."

I.e. because in my regular horoscope, my Moon is in Scorpio in the *third* house. The ninth house is the House of long journeys, exploration, and also visions and spirituality. Agrippa declared that the best time for dream divination was when the Moon transited one's ninth house (which occurs for a period of approximately two to three days every month).[108]

"I pray to my HGA to help me resolve all these new issues as well. Some meditation.

"Licence to Depart

---

[107] STEINBRECHER (1988), p141.

[108] AGRIPPA (1651), chapter 59.

"LBRP

"Total time (not including preparation) - 48 minutes."

*

I began to suspect that the mood between my fiancée and myself had vastly improved as soon as I got back to bed after typing up my journal. Indeed, the whole day turned out to be lighter – and hence better – than the previous few days.

After celebrating what Crowley would call "sacrament," I fell asleep in her arms. Strange and vivid dreams came upon me : esoteric colleagues both alive and dead (the dead chap referred to his deceased status as retirement) ; lots of yoga books in a shop or library ; discussing spa treatments with work colleagues in some sort of night-club. They did not appear relevant to anything, but I noted them down just in case.

Later that day at my fiancée's suggestion we performed a Golden Dawn-style ritual, taken from "The Golden Dawn Magical Tarot" – based upon the 10 of Cups. [109] My fiancée appeared unsettled : I remembered that she did not necessarily share my views on magick, so I made a conscious effort to go easy on her.

However : that evening, we performed a meditation that she had composed based on BOTA's Qabalistic doctrines of sexual polarity. As soon as we began operating in what she regarded as her home territory, a remarkable change came upon her demeanour. She suddenly revealed her self-confidence as she directed the ritual. This deeply impressed me, and made me so proud of her : she acted like the talented magician which I knew deep-down she really was.

---

[109] CICERO / CICERO (2012).

Day 50

01 June 2020

The Tarot ritual we performed yesterday obviously made a great impression on me – as I wrote in my journal :

"During night : Dreaming prominently about Sandalphon, in particular a telesmatic image I made of her several years ago. It occurs to me that yesterday we invoked the 10 of Cups - Malkuth in Briah, which is the plane of the Archangels - and the Archangel of Malkuth is of course Sandalphon ! So, this is evidence at least that the ritual did indeed make an impression on my unconscious. But is it evidence of anything more ? ? ?"

Malkuth is also the Sephirah which *777* associates with The Vision of the Holy Guardian Angel : hence if I were to conduct a Malkuth-based ritual to obtain this vision I would necessarily call upon Sandalphon as part of the process. One could explain why the dream manifested most simply by the fact that the tarot ritual and my own Abramelin practice reinforced one another. As to whether it *did* mean anything more, I still pondered…

In any event I went into my practice that morning feeling positive. The Middle Pillar Ritual, LBRP, and Bornless Ritual – especially the way in which I invoked each barbarous name as a god-form to assume – all went well. I performed the Conjuration and started the Confession of Sins by thanking my Holy Guardian Angel for everything it did for me : *"for enabling me to extricate myself from whatever situation in which I find myself."*

My thoughts turned to a short film I had recently seen by the artist Lindsay Seers. [110] One of the themes she keeps revisiting in her works is that of *Heterochromia*, a physical condition, which affects less than one in a thousand people, in which one has differently-coloured eyes. I myself have "sectoral Heterochromia," in that my eyes instead of being uniformly-green have strange brown-flecks in them. However, some studies have linked the rarest form, complete heterochromia (two completely different coloured eyes), to *Chimerism*, a condition where a person carries the DNA of an unborn twin inside them. In the case of such a "Chimera," one eye belongs to you, and the other eye to the unborn twin.

"I take responsibility for all karma of which I know and of which I don't know," I contemplated that morning. But then I thought : what if *I* am just such a

---

[110] *"S/he is still inside you,"* Lindsay Seers, 2020. The clip in question was on vimeo.com but it has since been taken down and is not archived via the Wayback Machine. Knowing Lindsay, she probably did that deliberately to make the point that some things just can't be captured in Time. (For details, see : https ://www.lindsayseers.info/work_node/520 ?page=1#2)

Chimera ? I would bear the karma both good and bad of *two* people. This would add up to schizophrenia if I actually had two selves in one body. (Statistically speaking, I probably do not have this problem. Chimeric complete heterochromia is the rarest form of the rarest form of a condition which itself is rare – I probably worried myself unduly).

Even so, meditating on my Holy Guardian Angel did lead me to a deep state of meditation that morning…

*

Having now completed seven weeks of Abramelin, my thoughts turned to looking ahead to the second two months - which would begin in a week's time. I therefore spent the day researching the fine details.

Apparently I had to prolong the morning ritual - and add in evening ritual as well. I actually looked forward to the prospect : "*this will give me an opportunity to meditate before going to bed, perhaps to re-develop my dream life,*" I thought.

I also composed a new conjuration for use during Phase Two, which consisted of adding in an extra paragraph to the one I used already. In this, I essentially paraphrased the wording of Dehn's version of what Phase Two required of me and expressed it in the form of a prayer. It clearly implied that from Phase Two onwards, in addition to the rituals I should perform morning and evening, I should also make a daily study of sacred writings – and hence my Holy Guardian Angel would lead me led into "Wisdom and Understanding."[111] I immediately noticed Dehn's bias as a translator : he expressed it in this manner to imply a connection to *Chokmah* and *Binah*, although curiously Mathers, himself a Qabalist, appeared to gloss over this.

But *what* sacred writings ? Did it mean the Bible, or any sacred book ? And what passages should I select for studying ? Should it have some order, or can I just select passages at random ? I would have to ponder this.

As part of my yen to study, today I also got hold of a copy of "The Sacred Magician" by William Bloom.[112] I felt reluctant to read this during the currency of my Abramelin Operation, as I feared Bloom's experiences might prejudice my own expectations. Instead, I thought I would find it far more fun to complete the Operation, and then take a look at Bloom's book afterwards, so as to make an objective comparison. Nevertheless, I could not resist the temptation to at least skim through a few pages…

---

[111] DEHN (2006), p94.
[112] BLOOM (1992).

A growing sense of unease gripped me. Bloom apparently had done both morning and evening rituals *from day one*. *"Eek!"* I thought. Was this right? Had I done it wrong? I snatched the nearest copy of The Book (Mathers' version) to check to see if I had mis-read it, but alas : I should have been doing an evening prayer session from the beginning!

My stomach churned. I felt like a complete fool. *"Oh well,"* I thought, trying to cheer myself up, *"this gives me lots of new sins to confess in the next two months."*

Nevertheless, the problem of what to do for an evening session vexed me all day. I wanted to rectify my practice straightaway, but the sudden change of plan would only cause disruption *vis à vis* my fiancée. That very night, she had in mind an evening of late-night yoga, followed by sex, although my pre-occupation put a damper on what should otherwise have proved a romantic evening.

Day 51

02 June 2020

During the night, I attempted to do the evening ritual astrally. I noted : *"It is not altogether effective, and worse, I am afraid I have upset [my fiancée] by attempting to do so. Most of the night is sleepless."* Clearly I would have to come up with a plan to do it properly, as lying in bed and attempting to have an out-of-body-experience just didn't cut muster. Although when astrally projecting in the past I have done so whilst lying down, and indeed lying on *top* of my bed, lying *in* my bed doesn't seem to work, at least not for me.

Nevertheless, I got up as usual for my early morning ritual. Every evening before going to bed I set my alarm back two minutes earlier than the previous day : this morning I awoke half an hour before sunrise, at 4.14am.

When I got to the Confession of sins this morning, I contemplated :

"Have plenty to confess in not performing the first 50 days properly. It makes me think that one has to rely on the Grace of God - if I were to believe otherwise, I would never be able to cope with every mistake I make. Humility is the key.

"Some sense of a deep meditative state ..."

At breakfast, my fiancée and I were able to reconcile our differences : also, we worked out how to accommodate my evening ritual to our mutual satisfaction. Apparently she welcomed the opportunity to fit in some reading of her own, whilst I retired early to spend some time in the Oratory.

Later that day, we performed a Golden Dawn style ceremony mainly to satisfy my fiancée's concerns about the four elements being left out after the 10 of Cups ritual which we did a couple of days ago. As part of the ceremony we performed the Middle Pillar Ritual : the energy we invoked felt powerful. My fiancée reported that "the room felt cleared."

She also said that at the point at which we invoked Daath, she saw a pixie-like alien sitting upon an artificial blue flower - and heard a name which she claimed sounded like *"Nikki,"* or *"Nikita."*

"Not 'Nitika,' by any chance ?" I said. I went and fetched my Magical Cashbook,[113] and explained how I had dedicated it to Nitika - and that I had been using it recently. However, despite the coincidence this shed no further light on her vision. Although I certainly thought it weird, I could think of no logical reason this Magical Cashbook had anything to do with Daath, nor why invoking that during the Middle Pillar Ritual should have produced that particular vision. It

---

[113] See : BRAND (2014)

didn't actually bear that much resemblance to my preconceived idea of *Nitika,* either.

That evening, I retired to my oratory and tried out my evening ritual for the first time properly. The structure I had devised for it consisted of : first, I would miss out the preliminary LBRP, LBRH, and Bornless Ritual, and instead I would start with just the Conjuration I had written. Then, the part where I confessed my sins would consist of me reviewing the events of the day in my mind, by visualising time going backwards. On this first occasion I did not just review the events of that day but of the entire past forty-eight hours. In effect, not only did I confess the sins which I had committed, but I also performed an exercise which I knew from past experience would improve my dream-life during the subsequent night.

Inevitably, this meant that by the end of reviewing the events of the day in this manner, I would naturally pass into a meditative state of consciousness.

I would then finish the ritual, by licensing any spirits trapped by the ceremony to depart.

On this first occasion of making a point of performing my evening ritual properly, I found it relaxing : I noted how nice it felt to have consciously improved my practice.

Day 52

03 June 2020

When it came to the "Confession of sins" of my morning ritual, my thoughts became pre-occupied by unhappy memories of my time as a member of a social organisation from many years previously. I.e., its founders intended it to operate as a club where people could enjoy themselves, but the dream went sour. As with many such organisations, a lot of petty politics, backstabbing and squabbling happened. I became distanced from friends I made. At the time I thought I did the right thing - but I suppose I acted self-righteously. I should have kept quiet, withdrawn, and let other people make their own mistakes without me interfering. "*Telling the truth to someone not ready to hear it is as bad as lying to them*" applied then especially - I told what I judged the truth, but I made no consideration as to whether people (including people I formerly regarded as friends) - were ready for it. I made a bad situation worse through my negligence. I consoled myself that that desire for Truth formed the kernel which lay inside an otherwise very Qlippothic outer husk.

I suppose that I did not have nearly as mature in my outlook on life as I do now. The exact details on the one hand proved painful for me to remember, but on the other an outsider would have found them too trivial to take an interest. However, suffering slander by people who deliberately acted out of malice also poisoned my memories of the time. I could, if I had had the money to hire a lawyer, easily have taken them to court, except that I did not feel vindictive enough. "Should I forgive ?" I wondered. "Or should I seek forgiveness from *them* ?"

Conflicting emotions washed through me : rage at having been made a victim, and at the same time anguish at whether I should blame myself for my predicament. And then shame for realising that my suffering ranked as *nothing* next to victims of serious abuse – I merely wallowed in self-pity by contrast. And then shame for allowing myself to be victim-shamed. And then...

I wondered : how can one ever break out of this guilt-anger-shame-cycle without reference to an external arbiter ? How indeed can one truly forgive oneself ? "Salvation can only come through the grace of God," I told myself by way of consolation.

I had to spend an extra amount of time concentrating on the presence of the Holy Guardian Angel. The whole memory of this debacle in my life left me feeling bad, but then - one cannot stir up the Dweller on the Threshold without shit like this coming to the surface, so ironically it indicates that the positive side of the process of spiritual development.

Later that day, long after I had finished my morning ritual, a remark by my fiancée led me to *more* unhappy memories from the same time period, as if I had manifested it. *"If only I could manifest wealth and riches and happiness just as easily,"* I noted in my journal.

By the evening I had calmed down. By chance I leafed through some Franz Bardon book (*Key to the True Quabbalah (sic)*) which sparked a random thought process, which eventually gave me an idea not connected with Bardon at all. I would focus on absorbing the psychic energy invoked during ritual into the physical cells of my body. "I always think about visualising my Body of Light," I wrote in my journal, "but what about deliberately drawing energy from it to the extent that I can physically feel it ?" I resolved to explore this later, and made a first trial of it during my evening ritual that day.

Day 53

04 June 2020

Despite performing the evening ritual in this manner for the first time, I did not immediately notice an improvement in my dream life : I recalled that I allowed thoughts about my old landlord, a man whom I did not particularly like or trust, to prevent me from dreaming about something interesting.

Nevertheless, when I got up that morning to prepare for my ritual, I deliberately tried to become conscious of my Body of Light as I did so. I recorded the results of that morning as follows :

"*Sunrise at 4.43am. Trying to physically absorb all the energies invoked ...*

"LBRP.

"Bornless Ritual. *Every barbarous name is a God-form which I assume. I draw energy from all of them.*

"Conjuration.

"Confession of Sins. *Thinking of all the missed opportunities from having missed the evening ritual up to now. But by the grace of God and my HGA it is possible for me to make up for it - I do nothing of myself.*

"*Thinking also about the nature of Qlippoth - i.e. They are the unpalatable husk or shell surrounding the juicy fruit of divinity. In the same sense, presumably everyone whom I perceive as having offended me had at their core what they believed was a good intention - hence they deserve my forgiveness. Assuming they are not absolutely evil, that is.*

"*Concentrating on the sense of I AM-ness leads to a deep state of meditation - good.*

"*Certainly more heartening than yesterday.*

"Licence to Depart.

"LBRP."

*

After my morning ritual this morning, I had an idea for how to solve the problems that the Magic Squares were throwing up for me : a magically authentic method, based upon something Crowley wrote in his *Confessions*. I noted in my journal that I could write this up as a blog post, so that it could also serve as a method of attracting money to my charitable fund-raiser. I will quote at length :

Abramelin Musings : Square Dancing[114]

Following on from my previous two posts on the subject (i.e. this one[115] and this one[116]), after having given more thought to the question "*How can you tell what is and is not an authentic Abramelin word-square ?*" it occurred to me that a convenient method of answering this had been provided by Aleister Crowley.

Figure 5 Better to shave it all off instead of having an embarrassing lockdown haircut !

---

[114] SUMNER (2020)

[115] *"Abramelin musings : dogs, lions and monkeys,"* 9th May 2020, in which I noted the difficulty of trying to work out which were the correct squares for chapter five of Book IV, and my discovery of the Leipzig Manuscript.

[116] *"Abramelin Musings : The Dresden Manuscript,"* 15th May 2020 - in which likewise I noted that the Dresden manuscript - and hence the versions of the squares therein - could be viewed online.

In his "Autohagiography" he described what happened when he tried teaching clairvoyance to a student :

> *I would, for example, give him a talisman which he had never seen before, and ask him to discover its nature. We would then compare the result of his investigation with the book from which I had taken the talisman, and he would find that he had judged correctly. (For instance, I would give him a square containing thirty-six characters in Enochian, which he could not read. He would pass in his astral body through an imaginary door on which this square was inscribed, and tell me that he had come out upon a balcony overlooking the sea, where a violent storm was raging. I would then refer to The Book of the Sacred Magic of Abra-Melin identify the square, and note that its virtue was to arouse a tempest.*

Crowley, Confessions, chapter 61.[117]

This, I would submit, suggests a practical solution to how to verify an Abramelin word-square, or reconcile apparent differences between different Abramelin source manuscripts. I.e. take the word-square one wishes to investigate, and pass through it as if going on a tattva-journey. By thus scrying one will get a clear impression whether the word-square is correct for you, or if there is something wrong and requires further investigation.

There is, however, one criticism which I would make of Crowley's method. At the time of the incident he described, Crowley had gone through the Abramelin operation, or at least purported to – he certainly did not complete the operation in the manner originally envisaged by Abraham the Jew, the author of the Book of the Sacred Magic. Nevertheless, if we accept for one moment that Crowley had completed the operation, *the student whose clairvoyance he was testing had not.*

The Golden Dawn says that when undertaking these sorts of scrying exercises, one should call for a guide to protect oneself on the astral landscape. An Abramelin alumnus, investigating a word-square in this manner, will have the best possible spirit-guide upon which to call – his or her own Holy Guardian Angel. Crowley's student presumably had not connected with his HGA in the Abramelin-manner or at all, and yet he attempted to scry into a word-square empowered by demons which Crowley had already evoked !

Needless to say, like a lot of people in Crowley's life, the student came to a bad end. This may not have been the Great Beast's fault, as the student had a pre-existing Cocaine addiction which compromised his mental health, but it would not be altogether churlish to speculate that Crowley's intervention probably didn't help. Hence, I would recommend that it is best to attempt this *after* one has attained KCHGA, just to remain on the safe side.

---

[117] CROWLEY (1929)

If you have enjoyed reading this article, please consider making a donation to my Just Giving page – raising money for poor and vulnerable families affected by the Covid 19 lockdown. All thanks to God and my HGA for being able to participate in the Sacred Magic.

*

Around that time I started to re-read *Confessions* more often : I developed a great sympathy for Crowley during this time, as I saw him as a man like me – trying to do the Abramelin operation as best he could. I was intrigued when I read him making a reference to a supposed super-duper "YHVH incense" : but I later realised Crowley merely referred to the well-known *Qetoret* incense from the bible.[118]

However much I admired Crowley, though, I never felt any inclination to fan-worship him, nor indeed anyone else from the history of the western mystery tradition. I try to remain objective about everyone I come across, and not assume that anyone stands above criticism. To my mind, when someone *does* say something good, that approach only makes it more valuable.

Unfortunately, I come across a lot of people who think that their favourite teacher *does* stand above criticism : so much so that one commits sacrilege by daring to evaluate their writings in a scholarly fashion – even if the conclusion ultimately proves favourable. I remember that day when I made a *faux pas* when I dared to suggest that my fiancée's beloved Paul Foster Case had said something wrong. In Case's defence, he probably wasn't wrong *per se*, it's just that I disagreed with my fiancée's interpretation of one of his writings (something about how energy circulates in one of his exercises). My attempts to explain that far from me behaving all nasty and horrible the subject genuinely interested me, fell on deaf ears : I decided to remove my ego from the argument by physically removing myself, and by going off to sulk.

My good intention consisted of my concern that by relying on teachers overly-much she didn't giving herself enough credit. In any case, my compassion for my fiancée became aroused when I received a snotty email from my former landlord (he had been on my mind because of the circumstances of me moving out of my old flat, to move in with my fiancée), and I realised there exist worse things and people in the world to deal with, than wasting time on what ultimately constituted a trivial argument. I apologised wholeheartedly to her. She for her part proved quick to forgive – our make-up "sacrament" turned out particularly good,

---

[118] Ibid.

buoying me to finish off the evening with the ritual I had established the previous day.

Day 54

05 June 2020

The evening ritual seemed to start to do some good. *"During night,"* I wrote in my journal, *"dreaming about jumping from car to car, to place to place, defying gravity. I recognise from my particular state of mind that if I carry on like this I will become Lucid ... and then the alarm goes off."* "Starting" being the operative word !

I dragged myself out of bed to face an unseasonably rainy morning. I recorded my ritual as follows.

"LBRP.

"Bornless Ritual. Whilst I was reading excerpts from 'Confessions' yesterday, I noted a passage where Crowley described his experience with the Bornless ritual when doing his own Abramelin operation. He described the 'Ar thiao section' as a projection to the infinite east - sort of like a rising on the planes, but horizontally - the same with the other directions (paraphrasing)

"Inspired by this I try to incorporate this sentiment into my own performance of the Bornless Ritual, i.e. Each section - east, south, west, north, down, up - is imagined as a 'rising on the planes' in that particular direction. Before I begin the final 'I am He, the Bornless Spirit ...' section, I pause to meditate on consolidating all these Risings. Powerful.

"Conjuration."

When it came to confession of sins, traumatic memories from over thirty years ago overwhelmed me. I seem to remember leading a dissolute life as a teenager – not particularly outrageous, and not harming anyone, except the one person who mattered – i.e. me. I did not necessarily sin against God, but against myself. But if I am God's creation, then that is *just as bad*.

"Confession of sins. I am uncomfortably aware of when I almost fucked up my life as a teenager, including what I now believe was a nervous breakdown ...

"But I held on - the Good at the heart of the otherwise unbearable Qlippothic husk was an indomitable inner strength. It kept me alive then, and through even worse situations to this very day. I meditate on expressing gratitude towards it.

"I remember from reading Bloom that when he experienced a 'heavy' in his oratory he responded by inviting it to pray with him.[119] This gives me the idea that I could do the same with all the negative impressions I encounter - I

---

[119] BLOOM (1992), p85.

mentally invite them to 'pray,' by which I mean I imagine them turning inward to contact their own inner divinity - as I turn inward to contact mine.

"This has a curiously comforting effect. It occurs to me that I could take this to its logical conclusion by not just inviting the 'heavies' which I encounter from time to time to 'pray' with me, but also all demons - and gods as well (such as the god-forms which are the barbarous names of evocation). But this is an idea to be explored and developed - as if it is too much to work out in this particular session.

*"**License to depart.***

*"**LBRP**."*

*

That day I made a start on compiling the word squares for chapter 15 of Book IV, "to have the spirits provide as much food and drink as one can eat and drink." The book listed only five choices - bread, meat, wine, fish and cheese. What about any other type of cuisine? What, indeed, about veganism or vegetarianism? Other alcoholic / non-alcoholic beverages?

My fiancée had a yen for Taoist things that day, as at her suggestion I read "The Secret of the Golden Flower," or at least the bit not written by Jung. I found it OK as a little book about internal alchemy, but unremarkable from my jaded point of view. Nevertheless, my fiancée interpreted my reaction as an excuse to get me to join in with some Taoist meditation which she wanted to do, before I retired for the evening to my nightly ritual.

Days 55, 56

06 – 07 June 2020

My reading of Crowley continued to influence me greatly. "*Everything is a rising on the planes,*" I thought, as I went into my morning ritual. Indeed, I perceived a tendency amongst occult hipsters to poo-poo the Great Beast, dismissing him as if he did not hold as much importance as he or his followers might like to believe. Now, however, I began to truly appreciate Crowley's achievement – because of me undertaking a course of action that he himself had done.

I perceived that disrespecting Crowley constituted a "sin" which I should confess as part of my morning ritual- now that I realised that I had not appreciated how much he did do. Turning to his own texts for guidance in the Abramelin process pointed out to me the irony of my situation.

More generally, everything which kept me from attaining my goal I labelled as a sin. On the one hand this could include distracting thoughts, but on the other it would also include my propensity for getting into arguments with my fiancée. I ought to have known by now the signs so that I could avoid doing so.

I found that *Jnana Yoga* – meditating on "I-AM-ness" – helped greatly over these two days. "*Trying to commune with the I AM ness - encouraging every entity in the universe to turn inwards and find their own 'central Ego,'*" I wrote in my journal. "*Meditating is good - by concentrating on the I Am-ness I am able to reach a deep state of stillness, which carries over to the subsequent final parts of this morning's ritual.*"

Actually, all my rituals over these two days I interpreted as "peaceful," and "Overall feeling positive."

I spent my days going through my latest BOTA lesson, which involved colouring in key 18, "The Moon," and also indulging my fiancée by taking part in one of her relaxation rituals.

Quite separately I plotted and schemed to organise the further development of my Rosicrucian Order (not associated with the Golden Dawn), an Order for both men and women based on sharing esoteric research. It amazed me to see the amount of interest this awakened, particularly amongst co-masonic groups, who had previously had no means of expressing this kind of interest.

On the evening of the final day of Phase One, I performed the nightly ritual, and then retired to bed. For some reason, my fiancée told me I had a vibration which made her think of "peanuts" (bizarrely enough).

PHASE TWO

Day 57

08 June 2020

Exactly eight weeks having passed since I first started, I declared today the first day of the Second third of my Operation. During the second Phase, one continues the morning and evening rituals as before ; but one also adds in a new requirement to one's devotions : praying that one can derive insight from studying the sacred writings.

I got up half an hour before dawn (i.e. at 4.11am) to prepare with the Middle Pillar Ritual.

When I started my actual morning ritual with the Lesser Banishing Ritual of the Pentagram, I decided, on a whim, to incorporate ideas on the Qabalistic Cross from a video by Damien Echols which I had seen whilst browsing YouTube the previous evening. I later discovered that most of the ideas had actually come from Israel Regardie, although Echols himself omitted to mention this. Anyway : the practice involves mentally preparing oneself by centring ones' consciousness in the astral body, then growing to giant form, so that not just the Earth, but the whole Universe is beneath one's feet. As one makes the various gestures, one imagines rays of power coming from and going to the limits of infinite space, i.e. :

"ATEH" - the infinite Height ;

"MALKUTH" - infinite depth ;

"VE-GEBURAH" - infinite south

"VE-GEDULAH" - infinite north ;

Etc.

The effect proved powerful, not least in that it stilled my mind and gave the subsequent ritual a greater depth - a more refined feel. As if I stood in infinite space itself when I drew the actual pentagrams.

I then performed the Bornless Ritual as normal, after which I premiered my New Conjuration for Phase Two. Actually this resembled the Conjuration I had used up to now, but with an extra paragraph added to reflect the new responsibilities of this new phase of the operation, (marked in **bold** below) :

"In the names YHVH, Tzebaoth and Adonai, who hath created all Nature and before Whom all Kings bow down and are subject - may I always practice Knowledge and Conversation of my Holy Guardian Angel, that I may have power and authority as did Moses, Aaron and Elijah.

"Oh YHVH ! Tzebaoth ! Adonai ! I entreat you to deign to command your Holy Angels to lead me in the True Way, and Wisdom, and Knowledge, by

studying the which assiduously in the Sacred Writings there will arise more and more Wisdom in my heart.

"In the names YHVH, Tzebaoth and Adonai - AMEN.

"In the names YHVH, Tzebaoth and Adonai, and my Holy Guardian Angel, I conjure all Spirits : turn away from evil and Honour God ; serve Him and humanity, and myself in particular ; keep safe from harm myself, all connected with me and with this place ; fulfil all my commands promptly, efficiently, and according to my interest ; speak truthfully to me without murmur or ambiguity in a voice clear and intelligible without equivocation ; appear before me in a fair shape without tortuosity or deformity ; and remain until I give thee licence.

"In the names YHVH, Tzebaoth and Adonai, and my Holy Guardian Angel - AMEN."

When it came to the "Confession of Sins," inevitably I contemplated the ramifications of what I had undertaken. It occurred to me that by adding in this new requirement for the second two months implied that I ought to make at least some study of scripture at least once a day ; and hence if I failed to do so, that would make a new Sin – i.e., a falling short of the target.

But what scripture ? I presume a Jew would use the *Tanakh,* but as a Christian I ought to be able to go over the New Testament as well, e.g. John 1 :1-5. NB : I say "As a Christian" but a long time had passed since I last went to mass, and obviously the Church would excommunicate me forthwith or worse if any priest or indeed any kind of regular Christian found out what I was up to.

As one who recognises a ray from the ineffable light in all religions, perhaps I ought to be able to read the Holy Book of *any* religion, and derive insight from any of them equally. However, I perceived that although it might prove Righteous of me to do so, to show how greatly I deserved the title of Sage by effortlessly finding the Truth in any religion to which I chose to apply my wisdom, I thought : *"Bollocks to this – I've got a better idea."* It went thus :

Instead of making a study of any old Holy Writings, I would deliberately select those passages of Scripture which would prove most useful to me as a Qabalist and as a Magician.

Thinking in this way would give structure and purpose to my studies, and furthermore it pointed me in the direction of where I ought to start. I had already done a lot of work with the Angels of the Shem Ha Mephoresh over the years. Now it so happens that a Qabalistic tradition dating back at least as far as the seventeenth century associates each part of the Shem Ha Mephoresh with a versicle from the Book of Psalms (except for one of them, which it associates with a versicle from Genesis). Hence by going over the 72 versicles corresponding to the 72 parts of the Shem Ha Mephoresh, not only would I fulfil my commitment to make a daily study of scripture, but I would revise and consolidate my knowledge of the Shem Angels. Also, I would challenge myself to improve my knowledge of Hebrew, as I intended to attack each versicle with the attitude of a Qabalist and examine it *in originale,* subjecting it to the rigour of gematria and so forth.

I fully expected that this would lead to an improved relationship with and understanding of the 72 Angels. I did not see this as practicing a different kind of magic to *Abramelin* during the course of the operation – which of course conflicts with the instructions in The Book – but as a way of incorporating the Shem Ha Mephoresh Angels *into* the Sacred Magic.

I also realised that if I studied one versicle per day, then seventy-two days would not take me to the end of my Operation. I supposed that if that happened, I would find other verses of scripture which were relevant from a Qabalistic and magical point of view – such as the first thirty-two verses of Genesis.

As I considered my overall plan, I mused :

"The kind of commitment required in this new phase is like going from Neshamah - the realisation of the higher intuitive mind - to Chiah - the turning of that intuition to discovering the esoteric meaning of scripture - from Adeptus Minor to Adeptus Major, or something like that. Does this mean that in the Final Phase I go onto discovering the Yechidah ?"

Apart from this, I noted in my journal for my contemplations that morning :

"THOUGHT : the great secret of the Tetragrammaton is that the Yod of Yod Heh Vav Heh stands for 'Yechidah' - hence when I realise the divine spark within me, I really do realise Divinity.

"Meditation on I AM ness leads to a very deep state."

I finished my morning ritual with a Licence to Depart, and by performing the LBRP in the manner I had done at the before, extending my visualisations into Infinite Space.

*

Later that day, I made my first attempt at making a Qabalistic study of scripture : starting with Psalm 3 :3, the versicle associated with *Vehuiah,* the first of the seventy-two angels. I had first started working systematically with them in 2016 when I made a bold attempt to invoke each of the Angels at least once, for the purpose of trying to become familiar with them. From this I compiled my own personal grimoire, which I entitled *"The Angels of the Shem Ha Mephoresh"* (I do not expect to publish this, as I made it just for my own use). Now, I proceeded by revisiting my grimoire and adding in the analysis I made of each versicle under the corresponding Angel's entry.

I do indeed count myself lucky to live in the age of computers and the internet, as ceremonial magicians of more than a generation ago would have found my own chosen method of scriptural study, for the purposes of my Abramelin Operation, impossible. Thanks to the world wide web, I had at my fingertips electronic copies of the Book of Psalms in both English and in Hebrew, as well as numerous reference documents such as Hebrew dictionaries and pronunciation guides, *777*,[120] and other works on Shem Ha-Mephoresh Angels. Thus I could quickly compile all the data relating to a particular versicle, which held relevance from a Qabalistic point of view, so that I could proceed to the meat of the exercise, i.e., attempting to intuit the real *inner* meaning of the piece of scripture in front of me.

   Suffice to say, by going through this particular versicle and then contemplating my findings, I entered a powerful state of meditation – which I took as indicative of the actual presence of Vehuiah, and of his willingness to integrate with my own Holy Guardian Angel. One source says of invoking Vehuiah that "*one may become illuminated by the spirit of God*,"[121] so the experience felt curiously appropriate.

My first attempts at scriptural study in this manner so encouraged me, that I hypothesised a new method of working with the Shem Ha Mephoresh Angels. I jotted down the following in my magical journal :

- Go to the appropriate versicle, verify how this is written in Hebrew and how it is pronounced.
- Work out the gematria of each word : consult *Sepher Sephiroth*[122] and note down correspondences. Note down any other insights.
- Invoke Holy Guardian Angel and meditate on the versicle by mentally repeating it in Hebrew (whilst remaining cognisant of its meaning), all the while aspiring to grasp the deeper meanings or meaning indicated by ones Qabalistic research.
- Invoke Angel itself by name, petitioning it that it recognises one's Holy Guardian Angel, and grant whatever its special boon is supposed to be. Talking Theurgy here - nothing superstitious or what not.*
- Commune with Angel as appropriate. The presence of the Angel ought to reveal itself, but at length, one should thank it and one's HGA, and close in the proper manner.

---

[120] CROWLEY (1909)

[121] LENAIN (2020), p56

[122] Ibid. I also worked from a version entitled *"Sepher Sephiroth (Revised) "* – BENNETT *et al* (2003)

* The reference to "superstition" came to birth from the awareness that several books on the Shem Ha-Mephoresh angels published nowadays focus on the *thaumaturgic* aspects of invoking them, whilst ignoring the theurgic side. I however wanted to focus on integrating the positive, spiritual aspects of these angels into my personality : mainly because it felt important for me to maintain the compatibility with my *Abramelin* Operation. If I instead had merely focussed on the material aspects of what these books promise as a result of invoking these angels – that for me would have gone against the spirit of my Abramelin Operation – a big no-no.

The beneficial effects of invoking Vehuiah remained with me for the rest of the day. In a fit of inspiration, I found the manuscript from which Mathers himself worked - the one at the Bibliothèque de l'Arsenal : it had been digitised so that anyone can view it online. I blogged about it, for no other reason than so that I myself could find it again quickly when I went online.

I also felt particularly energised when I performed my evening ritual later. I celebrated the fact by "rejoicing" with my fiancée before going to sleep. For some bizarre reason she told me that my spirit animal was a *Tiger*, the significance of which – unless of course my prowess had inspired her – I did not fully appreciate at the time.

Day 58

09 June 2020

I had previously[123] thought of dealing with "heavies" – negative thoughts, feelings, etc, characterised as entities – by inviting them to pray with me, following an idea by Bloom. However, what if, instead of treating the negative entities as such, I treated *all* such entities as well ? I.e. not because they are negative as well, but so that the One ultimately absorbs all things ?

I tried this out during this morning's ritual. I began in the normal manner (incorporating my new conjuration which I had started using the previous day). Then, when I got to the point of confessing my sins, it occurred to me :

"The 'heavies' which I invite to pray with me i.e. Turn inwards and connect with the I AM ness - are the godforms I assumed in the Bornless Ritual, and my own past lives themselves.

"Meditating again leads to a deep state of I AM-ness."

I later realised that the same principle could be applied not just to my Abramelin rituals but also to troubling situations in everyday life – as a practical method for shaking off unpleasant moods, etc.

*

My Spirit-Animal stared at me with what seemed a bored expression which nevertheless masked a deadly desire to pounce on me for the kill. I stood rooted to the spot : partly in terror, but also partly in amazement that it had manifested to visible appearance at all. What unholy, perverse, magical rites had my fiancée and I actually done ? I had heard of demons manifesting before their due time in Abramelin operations before (probably from reading Crowley) : could the same thing now happen to me ?

I decided to do the only thing that someone faced with something bearing the resemblance of a Tiger would do. I shot it. I.e., with my camera – and posted it on social media.

During these early days of Summer, with the weather was so warm, we would leave the door from the conservatory to the back-garden open all day and into the evening, to provide a welcome draft. Hence today, I happened to walk through the house in the direction of the garden, and found the nearest thing to my Spirit Animal which the local fauna could provide – a domestic cat with golden, almost tiger-like fur – settled quite comfortably in an armchair we had set up there.

---

[123] i.e., on day 54 – *vide supra.*

Despite not literally being a demon (after seeing it in the vicinity, I guessed it to be a neighbour's pet), I could not help thinking that the magic in which I indulged might have attracted it to the house, nonetheless.

Briefly going through my social media in general, I noted that my blog-post from yesterday, though earnestly meant, had not picked up much interest – a few "likes" but nothing more. Obviously, scholarship on original Abramelin manuscripts did not appeal to many people's interest. But I ought not to complain (I thought), because I had made the blog-post for my own benefit rather than anyone else's.

I then came back to the post about the Cat, and found that it had picked up as many "likes" in five minutes of being online as my scholarly and worthy blog-post had done in almost twenty-four hours. "*I should stick to posts about Cats and Aleister Crowley, if I want publicity,*" I noted at the time.

Social media proved itself a very fickle thing : a photo of a new book which my fiancée got from Amazon, by Anna Kingsford, went on to get even more likes that the Cat. The only reason this concerned me at all lay in the fact that as a writer I try to hit upon the "right" social media strategy in order to publicise my works – preferably one which doesn't involve paying a marketing expert to do it all for me.

Apart from worrying myself about Cats and demons, I did accomplish something useful today (in addition to my morning and evening rituals) by continuing my scriptural study, and analysing the versicle associated with Jeliel, the second Shem Ha Mephoresh angel. I noted in my journal :

"Going by Gematria, 'but thou Oh LORD are not far away...' could also be code for 'but thou oh LORD are God, the Angel of the Covenant...'"

Day 59

10 June 2020

I managed to put a positive spin on the vegetarian food weighing heavily on my alimentary canal. *"Up at 4.10am for Middle Pillar and elimination,"* as I described it in my journal. *"Whereas before I had assumed the latter was a distraction, far from it - it is a* banishing *- so that I am not distracted during the main ritual."*

I recorded my actual morning devotions as follows :

"LBRP.

"Bornless Ritual.

"Conjuration.

"Confession of Sins. *Yesterday, I realised that I had memories of past regrets which keep a neurotic hold over my consciousness. More worryingly is that when they rise to the surface (as it were) I am momently 'possessed' until I assert conscious control over them - by which I mean I am repressing them again. I pray to my HGA that I learn to not repress them, but to treat them as a 'heavy' and instantly invite them to 'pray' with me.*

"I realise that I had spiritual pride without realising it. When I started the Abramelin Operation, I thought the states of consciousness I was attaining were the bees-knees. However, now I have discovered that the true extent of Abramelin is even greater than I had assumed - e.g. Through the simple fact of integrating my qabalistic studies of the Shem Ha Mephoresh angels. Hence I made a serious error in thinking that I had achieved anything whereas I had merely entered within the porchway of what is possible.

"The solution is that I should get into the opposite habit - that the true extent of the Sacred Magic will always be even greater than I can assume. E.g. Whilst I think incorporating the Shem Ha Mephoresh is or has the potential to be awesome, I must remember the possibility that there will be even more to discover at which I have not yet guessed.

"Trying to contact the stillness ...

"Licence to depart

"LBRP."

*

After getting up from going back to bed for a lie-in, my fiancée told me that she had dreamed about me as Prometheus, stealing fire from Heaven, not just once, but day after day (she guessed this referred to her interpretation of what she supposed I did with my Abramelin operation). She also mysteriously said "Merlin was there ..."

"Perhaps Prometheus and / or Merlin are some of my past-lives ?" I mused. Neither idea had ever occurred to me before, as both seemed too fantastic.

Less improbable but just as magical, I attained a profound state of meditation whilst researching the versicle associated with Sitael, the third Angel of the Shem Ha Mephoresh, as part of my daily scripture-study. So my prediction from my morning ritual appeared to prove *true*.

I did my evening ritual again later, and retired to bed.

Day 60

Corpus Christi - 11 June 2020

The Chickpea pancakes and Cajun Quorn which my fiancée tried out last night induced a mixture of dreams : some pleasant (memories of people I knew from the Golden Dawn) ; some emotionally neutral, such as going on a trip by train or plane ; and some unpleasant, which had probably been inspired by recent news stories about Prince Andrew.

I prepared with the Middle Pillar Ritual : feeling the invoked power thereof reminded me of the *Shekinah*, the Divine Presence of God. I recorded the rest of my morning ritual as follows :

   "Bornless Ritual - *the vibration of each barbarous name itself becomes a Godform which I assume. Powerful.*

   "Conjuration.

   "Confession of sins. *Troubled by thoughts of Atheism."*

I.e. for one moment I wondered whether I really *knew* that God existed. My contemplations continued :

   "Regarding this as a 'heavy' - it occurs to me that this is a Qlippah, hence - what is the Divine spark at the heart of this ugly shell ? The good intention is that at the root of atheism is a desire to turn away from all that is bad about religion, especially as it has existed historically - and a desire to turn towards the Good. Ironically, however, the Good towards which I wish to turn is the real God - the real spiritual principle of the Universe ! 'The fool hath said in his heart "There is no God."'

   "Licence to Depart.

   "LBRP."

*

I tried to return to bed to get some shut-eye, but my fiancée – being wide-awake, infuriated me by insisting on talking about random stuff whilst I tried to sleep. It would not have been so bad but she kept straying from topic to another.

Eventually, however, I got up and addressed myself to my daily scripture reading. I made a study of "*Turn thou towards me, oh LORD, and save my Soul, deliver me for the sake of Thy Mercy,*" – associated with Elemiah, the fourth of the Shem Ha Mephoresh angels, upon which I meditated. Comparing the King James Version with the original Hebrew certainly proved eye-opening. What I had not realised up to then was that it should more literally be translated "*Turn thou towards me, oh LORD, and save my* Nephesh, *deliver me for the sake of Thy Mercy,*" i.e. the psalmist actually refers is the lower Soul or animal nature.

Later : it being Corpus Christi, the day which the Golden Dawn equates with "Day C" of the *Fama Fraternitas,* today all good Adepti ought to have assembled in the *Domus Sancti Spiritus*. Unfortunately, Covid-19 restrictions rendered this impossible this year, so the Chiefs hatched a plan whereby we would astrally project there instead.

That afternoon, therefore, I went for a lie down and attempted to project myself and commune with my fellow Adepti, whilst the Greatly Honoured Chiefs re-consecrated the Vault in the privacy of their own home. I later got emails from my fratres and sorores along the lines of "Oh yeah, I was there, and it was fun to meet everyone !"

My fiancée, however, wore a sad expression on her face : as a member of the Portal grade, she had convinced herself she could not join in, so she spent the afternoon sulking. I tried to console her that evening by rehearsing some inner order rituals with her, but it held small comfort. So eventually I retired for the evening, performing my nightly-ritual.

Day 61

12 June 2020

Sigmund Freud once claimed that when we dream of gold, we actually think, unconsciously, of our own feces, and all the hang-ups we associate with the anal-stage of our psychosexual development. Hence the reason a lot of people think describe money as somehow "dirty" or "unclean" – they exhibit unconscious biases formed from childhood experiences – or even trauma.

Did this mean, I wonder, that, conversely, if one dreams of excrement one actually dreams of money ? I hoped that this proved true, because otherwise all this vegetarian food affected my oneironautical activities throughout the night.

Incidentally, I apologise for writing a lot about my bowel movements, but I considered it a serious matter at the time. I only hope that it does not put my readers unduly off the *Abramelin* operation – or vegetarian food for that matter.

In any event, I awoke at 4.10am that morning for preparation with the Middle Pillar. I was trying to cultivate an attitude of "Body Asleep, Mind Alert But Still," which the astral projection training of The Monroe Institute had inspired. I had read about it a lot, as I always wonder if other people find it easier than I do. In any event, thinking in this manner helped me attain a deep state of relaxation whilst performing the ritual, although I did not project astrally *per se*.

As regards my main ritual that morning :

"LBRP.

"Bornless Ritual. I rush through this, on the supposition that the less time I waste, the less chance my mind has of being distracted. Hence : I assume the Godform of the vibration even as I am vibrating - chop chop ! Need to find my rhythm though - I don't want to go too fast."

(This, however, should be read in the light of my subsequent efforts to find the right pace at which to perform the Bornless Ritual – *vide infra*.)

"Conjuration.

"Confession of Sins. If my life is not 100% perfect, that is evidence of at least some kind of sin, even if I can't think of something particularly wrong.

"Thinking about extending mercy to all my past lives ...

"An idea - an extension of my theory about the Qlippoth i.e. That if one identifies a thing as a Qlippah or evil outer husk, there is a kernel of goodness at its heart - i.e. A good intention which motivates the evil action. This is equivalent to the Divine Spark, which is of Atziluth, at the heart of the Qlippothic outward manifestation which, naturally, is of the realm of the Qlippoth.

"HOWEVER, what if one were to take this further, by - after identifying the kernel of goodness at the heart of the Qlippah, to treat even this as a 'husk' or

Qlippah in relation to an even greater kernel of Goodness ? In other words, one is ever seeking inwards, so that if ever one experienced what one at first thought was perfection, one should not believe it to be so, but instead think : 'Even this is but a poor reflection of the Divine reality.' Then by treating this as the new husk, one seeks out what is at the heart of even this.

"I apply this mode of thinking to my own Peak Experiences, and find myself entering a profound state of meditation (which, by my own admission, is but a poor reflection of something even greater).

"Licence to Depart.

"LBRP."

*

During the day, for my daily scripture-reading I made a study of the versicle associated with Mahasiah, the fifth angel of the Shem Ha Mephoresh. "*I sought the LORD and he answered me ; from all my troubles he has set me free.*" Google Translate proved, needless to say, next to useless in helping me figure out the meanings of individual Hebrew words, so I had to spend some time looking for a reliable on-line Hebrew dictionary. I had a long distrust of Google Translate, despite its easy availability out of all online translation tools. Previously I had to deliberately tell Neophytes coming into the Golden Dawn *not* to attempt to use it to come up with a motto, but instead express what they wanted to say in their native tongue and get it translated by someone who actually studied Latin at school. It would not have surprised me to learn that Brian had used Google Translate when he first tried to figure out how to say "*Romans, go home !*" before setting out on his ill-fated graffiti-escapade : that is how bad some of its results have been.

Evening ritual accomplished.

Day 62

13 June 2020

I remembered a disagreement I had with my fiancée the previous day. She had some opinion (I can't remember the specifics) which struck me as a disempowering self-belief. However, I found out to my cost that it's not tactful to try and empower the other person by pointing this out, because then one runs up against cognitive dissonance, i.e., "*it may be a disempowering self-belief, but it's* my *disempowering self-belief!*" I paraphrase. Anyway, this preyed on my mind during my morning ritual :

"*Up at 4.09am for preparation with Middle Pillar Ritual.*

"*Sunrise at 4.39am.*

"**LBRP**.

"**Bornless Ritual**. *Taken at a slower pace than yesterday, I imagine the vibration in my heart is the godform I invoke, which I then assume - and direct my attention inward in contemplation. The combined effect not only feels more relaxed and gentle, but also more powerful - it carries over to the subsequent rituals*

"**Conjuration** - *good*.

"**Confession of Sins**. *I got into arguments yesterday with A, so I must be doing something wrong. The good intention is that I want to convince her she is more powerful than she thinks she is, that she is worthy ... But she gainsays me when I try to do so. Is it my way of telling her?*

"*In any case - concentrating on the stillness leads to a deep state of meditation - but I need to go deeper.*

"**Licence to Depart**.

"**LBRP**."

*

A strange series of events occurred today. My fiancée was chatting away on some point on which I happened to disagree. Unfortunately, I made the mistake of saying so – at which juncture my fiancée got mightily offended. I personally considered the precise details of the discussion as immaterial : however, I became seriously upset by her seeming to think that if I disagreed with her that I meant it personally against her, which I felt tantamount to accusing me of bad faith. Being accustomed to debating ideas in a scholarly fashion, her holding a different opinion to me did not bother me : but because I failed to convince her of my intentions, I upset her, which in turn made me upset as well.

I beat a retreat, and forced myself to continue with my daily scriptural study. Today I investigated the Psalm versicle associated with Lelahel, the sixth angel of the Shem Ha Mephoresh : "*Sing praises to the Lord, which dwelleth in Zion : declare among the people his doings.*"[124] As I examined the gematria of the Hebrew original of this verse, I realised that the phrase "which dwelleth in Zion" could stand for "*which renews limpid blood.*"

I did a double-take : Lenain had written of Lelahel that "*[o]ne invokes this angel to ... cure illnesses,*"[125] and here the gematria pointed to Lelahel's role as a *healing* angel. I immediately began to realise that someone (e.g. Lenain himself) must have gone through the gematria of these versicles himself hundreds of years ago, and I was rediscovering the fact now : I thought it too much of a coincidence to regard it as all arbitrary.

In any event, briefly meditating on the versicle and the thoughts that arose from my discoveries had a calming effect, and did much to alleviate the bad mood I had acquired from earlier.

Then, however, the real miracle happened. When I ran into my fiancée again later that day, the situation between us calmed down greatly, and we effected a reconciliation from earlier. I could not help but think that this occurred after I had contemplated Lelahel – whom I had identified as a Healing Angel. I had assumed that this meant he cured *physical* illnesses, but perhaps Lelahel also worked to heal what was wrong with us ? Perhaps it meant that Lenain hadn't just *decided* that Lelahel was a healing angel, the gematria had enabled him to make contact with the actual entity, who gave him the "correct" answer, as it were.

In any case I believed in the reality of Lelahel presence that day : I could thus complete the rest of my rituals that day with confidence.

---

[124] *Psalm 9* :12
[125] *Op. cit.*, p58.

Day 63

14 June 2020

My fiancée had come up with a plan to create a double-cubical altar for her own magical practice, by ordering two cubical boxes via the internet and simply gluing them together, before covering the whole thing with a large black altar-cloth. This got off to a bad start, as on her first attempt to do so, the boxes which arrived measured 18 *centimetres* not 18 *inches*. It transpired that she had never seen the film *Spinal Tap,* so my attempts to make comedy out of the situation went unappreciated.

Nevertheless, after sending them back, she tried again and this time found cardboard boxes the right size : they came delivered in the form of flat-packs, during the preceding day. As it happened, that night I had a vivid dream about assembling altar from the boxes that she had had delivered, which I interpreted as a sign.

When I got up, my ritual went well that morning right from the outset, right from my preparation with the Middle Pillar ritual.

I performed the LBRP. As I recorded in my journal afterwards :

"NB : the idea of visualising one's astral body standing upon the Universe and receiving rays of influence from the infinite height / depth / south / north - which I first got after watching a Damien Echols video on YouTube - in fact comes from Golden Dawn Magic *by Chic & Tabby,[126] i.e. He plagiarised it ! Nevertheless, it is a worthwhile addition to my practice."*

Perhaps "plagiarism" is too strong a word – Echols hadn't specifically claimed the idea as his own, it's just that he neglected to say that he didn't. Indeed, I had made the criticism of his first book[127] that although he described many magical techniques suitable for beginners, he had not included a bibliography of his sources which the same beginners could use to further pursue their researches. E.g., in contrast to *Modern Magick,*[128] which had enabled me, as a beginner, to get started.

This has caused me to formulate a general theory, which I call the "*Steve Jobs Approach To Occultism."* I.e. Steve Jobs made a success of his time at Apple – or at least, his *return* to Apple – by theorising that his customers didn't want to know *how* his products worked, just so long as they *did* work, and looked beautiful. To this extent he created products (or rather he had his minions do it – he himself played the role of Key Person of Influence in the process) which

---

[126] CICERO, CICERO (2019)
[127] ECHOLS (2018)
[128] KRAIG (1996)

looked and felt aesthetically pleasing, but which provided no opportunity for the users to open the casing, as it were, to do their own repairs, or make their own expansions or additions. He saw users as consumers only, not as hobbyists.

Similarly, I have noticed a trend in Occultism in which occultists are viewed as people who don't want to know *how* their occult products work, just so long as they *do* work, and look beautiful. For example, Occult books and descriptions of magical practices with slick, glossy covers, and which provide just enough information to accomplish their stated purpose – but no more : no bibliography, scant (if any) mention of external sources, no background to provide context. In other words, there exist a number of Key Occultists of Influence who do to Magick what Steve Jobs did to Apple.

Were I a cynic, I would say that if the Occult book had a sufficiently beautiful cover, a large part of the potential market would not enquire too closely whether it *did* work or not.

I do not mean this, however, as a condemnation of either Steve Jobs' memory or of these Steve-Jobs-style occultists, because, after all, Apple products do work, people do enjoy them, and also what these occultists publish does contain a lot of valid material. In a sense, Jobs' had a spot-on marketing strategy : just because one wants to use a computer, does not mean that one needs a computer on which one would train as a coder or a computer engineer. Likewise, not everyone who wants to make use of the occult wants or feels the need to become a creator of original occult rituals, which a system like the Golden Dawn effectively aims at doing : instead their practical needs number so few that a full system of occult development would go wasted upon them, and hence simple Steve-Jobs-Occult resources would entirely suit them. The only really annoying thing lies in the fact that these Key Occultists of Influence seldom make explicit how someone could cease their dependence upon them and learn how to become an original thinker in their own right – as they would then be reducing their own customer base. Taken to its logical extent, this would become the way of the charlatan.

But I digress. I performed the Bornless Ritual, like the previous day, at a slowed down pace, and felt pleased by the results. After the Conjuration, I got to the Confession of Sins, where my mind turned to the trouble I had the previous day. I wrote in my journal :

"Getting into an argument yesterday and more to the point, not being wise enough to avoid it - that is an obvious 'sin.' Harbouring resentment, anger, etc - more sins. I petition my HGA that my Nephesh is able to expel these out of my personality into my evil persona, and to sublimate the power which animates them for the good of my higher self.

"Remembering how I believed that the Shem Ha Mephoresh angel Lelahel had helped yesterday, I give thanks for this occurring.

"Contemplating the I AM. Contemplating assuming my HGA as a god-form. Deep state of meditation. Wary, as I remember the last time I did that, twenty years ago."

I.e. when I reached such a deep state of meditation after contemplating my Holy Guardian Angel in such a manner, I subsequently had a particularly bad "Dweller on the Threshold" incident. It didn't help that I went through a Saturn-return at the time (although this did not apply now).

I finished the ritual in the usual manner, with the Licence to depart and LBRP.

*

During the day : I attended a Golden Dawn meeting online in which we practiced "Rising On The Planes" – actually an exercise written by Chic & Tabby Cicero from "A Garden of Pomegranates."[129] Obviously it could not take the place of a real Golden Dawn meeting, but despite the limitations of the ZOOM format, I did feel at least some benefit from taking part.

Afterwards I helped my fiancée assemble the very altar from the boxes of which I had dreamed the night before ; as well as going through the formations of officers in various rituals with her. On the whole, the day went pleasantly, and entirely free from the arguments of yesterday : the first sign of our strawberry plants bearing fruit struck me as an appropriate metaphor for a new phase of life.

I only got round to my scriptural study late at night, when I contemplated the versicle of the Psalms associated with Achaiah, the seventh angel of the Shem Ha Mephoresh : after which I completed my evening ritual.

---

[129] REGARDIE *et al*, (2002), pp 205-215.

Day 64

15 June 2020

For some reason, thoughts about Builders of the Adytum occupied my mind during the night. I dreamt of how I might relate the Tarot trumps to the various officers in a BOTA pronaos. The dream itself only offered a vague idea of the validity of such a concept : it did not go into details. Nevertheless, on later reflection whilst awake, I figured that one could make the association between Pronaos Officers and Tarot keys. Having relatively little experience in the Pronaos, I had received scant information thereon, but the various intimations I had picked up clearly suggested that such officers represented definite Qabalistic forces. Hence one could work the whole thing out if necessary.

BOTA strike me as a funny lot. Although their pronaos officers do represent Qabalistic principles and their movement around the ritual space supposedly reflects how energy flows around the Cube of Space, many of them would blanch if one were to say they were performing *magic*. Or that their calling upon Qabalistic names of deity were tantamount to *invocation*. They remain very non-occult about their occultism, to ensure that they appeal to the widest possible range of people.

In any case, I got up at 4.09am for preparation for my morning ceremony with the Middle Pillar Ritual. The ceremony itself proceeded in the usual way : the Bornless Ritual continued to feel powerful. When I got to the "Confession of Sins," my contemplations ran as follows :

"Giving thanks to my HGA for having the ability to mend my faults and mistakes.

"Petitioning that I always have this power, not backsliding. Praying that I achieve this feat for all the Karma for which I am responsible : that I am brave enough to face the Dweller on the Threshold. Meditating on 'Adonai' - contemplating stillness. If the raising of the Kundalini resolves Karma, then this ought to be the key to dealing with the Dweller on the Threshold as well.

"THOUGHT : why not actively use the Sacred Magic to complete the charitable fundraising I originally intended to do ?"

I finished the ceremony with the Licence to Depart and LBRP (again).

Later, I spent time researching the versicle of Psalms relating to Cahetel, the eighth angel of the Shem Ha Mephoresh.

Also - possibly prompted by my dreaming about BOTA during the night – I decided to get round to reading my next weekly lesson. I say "weekly" but in fact I did not, at the time, get through one every seven days by a long chalk : sometimes I would leave long gaps between lessons, only picking them up irregularly. Perhaps my Unconscious stirred me to action.

In any case, I looked through lesson forty of the "Tarot Fundamentals" course, which dealt with Key 18 - on "The Moon." As I read it, memories of one of the arguments I had had with my fiancée over the weekend suddenly overwhelmed me, causing waves of emotion to attempt to overcome me. But what really caused this reaction lay before me on the printed page : Paul Foster Case in fact agreed with *me* over one of the items which had provided a serious point of contention.

I shook my head in exasperation. I could not bring the matter up now without appearing churlish and petty, so I would just have to forget all about it. It would have been wise to forget all about it anyway.

Later, I attempted to amuse myself by watching Ramsey Dukes on YouTube talking about Abramelin. His views revealed him as one of a depressing number of people who consider Georg Dehn's book better than Mathers'. What ! Have none of these people actually attempted to use it as a working grimoire ?

But despite the cynicism I had felt during the day, after I performed my evening ritual, I found my fiancée pleased to see me crawl into bed. At her instigation, we took part in the Middle Pillar ritual, which led to much *rejoicing*.

Day 65

16 June 2020

During the night I had a strange dream about someone lecturing senior members of the SRIA about Enochian magic. On waking I realised the incongruity of it ought to have made me Lucid. In real life, I would hardly expect *senior* members of the SRIA to willingly attend a talk on Enochian magic, or indeed any kind of magic, as they mostly comprise respectable Freemasons with their eye on attaining grand rank, and would run a mile from anything that contained the merest whiff of scandal. This despite the fact that they have named two of their "colleges" John Dee and Elias Ashmole, the originator and first practitioner of Enochian magic respectively.

The rank-and-file members, on the other hand, would have a lot of enthusiasm for it, as many of them would have joined the SRIA thinking it was a masonic organisation where they could at least get to hear about some decent esotericism, only to find their hopes cruelly dashed.

The SRIA, therefore, mostly comprises a bunch of Freemasons playing at being esotericists. Unlike me, who consider myself an esotericist playing at being a Freemason. To be fair, though, some members do make a good job of maintaining a healthy Freemasonry/esotericism life-balance, but I rather fear they number in the minority. As one frater who attended a talk on an occult topic said: *"Approximately only thirty percent of the members of the SRIA would be interested in a talk like this. But that's still a higher proportion than in Freemasonry as a whole."*

In any event, I got out of bed and prepared for my morning devotions with the Middle Pillar Ritual as usual.

When I got to the LBRP, I realised that my reactions to Ramsey Dukes' video on Abramelin, which I saw the previous evening, still fired me up. Recognising this as an obsessive thought which might disturb my rituals, I preceded the LBRP by expelling my obsession with RD from my aura. This I did by visualising it as a football with RD's face on it. Then, as I did the LBRP, I imagined the football deflating and eventually disintegrating outside the perimeter established by the pentagrams.

(NB: I should emphasise that I directed my actions against my obsession, not against Dukes himself. Whilst preparing this book for publication I checked his YouTube channel and found that he had posted one new video in September 2020, two months later - so he had managed to survive this incident.)

This helped my frame of mind: when I performed the Bornless Ritual, the discipline of doing it with the full vibrations and visualisations calmed me right down.

I performed the Conjuration, and then got to the Confession of Sins. It occurred to me that I had *almost* got into another argument with my fiancée the previous day, but this time I had succeeded in averting it. I had made an obvious mistake in allowing it to arise at all : however I gave thanks to my HGA that I was able to resolve it immediately.

I gave thanks to my HGA generally. I imagined the Dweller on the Threshold as a great mass which could be transformed by the power of love, by kundalini - by the forces represented by the divine name 'Adonai,' in other words. By angels too, rushing to lend their assistance. I found I could briefly meditate on the stillness … before eventually finishing that morning's session with the Licence to Depart and LBRP.

When I returned to bed afterwards, I found my fiancée in a happy mood that morning. She speculated that the Bornless Spirit having "sight in the feet" might refer to the fact that Mathers mentions the letter Heh as being connected with the feet (as in the final Heh of YHVH) ; and the BOTA way of thinking connects the Tarot Key associated with Heh, i.e. Key 4, "The Emperor," with sight. Sacrament proved good that morning.

During the day I investigated the versicle associated with Haziel, the ninth angel of the Shem Ha Mephoresh. In the evening, we tried to do Yoga Nidra together but I kept falling asleep. I struggled through my own ritual : I think I had over-indulged myself at dinner that evening.

Day 66

17 June 2020

During the night, I dreamt of getting home from two counties away, with the notion that I have done this before ... Depending on which dream interpretation site one looks at this could either mean that I felt confident and on course to achieve my goals, or it could actually mean the complete opposite, that I felt insecure and worried I would never do so.

I got up at 4.09am, feeling crapulent – my concerns about last night's dinner confirmed. The combined effects of the Middle Pillar ritual - and elimination - relieved this. Indeed, after I performed the LBRP and Bornless Ritual, I could quite definitely feel my natural energy restoring itself.

After the Conjuration and during the Confession of Sins, I focussed on sublimating the Dweller on the Threshold by "kriya yoga" style meditation. In a nutshell, my technique consisted of identifying the Dweller on the Threshold with my karma, and resolving it by pulling the kundalini up the *sushumna* (the energy channel corresponding to the spine) on each *in-breath*. I had practiced this several times in the past and found it very powerful. Afterwards I finished the ritual in the usual manner.

During the day I investigated the versicle relating to Aladiah, the tenth Angel of the Shem Ha Mephoresh - Psalm 33 :22. Gematria revealed a good number of insights, e.g. : the gematria of the Hebrew for "We hope in Thee" – *Yichelnav lakh* – was equivalent to "Tzaddi" and "N" (the letter Nun) respectively. Hence "We hope in Thee" is equivalent to the Fish-hook and the Fish, or the Meditation and the object of Meditation. The state of contemplation I achieved thereafter felt especially satisfying, which I took as evidence of the presence of Aladiah himself.

I also spent time scanning the list of demons given in Dehn, OCR'ing it and converting it into a Word document, to make it easier for me to compose a set of conjurations for the final three days of my Abramelin Operation, the *Convocation of the Evil Spirits*. Aside from writing conjurations, at least one point during those three days, I would require a hard-copy of a list of all the demon's names as part of the ceremony, so this would come in doubly useful.

My fiancée herself spent the day intent upon writing her portal thesis : from the way she acted I perceived that I could not have offered her any advice about it even if it had been well-meant.

In the evening, after a dinner of Pasta with chilli oregano and sardines, with *homegrown* rocket (i.e. from our own garden), I received some news which left me with mixed feelings. The first Hierophant of my Golden Dawn temple – who also proposed me into Freemasonry and Rosicrucianism – had passed away. I had found him a very ego-driven man (a typical Leo) : on the one hand this trait gave him great motivation to achieve what he set his mind to, but on the other he managed to rub a lot of people up the wrong way with a combination of arrogance, chauvinism, and out-and-out delusional behaviour. Many of his friends and associates either broke-off contact with him or kept him at a distance. I myself had a fractious relationship with him in the end : I became so exasperated that I walked out on his Golden Dawn temple – *in the middle of a ritual*.

Eventually, however, after experiencing a run of bad-luck in both his professional and private life, he decided to emigrate to Peru, *to escape the coming apocalypse* which he felt certain would engulf Europe and North America – arguably one example of the delusional behaviour which affected how a lot of people reacted to him. Unfortunately the end of the world did come – for him – whilst living there, as he died of a stroke at a comparatively young (66) age.

However, I felt most galled by the fact that he had actually tried to contact me via Facebook back at Christmas time, but I had ghosted him – and never heard from him again. I wondered if he realised he was ill, and actually wanted to reach out to make peace with those he had offended ? But before I could feel too guilty, I reminded myself that I didn't know at the time – and I still didn't know now – so it could amount to beating myself up for no good reason.

Nevertheless I still felt vaguely uneasy as I carried out my evening ritual, and went to bed.

Day 67

18 June 2020

I woke up the next morning, and tried to go through the motions of the Middle Pillar Ritual, but I felt distracted. My first Hierophant's death yesterday obviously affected me more than I realised. Inevitably, therefore, processing my feelings for this man took up most of this morning's ritual.

I began in the usual way with the LBRP, Bornless Ritual, and Conjuration. When I got to the "Confession of Sins," I recalled – in addition to failing to learn how to avoid arguments -

"On the one hand I feel guilt over how I treated this man ; on the other - irritation at his death distracting me could also be a sin, as I am not giving voice to natural grief."

People posted tributes to this man on social media. I realised I could identify another of my sins : jealousy at all the attention that he got and I didn't. My own selfishness over the issue now appeared before me. I identified the kernel of goodness – which I had theorised is at the heart of every sin – as the fact that wanting to do my best for the temple which he had both built up motivated my feelings : but so too did the extent to which he had also towards the end almost caused it to run down.

I imagined all these powerful emotions as "Heavies" which I invited to pray with me. In the end, I decided that - due consideration for the eternal soul of this man notwithstanding - thinking about it to the extent that I did counted as an *Obsession :* one which I needed to banished. Hence, after the Licence to Depart, I projected an image of him outside my aura which I then sealed off before beginning the LBRP.

*

Later that morning, I studied the versicle associated with Lauviah (11th Shem Ha Mephoresh angel) and got into a good state of meditation as a result of doing so.

During the afternoon, I took part in a meeting (via ZOOM) of a Masonic Study Group, at which the question came up : *"Speaking as a Freemason and a spiritual person, how have you been coping with the lockdown caused by COVID-19 ?"*

We were told in advance that we would discuss this question : by giving some thought to it I came up with an answer which excited me greatly, to wit :

"I have been fortunate during this lockdown, as I have a permanent job in the public sector. Consequently, instead of being furloughed, I was paid to work from home. NB : the nature of my job is that it can't be done from home, hence I effectively had a free holiday on full pay.

"I've taken the opportunity to complete a number of personal projects such as moving out of my old flat and in with my fiancée ; but more relevant to this present discussion, I have used the time to start undertaking the Abramelin Operation. I may write a fuller report on it sometime after I finish it, as I still have a long way to go.

"Now in the popular mindset, the Abramelin Operation is supposedly about gaining occult powers, but in my experience, this is the wrong way of looking at it. It basically involves me following a strict regimen of daily meditation, self-examination, particularly of my conscience, and making a study of the Volume of the Sacred Law with a view to making a daily advancement in knowledge. Viewed in this way, it is a practical way of doing exactly what our Masonic rituals say we Freemasons should be doing !

"One feature of the Abramelin operation which does not get mentioned by modern practitioners is that when Abramelin first conferred the Sacred Magic on Abraham the Jew, he did so in a ceremony of initiation which required Abraham, the initiate, to make a massive donation to Charity – specifically to relieve poverty – again, another rather obvious Masonic parallel. I actually believe this is an important key to the Abramelin, so what I've done is set up a Just Giving page in order to raise money for a food bank charity which helps poor and vulnerable families affected by the pandemic."

I took a risk in mentioning me undertaking the Abramelin Operation, because I felt now I really would obligate myself to finish it *and* achieve Knowledge and Conversation of my Holy Guardian Angel – otherwise I would lose face publicly. I also had the consideration of the Fourth Power of the Sphinx at the front of my mind, and the superstition that by mentioning it before finishing it I might jinx the project.

However, I could indeed see parallels between the Abramelin operation and Masonic ideals. Indeed, the more I thought about it, the similarities proved even greater than I first realised. For example, apart from the obvious point about Charity, I could perceive a correlation between the three phases of the Abramelin Operation and the three degrees of Craft Masonry, i.e. :

Phase one : every day examine one's conscience and confess one's sins.	Entered Apprentice : become acquainted with the principles of *Morality*.
Phase two : in addition to the above, make a daily study of the sacred writings.	Fellow Craft : become acquainted with the principle of *Intellectual* Truth.

Phase three: add to the preceding more rituals – i.e. morning, noon and night – specifically aspiring to enjoy the company of the Holy Angels.	Master Mason: contemplate Death – which I saw as a metaphor for contemplating *Spirituality*.

When one adds in the fact that Eckartshausen described the three doors to the Interior Church as those of Morality, the Intellect, and Spirituality,[130] this made me sure that a pre-existing Tradition must have inspired both the authors of the Sacred Magic *and* Freemasonry. At least one source has described Eckartshausen himself as a Freemason (amongst other things):[131] if so, then his inspiration would have a rather more obvious source. My instinct told me that it seemed unlikely that the Sacred Magic inspired Freemasonry, but there must exist a common source for both: so, I resolved to investigate whether I could find evidence of this putative Tradition in more ancient writings, such as Greek philosophy. At the very least it would make for a good paper which I could present at a future study circle meeting.

As it happened, I did not throw myself into starting to research the finer details of this theory until after I had finished the operation. Evidence of this three-fold illuministic structure proved hard to find outside the three sources of Craft Freemasonry, Eckartshausen, and Abramelin itself. Only in Aristotelian Ethics could I find anything which came close to it.

Aristotle taught that Virtue has to do with the proper function (ergon) of a thing. For example: one only thinks of an eye as "a good eye" in so much as it can see, because the proper function of an eye is Sight. Aristotle reasoned that humans must have a function specific to humans, and that this function must derive from an activity of the *psyche* (soul) in accordance with reason (*logos*). Aristotle identified such an optimum activity (the virtuous mean, between the accompanying vices of excess or deficiency) of the soul as the aim of all human deliberate action, referring to it as "Bliss," (sometimes rendered as "happiness" or "wellbeing.")

He further taught that to have the potential of ever being "happy in this way" (i.e., having Bliss) necessarily requires a good character (*ēthikē aretē*), often translated as moral or ethical virtue or excellence.

To achieve a virtuous and potentially Blissful character requires a first stage of having the fortune to have good habits ingrained into oneself not deliberately, but by teachers, and experience: leading to a later stage in which one consciously chooses to do the best things. This, I would suggest, constitutes the Moral aspect.

---

[130] VON ECKARTSHAUSEN (1909)
[131] VON ECKARTSHAUSEN (1989)

When the best people come to live life this way their practical wisdom *(phronesis)* and their intellect *(nous)* can develop with each other : i.e., the Intellectual aspect.

This leads towards the highest possible human virtue, the wisdom of an accomplished theoretical or speculative thinker, or in other words, a philosopher. This, I would suggest, makes up the Spiritual aspect.

Hence, the *Nichomachean Ethics* contain allusion to the three-fold illuministic structure which I sought. However, the real kicker for me lay in the precise word which Aristotle used, translated as "Bliss" or happiness. The original Greek term is *Eudaemonia* (Ευδαιμονια). This literally means "good spirits," hence the modern expression : but, of course, one can also translate it as "Good *Spirits*" – such as the Holy Guardian Angel. This would be akin to saying Virtue consists in the proper *ergon* of human deliberate action : Knowledge and Conversation of the Holy Guardian Angel.

Hence (to digress slightly), Joseph Campbell landed closer to the mark than many people realise. When he said, "follow your Bliss,"[132] one can interpret this, according to my line of reasoning as stated above, as "follow your Holy Guardian Angel."[133]

This actually amounts to a bigger claim, to my mind, than saying that one has attained KCHGA : that I bear the mantle of Aristotle's true interpreter, and that everyone else for the past two thousand, three hundred and forty years has had the wrong end of the stick. Clearly this claim would exceed the limits of bombast and ego-aggrandisement were I to make it, so I shan't.

But the real puzzle – one which I have not resolved at the time of writing this book – lay in why this interpretation of Aristotle had not reached a more widespread audience. I would have expected to see some sort of tradition stretching from the time of Aristotle stretching to the fifteenth century or later, the time of the supposed authorship of *Abramelin,* but history had remained silent.

*

During the day, a friend emailed me with a major life-affecting question that he needed answering : could I therefore do a divination for him ? I agreed, principally because I saw it as an opportunity to practice my skills for my Golden

---

[132] CAMPBELL (1988), chapter IV, "Sacrifice and Bliss," *et passim.*

[133] "**MOYERS :** Do you ever have this sense when you are following your bliss, as I have at moments, of being helped by hidden hands ?

"**CAMPBELL :** All the time…" *Ibid.*

Dawn work. He offered to pay me for my services, but I declined : although I did suggest that he could make a donation to my JustGiving page (which he did).

I therefore did a combined "Opening of the Key" (i.e., Tarot), Horary Astrology, and Geomancy reading. My usual *modus operandi,* in such cases, consisted of recording the time, date, and place of when the Querent had first asked the Question for the Divination– or where it formed fully articulated in my head – before dealing out the tarot cards. That way I could use Horary Astrology to cross-check the results of the other divinations which, after all, had been born at the same moment.

The "Opening of the Key" forms the Tarot spread which Mathers specified for use, in the Golden Dawn's inner order instructions on divination. As an Adeptus Minor I ought to have been able to use it, although it had long put me off, because I thought it far too cumbersome. For most everyday questions I preferred to use far simpler tarot spreads. The "Opening of the Key" had such a detailed procedure, I thought, that I ought only use it for determining major life-affecting questions – which ironically was precisely the case in the present instant.

But despite my reluctance towards the "Opening of the Key," I had developed some strategies for making it more palatable for me. I got into the habit of, when looking at a card or pair of cards, to come up with only the first *word* (or couple of words at most) which inspired me, before moving onto the next one. Then at the conclusion of each of the five operations, I would articulate this string of words into a coherent sentence.

Also, I used a digital Dictaphone to record my Tarot divination, as it enabled me to note down all the details without interrupting my flow. I could then write (i.e. type) the whole thing up afterwards at my leisure. I certainly preferred this to writing down my results as I did the divination itself.

Both the idea of concentrating on just one word at a time, and of using a Dictaphone, I used as tools to ensure I did not get bogged down, which I felt would induce ennui and get me out of that state of divine afflatus or psychic receptivity which really forms the key to a good divination.

After I had finished all three – tarot, astrology and geomancy – I typed up the results and sent them to him. He appeared pleased with the results, as I had managed to reassure him that his life-ambition proved a sensible one, so long as he took certain precautions which I specified, but otherwise he would meet with success.

*

My fiancée *still* felt anxious about her portal thesis – it became a touchy subject around the house. It didn't help that she felt insanely jealous about the inner order of the Golden Dawn, as she saw it as depriving her of *me*. Sometimes she pretended not to care about it, but from the way that she slammed down tea cups, clattered plates and banged doors behind her as she moved through the house I could have easily discerned her true feeling even if I *didn't* have any psychic ability.

I accomplished my Evening ritual and went to bed.

Day 68

19 June 2020

Ihad a problem : the anxiety my fiancée exhibited regarding her thesis, combined with her feelings towards the inner order, made life around the house feel like walking on egg-shells. More to the point, it seemed that anything I tried to do to help seemed to backfire. Hence, when it came to the Confession of sins during my morning ritual : I prayed to my HGA to remind me : *trying to help someone against their will is like attempting to heal them without their consent, i.e. A Bad Thing.* I ought not to offer to help unless it is asked for. I prayed that my HGA might ever remind me of this like Socrates' Daemon, in other words.

The mistake which I had made slammed into me : *I didn't completely trust her.* Offering to help her proceeded from a desire to make sure she did well for herself, but it resembled the parent who mollycoddles their child instead of trusting them to go out into the big bad world.

I tried to think of a solution to my problems. Not joining in with my inner order activities upset her, even though I *had* offered to give her personal tuition in magic that technically constituted inner order material all the same. I had done this so that I did not break the vow I had taken to keep the inner order and outer order separate. But now, I thought : what has more importance – my vow, or indulging my fiancée ? I prayed that my HGA would guide me to do the *right* thing, e.g. Finding some compromise that gave her what she wanted without me offending against my conscience.

Thinking through all my various faults and failings like this seemed to lift a burden from my soul, and enabling me to turn my concentration to something more peaceful. I noted ;

"Taking extra time to concentrate on the I AM-ness. Instead of just getting 'heavies' to 'pray' with me, I will that all entities - divine, angelic and demonic - invoked or potentially invokable, turn inwards and contemplate, as they are all potentially 'heavy.' I will that Nirvikalpa Samadhi *itself turn inward and contemplate.*

"At length I get the welcome sense of deep meditation which I associate with the presence of my HGA."

*

During the day, my fiancée's sensitivity had not abated since yesterday, and in fact if anything had increased. I spent most of the day staying out of her hair : I continued my scriptural study with the versicle associated with Hahaiah, the 12th angel of the Shem Ha Mephoresh ; in addition, I finished typing up the results of yesterday's divination. I felt melancholy over the whole situation. My fiancée seemed to have better spirits by the latter part of the day, but I still felt afraid to upset her.

I performed my Evening ritual as normal and went to bed.

Day 69

20 June 2020

My mind bridled under the oppression of having to perform such a well-known, *well-worn* ritual day after day *after day*. "Why am I doing this ?" I thought. "What does it all mean ?"

I suppose that, partially to stave off boredom, I turned to contemplating the actual meaning of the words I invoked as I did so. From the dirt of such unworthy motives sprang some surprisingly beautiful flowers. For example, whilst performing the Lesser Banishing Ritual of the Pentagram that morning I came up with the following idea :

"Thought : 'EHEIEH' is essentially a Destructive *formula, because in order to get to the Eheieh one has to destroy all things, including the destroyer."*

I.e. in order to experience the pure sense of "I am," one has to exclude everything "I am not." Hence the closer one gets to the "I am," the more the rest of the Universe dissolves away : in this I thought precisely of the occasion I experienced *Nirvikalpa Samadhi.*[134]

"Whereas, 'ADONAI' is constructive - it shows how out of the 'I' ness (Eheieh) comes the seed or root of all existence - the yod of YHVH."

I.e., I mentally re-visited the analysis of "Adonai" as a chain of Atziluthic correspondences which I had noted a month previously.[135]

I performed the Bornless Ritual and Conjuration as usual. When I got to the Confession of Sins, I took the opportunity to thank my HGA for being able to control my temper and not get into further arguments. However, the apparent resolution of one thing only opened the door to me becoming aware of a whole new charge-sheet of misdeeds.

I recalled some of the incidents of black magick from my life which had most shocked me. I later realised that I had already confessed them, right at the very beginning of my Abramelin operation : i.e., they shocked me so much, I had no difficulty in remembering them. But if I had already confessed them, what advantage lay in recalling them now ? Unless I had not fully resolved them – or had only confessed them insincerely the first time. I admit I felt ambivalent about the situation. I felt ashamed of *myself* for letting or almost letting the black magick get out of hand : but I did not bear any ill-will to the demons involved, whom I regarded as forces of nature, or "Just doing their job." I certainly hadn't been put off black magick itself, as I had later gone on to work with the same demons *but*

---

[134] Day 11 – *vide supra.*
[135] Day 42 – *vide supra.*

in a more responsible manner. In any case, here I found myself, attempting to conjure the Four Kings of Hell, the Eight Princes, and all their attendant spirits …

I thought : *"Allowing myself to be affected by depression / depressing thoughts yesterday = sin."* Obviously one should never attempt to shame people with *genuine* mental health problems, but I felt worried that *my own* behaviour hadn't been completely genuine. If, for example, I could have helped myself but did not, then I bore at least part of the blame for my own predicament – I would have committed a sin against myself.

I identified a "potential sin" – i.e. the thought of a sin arising before it actually took place, that of harbouring resentment towards my fiancée for making me feel the way I did over her behaviour towards my involvement with the inner order of the Golden Dawn. By becoming aware of it *before* it happened, I could modify my behaviour in advance.

I tried concentrating on the I AM ness, and got to thinking about my past lives. Again the memory of sins to which I had already confessed assailed me : this time the memory of the brother who died before my birth, and my fear that "I" – the being that exists in eternity – held responsibility for his death, that I had murdered him by the act of *my own incarnation.* I despaired at what I could do about it, trying to remind myself that I could only rely on the Grace of God. Feeling unsatisfied that I had issues which I still had not resolved, I ended my morning ritual for the time being in the usual manner.

*

What with the woeful state into which my morning ritual had plunged me, the rest of the day could not fail to seem lighter and happier by comparison. I analysed the versicle associated with Iezalel (13th Shem Ha Mephoresh angel), whilst later I performed another combined Tarot (Opening of the Key) / Horary / Geomancy divination – as I had two days ago – this time for my fiancée herself. The fraught atmosphere between us calmed down noticeably today – she finally acknowledged that she had overreacted Thursday and Friday.

Evening ritual performed as usual.

Day 70

21 June 2020

Iwoke up at 4.10am : this being the Summer Solstice, I reflected that I would not have to set my alarm any earlier than this, as the days would get shorter from here on.

After preparing with the Middle Pillar ritual – and some timely elimination – I began my morning ritual in the usual manner.

When I got to the Confession of sins, I came back to the idea that my higher self had "killed" my brother in order that I could incarnate as me. I prayed that my Holy Guardian Angel would enable me to resolve the karma that I had inadvertently gained for myself - both the responsibility for his fate, and his karma itself.

Ironically, even if I my brother had not reincarnated as me, I had his karma anyway. It occurred to me that I could only resolve this by becoming the best person that my family would want me to be : I prayed to my HGA that this would happen.

My meditations turned to focussing on the I AM ness as a *Destructive* concept, I found that because it excluded all notions of what I AM not, curiously, it helped the one-pointed concentration because it empowered the thoughts upon which I did choose to concentrate. I found myself able to attain a deep meditation this way.

I ended the morning ritual, as usual, feeling considerably better than I did at the same point yesterday morning.

*

During the day, I became concerned that I had lost a couple of things, and wondered if someone might have stolen them ? I petitioned Andromalius, my favourite spirit of the Goetia, to recover them – they soon turned up. I didn't record any further details in my magical diary at the time, so I must have thought that apart from the fact that Andromalius came through *as usual*, the items themselves amounted to no more than trivialities.

I should point out that I did not go through the rigmarole of doing a full-on Lesser Key of Solomon type evocation, although I do have all the equipment stored away in case I ever need to do so. Rather : Andromalius perfectly exemplifies a spirit for whom I had done a full evocation in the past, and got him to agree that in future he would consent to me contacting him by only the briefest of rituals – I established a "short-cut," in other words.

There used to exist a great prejudice against making "pacts" with demons : writers like A E Waite succeed in repeating and reinforcing this prejudice for a very long time. His book, *The Book of Black Magic*, must surely qualify one of the most unhelpful studies ever in terms of serious scholarship on magical texts. [136] In this book, Waite focusses on grimoires, such as the Grimoirum Verum, which imply that making Pacts necessarily involves selling your soul to a demon. Crowley, even though he never missed an opportunity to excoriate Waite on any other occasion, in writing himself about black magic unwittingly followed this trope without question [137] – as did many other occultists of the twentieth century – because they knew no better.

We now know, however, thanks mainly to the research of people like Stephen Skinner and David Rankine, that other less well-known grimoires exist which paint a much different picture – that a Pact is simply where you get an evoked spirit to agree that it recognizes the authority by which you have summoned it, and that it agrees to perform your instructions. [138] A E Waite could have accessed the Mss with no less difficulty than those of which he eventually made use when writing his Book of Black Magic, so why did he not refer to them at the time – to provide a more balanced view of the subject ?

The frank answer can only be that lurid, sensational tales of Faustian pacts, satanic rites, and diabolical sorcery *sell* books : whereas people find balanced and scholarly works quite boring. Far from being the man of integrity as which Waite wanted to portray himself, he deliberately pandered to the salacious fascination of his readers, because he wanted to make money from his book.

In this sense I have made "pacts" with demons aplenty, but I have never attempted to sell any of them my soul. My negotiation with Andromalius to establish a short-cut to working with him in effect constituted a "pact" – one of the *balanced and scholarly* kind – I have entered into similar arrangements with other spirits which I have evoked, just because therein lies the method responsible ceremonial magic. Indeed, one can effectively describe the whole *Abramelin Operation*, especially the workings of the last seven days, as a *meta-pact*, in that one essentially gets all the demons of hell to agree to recognise the authority of one's Holy Guardian Angel.

*

---

[136] WAITE (1911)

[137] "THE MASTER THERION" (1929), chapter XXI part II.

[138] See, for example, RANKINE (2009).

Later, I made a study of Psalm 9 :10, in connection with Mebahel, the 14th angel of the Shem Ha Mephoresh.

I came to a decision about how to try healing all the arguments that had arisen with my fiancée over her not being in the inner order of the Golden Dawn. I decided to give my apologies and absent myself from the inner order meeting, out of consideration for her feelings. However – I reasoned – although the inner order would have to wait for my fiancée, I thought it unfair to make *her* wait for *it*. I therefore offered to share some practical magic with her, as my way of satisfying my doing my best by her without breaking the obligations I had sworn. I focussed on this occasion on teaching her the rudiments of scrying into Tattvas, starting with the Earth Tattva. She had previously attempted scrying of sorts, but she did not have experience in the Golden Dawn style of doing so. I therefore talked her through the Earth Tattva, making a guided meditation out of it : in doing so I described exactly how one would enter properly, use the correct signs, divine and angelic names, test and work with a guide, and test everything else that appeared, and finally how to exit properly as well.

I noted that my evening ritual accomplished felt better than usual, as I attained a deep state of meditation through performing it.

Day 71

22 June 2020

I dreamt about a train journey, as I often do. On the one hand this did not seem so unusual for me as I often do a lot of travelling by train in waking life, mainly up to London and back. Or at least I *did* before the lockdown happened. Since most of my friends and associates lived across the country, London formed a convenient central meeting place for us all to socialise : I also did all my Masonry and esoteric activity there.

On the other hand, whenever I dreamed of a train journey, it never coincided with one which existed in waking life. Often, it went via a route which simply did not exist. Lines which lay where no lines normally ran : stations which were mere stops in the wake-world, but astral junctions nocturnally. I often dreamed that I returned home, but along a completely bizarre and fantastical route.

Aside from this rather obvious metaphor, I also dreamed about a guitar synthesiser - which really puzzled me, as I've never had or played one, although I do own a guitar.

Despite this, my morning ritual began in a conventional manner. When I got to the Confession of Sins, my thoughts returned to the concept of myself as a "killer" which had occupied my mind these past few days. My higher self must have decided that I needed to incarnate at this particular time, because the lessons of this age were *my* lessons (I reasoned). Hence, *how many more people have died because of my higher self?* I had only been able to do this Abramelin operation now because of the COVID-19 outbreak. Did this mean that I bore responsibility for the suffering of all those who had died because of it ?

If my destiny comprised learning by forming an antithetical reaction to the evil men & women of this time, does this mean that my higher self had caused their evil deeds ?

Nevertheless, I concentrated on the I AM ness through *jnana yoga*, and managed to attain a degree of stillness. I ended the ritual as per usual.

*

During the day, I analysed psalm 94 :22, which is associated with Hariel, the 15th Shem Ha Mephoresh angel, as part of my daily scriptural study. I also typed up the results of the divination I did two days ago. I was only one "Opening of the Key" from going for my divination exam.

My fiancée came to me, looking deadly worried. She told me that she felt concerned about some kind of entity which she had encountered during what she took to be a vivid astral experience. She fought off the entity and returned to her body safely. At my suggestion we performed the Middle Pillar Ritual together.

Nevertheless, she remained convinced that the Tattva journey we had performed yesterday had somehow "gone wrong." I immediately reacted by telling her I couldn't understand how, since we had used all the correct divine and angelic names, all the safeguards, and banished thoroughly.

However digging a little deeper I began to understand : my fiancée could not parse her encounter with the entity in terms of anything she knew, which mostly meant Builders of the Adytum teachings. Apparently BOTA – according to her – did not *do* either astral projection or clairvoyance at all. Hence her experience had left her singularly unused to astral phenomena, and she had convinced herself that anything of that ilk which did occur must have inherent danger.

So for example, when she went into more detail about the entity she had fought off, it turned out that this being hadn't actually done anything. The fact that it had turned up at all proved enough to freak her out.

I protested it as unfair to assume that the appearance of this entity had a link to the tattva meditation we had done the day previously. Besides (I told her), this was nothing that a good old LBRP could not fix. However, she remained agitated, despairing about the efficacy of the Pentagram ritual in general, and magic in general. I did not press the matter : she eventually calmed down – for the time being at least…

Day 72

23 June 2020

For some reason I dreamt through the night of NOX signs ; which, I found strange, not being a Thelemite, and never having performed any ritual which makes use of them in my life. Although obviously I do read a lot of Crowley, so I'm vaguely familiar with them.

I got up at 4.10am for preparation with the Middle Pillar Ritual. Feeling tired. I then started my ritual with the LBRP and the Bornless Ritual. In my weary state I experienced distracting thoughts, so I concentrated on incorporating "I AM ness" – it helped to still my mind.

After the Conjuration, I first confessed as sins, obviously enough, the distracting thoughts I had just experienced : after all, my ritual had gone consciously less than perfection. Then, however, my contemplation turned to the disagreement I had had the previous day with my fiancée about the nature of her astral experience. I sensed she felt sensitive to me disagreeing with her even about something impersonal. I thanked my HGA for always helping me solve problems and mend wounds.

For some reason I started thinking about storytelling : potential plots for a new novel : I used this as a frame for my thoughts upon the nature of the astral plane. I wrote down my cogitations in my journal afterwards as follows :

> "Thought : an adventure based on 'Hero with a Thousand Faces' but he is venturing out on to the Astral plane (as opposed to, e.g. Outer space as in Star Wars, or the forest / wilderness / etc of mythology). We think we can explore the Astral Plane by imposing the known on the unknown, but how much do we really know ?

> "Come to that : when has there ever been a tale in mythology of someone venturing out into the wilderness and coming back successfully ? Except, perhaps, the Hero is on a quest. Hence, what if I applied the same principles to the real-life Magical Quest ?"

Afterwards I passed into a deep state of meditation by concentrating on the I AM ness : so at least I ended this ritual in a better mental state than when I began. I finished in the usual manner.

*

During the day I researched Psalm 88 :2, which is associated with Haqamiah (the 16th Shem Ha Mephoresh angel). I managed to do this at work : I had one of the few jobs in the country which one could not do from home, it required my physical presence in the office. However, because the lock-down still operated throughout the country, the echoes in the deserted corridors returned silence. I had less duties than normal, except to remain on standby for the next assignment. Hence I could do my scriptural study – and even some meditation – undisturbed, sitting at my desk in front of my computer.

Even so, my employers (who mainly worked from home themselves) let me leave early if I did not have too much action on any given day. Because I had had a permanent contract for several years now, they could not have furloughed me or reduce my hours without first making me redundant, which they obviously must have thought would have given them too much trouble.

Consequently, that afternoon I managed to come home early and catch two hours sleep. I had some prolonged OOBEs - my first in a very long time. I had to assume that deliberately making time to catch up on the ZZZs had caused it. I did not believe Haqamiah responsible *per se*, as astral projection did not feature in the description of his powers and abilities, unless it came about as a side-effect of doing the scriptural study in general. Instead, I felt gratified that once I tried to catch up on extra sleep, the knack of having an OOBE came back immediately, and quite naturally. (I have long suspected that success in lucid dreaming comes from being well-rested to begin with).

I took the opportunity of my extra-corporeal sojourn to invoke my Holy Guardian Angel by the method I had discovered for myself over twenty years previously (I had used this so often I habitually called it "The Method").[139] I also practiced rising up to infinite height, prior to performing the Middle Pillar Ritual. This felt especially satisfying, as I thought it would give me some kinaesthetic reference when performing the ritual in the physical the future – i.e. I wouldn't have to *imagine* rising to infinite height as per Israel Regardie's instruction, I could *remember* doing so.

Ironically, after I had returned to the physical and met up with my fiancée, she started talking straightaway about her own astral experience of two days previously. She now claimed that the strange being she had encountered had not merely turned up, but had attacked her as well, although I suspected her of being melodramatic. I theorised that by taking the proper precautions one ought to be able to control one's experience so that one could adequately defend oneself on the astral plane : buoyed by my peregrination earlier that afternoon, I felt fully confident of the fact.

My fiancée, however, perturbed by my apparent lack of concern, expressed horror that one would willingly go to the astral plane where unknown nasties could make one their victim.

---

[139] See Day 15 for a fuller explanation.

"But you successfully fought off the entity," I reminded her. "That means that far from being a *victim*, you are in fact a *winner*." It concerned me that by concentrating on the horror of the thing, and not on her success in dealing with it, she replayed a disempowering narrative in her head. I wanted to restore her confidence by making her re-frame her self-image from "*someone who gets attacked by astral nasties*" to "*someone who can easily defend herself from astral nasties,*" which was how I saw her myself.

It made me think, though : how often had I handicapped myself by having a disempowering narrative in my own head ? Did I still do so ? Perhaps my Holy Guardian Angel and / or the subtle forces of Nature were indirectly giving me a life-lesson, by showing up our differences in approach to the astral plane.

Evening ritual completed.

Day 73

24 June 2020

During the night : a dream inspired by *The Walking Dead* - people going down a staircase to escape from Zombies, then coming back up the other side, disguising their scent with dead bodies. We had watched this the previous evening : we had a boxset of the first five series on DVD which we steadily worked through. Given our confinement at home during this stage of the pandemic, television assimilated that part of our lives where we would have gone out for entertainment. Our tastes involved old series like (in addition to the above) *Game of Thrones* (my idea), *Stargate SG-1* (my fiancée's) and a whole host of movies on *NowTV*, *Netflix*, and very occasionally *YouTube*. We avoided the BBC, as we disapproved in principle of having to pay for a TV licence, even though we had enjoyed David Attenborough documentaries. As for commercial TV it did not even exist, as far as we were concerned.

I felt intrigued though. I would have thought that my evening ritual would have released the hold of the previous day's memories on my mind, so that they would not interfere with my dreams. Either this Zombie scenario wanted to communicate a mysterious message, or I wasn't trying hard enough with my ritual.

Actually a third alternative occurred to me later : after doing the Middle Pillar ritual I had to go the toilet immediately before my main morning session, so perhaps my digestion had interfered with my dreams. The Zombies came to attack me in revenge for having eaten too heavily the previous evening, as it were.

Once restored to equilibrium, however, I prepared for the ritual proper with an extra five minutes of contemplation - of "Shaddai El Chai" as it happened.[140]

I opened with the LBRP. When I did the Bornless Ritual, I contemplated Rising On The Planes but in the six directions, following the method taken by Crowley. As I noted in my journal :

> *"Here are the godforms, represented by the barbarous names of evocation ; their source comes from the direction in question, but what is the source ? What sends them forth ? What emanates them ? And : can I identify with that emanating power ?"*

I performed the Conjuration. When I got to the Confession of Sins, I started by focussing on resolving the karma of my past-lives, and managed to attain a state of Stillness.

An unconventional idea occurred to me :

---

[140] See : Day 42, *supra*.

"Thought : 'Nephesh Ha-Messiah' is supposedly an Archangel of Malkuth. Hence : Jesus' lower soul - which is the soul of He who is Perfect Man and Perfect God - is Archangelic in nature. If Jesus' Nephesh is archangelic, this would literally make Jesus Himself greater than Archangelic - which is only to be expected if one were following conventional Christian theology. However - if Jesus is my role model as a human being and one on the spiritual path, does that mean I can at length (with the grace of God) transform my own Nephesh into an Archangel ? What would that entail ? "

I ended in the usual manner with the Licence to Depart and LBRP.

*

The bright summer outside caused the plants in the back garden to grow and bloom enthusiastically. New strawberries ripened on the little plant we had bought from a local shop. Unfortunately, juggling my spiritual and mundane activities on my computer kept me stuck inside.

I had a brief headache whilst trying to organise a forthcoming meeting of my Royal Arch chapter. Just about every Masonic order had had its meetings suspended by its governing body (in this case, the Supreme Grand Chapter of England & Wales). However, we still wanted to meet up via ZOOM. Luckily I managed to sort this later in the day.

My fiancée once accused me of belonging to too many orders. I disagreed with her : therefore to settle it I made a list of what exactly I belonged to. It went like this.

Men-only Masonic.

1 * Craft Lodge ;

1 * Royal Arch Chapter ;

3 * SRIA Colleges ;

1 * lodge of The Hermetic Order of Martinists ;

1 * Commandery, CBCS (OM&S lineage) – *had been meeting infrequently prior to the lock-down.*

Co-masonic

2 * Craft lodges, one working the Bessant ritual, the other the Wilmshurst ritual ;

1 * Royal Arch chapter ;

1 * Rose-Croix chapter.

1 * Mark lodge *(had only attended one meeting so far, my own advancement).*

1 * Knights Templar commandery *(likewise, only one meeting so far, my own installation).*

Infrequent guest at Memphis Misraim *(various different lineages).*

Non-masonic

"The True Order of the Rosy Cross," a Rosicrucian order which I and a team of others had been founding before the lock-down hit ;

Invited guest, Ordre Martiniste & Synarchique ;

1 * Elu Cohen temple *(lineage too difficult for me to describe accurately)* ; and obviously -

The Golden Dawn, which included one temple and two associated study groups.

This list at least was accurate at the time I drew it up : I later resigned from all three SRIA colleges for reasons which I describe later on. I have not included on this list a couple of orders which I joined, but left after only a few meetings. In both cases I did so for the same reasons : they lay too far away for me to travel to them ; and they were too full of conventional Freemasons rather than esotericists. Hence, I felt doubly disincentivised to remain a member of them. I only mention the SRIA because it did play a large role in my life for over twelve years.

A lot of the Co-Masonic and Non-masonic orders doubled-up, so they would have two ceremonies in a day – one of one thing, and one of another. Because the same people mostly organised them, it saved money on venue hire. The Co-masonry in particular, comprised not lots of different organisations, but one organisation working different rituals at different times.

Another reason I belonged to this number of orders lay in that in finding ingenious ways to save money, many of these cost no more to join than I had already paid, or in fact cost nothing. I would not, for example, have thought of joining either Mark or KT under men-only Freemasonry, as this would have proved far too expensive. However, as I effectively had a free opportunity to do so under co-masonry, my curiosity got the better of me.

When my fiancée first saw this list, she stared wide-eyed in disbelief at it, because it seemed *so many*. I pointed out, however, that I knew plenty of Masons who actually belonged to more than this. I once sat opposite a member of the SRIA whilst dining who told me, because he had recently retired and Mark Masons Hall had recently put its charges up, he had decided to resign from *forty units which met there*. This was probably exceptional : an acquaintance whom I had reckoned as being into everything, when I told him this, exclaimed : "Forty ! And *I* thought *I* belonged to a lot !"

Incidentally, it probably says much that he referred to all the different things of which he had been a member as "units." Owners of masonic venues use "masonic unit" as a dreadful term to reduce the organisations which meet there to the status of commodities. It doesn't matter if your Order is deeply spiritual, or has a long and noble tradition, or it meets as a Temple, a Lodge, a Chapter, a College, a Commandery, or has valuable and precious symbolism in its ritual which its members find important : a venue owner only concerns himself with three things : does it pay to use the meeting room ? Does it pay for a standard-issue storage box in which to put its equipment ? Does it pay for dining ? Money, money, money !

Unfortunately many of the appendant orders in men-only masonry are full of people who treat the organisations to which they belong with as much care as a venue manager looking down his or her list of who has hired what each day. In the SRIA for example, one could easily spot the serial-joiners who worked their way through the book *Beyond The Craft*[141] : the SRIA comes towards the end of the list of orders mentioned therein, and – lo and behold – they only apply to join the SRIA after they have joined every other order as part of their "masonic journey." In addition, I have had the misfortune to attend festive boards where, because no-one else had any interest in anything esoteric or spiritual, listing all the various orders to which one belonged and inviting one another to join each other's orders provided the sole topic of conversation.

In fact, my own policy consisted of *refusing* to join a new order unless someone I knew and trusted well strongly recommended it to me. (I also had a standing invitation to join a whole host of other interesting esoteric degrees, but I had never taken it up, because it would have been too difficult to get to the meetings). Because I only hung around with esotericists, any order that they recommended to me I assumed would comprise like-minded people. Unfortunately this approach had failed to work on two occasions, when I ended up joining two orders which, although an esotericist had invited me, the order itself turned out to be run by Freemasons. In my experience, having the right people in a lodge (etc) forms the *sole* criteria for making it into a successful venture, which from my point of view meant running it as a spiritual or esoteric organisation to which I would want to belong. After all, the right people could take any ritual, even one apparently not spiritual, and make it spiritual through the way in which they performed it. Conversely, the wrong people if given the most spiritual ritual ever written would not fail to make a pig's ear of it. I resigned from both of the orders I had joined by mistake after I saw them from the inside.

*

After I had dealt with my masonic concerns, I continued my scriptural study that day by researching the versicle associated with Lauviah (17th Shem Ha Mephoresh angel). I noticed that this supposedly shared the name of the 11th angel as well, so instantly I went on the alert : had a mistake crept into the list from

---

[141] JACKSON (2012)

which I worked ? I felt my fears compounded when I saw that Stephen Skinner had listed the name of the 17th angel as something else entirely.

I could think of only one way of verifying the correct names : I went into the original Hebrew text of Exodus 14 :19-21 to get the proper spelling. I did not do this regularly, but after much searching I found an online version of *Shemot* which I could use.[142]

One counts from the first letter of verse 19, the backwards from the last letter of verse 20, then forwards from the first letter of verse 21. Lamed, Aleph, Vav. Lamed, Aleph, Vav. Yep, the 11th and 17th angels were spelled identically. In shock, I realised: Skinner had made a mistake !

Having sorted this out, I felt intrigued that *this* Lauviah's function and powers did not seem (according to Lenain) to correlate to the *Magical Use of the Psalms*. I.e. Lenain said that Lauviah " *... serves against spiritual torment, sadness and to sleep well at night,* "[143] whereas the associated versicle – Psalm 8 :2 – would. I supposed, help to "*bring customers to one's business.*" But then I looked at the gematria of each word making up that versicle, and realised that one could effectively substitute "*O Lord our Lord, how excellent is thy name in all the earth ! Who hast set thy glory above the heavens,*" with the phase "*Nocturnal vision will be exalted in sleep through meditation, advancing firmly, who has set thy limit upon the Neshamah.*" Sleep well at night, indeed ! Lenain (or his source) must himself have gone into the gematria of the Hebrew to figure out the meaning of the angels.

Apart from this, I managed to fit in reading BOTA's "Tarot Fundamentals," lesson 41, and colouring in Key 19, "The Sun," before eventually doing my evening ritual as per usual.

---

[142] https ://www.chabad.org/library/bible_cdo/aid/9875 accessed 2020-07-07
[143] LENAIN (2020), p64.

Day 74

25 June 2020

T his morning I got up at 4.11am for preparation with the Middle Pillar Ritual. I attempted to do it Astrally ; I lay on the hard floor of my oratory and transferred my consciousness to my Body of Light in order to perform it.

I re-centred my consciousness in my physical vehicle to do my regular ritual : first the LBRP ; then the Bornless Ritual, where I attempted to contemplate the "source" of the barbarous names, in the manner I had done yesterday. It proved a powerful experience.

I performed the Conjuration. When I first started "confessing my sins," I first thought of harbouring angry thoughts, although the last occasion I had done so had resolved itself, thanks to God. My contemplation then, however, turned to my feelings towards my fiancée. "*She worries me with her atheistic left hand path tendencies,*" I noted in my journal. She did not deliberately follow the left-hand path, nor did she ever do anything in any way evil. She just seemed to have an overly materialistic view of spirituality, the like of which I had previously only seen in people who openly admitted to following the LHP. As regards atheism, she seemed equivocal on the subject, talking one day as if she assumed God existed, and then denying the same the next. She certainly hated the religion of her upbringing and inferred that because she had had a bad experience, then *all* religion must be bad.

I continued :

"*E.g. with regard to death and Resurrection. This is not just an article of my Christian faith,*"

I should here point out that although I say, "*my Christian faith,*" I could hardly describe myself as the world's most religious person. I had practiced the occult since before I stopped attending church, an extremely long time ago. A conventional Christian could easily point out innumerable reasons where my behaviour does not accord with the strict letter of (their interpretation of) the Bible.

Instead, my "faith" consisted of believing in the literal truth of the New Testament – whilst at the same time averring that regular Christianity had misinterpreted it all this time, even to the point of tying itself in theological knots which ought not to have existed at all. I regarded the concept of "Faith" itself as a particular bugbear. Nearly everyone I spoke to assumed that it meant to believe without evidence. However, when Saint Peter made his profession of faith – which theologians refer to as *The* Profession of Faith – Jesus actually said something quite different : "*... for flesh and blood hath not revealed it unto thee,* *but my Father which is in heaven.*"[144] "Faith" for Saint Peter, therefore, did not involve just blind acceptance, but consisted of the natural *intuitive* reaction of his soul to *divine inspiration* – the good Lord himself said so. And being an occultist, I recognised the importance of Intuition and Divine Inspiration, since I regarded them as very real phenomena.

The mystery of the Incarnation, Christ being simultaneously real-man and real-God, the essential truth of the Sermon on the Mount, the miracles, the transfiguration, the death, resurrection, ascension – I accepted all of it, mainly because an occult or Qabalistic explanation existed for each of them. I even had sympathy for St Paul, despite his obvious chauvinism, as I felt the exoteric Churches had misinterpreted many of his important teachings as well.

But to return from my digression to my thoughts that morning about Death and Resurrection in particular :

"I see the parallel between the Resurrection-Body and the Arcana Arcanorum ('AA') of Alchemy. I.e., in order to attain the AA, one must, at the very least, posit the possibility that it exists ! Curiously, at other times my fiancée says that she has her own Body of Light, but she does not make the connection to the Resurrection Body herself. But the real question is : to what extent should I stand-up for my conscience as opposed to just leave it ? I hope that by giving the gentlest of remonstrances that she takes the hint, it seems awful 'bearing witness to Christ' involves forcing her unnaturally."

Following this, my thoughts turned to an idea which I had first had the previous day :

"Meditating on the Nephesh Ha-Messiah - my Nephesh becoming the 'NHM,' whilst my higher consciousness is transformed into an Angelic nature by my HGA. Deep. Powerful."

I finished that morning's ritual in the usual manner.

*

Later, as part of my scriptural study, I spent time going back over Lauviah from yesterday : and also researching Psalm 7 :9, associated with Caliel (18th Shem Ha Mephoresh Angel) : *"Judge me, O Lord, according to my righteousness, and according to mine integrity that is in me."* I noted :

"There is a wealth of Qabalistic knowledge here - the coincidences revealed by the gematria - all on topic with the theme (!) of Justice - is astounding."

I unconsciously came up with "Theme" as a play on words : the Hebrew word for "my innocence" – *themai* – appeared almost identical to the Coptic *Thme*, i.e.

---

[144] *Matthew* 16 :17

the Goddess Maat, as well as the Greek *Themis*. In any event, for me it seemed like further evidence of what I had posited yesterday, that Lenain had gone into the gematria of the versicle associated with the angels to establish their meaning in practical magic.

Evening ritual accomplished.

Day 75

26 June 2020

The next morning as part of my preparation I again attempted to perform the Middle Pillar Ritual astrally. I started my regular ritual with the LBRP, Bornless Ritual, and Conjuration. When I got to the Confession of sins, I thought :

"Even if I have not done anything majorly evil, simply falling short of perfection at any time is a kind of sin. If I have past-lives, I must have been less than perfect so many times to have to keep reincarnating.

"Meditating on my HGA : transmuting my nephesh into 'Nephesh Ha-Messiach' and my higher consciousness into that of an Angel. Good. As to 'Knowledge & Conversation of my HGA' : it is one thing to be able to deduce the presence of my HGA, but how do I convert that into Knowledge and Conversation per se ? Perhaps the answer lies in treating 'the presence of my HGA' as a thing into which I can actually go, i.e. Astrally project, there to commune with my HGA as an actual being. It occurs to me that this is comparable to Eckartshausen's notion of the 'Interior Church.'"

I finished as per usual.

*

I headed off an argument with my fiancée – an achievement I attributed to the intervention of my Holy Guardian Angel. We found ourselves disagreeing over the interpretation of some passage (I forget which), when by chance I said : "Have you considered that it might just be a metaphor ?"

My fiancée reacted as if thunderstruck by the idea. For several years she had tried to get her doctor to diagnose her with ASD : apparently, not taking everything literally does not occur to people who are on "the Spectrum," at least not in 100% of cases. I couldn't believe I could have avoided all these arguments so easily ...

*

Later that day I researched Psalm 40 :2, associated with Leuviah (19th Shem Ha Mephoresh angel), and experienced a deep state of meditation as a result (which I interpreted as the presence of Leuviah himself). I suppose that I must have had a special affinity with Leuviah, as I had recorded having a good experience when I first tried to invoke him four years previously.

At the time I took the details of the associations and roles of each Angel from *Practical Kabbalah* by Robert Ambelain : however in the English translation from which I was working, the entry for Leuviah omitted a number of details, i.e. two paragraphs of text. I wondered if the lack of explanation mirrored the difficulty I had in finding adequate English equivalents for all the Hebrew words, i.e. that Leuviah didn't *want* anyone explaining him, but in the end I figured that Google Translate was just playing silly buggers again. (After the Operation had ended, I got hold of a copy of Lenain's original version of the Shem Ha Mephoresh Angels, as well as Ambelain's text in French,[145] both of which supplied the missing details. It turned out that Leuviah's special function aligned with that indicated by the versicle's meaning in the magical use of the Psalms.)

Evening ritual accomplished.

---

[145] AMBELAIN (1951), p264

Day 76

27 June 2020

Watching someone *masturbate*, according to one online dream dictionary, supposedly indicated one's own inhibitions, but not necessarily in a sexual sense. This did not impress me. Such websites pose a danger through being far too general. I personally could think of at least two other explanations at least equally plausible : that the dream came from either a memory of watching some lesbian porn, or of a scene from an Alex Sumner novel. I seem to recall the last time I wrote something like that, I did so to describe a strong female character taking control of her sexuality in order to cast a magic spell.

Needless to say, life imitates art. I have often found that if I try to think up the grossest, most disgusting method of trying to do magic, I later discover that members of the Illuminates of Thanateros have beaten me to it and already tried it out. Indeed, I clearly remember one lady Chaos Magician tell me, looking me straight in the eye, that she used this very method to attain gnosis when summoning up Goetic spirits.

This, incidentally, highlights one of the great ironies of Chaos Magicians. I have it on authority that the IOT has used, and perhaps still does use, every conceivable method of working sorcery, no matter how shocking or outrageous. And by that I mean "shocking or outrageous" to other magicians whom one would expect to have a broad mind about such things. However, the IOT can hardly publicly mention 99% of the activities they get up to without attracting the unfavourable attention of the police and / or press, so the only stuff that gets talked about ends up as some *boring* old Sigil magic.

In any event : I roused myself from my slumbers early that morning, and performed the Middle Pillar Ritual astrally, as I had done before. I performed the LBRP, Bornless Ritual, and Conjuration : when I got to the Confession of Sins, I noted :

> *"In the midst of the ritual I feel an urge to eliminate which threatens to compromise my appreciation of the thing. Hence - one obvious sin is making the mistake of eating food late at night (and, as it happens, allowing myself to become dehydrated due to the hot weather). I pray my HGA that I will know better and act accordingly in the future.*
>
> *"Nevertheless, I try to concentrate on the presence of my HGA as best I can. I find doing so eases my bodily discomfort - as if the HGA can give me the wherewithal to overcome such difficulties. When I turn my attention away to the rest of the ritual, the discomfort returns. I therefore keep the rest of the ritual short."*

I closed with the Licence to Depart and LBRP as quickly as dignity would allow, so as to be able to leave my oratory for a much-needed comfort break. The total time had only been 40 minutes, which by that stage of my operation seemed unusually short.

*

Later that morning, I received a strange message from someone I knew via a magical friend, who wanted me to do a spell to help her get rid of an irritating housemate. This posed a dilemma : my correspondent obviously had a real problem : however the only spells I knew for getting rid of people consisted of ones which I would not, in any conscience, want to use. Perhaps instead I could recommend something – some magical technique – to my correspondent, to enable her to help herself ?

My mind flitted back to the dream I had had that morning, and the memory of the lady Chaos magician. I dismissed the idea.

In the end I suggested that my correspondent think in terms of protecting herself from the negative vibes she felt from this housemate, by using the Lesser Banishing Ritual of the Pentagram. I heard no more about this from her, so this appeared to conclude the matter.

Apparently my correspondent asked me because our mutual friend recommended me to her. Either they recognised my superior sorcery skills, or they just didn't want to get their hands dirty, and thought Alex wouldn't be above that sort of thing. In my experience however, one can solve many magical problems through non-evil magic, fortunately enough.

*

During the day, in a hurry I tried investigating Psalm 120 :2, which my copy of the Ambelain text associated with Pahaliah (20th Shem Ha Mephoresh angel).[146] I felt rushed partly because I also took part in a Golden Dawn study group that day, in which I revisited a paper I wrote for *The Light Extended,* entitled "Skrying In Theory & Practice."[147] As it happened, this led afterwards to a discussion with my fiancée who had much sensitivity about astral projection. Perhaps she still associated her last attempt at skrying with the strange experience she had had the following day. She could not see why I considered astral projection as *fun*.

---

[146] NB : I shall have more to say about this on Day 97 – *vide infra*.

[147] SUMNER (2019)

"I don't mean 'fun' in the sense of being frivolous," I said. "I mean 'fun' in the sense of treating these things light-heartedly."

This did not help: apparently my fiancée had never had a positive astral experience, either frivolous *or* light-hearted. She seemed to have had uncontrolled astral experiences which had turned out unpleasant in the past, and hence she assumed that all such phenomena must remain unpleasant, despite me trying to reassure her otherwise. "It's possible to control how you astrally project – by preparing yourself beforehand," I would say. "So that instead of projecting to some random place, you only project to where you want or need to be. The Golden Dawn method in particular has built in safeguards: all that vibrating of divine and angelic names is meant to ensure you turn up in the right place, and are protected when you get there."

Alas, such words provided little comfort: since she characterised the astral plane as uniformly bad, she couldn't believe that "right place" could ever exist to which to project. Nevertheless, out of habit, she persisted in trying to make use of Robert Monroe's Gateway programme all the same, though for years she seemed to make little headway.

Evening ritual accomplished.

Day 77

28 June 2020

From my magical journal :

   "During night : dreaming about being crowded by members of the GD or SRIA whom I know. Getting angry ...

   "Up at 4.12am for preparation with Middle Pillar Ritual - again, practising in the astral.

   "Sunrise at 4.42am.

   "LBRP. *Before doing the Qabalistic Cross I try expanding my consciousness in the manner suggested by Damien Echols in his YouTube video (which I subsequently found was an original idea of Chic & Tabatha Cicero). It occurs to me that with each successive expansion, the sephiroth of the Tree of Life in my microcosm represent : firstly, the planets - or the souls of the planets (the gods) ; then whole solar systems (stars) ; then constellations ; then local galaxies ; then local clusters ; then Universes ; then Infinities. This is an intriguing thought ...*

   "Bornless Ritual. *I can rely on my own Body of Light to act as if autonomous in assuming the god-forms which the barbarous names of evocation represent ...*

   "Conjuration.

   "Confession of Sins. *In the dream I had (see above) : the anger represents resentment I harbour against being constricted. Perhaps it is repressed anger against the people in the dream, but perhaps it was also caused by inadvertently feeling resentment towards my fiancée ? I concentrate on trying to sublimate this anger - to both them and her - trying to solve it, convert it into something better, more useful.*

   "Concentrating on my HGA. My nephesh is Nephesh Ha-Messiah. My Ruach is the Akasha, the consciousness of the Universe itself. My higher self is angelic in nature : my Yechidah, Chiah and Neshamah are the corresponding macrocosmic equivalents. In more depth I try meditating upon the concept of expanding my consciousness in the manner I briefly identified when I was doing the LBRP. Stillness.

   "Licence to Depart.

   "LBRP. *Resolving to do the best LBRP ever, I focus on the expanding of consciousness even more fully, the real manifestation of Divinity represented by the four Holy Names, the Archangels, etc.*

   "Total time : 1 hour 7 minutes (not including preparation)."

*

Looking further at Pahaliah from yesterday : I worked out that every other source apart from the text from which I had worked associated this angel with Psalm 116 :4 instead. Although I felt irritated to know I had laboured under a mistake, I at least felt gratified to have finally found the "correct" answer.

I also spent time investigating Nelchael, the next i.e. 21st Shem Ha Mephoresh angel, associated with Psalm 31 :15.

In the afternoon, I took part in a BOTA meeting via ZOOM. We studied "Tzaddi" i.e. "The Star," and did an Anne Davies meditation – the same one which we had done previously, which had inspired me with regard to placing my consciousness in various points in my microcosmic tree.

Apart from this, I spent the day cultivating more strawberries from our plant which actively tried escape from the pot in which we had bought it. I also took the time to reply to a question on Quora about why if precognition was real did psychics not predict 9/11. (Answer : they did, but because not all of them had 100% accuracy in every detail, their predictions proved utterly useless for preventing disaster. The authorities had no way of telling a good psychic from a bad psychic, so they found it far easier to ignore all psychic advice than to evacuate every large building in Manhattan for an indeterminate time in the second week of September. Or possibly the third week. Or possibly Jersey City, or Queens or… you get the idea.)

Before going to bed, my fiancée and I decided on a whim to listen to old Israel Regardie recordings on YouTube. I realised that this whole Damien Echols idea which I had first attributed to Chic & Tabatha Cicero in fact went all the way back to Regardie himself !

Evening ritual accomplished.

Day 78

29 June 2020

I got up at 4.13am and, like previous days, prepared for my morning ritual with Middle Pillar Ritual in the astral. When I began the main ritual, I again did the LBRP in a similar manner as the previous day.

When I did the Bornless Ritual, I found I could rely on my Body of Light to assume the God-forms in question, and feel their energy coming in from the six directions.

I performed the Conjuration. For the Confession of Sins, I noted in my journal.

"Focussing on awareness of my HGA. Thought : the meditation on the Akasha tattva on Saturday provides me with a rationale for being able to attain awareness of my past lives."

I.e. my talk, "Skrying in Theory and Practice,"[148] featured a guided meditation of the Akasha Tattva. It came from an old document of the Stella Matutina, dating from 1916 or earlier.

"I therefore attempt to go on a quick tattva-journey – I meet a dark, winged guide (who tests well by LVX signs) – we ascend to that part where knowledge of past lives is attainable. I petition my HGA that – just as it enables me to resolve the karma of my present life, that it can resolve the karma of my former lives as well. Return and thank guide.

"I become aware of the transmutation that the presence of my HGA causes – i.e. My nephesh = Nephesh Ha-Messiah, my higher self is angelic, my self-consciousness is the consciousness of the universe, my evil persona is hell itself. I will that the respective parts of my soul thus transmuted are absorbing energy from the universe. DEEP. POWERFUL.

"Licence to Depart.

"LBRP.

"Total time not including preparation : 1 hour 7 minutes. At first I felt not really connected, although my astral awareness definitely improved during the Bornless Ritual so that by the time of meditation during the 'Confession of Sins' I was buzzing."

*

Apart from this, I spent the day investigating Psalm 121 :5, which pertains to Ieiaiel, the 22nd Shem Ha Mephoresh Angel, who protects when travelling : and

---

[148] Op. cit.

then performing my evening ritual as per usual, as well as enjoying "sacrament" with my fiancée.

Day 79

30 June 2020

I got up at 4.14am for preparation with Middle Pillar Ritual – this time done physically. I noted down my morning ritual thus :

   "LBRP.

   "Bornless Ritual. Body of Light's ability to "rise on the planes" and contact the Truth which the source of the Godforms in each direction represents comes easily today. Good.

   "Conjuration.

   "Confession of Sins. Anger at imaginary critics. Concern for A and her thesis. I almost allowed them to distract me. I treat them as 'heavies' and invite them to 'pray' with me. Anger *I task with protecting me from such critics in real life, whilst* Concern *I task with teaching me to be careful to handle A sensitively, with diplomacy etc. They integrate with my Evil Persona.*

   "The Karma of my past lives - I integrate that into my Evil Persona, so that in effect I not only have their past wisdom, but the energy contained within their sins as well. If I am going to seek forgiveness for their sins, I want all of their sins in one place.

   "Concentrating on the presence of the HGA and the transmuting effect that it has on all parts of my soul. Good.

   "Licence to Depart.

   "LBRP.

   "Total time : 1 hour 2 minutes.

   "Trying to think of a new word to express what the Evil Persona is made out of. 'Sin Energy?' 'Dark Energy?' The point being that although it comes from a seemingly unpleasant source, in its proper context it gets put to good use."

*

Having gone back to bed to catch some Zzzs after typing up my journal, I was forcibly roused from my slumber by my fiancée, who wanted to talk about sex magic, specifically BOTA's teachings on sexual polarity. Whilst interested in the subject generally, my attitude was like *"enough with the theory, let's get to the practical application."* My fiancée, however, *kept on talking.*

Eventually, the encounter ended abruptly and not in the most ideal manner. My fiancée happened to mention that Anne Davies formulated her theory about the *Nephesh* after she meditated on Smokey, Paul Foster Case's pet cat, and reached a state of meditative awareness so deep, she found it *orgasmic* in its intensity.

"I wish *I* was Smokey the Cat," I said, finally getting a word in edgeways. "He seemed to have had more luck with Anne Davies than I'm getting right now."

The effect proved *appalling*. My fiancée reacted furiously to me making such an improper remark about her beloved Anne. She got even more furious when I reacted to her outrage with uncontrolled mirth. I tried to explain that despite lowering the tone with humour, I actually agreed with her in her desire to explore the polarity teachings, but unfortunately she refused to listen : I had no choice but to get up, shower, and go in search of breakfast.

I spent most of the day hiding from my beloved's wrath in my office. This gave me the opportunity to contemplate Psalm 120 :8 as part of my ongoing scriptural study, associated with Melahel (23rd Shem Ha Mephoresh angel). The meditation arising therefrom happened to prove very powerful.

When I did resurface, metaphorical egg-shells lay all around. My fiancée made a remark about her thesis, and instantly became sensitive when I suggested in the mildest terms how she might improve it. Her reaction bewildered me, as I had no conception of behaving tactlessly (on this occasion).

Her mood continued all evening. We got into a disagreement over a point in Regardie's 'Art of True Healing' - i.e. Regardie said one thing about how energy circulates in that book, but the Golden Dawn teaches otherwise. Does the circulation take place only within the body, or does it swirl through the aura ?

I opined that Regardie said different things in different places, but even so, the distinction had no practical difference. It would make sense to say that energy circulates around the aura, because it would fit in with the Golden Dawn's teachings of the "Tree of Life Projected in a Sphere." Although the question interested me, whether a practical difference did exist between circulating energy in the aura or in the physical body alone. I suspected that my fiancée did not actually want an intellectual discussion on the point, but rather wanted to get back at me for my remarks about Smokey the Cat earlier.

Evening ritual accomplished.

Day 80

01 July 2020

I got up at 4.14am for preparation with the Middle Pillar Ritual. When I got to the part where I circulate the Light around / in front and behind / up and over / spiralling about me, I found my thoughts disturbed by the memory of the aura vs body argument. Does it make a difference ? Perhaps the argument made the difference, not the distinction.

Come sunrise, I expelled the obsession with the whole disagreement from my aura, and disintegrated it with the LBRP as I began my main ritual of the morning.

Then, when I started the Bornless Ritual, my thoughts calmed right down immediately when I said, *"Thee I invoke, the Bornless One."* I got the idea - perhaps I had a learning opportunity ? I thought :

"Perhaps I should be turning my attention to the Macrocosm as well - in which case I should be incorporating the Hexagram as well as Pentagram rituals into my daily practice. Perhaps far from being an attack, it's a challenge for me to do better - to up my game. I ought to thank *my fiancée for this !"*

Then, in the middle of the Conjuration, I realised the resolution of the apparent dichotomy which had caused my mental upset.

"I am mistaken to identify with merely the Physical Body. My subtle bodies extend beyond my physical bodies - hence there is no distinction between my aura and the real body, or self."

Hence, when it got to the Confession of Sins, I was able to thank God and my Holy Guardian Angel for all the spiritual gifts I had received so far, e.g. Being able to resolve the problems which seem to beset me, including this one. I thought :

"Allowing myself to be distracted by this aura problem at all is a sin. The incorporation of the LBRH into my ritual is a sensible solution. (Not doing it beforehand might also be considered a 'sin' - as in falling short of the correct standards).

"Issues with A to the extent that they are my fault - or indeed responsibility - amount to failings on my part and hence sins. BUT ... How to deal with them ? Clearly by changing myself somehow, attempting to change A would be wrong even if it were possible. I ought to preface every remark I make by emphasising how much I love her. But how to say anything at all without her taking it the wrong way ? Hmm ...

"Concentrating on my HGA - my subtle bodies being transmuted ..."

Thus, when I finished my ritual that morning, after the Licence to Depart I did both the LBRP *and* the LBRH, the first time I had done so. Henceforth for the rest of my operation my morning rituals rarely dipped below an hour in duration. To think that the first one had taken a mere 15 minutes ! It seemed unbelievable now.

*

During the day I noticed that my fiancée appeared better disposed to me than she had last night, so I fancied that something of a reconciliation might be in the air.

As part of my scriptural study I investigated Psalm 18 :33, which according to Ambelain and Lenain is associated with Chahaviah (or "Hahuiah" as they put it), the 24th Shem Ha Mephoresh angel. *However :* I realised that other sources, such as the Rose Croix D'Orient, attributed Psalm 147 :11 to this Angel instead. I could see how the confusion might arise : both versicles have similar wording, i.e.

"Behold the eye of the Lord is upon them that fear Him, upon them that hope in His mercy."
(Psalm 18 :33).

"The Lord taketh pleasure in them that fear Him, in those that hope in His mercy."
(Psalm 147 :11)

I therefore ended up investigating *both* versicles : in any event the gematria proved fascinating.

In the evening : I attended a ZOOM meeting which took the place of my Royal Arch Chapter meeting. My mother Chapter being unusual amongst Freemasons in that it comprised esoterically-minded Companions, we had a high level of discussion that evening. One person made the remark that finding the Lost Word in the Vault was akin to making contact with Spirit guides – such as the Holy Guardian Angel.

Afterwards, my fiancée had brightened up considerably. Together we performed what YouTube described as a "Relaxation Ritual" by Israel Regardie, though my fiancée had originally wanted to put on "Body Awareness." I then read out a meditation from "Ritual Use of Magical Tools"[149] for her, after which we performed the LBRP. I felt myself transformed into a giant synthesis of not only me but also the Archangels, the Pentagrams and the Six-Rayed star, which ended up performing the final Qabalistic Cross all together,

I completed my Evening ritual, after which we enjoyed the kind of polarity workings that she had first described the other day, which I got through without mentioning Smokey the Cat, or making any meowing noises whatsoever.

---

[149] CICERO, CICERO (2000)

Day 81

02 July 2020

For some reason I had a vivid dream during the night, of shopping in Harrods in the lockdown. I had seen a news story the day before, about the axing almost of 700 jobs from the store, reflecting a trend amongst retailers at the time. Had that 700 included the owner of Harrods it would have provided a cause for celebration, rather than the tragedy it became. I could see Society collapsing around me, and here I was engaged in an elaborate ritual to summon and bind all the demons of Hell.

Whatever the significance of the dream (it might have meant nothing more than the fact that I had remembered the news story), I got up early for my usual Middle Pillar Ritual. I felt tired, but I reflected that at least I was found myself in better humour than yesterday.

From today onwards, I performed the Lesser Banishing Rituals of both the Pentagram and Hexagram, at the start and at the end of my morning rituals.

After the Bornless ritual and the Conjuration, I got to the Confession of Sins. I thought :

"Expressing gratitude to God, my HGA, and all spiritual guides and teachers, living and dead (passed on), discarnate & incarnate, that have, do and will guide or guided me. Whilst I am not perfect, that is technically a sin, hence I will not be completely free from sin whilst I am still on the path before completing my goal.

"I am responsible for all the sins (karma) of my past lives. Trying therefore to resolve them is not unlike 'The Harrowing of Hell' - establishing the Christ power in 'Hell' so as to liberate the souls of those who have died before. Taken to its full conclusion, I would be responsible in some way for the liberation of the human race.

"Concentrating on my HGA..."

I closed the session with Licence to depart and the LBRP & LBRH – the "new normal," to borrow a phrase that had become a media buzz-word.

Later, during the day, I investigated Psalm 9 :2, associated with Nith-Haiah (25th Shem Ha Mephoresh angel). The meditation arising therefrom proved especially good that day.

In the evening, my fiancée persuaded me to do some "Yoga With Adriene" (i.e. the popular YouTube channel) with her. She had found a video especially for me : "Yoga for Writers."[150] Although mostly *asanas*, Adriene did slip in the *sangkalpa* "When I sit down, ideas flow freely."

---

[150] https ://www.youtube.com/watch ?v=bQWwWaWXPS0 accessed 2021-06-03

Evening ritual accomplished.

Day 82

03 July 2020

During the night : dreaming about trains *again*. Trying to catch a train somewhere with my fiancée, but we had difficulty getting on it, and once aboard it did not seem to go to the advertised destination, but somewhere where it would get lost...

I got up at 4.16am for preparation with the Middle Pillar Ritual. Come the main ritual of the morning, I recorded it thus :

*"**LBRP**. As previously..."*

i.e., by extending my consciousness into the infinite, in the manner described *originally* by Israel Regardie.

"When I complete the last invocation, '... And in the column shines the six-rayed star,' I visualise the whole thing, pentagrams representing divine forces, Archangels and six-rayed star doing the final QC. Then when I do the ...

*"**LBRH** - I imagine the whole shebang rising to the Macrocosmic level to perform this.*

*"**Bornless Ritual**.*

*"**Conjuration**.*

*"**Confession of Sins**. I begin by thanking God and my HGA for everything they do, when I have a brilliant idea as to why for all these years, I keep seeing trains in my dreams. It seems so obvious that after I bring it to the surface of my consciousness, I perceive how foolish I was not to guess it before. (Ironically this is a sin to confess - a recognition that I have been falling short of confession).*

"The big realisation is this : Recurring Imagery in a dream signifies a message that one's unconscious is trying to tell oneself - but is continually being ignored. If the Conscious Mind realised the significance of the message, and resolved it accordingly, the imagery would cease to be recording. Hence : the Train imagery tells me there is something my unconscious has been trying to tell me all these years but I have not realised its full meaning. UNTIL NOW ...

"I believe that the Train is a symbol of POWER - power to direct my life. The fact that these Trains are not necessarily going where I want or expect them is telling me that I am not making full use of this power.

"Moreover, the Train imagery gives me a key wherewith I can start working on resolving this - i.e. By thinking in terms of Taking Control of the Train, and deliberately driving it to where I do want to go, e.g. KCHGA. I have always told myself that I am a Lucid Dreamer, so I ought to be able to work with this dream-imagery in literally the way I describe.

"(? Was this caused by Yoga for Writers yesterday ?)
"Licence to Depart.
"LBRP ; LBRH.
"Total time not including preparation : 1 hour 6 minutes."

*

For my scriptural study today I investigated Psalm 119 :145, which has to do with Haaaiah, the 26th Shem Ha Mephoresh angel.

An unexpected piece of good fortune occurred today. A Companion who had participated in the ZOOM call in which I took part the previous Wednesday, decided to gift me a collection of W L Wilmshurst's lodge papers for Lodge of Living Stones. The Lodge did not normally circulate these outside its own members, so I was very lucky to get hold of them. They fascinated me – not only did they more fully set-out Wilmshurst's vision of mystical Freemasonry, but they also provided a lot of insight into the history of Lodge of the Living Stones itself. Unfortunately, the collection did not include the one I really wanted – *The Book of the Perfect Lodge* – but I ought to have expected that, as Living Stones retains all copies itself. Nevertheless, I resolved to examine them further at length.

At the end of the evening when performing my last ritual of the day, I attempted to create a sigil that would help prepare my mind for the kind of dream work I identified in my morning ritual.

Day 83

04 July 2020

The sigil, however, never got the opportunity to prove its capability. During the night, my fiancée woke me up, as a strange dream she had had quite excited her : she insisted on sharing all the details with me. She fell silent, however, when I pointed out the time. I tried to get back to sleep : I started to have a sexy dream which, depending on which interpretation I read, could either mean I felt comfortable with myself or the exact opposite… but before I could become lucid and do the dreamwork I had intended, my alarm interrupted me.

I got up and performed the Middle Pillar Ritual. This time I reached a deep state of meditation whilst doing so. I deliberately excluded obtruding astral phenomena by first focussing on "I AM."

Feeling buoyed I went into my main ritual :

"*LBRP*.

"*LBRH*.

"*Bornless Ritual. The energies coming in from the four cardinal directions are modulated by the Archangels, but only latterly does it occur to me that the energies from zenith and nadir are modulated by the "six-rayed star" - this needs further investigation.*

"*Conjuration.*

"*Confession of Sins. Sigil did not discernibly work during night. Hence the fact that this is not yet perfected is a sin.*

"*Allowing past trauma to affect me - to distract me - is a sin. The trauma may have been caused by someone else, but it is my responsibility to deal with it.*

"*Thinking about* Samyama - *what would it be like to do* Samyama *on my HGA ?*"

The inspiration for this thought came from a book my fiancée had read regarding Patanjali's Yoga Sutras round about that time : *or so I remembered*, but when I went back to look for it, to provide a citation for the bibliography, I couldn't find it, even after getting powerful demons on the case to help me retrieve it. Nevertheless, I felt sure that I hadn't just dreamed it – unless of course I had yet again shifted diagonally through time. My differently-remembered version of what I had read proved so influential that it affected pretty much all of the rest of my Abramelin practice. I will try to reconstruct from memory what I had read in a different timeline, to wit :

As I understood it, *Samyama* was a practice in which Concentration *(Dharana)*, Meditation *(Dhyana)*, and "Contemplation" *(Samadhi)* became integrated into one : it provides the key to attaining the Siddhis. Actually, "contemplation" is a poor translation of the term, in my opinion. A better word would be "grok," in the sense of becoming one with the object of knowing. However, the commentary I now remembered reading phrased it a little differently : *Dharana* meant to meditate on the "outward form" of an object ; *Dhyana* referred to perceiving its inner or psychic form ; but *Samadhi* would entail becoming one with the process of that inner perception. Hence :

> *"Experiencing how the HGA manifests (e.g. The transformative affect it has on me) would be the outward form. The inner form is the inner psychic nature of the HGA. But the contemplation would be to become that inner psychic nature."*

The closest I could find to my conception of *Samyama* was in a book about "Kriya Yoga." Referring to *Dharana, Dhyana,* and *Samadhi,* it said :

> *"Furthermore, these three stages of yoga, held in time, produce what is called the clear gem, often referred to as the jewel of wisdom. This jewel is achieved when the subtle principle of the mind crystallizes into a pure, clear, colourless light. Consequently, if this gem is set upon something it will take on the colouration of that upon which it is resting ...*
>
> *"The technique of* Samyama *consists of the following processes : 1. Taking the clear gem and setting it on any object, gross or subtle ; 2. Perceiving the colouration of the gem ; 3. Removing the gem and remembering the perception when the* Samyama *has been concluded."*[151]

In effect I proposed to place this "Clear Gem" of *Samyama* upon my own Holy Guardian Angel : "experiencing how the HGA manifests" – *Dharana* – the placing of the Gem ; perceiving the inner psychic nature of the HGA would equate to perceiving the colouration of the Gem or *Dhyana ;* whilst becoming one with that psychic nature would mean the conclusion of the *Samyama,* i.e. *Samadhi.*

I would come back to this idea in the future. Meanwhile, my contemplations shifted to pondering the nature of my consciousness itself :

> *"It occurs to me that as I create my own Universe I would be the HGA for the people of my cosmos. I am the God of my own Imagination (not : in my imagination). Needs to be meditated upon more.*
>
> **"Licence to Depart.**
>
> **"LBRP.**
>
> **"LBRH.**
>
> *"Total time taken (not including preparation) 1 hour (ending was rushed as by that time I had the urge to eliminate)."*

---

[151] G. KRIYANANDA (1992), pp328-329.

*

A strange discussion ensued when my fiancée and I happened to talk about Alchemy. I voiced the opinion that I categorised all real Alchemy, including the physical (External) Alchemy, as spiritual, and that if one takes the spiritual out of the alchemy, it ceases to be *real* alchemy. In other words, one cannot sensibly think of physical alchemy as something different from "spiritual alchemy," because even the lab work is spiritual to some degree.

My fiancée however looked at me as if I had grown an extra head. She refused to believe that physical alchemy was spiritual – I could only assume that she and I were talking of different things without realising it.

As it happened, she had a book called *Real Alchemy* on her bookshelf which she had bought and never read. I opened it up to page one, to the Foreword written by Dennis William Hauck :

> *"It is true that alchemy reflects the highest aspirations of the human soul, for our gold has always symbolized the hastened perfection of Man as well as matter. However, any alchemist worth his salt knows that lasting transformation only takes place when the work is accomplished on all levels of reality – the mental, the spiritual, and the physical."*[152]

To me this sounded perfectly reasonable, but my fiancée looked flabbergasted by it, as if she had just listened to some unspeakable heresy. I myself couldn't understand the opposing point of view, that there might exist some kind of alchemy that didn't have some spiritual aspect to it. I had, I have to admit, long rejected the purely psychological view of Alchemy. From my point of view, if Carl Jung finds it helps to get meaningful results by describing his theories in alchemical terms, that only proves the alchemical nature of psychology – *it does not prove the psychological nature of alchemy* (and, indeed, arguing upon these lines would lead to a logical fallacy). Besides which, I had grown increasingly aware of both a modern revival of practical alchemy, pioneered by people like Frater Albertus and Jean Dubuis, which had occurred *after* Jung formulated his ideas ; as well as the contemporary existence of certain esoteric currents which had pre-dated him.

This did not succeed in convincing my fiancée, so I dropped the subject. I felt worried that she genuinely thought that just because I disagreed with her that I meant to have a go at her, which in turn meant that I could not "win" the argument even by being correct.

---

[152] BARTLETT (2009), p1.

Later : contemplating Ierathel (27th Shem Ha Mephoresh angel), and its associated versicle, Psalm 140 :2. The first word, "Chelatzinai" (i.e. "Deliver us") had the same Gematria as the phrase "the Master of the Nose," a recondite name in the Zohar for God, associated with Kether. I thought : "*I learn something new every day !*"

Afterwards, I found that my fiancée had calmed down, so we spent the rest of the day pleasantly. Evening ritual accomplished.

Day 84

05 July 2020

Today was the end of the first three months of the operation. I had, however, already planned to go slightly over the prescribed six-month length, so I had not reached half-way *just* yet.

I got up at 4.17am for preparation with the Middle Pillar Ritual. Then my main ritual of the morning :

"LBRP.

"LBRH.

"Bornless Ritual. Integrating visualisations of LBRP and LBRH into one big synthesis. Trying to imagine what Samyama on the energies coming in is actually like as I think of the six directions."

I.e., I was trying to incorporate my ideas on Samyama from yesterday.

"Conjuration.

"Confession of Sins. What keeps me from perfection is a sin per se. The terrible arguments with my fiancée yesterday are evidence that I have not yet mastered the knack of not rising to obvious provocation ! I pray that my HGA teach me good humour without flippancy, speaking the truth as much as another can bear it, without being deliberately misleading, and the value of silence and self-effacement.

"Developing the idea of making Samyama on my Holy Guardian Angel. A deep state of meditation. Good.

"Licence to Depart.

"LBRP.

"LBRH.

"Total time taken not including preparation : 1 hour 13 minutes (longer meditation during confession)."

*

An intriguing question on Quora.com : "You start a secret society. What would you do ?" I guess the querent meant it flippantly, but I wrote a reasonably serious answer all the same, i.e. read a good book on how to actually run a secret society. Such as *Inside a Magical Lodge* by John Michael Greer which, incidentally, my co-masonic obedience had used extensively when establishing itself. I then realised that the book had gone out of print : the means of running a secret society *had itself become secret*. (Since then, a new edition has become available).

For my scriptural study, I investigated Psalm 71 :12, associated with Sheahiah, the 28th Shem Ha Mephoresh angel.

My fiancée felt out of sorts, depressed over her latest attempt to give up smoking. I decided to ask her a question about a subject with which I knew she was familiar, not because I wanted to know about it, but because I knew she could talk for an hour or more about it non-stop – which she did. Miracle upon miracles ! Launching into her favourite topic caused her to completely forget the slough of despond through which she had trudged, so that by the time she finally paused for breath, she had become her happy self again. I had played a trick on her, but my darling's happiness merited me sacrificing my personality. I'm not sure if she realised what I had done : I didn't mention the subject.

Evening ritual accomplished. I meditated on the sigil I had created several days ago, intent that tonight I would direct my dreams as I wished.

Day 85

06 July 2020

My fiancée pestered me for "Sacrament" during the night, so I used the opportunity for finding a new reason to chant "*Om Mani Padme Hum*" for half an hour or so. Of course, I enjoyed the experience, but afterwards I reflected on the irony : twice I had now tried to use that sigil for lucid dreaming, and twice I had got distracted from doing so.

I got up at 4.18am for preparation with the Middle Pillar Ritual. I could feel my Body of Light well that morning. Then my main morning ritual :

"*LBRP*.

"*LBRH. Absorbing the cumulative effects of these two rituals within me. Then -*

"*Bornless Ritual. Contemplating each direction, the effect is surprisingly powerful.*

"*Conjuration.*

"*Confession of Sins. Identifying with a mortal personality at all is potentially sinful, as being finite, I am doomed to fall short of the infinite. Hence I should identify with the infinite ... Lustful thoughts, memories of past trauma - all absorbed into the Evil Persona. The Sin-Energy of all past lives - I absorb into the evil persona.*

"*THOUGHT : the power to succeed in this operation - that too I have inherited from a past life.*

"*Deep meditation upon the presence of the HGA. Very still, very good.*

"*Licence to Depart.*

"*LBRP ; LBRH.*

"*Total time not including preparation : 1 hour. Focussing attention on the Body of Light and the importance of its role in this ritual is definitely the right thing to do.*"

*

For my scriptural study that day I investigated Psalm 54 :6, associated with Reiiel, the 29th Shem Ha Mephoresh angel.

That evening after dinner, my fiancée fancied trying out a Relaxation Ritual, so we found one narrated by Israel Regardie on YouTube. To our surprise it proved briefer than we were expecting. I used up the time by trying to teach her the rudiments of the Hexagram Ritual.

I carried out my Evening ritual. When I turned into bed, my fiancée again successfully distracted me from attempting to use that sigil.

Day 86

07 July 2020

I tried out a so-called "Genius Mind" vitamin / herbal supplement, which I had received as part of the Amazon Vine programme. It had no discernible effect. I had no idea whether it didn't work because one cannot improve on perfection, or because it didn't work generally : I suspect the former, obviously. In any event I set to that morning, by concentrating briefly on making Samyama on each of the Sephiroth as I performed the Middle Pillar ritual.

This proved powerful, but it also meant that I started my main ritual of the morning 4 minutes late :

"*LBRP.*

"*LBRH.*

"*Bornless Ritual. Attempting to make* Samyama *on each barbarous name as I vibrate it as well as the source in each direction. As if it is all a Vinyasa on the spiritual level. Powerful !*

"*Conjuration.*

"*Confession of Sins. This added depth to the Bornless Ritual must have been more powerful than I realised, because it has stirred up shit, which suddenly seizes my consciousness whilst I try to meditate - neuroses of one kind or another. But then I meditate on them rationally - I treat them like 'heavies' and invite them to pray with me. Thinking of them as 'qlippoth' I consider : what is the kernel of goodness at the heart of these seemingly unpleasant nasties ? I reflect : they wanted to protect me from getting myself into harmful situations. Hence the good-kernel is the benevolent intention of protecting me. Hence, further, I speak to them, thanking them for their efforts, and willing that they apply their energies to protecting me again, but this time in a way which I find more palatable.*

"*The act of going through this re-framing process with these quasi-Qlippoth has a calming effect - as if it is the tonic that I needed. All thanks to my HGA.*

"*Licence to Depart.*

"*LBRP.*

"*LBRH.*

"*Total time : 58 minutes.*"

*

I found researching Psalm 71 :5, associated with Omael (30th Shem Ha Mephoresh angel), especially fruitful. Firstly I attained a deep state of meditation whilst contemplating the whole thing, which always struck me as a good sign, an indication of angelic presence. More curiously I uncovered some Gematria which I thought so remarkable that I noted it down at length :

"THOUGHT : 'Nour' (Youth) is a title or the synonym of a title of Metatron. It is also Gematrically equivalent to 'Yeheshuah.' Hence 'Yeheshuah' is equivalent to 'Metatron !' In a sense there is an obvious explanation - each in their own way is considered as the Son of God, the former because He is the Christ, and the latter because he is the foremost of all the Archangels."

*

I opened my emails and found out that I had won a competition: a signed copy of the *new* edition of "Sacred Magic" by David Goddard. The first edition of this book had previously provided me with inspiration, particularly through its exposition of Madeline Montalban's system of Angel magic.[153] At least I hope I had "won" it – as in, the publisher supposedly drew the result out of a hat, but I wonder if the fact that I often do book reviews on my website made it less random than it first appeared ? Whatever the explanation, one of Madeline Montalban's most important teachings is that one can deduce the presence of Angels by noticing omens and portents occurring within one's life. For example, if one were to invoke a particular angel, and then one started noticing symbolism consistent with that angel cropping up as coincidental events and objects, as one went about one's daily business. What, then, would Madeline Montalban have made of me undertaking the most intensive regimen of angel-invocation, and finding myself gifted with a free book on angel-magic ?

Later, I made a *faux pas* when my fiancée asked my opinion about her portal thesis : I suggested it could be successful after a few edits, such as re-writing bits. However, she only heard the word "re-writing" and assumed (wrongly) that I meant re-write *the whole thing*. I tried to explain that I only meant a few paragraphs here and there, but I seriously misjudged how sensitive she felt about it all at that moment, so my protestations fell on deaf ears. I should, of course, have simply said *"Yes, dear, it's perfectly fine, there's nothing wrong with it at all."*

I emerged from hiding later to find that she had sufficiently calmed down that we could go out for a rare trip to the local pub. Lockdown restrictions had partially eased, so we availed ourselves of the opportunity of getting out of the house for the evening. We found it strange to see a half-empty pub, providing table-service only, on what should otherwise have been a busy summer evening (nevertheless

---

[153] See : Days 35, 36 *supra*

the place had as many customers as restrictions would allow). What with the state of the world at that time, I felt a bit like Shaun of the Dead – waiting for it all to blow over. This of course happened before the resurgence of Covid-19 which would cause lockdown restrictions to return. Had we known what would happen, I would have appreciated the opportunity more.

My fiancée said something strange, which almost caused me to have an argument, but I bit my lip as best I could. She revealed that earlier in the day she had attempted to invoke Water – but without the corresponding Spirit Pentagram. Being new to the whole business of the Supreme Invoking Ritual of the Pentagram, I suppose she had made an honest mistake. This of course would normally count as a basic error, but because I still picked my way over the proverbial egg-shells, I realised that if I pointed this out she would *not* appreciate it, given her troubled mood. As it happened it put a damper on the rest of the evening.

Feeling uneasy, I did my evening ritual and went to bed.

Day 87

08 July 2020

Up at 4.20am for preparation with the Middle Pillar Ritual. I now felt awful after that business with the thesis yesterday, so before performing the LBRP and LBRH, I treated my feelings like an "obsession" i.e. I visualised them as a ball of evil which I expelled from my aura, then imagined that the Banishing rituals caused it to disintegrate into nothingness.

When I performed the LBRP, I applied some of the insight I had garnered from working with Omael the previous day.

"THOUGHT : Each Pentagram before me = 'YEHESHUAH.' This, from my Qabalistic studies yesterday, is equivalent to 'NOUR' which itself is equivalent to Metatron, and hence Kether. Hence, further, Yeheshuah - and the Pentagram - is thus associated with Kether.

"Alternatively, the Pentagrams which I cast each represent 'Metatron' whilst the inner subjective feeling which they arouse - the Shekinah - represents 'Sandalphon.'"

It occurred to me that the Golden Dawn expects each Adept to make a Pentacle, bearing a "six-rayed star." This represents Earth and has the colours of Malkuth, which has Sandalphon as its Archangel. Now it so happened that Damien Echols had created his own version of the pentagram ritual in which he added Metatron and Sandalphon to the four archangels, as zenith and nadir respectively.[154] Ironically, I came to realise that perhaps they *did* feature in the pentagram ritual – but not in the way that Echols has imagined, i.e. Metatron, being the circle of pentagrams, represented the Periphery, whilst the six-rayed star represented that of *the Pentacle*, and hence Sandalphon, through its association with Malkuth – and *the Centre*. I did not change the wording of the pentagram ritual *per se*, I just viewed this as a new layer of symbolism to keep in mind.

I performed the LBRH, Bornless Ritual, and Conjuration. When I got to the Confession of Sins, I thought :

"If I carry on allowing arguments with my fiancée to happen and thus disturb my mind, this could potentially spoil this whole operation - hence that would be a Major Sin. Hence each instance of succumbing to an argument now is either potentially or actually sinful.

"Instead, I ought to be able to rely on my HGA to guide me and influence me in the best way to complete this operation successfully. Hence, by tuning into and heeding the guidance of my HGA, I can realise the best way to avoid and alleviate all such arguments. E.g. By not mentioning her thesis, keeping

---

[154] ECHOLS (2018), chapter 13.

Silent generally, unless it be to praise - and then to do so only in a T-A-C-T-F-U-L way.

"The kernel of Good at the heart of my concerns is my love for A, after all.

"I am grateful to God and my HGA for empowering me to be able to avert danger in advance."

A thought popped into my head : my fiancée had displayed an overly sensitive mood yesterday ; she had also admitted to attempting to invoke Water but in a mistaken fashion. *What if the two were connected ?* That she had inadvertently conjured some sort of Water Elemental without realising it ?

The whole rationale of conjuring the elements in the Golden Dawn's particular manner extrapolates from the tradition of Elemental beings – first articulated by Paracelsus, but in reality stretching back before the dawn of history. Some sources have described Elementals as wild and chaotic ; but other sources describe them as genuinely helpful beings who assist in an individual's progress upon the path of return. Why the dichotomy ?

The answer lay in Spirit, by which I mean a soul-connection with God. According to the western tradition of Elementals, every human being naturally has that connection, making them actually spiritually advanced creatures, even if you would not think it to look at various members of humanity.

Elementals, however, according to the same Paracelsian tradition, don't automatically have Spirit within them – unless one can somehow fashion a connection artificially. An elemental unconnected to Spirit remains a wild, chaotic, blind force of nature : but a Spirit-connected Elemental becomes a being that a responsible magician would want to work with in order to further the Great Work.

Two broad methods exist of linking the elemental to Spirit. The first consists of prayers and invocations. The Golden Dawn's incorporation of Spirit pentagrams into its Pentagram ritual exemplifies this approach : I also believe that certain pagan traditions and practices can achieve the same thing.

The other, however, consists of what one may quaintly term an "Elemental Marriage," or less quaintly, sexual intercourse with an Elemental. The original Golden Dawn did not teach this method, probably because it arose in a climate of Victorian prudishness. The subject did, however, provide a hot source of gossip amongst Golden Dawn members – precisely because they lived in a climate of Victorian prudishness. This method first came to light in *Comte De Gabalis* by Abbé Nicolas-Pierre-Henri de Montfaucon de Villars – a priest, no less, who appeared to use satire to ask just how gullible *are* these Occultists ?[155]

[155] DE MONTFAUCON DE VILLARS (1913)

However, the members of the original Golden Dawn formed a consensus that *"methinks the Priest doth protest too much,"* i.e., the book did in fact contain the real deal. I personally fail to see why one should prefer the prayers & invocations route to that of Elemental Marriages, unless it really does boil down to a hangover from a Victorian idea that conjuring an entity just to commit *Spectrophilia* had something *icky* about it. Either that, or instead of just sex magick, it really involved a *Marriage* of sorts, with a correspondingly high level of commitment. Hence it would not appeal to many horny-but-flaky occultists (i.e. the vast majority).

Still, perhaps the racial memory still has some notion of the instinct to unite the Elementals with Spirit through copulation : hence the tradition of shouting, "Oh God," whilst doing so.

In any event : returning to the quandary which presently beset me :

> *"It occurs to me that if bad feelings did result from my fiancée not doing rituals properly yesterday, I ought to do something about the wild Water Elemental myself.*

> *"Trying to concentrate on my HGA, albeit briefly.*

> ***"Licence to Depart."***

I considered that despite my thoughts about Elemental Marriages, I did not want to start experimenting with it at that particular moment. I therefore decided to take a more conventional and boring approach. Before closing the ritual that morning, I performed an astral Supreme Invoking Pentagram of Water (with the proper Spirit pentagram), to unite the putative Water elemental about which I had theorised with the element of Spirit. This being done, I conjured the Elemental to behave appropriately at all times, and then licenced it to depart. I closed with the LBRP and LBRH as normal. These last two rituals felt rushed as I had a need to Eliminate. Perhaps physical crapulence had caused or exacerbated it ? In any case, after attending to the needs of my body, I felt a lot better.

*

For my scriptural study that day, I investigated Psalm 71 :16, which is associated with Lecabel, the 31st Shem Ha Mephoresh angel.

Quite separately I took the opportunity to read through the Wilmshurst papers I had received, starting with his address on the consecration of Lodge of the Living Stones. It struck me as highly interesting, but I also realised that Wilmshurst had lived in an entirely different world to today. Wilmshurst had founded a blatantly esoteric lodge, a regular lodge under the United Grand Lodge of England which yet incorporated meditation into its rituals and treated its ceremonies with as much care as that of a magical order. Tellingly, however, he had done so with the full consent and co-operation of the Province of West Yorkshire. The papers revealed the consecrating officers, including the Provincial Grand Master and Provincial Grand Chaplain, as members of Wilmshurst's circle – or, the Province looked upon Wilmshurst himself as an insider, "one of the lads," as it were. Hence, Wilmshurst in his founding address could speak confidently about the future of the new lodge, remarking that he had the support of both the officers and rank-and-file brethren of the Province, and looked forward to approximately *sixty* attendees per meeting as a reasonable number neither too large nor too small.

Sixty! What I wouldn't give to have more than twenty, let alone sixty, attendees per meeting of my mother-lodge. It came into being in the late 1980s as a sort of Wilmshurst-style lodge, with the same rituals, practices and ethos, but based down in London. However, one could not have found a wider contrast than between its founding and that of Lodge of the Living Stones. Whereas Wilmshurst had founded his lodge as a happy-collaboration with the Province of West Yorkshire, the founders of my mother-lodge had to operate *in spite of* UGLE, which at that time (i.e., fifteen years before the formation of the Metropolitan Grand Lodge of London) administered London lodges directly. Whereas the consecrating officers of Living Stones had made speeches deliberately praising Wilmshurst's efforts, the chief consecrating officer of my mother-lodge (actually the then Grand Secretary) made a very snooty address in which he deliberately warned the brethren to focus on the material and not the spiritual. Otherwise, they might end up following the freakish ideas of *that awful Wilmshurst chap*!

Unless he was a complete idiot *(which one cannot entirely rule out)*, I presume he spoke in a purposefully ironic manner in regard to our founders' intentions. Nevertheless, the privilege of consecrating a lodge rests with the Grandmaster or his personal representative – so one can assume that one could take the Grand Secretary as the voice of The Establishment within UGLE at the time. For several years UGLE viewed my mother-lodge with something akin to horror, until at one point a visiting grand officer sent a highly critical report to his superiors stating that he observed Brethren in the lodge performing a strange ritual *(i.e. Wilmshurst's ritual as he originally intended it)* and behaving in a sinister manner *(i.e. sitting in silent meditation)*.

This had a catastrophic effect: UGLE immediately acted by banning my mother lodge's use of the Wilmshurst ritual; and at the same time communicating to the members of the lodge, *"you can either have a chance of honours in Masonry, or you can remain a member here."* A large number resigned straightaway, leaving only a husk comprising a few dedicated hardcore members.

(Living Stones, incidentally, escaped such censure because its Province supported it, as it had in the beginning. One can discern a clear lesson here : don't found a lodge without the willingness of your Provincial Grand Master to act as "project champion," to borrow a phrase from Project Management.)

Sometime later, however, the leadership at UGLE changed, and Freemasons who *did* have sympathy to esotericism found themselves in positions of power and influence. The lodge began to slowly recover, although it never again reached the membership levels it had at its founding. Thus did I find the lodge when I myself first entered it.

Now, as I write, the leadership at UGLE has changed again, and those who had had sympathy to esotericism have departed, to make way for a generation more wary whilst remaining outwardly less hysterical towards it. It may well occur that the prevailing mood at UGLE changes again – multiple times – during the rest of my life. In any event, I perceive quite clearly that esotericism lies most definitely outside the norm in mainstream freemasonry, and the fact that it exists at all defines the very meaning of "precariousness." Ironically, Wilmshurst himself noted that the widest influence his writings had was not in mainstream Freemasonry, but instead in Co-masonry, which UGLE regards as clandestine, but which has always remained more receptive to spiritual ideas.

*

During the day, I realised that although my method of dealing with that putative Water Elemental had helped *me,* my fiancée still felt sensitive about the disagreements of the previous day. It bemused me as to why she kept talking about the unfairness of her thesis, if she knew full well she would trigger herself by doing so.

Then, however, I had a brainwave. I offered to teach her the Banishing Ritual of the Hexagram, intimating it as the kind of cute thing that couples do – something to bring us together, and so forth. Being an actual magical woman, my beloved was the only woman in the whole world on whom I could have used this line and have a hope in hell of it working : which it did. As it happened, I took the opportunity to cast both the LBRP and LBRH around us : the atmosphere noticeably lifted as the residual negative energy got banished from our environment, leaving the whole place feeling fresher and lighter.

My work there being done, I retired for the evening and did my concluding ritual of the day, feeling a lot better than I had earlier.

Day 88

09 July 2020

I tried that "genius mind" herbal supplement immediately before going to bed to see what effect it would have. In the morning I vaguely recall vivid dreams, but I didn't fully remember them. So perhaps taking the herbal supplement worked, but overall the test produced inconclusive evidence.

I got up at 4.21am for preparation with the Middle Pillar Ritual. My morning ritual went as follows :

"LBRP.

"LBRH.

"Bornless Ritual.

"Conjuration.

"Confession of Sins. Sort of avoided a large argument yesterday but still not perfect. It is a continual learning process. I pray that my HGA guide me into saying and doing the right thing.

"Thought : the fact that I have had arguments with my fiancée up to now was my fault because I chose to go out with her in the first place, to drag her into my life. She is my karma ; therefore I pray that I have the strength to deal with it properly - to treat her in the proper manner.

"Concentrating on my HGA - feeling the stillness ...

"Licence to Depart.

"LBRP.

"LBRH.

"Total time not including preparation : 1 hour 7 minutes.

"The fact that I keep mentioning my troubles with A indicates it's not getting better... Yet. I ought to be able to knock this on the head - perhaps by casting a spell on myself ..."

*

Today I investigated Psalm 33 :4, associated with Vasariah, the 32nd Shem Ha Mephoresh angel.

I found more masonic treasure in the Wilmshurst trove than I first realised. Apparently, Wilmshurst expected all members of his lodge to have a daily spiritual practice consisting of Masonically themed personal rituals which he prescribed : not just for their individual benefit, but also to strengthen and maintain the egregore of the lodge as much as during the time they spent *physically* apart from it as when they met together. I and other members of my mother lodge had wanted material like this for some time.

Later that evening, I tried an experiment. Being fed up with having to worry about my bowels early in the morning, I deliberately drank caffeine late at night to encourage elimination before I went to bed. In addition to the effect I hoped it would have the following morning, I hoped it would also encourage dream-work.

My fiancée had calmed down a great deal during the day. Perhaps it helped that I deliberately made an effort to avoid anything provocative. Relations between us seemed to improve a lot that day, so it came as a welcome relief when sleeping together after my final ritual that evening.

Day 89

10 July 2020

U p at 4.22am for preparation with the Middle Pillar Ritual. Feeling better today. I noted down my main morning ceremony as follows :
     "LBRP.

"LBRH.

"Bornless Ritual.

"Conjuration.

"Confession of Sins. Thanking God and my HGA for the grace which solves my problems.

"Distracting thoughts - less than perfection - hence sinful. The Kernel of Goodness is that my nephesh wants happy thoughts with which to engage. So let it engage with happy thoughts of successful meditation !

"Concentrating on my HGA. Stillness. Better.

"Licence to Depart.

"LBRP.

"LBRH.

"Total time (not including preparation) : 57 minutes."

*

Later : investigating Psalm 94 :11, which is associated with Iehuiah (33rd Shem Ha Mephoresh angel).

Generally speaking I felt positive all day. I wrote in my journal :

"I feel I am better able to control the arguments situation, thanks to my HGA, but it is still the case that my fiancée gets into a tetchy mood whenever she starts thinking about her thesis.

"Evening ritual accomplished. Meditating intensely on being a lucid dreamer."

Day 90

11 July 2020

My attempts at lucid dreaming again proved inconclusive. I did not get much sleep : the only dream I managed to record involved someone telling me "... *Because I smell.*"

Up at 4.23am for preparation with the Middle Pillar Ritual as usual : then my main ritual :

*"**LBRP**.*

*"**LBRH**.*

*"**Bornless Ritual**. Being worried by obsessive thoughts - actually some random thought that keeps cropping up, which is just distracting me from my higher self - I expel it from my aura and do an extra LBRP at it.*

*"**Conjuration**.*

*"**Confession of Sins**. Allowing myself to be distracted by obsessing thoughts is Sinful - because it is less than perfection - but by the grace of God and the intercession of my HGA, it is something I can solve and overcome.*

"So indeed are all supposed problems with which I am faced : I am grateful to God and my HGA for the ability to overcome.

"As I meditate more, I feel my mind relaxing, releasing from my problems, and more and more able to concentrate on my HGA. I am able to perceive the beneficial, transmuting effects that my HGA has on me.

"Successful meditation causes shit to be stirred up. Hence : I should be prepared for this shit in order to be able to succeed in meditation. Also, I must remember that the healing process is not necessarily immediate, but happens over time - I must prepare myself for the long haul, and have Faith that the act of continually invoking my HGA will work - and it does work.

*"**Licence to Depart**.*

*"**LBRP**.*

*"**LBRH**.*

"Total time : 1 hour."

*

Investigating Psalm 131 :3, associated with Lehahiah (34th Shem Ha Mephoresh angel).

My fiancée believed that a discarnate spirit hung around her, and had done so for many years : it manifested its presence by occasionally poking her, on random parts of the body, once a day or once every couple of days. It did not do any harm, or indeed anything else at all : but the fact that she kept being touched at all caused her a great deal of concern.

Banishing seemed to do nothing : the fact that it seemed to manifest within a sacred circle once made my fiancée think that the LBRP wasn't powerful at all. I, however, theorised that one could explain the "Toucher" more likely not as a separate spirit at all, but as a part of her herself : hence, it manifested in the sacred circle because she brought it in with her, and one couldn't banish it without banishing her as well.

My fiancée did not like this theory, as it implicitly reduced a sinister and mysterious (and hence exciting) Entity to a psychosomatic condition. I tried to placate her, but to no immediate avail. Eventually, however, I came up with a plan which mollified her : I would examine this "Toucher" magically. This I did by astrally projecting and examining her with the aid of a good friend of mine, "Y.," a Mercurial spirit guide whom I had first contacted several years ago and with whom I had worked several times in the past. We established that, notwithstanding the technical explanation, the Toucher was "real-enough" and if so treated would act accordingly. Y. and I further established specifics as to why this kept happening and what caused it.

I have deliberately left out details here : I figured that, if a healer ought to maintain confidence with their patient, then I had an even greater responsibility of confidentiality, given that I did this not for a patient but for the woman I love. Suffice to say, in order to give sense to an unresolved "psychic wound" to her etheric body which she did not consciously understand, her unconscious mind had reified it as this Entity called "the Toucher." Dealing with it, however, would prove relatively simple : establish its name (e.g. By Ouija board or something similar), conjure it and bind it to co-operate with her conscious Self – this would lead to a natural healing effect.

Y. also told me to make the story sound fantastic – if I tried to sound sensible it might offend her or make her disinterested in co-operating. I suppose he meant that in order to deal with other people, one ought not to reject Charlatanry outright, but learn how to put it in service to genuine magic. The successful magician needs to be part Gandalf and part P T Barnum.

At the conclusion of my session I thanked Y. who left : I returned to my body and made the sign of silence.

(Ironically : after going through this "healing" my fiancée felt a strong urge to quit smoking, whereupon "the Toucher" disappeared of its own accord. I believe that although the phenomenon technically had a scientific explanation, by treating it as if it *were* magic, we enabled the discovery of the scientific explanation.)

The whole session made me think : perhaps the key to good Astral Projection comes from visualising oneself in one's astral vehicle, and then to make Samyama thereon, so as to achieve a full (immersive) astral experience ?

(Quite separately the evening ended on a sour note as we got into a disagreement over something else entirely : I try to explain my theory of good-and-evil using the example of the Qlippoth, but she refused to listen to it. I think the idea that the Golden Dawn acknowledges their existence at all horrified her, as apparently BOTA protects its members by not mentioning them. I however had an idea that although one could view the Qlippoth as unpleasant they are not as terrifying as many people suppose... But it would have proved fruitless to press the point. I tactfully excused myself, so I could go and do my evening ritual.)

Day 91

12 July 2020

I got up at 4.24am for my usual Middle Pillar Ritual, and then launched into the main event :

"*LBRP.*

"*LBRH.*

"*Bornless Ritual. An idea occurs how to rid myself of distracting thoughts. Instead of letting my mind think of thoughts which are not to purpose, force it to echo that upon which I am concentrating on that particular moment. In this way I am making use of my mind's tendency to wander but making it wander towards the place I am going anyway, instead of wandering-off.*

"*Conjuration.*

"*Confession of Sins. The idea I had in the middle of the Bornless Ritual is the solution to the 'obsessive' tendency I identified during yesterday's morning-ritual. Hence, when I asked my HGA to solve this problem, my HGA came through and delivered ! I thank God and my HGA for doing this !*

"*My continued tendency to get into arguments is a big no-no. I realise : I take the bait, as it were, because I feel my ego is threatened. However if my ego were not threatened, I would not take the bait. Hence : without realising it I had fallen into an inferiority complex myself ! The solution, I realise, is to remind myself :* 'I speak from a position of self-confidence, security and superiority, and I thank my Holy Guardian Angel for transforming me in this manner.'

"*Hence, my reminding myself that I am not inferior and my ego is not threatened, I ought to be able to rise above any provocation. Meditating on this affirmation brings peace - the presence of my HGA.*

"*Licence to Depart.*

"*LBRP.*

"*LBRH.*

"*Total time not including preparation : 1 hour 10 minutes.*"

*

After catching some Zzzs, we got up and went for breakfast at a café run by the local Buddhist centre. We mainly did it to celebrate the partial easing of lockdown restrictions. The place lay right on a busy road, but they had made a covered ornamental seating area out of their back-yard, which provided an oasis of calm. I had assumed they would have served only vegetarian food although there did seem to have some animal products on the menu : nevertheless I restricted myself to a breakfast baguette with avocado and vegan bacon.

My fiancée had a large slice of cake – which improved her spirits no end.

That afternoon, I spent time investigating Psalm 116 :1, associated with Kavaqiah, the 35th angel of the Shem Ha Mephoresh – of whom it is said :

"This angel rules over testaments, successions and all amiable distributions ; he supports peace and harmony in families."[156]

Afterwards, we had a ZOOM meeting for members of our GD temple in which we did the Middle Pillar ritual, and sent out healing, etc.

I noticed that I and my fiancée's relations improved generally today. It only occurred to me much later that perhaps Kavaqiah had worked his wonders without me realising !

Evening ritual accomplished.

---

[156] LENAIN (2020), p74.

Day 92

13 July 2020

My early morning Middle Pillar Ritual went remarkably well that particular day. I went into my main ritual feeling especially positive.
"*LBRP.*

"*LBRH.*

"**Bornless Ritual**. *I am attuning myself to pre-existing, ancient Energies. Better than yesterday ...*

"**Conjuration**.

"**Confession of Sins**. *Thanking God and HGA for improvement in relations with my fiancée. Realisation of affirming that I am speaking from self-confidence etc did have an effect - my HGA did indeed come through. I can detach myself from negative mental patterns as easily as giving up smoking. I.e. As easily as I believe giving up smoking is according to my experience!*"

NB : I should explain : as a teenager / young man, I smoked regularly averaging about ten a day or more if I went out clubbing in the evening : this went on for eight years. I quit eventually at the same time I started a new fitness regime, involving taking up Iyengar Yoga. *Pranayama,* the control of the life force through breathing, having such an important place in the practice, it seemed obvious to me that having a healthy pair of lungs went as a *sine qua non.* So I quit, going cold turkey : I experienced some side-effects such as expectorating a lot of phlegm as my lungs cleared, but this lasted no longer than a few days.

However, to beat the more serious problems of psychological dependency, I hit upon an unconventional solution : I actively used my new yoga practice to take my mind off the cigarettes. I would think nothing of doing at least two hours' practice of asana and pranayama every day, in addition to meditation. I actually became very proficient at it – at one point I even considered training as a yoga teacher, although this did not come to pass.

In effect, I had quit smoking by replacing an addiction to something unhealthy with an addiction to something healthy – and I felt proud to have done so. I considered it – and I still do – as one of the most sensible decisions I had taken in my entire life. I had no illusions as to what I had done. Indeed, if people came up to me wanting advice on how to quit smoking, I would give them my testimony and suggest that they themselves could use the idea of achieving excellence as a practitioner of yoga, tai chi, jogging, or whatever fitness regime they preferred, as motivation to help them give up.

This of course did not actually work in many of the cases, because they found the idea of breaking a sweat anathema. Either that or they could not relate to the concept of *enjoying* being fit : and as to the benefits of meditation, I could just as well be talking *Sanskrit*.

Hence : I firmly believe that although some people may find giving up smoking difficult, *it can be done*. I have almost forgotten what it is like to smoke : it certainly doesn't occupy my day-to-day thoughts. I identify as a non-smoker, as it were.

Unfortunately, this subject proved delicate in my household, as my fiancée still smoked regularly. She disagreed with me entirely about quitting being easy (or indeed possible). Ironically I didn't even try to get her to quit, she had done that continuously of her own volition for over twenty years. She therefore claimed greater expertise in the subject : she had more experience, as she had quit many times, but I had done so only once.

Recently, however, she had resolved to get on a health kick, and suggested it would do us good to go out walking of an evening, as a change to sitting in front of the TV and watching *Netflix*.

Anyway : back to my contemplations that morning :

"Harbouring resentment against other people apart from my fiancée is also a sin, but the solution is really the same - to realise that I speak from a position of security, etc. I should make that my constant mantra.

"If I am responsible for my fiancée's karma, does that mean my HGA can help resolve hers as well as mine ? Thinking about the karma of my past lives ...

"Concentrating on my HGA. Stillness.

"LBRP.

"LBRH.

"Total time not including preparation : 57 minutes. End was rushed due to feeling the need to eliminate. Not taking steps to ensure this is not a problem is a Sin to confess tomorrow. Thought : perhaps take my fiancée up on her offer of going out for a walk this evening ?

"Thought #2 : Making Samyama *on everything which I attempt to invoke definitely strengthens the power of the invocation. I ought to adopt this practice as a general rule."*

*

Later : researching Psalm 26 :8, associated with Menadel, the 36th Shem Ha Mephoresh angel. Lenain says :

"This angel is invoked to retain one's employment, and to preserve the means of existence which one enjoys..."[157]

Then, just a short while after I had been meditating on this versicle, my fiancée texted me to say she had got a job interview - her first in several months. Just in case Menadel did assist with this, I paid public tribute to him on social media.

I noted my relations with my fiancée improving during the day : I believe the prospect of a new job had contributed greatly to her improved mood. As it happened, she herself did not want to go out for a walk this evening, claiming tiredness and wanting to watch *Netflix* instead. I resolved to be proactive in insisting the following evening.

I performed my Evening ritual, and turned in, feeling very tired.

---

[157] Op. cit. p75.

Day 93

14 July 2020

During the night : I dreamed I attended a meeting of the inner order of the Golden Dawn in America, where I alone amongst all the Adepti stood up to the Greatly Honoured Chief. I had nothing against him in real life, so I presume it indicated my desire to take control of my life, or something like that.

I got up at 4.26am for my usual Middle Pillar Ritual. My bowels temporarily called me out of my oratory, but at least I had got it over with in time for my main morning ritual, so it didn't distract me like the previous day. As I noted afterwards :

*"**LBRP**.*

*"**LBRH**. I visualise myself as the man in the Flammarion engraving, poking his head out of the boundary of the Universe, when I get to vibrate ARARITA in each direction.*

*"**Bornless Ritual**.*

*"**Conjuration**.*

*"**Confession of Sins**. Perhaps, to get an idea of what sins I myself should confess, I should make a note of what I criticise in others ? In case I am projecting, etc.*

"Concentrating on the stillness.

*"**Licence to Depart**.*

*"**LBRP**.*

*"**LBRH**.*

"Total time not including preparation : 1 hour 11 minutes."

*

When I got back to bed, my fiancée's excitement at having a new job had only increased since yesterday : so much so, that she felt in the mood for "rejoicing." I happily obliged her.

During the day, I investigated Psalm 80 :8, associated with Aniel, the 37th angel of the Shem Ha Mephoresh. Lenain said that Aniel "*reveals the secrets of nature and inspires wise philosophers with their meditations.*"[158] I concluded that the *gematria* of the versicle in question inspired this function ; whereas the Magical Use of Psalms describes the same versicle as helping to overcome plots against

---

[158] Op. cit. p75.

oneself, and saving oneself from grievous error. In any event my meditations upon Aniel felt very rewarding today.

Later : I received my copy of David Goddard's "Sacred Magic of the Angels,"[159] which I had supposedly "won."[160] As I already had a copy of the first edition of this book, I thought I could have a wizard-wheeze by spending some time comparing the two versions. However, the more I did so, the more my horror grew. Apart from Goddard appearing to have dumbed the text down, the biggest change in the new edition consisted of him deliberately downplaying the significance of Madeline Montalban in the development of this style of Angel Magick. In fact, he had done a complete one-eighty : the first edition praised her, but the latest edition dismissed her importance almost entirely. I suspected that politics or ego games lurked in the sub-text. But, worst of all, I couldn't post a review on my blog or Amazon saying what I really thought of the book, as David Goddard *now knew where I lived.* Fuck.

Evening ritual accomplished.

---

[159] GODDARD (2019)
[160] See : day 86 *(vide supra).*

Day 94

15 July 2020

During the night, I dreamt of myself in a vineyard, of all places, making a career as a vintner. I had never visited a vineyard in real-life, nor thought of changing career in such a manner. Several sources describe this as a good omen : it denotes *"favourable speculations and auspicious love-making,"* or the *"promise of happiness and prosperity for endurance and hard work,"* i.e. the success of my Abramelin operation. Or, of course, it might have derived from red wine's pre-eminence as my favourite tipple to go with my evening meal.

In any event, I got up at 4.28am for preparation with the Middle Pillar Ritual. This morning I tried doing it in the Astral. My Solar Body felt like a separate being, meditating upon itself - it just so happened that my consciousness stayed there as a guest. I found it a curiously powerful experience. This, added to remarks on Day 90 (i.e. about visualising oneself in one's astral vehicle and making Samyama thereon), strengthened my Astral Projection practice.

I noted down my main ritual as follows :

"**LBRP**.

"**LBRH**.

"**Bornless Ritual**. *This I do in the Astral as well. Whilst physically sitting in padmasana I place my consciousness in my Solar Body. It is as if I am bilocating. Ritual is good.*

"**Conjuration**.

"**Confession of Sins**. *Allowing myself to become distracted is a constant niggle. In fact, everything about me that is not perfect is technically a Sin. Hence I will always be a sinner whilst I am not perfect, which is united with God.*

"But what would perfection actually be like ? I attempt to do what I have always theorised the Hermetic path is ultimately about. In my Solar Body, I rise on the planes until I break through the last barrier at the outer edge of the cosmos, and concentrate on merging / uniting with the actual God. Interesting, but I am too distracted by the sensations of my physical body to fully appreciate the experience (i.e. A Sin !).

"However : it occurs to me that assuming this is a real phenomenon, there must have been great sages in the past or existing now who have already achieved it. I should go to seek them out, e.g. By historical and scholarly research. (I return to my physical body and normal consciousness).

"**Licence to Depart**.

"**LBRP**.

"LBRH.

"Total time not including preparation : 1 hour 6 minutes."

*

Most of the rest of the day passed uneventfully, apart from answering a question on Quora "Do co-masons get to date other members of the lodge ?" (answer : yes if they were single ; but in practice most of them joined because it was something to do with their significant other together – so most of them are already taken).

I spent time researching Psalm 91 :9, associated with Haamiah (38th Shem Ha Mephoresh angel). A fun fact I discovered : the word "Tav" (i.e., the name of the twenty-second letter of the Hebrew alphabet, literally a "cross"), equates (by Gematria) to "Atah," ("thou art,") the first word of the Qabalistic *Cross.* It occurred to me that "Atah" was a divine name : for if God refers to Himself in the first person as "Eheieh," and is referred to in the third person as "YHVH," logically one would speak to Him in the second person as "You are who you are." God must find it weird to have a name which actually *conjugates.*

Evening ritual accomplished.

Day 95

16 July 2020

That night, alchemical images filled my dreams – the phrase "Dreams : the Alchemy of Thought itself" cropped up significantly. Actually it would have surprised me more if I had *not* dreamed about Alchemy. I had, after all thought long about my Solar Body the previous day, and one could view the whole Abramelin operation as alchemical in a metaphorical sense. What with my interests, at any given time I might have alchemy on my mind, even if I weren't concerned with this operation.

I got up at 4.28am for preparation with Middle Pillar Ritual : as yesterday, done in the Astral. "*Good,*" I thought, "*makes me want to spend more time in the astral doing things, going places ...*"

My main ritual of the morning then went as follows :

"LBRP.

"LBRH.

"Bornless Ritual - *done in astral.*

"Conjuration.

"Confession of Sins. *The fact that God is infinite whilst I am finite means that by default I fall short of perfection, and hence a sinner. Allowing myself to become distracted, not practising meditation or astral projection (etc) to a perfect degree - all sins to be confessed to God and my HGA.*

"*An idea regarding how I might improve my relationship to the Shem Ha Mephoresh angels. Throughout the Lenain (Ambelain) text reference is made to different, foreign, names of God which up to now I have been ignoring. But what if they are important ? If so - that is a concrete example of a sin, in that I have been failing to do something which might better lead to perfection. I should start incorporating them into my daily meditations.*

"*Actually, it occurs to me that yesterday I concluded I should seek out exemplars of Hermetic ascent. However, because I was very busy at work (i.e. I allowed myself to become busy) I didn't get round to doing so. An actual sin ! Giving thought to it now, I can think of (off the top of my head) : Jesus ; Enoch ; Elijah ; probably Plotinus and Iamblichus.*"

It occurred to me afterwards as I wrote my journal up that I should have included - and hence should include tomorrow - Christian Rosenkreutz - as after all, I do belong to the Rosicrucian current.

"*I concentrate on the stillness of my HGA's presence ...*

"Licence to Depart.

"LBRP.

"LBRH.

"Total time not including preparation : 1 hour 2 minutes."

*

Later, over breakfast, the conversation with my fiancée hit an out-of-tune note : it didn't help that we had gotten into a discussion on Freemasonry, with which she had a strained relationship despite being a co-mason herself. I forget what point I wanted to make – probably something quite trivial in the great scheme of things. However, my fiancée seemed to think that because I disagreed with her over an issue that I meant it personally against her. At this point I should have set a guard upon my lips and risen above the obvious provocation. Instead, I foolishly accused her of upsetting me, which in turn upset her, whereupon the whole thing degenerated. I left for work, feeling angry and frustrated that I had an unresolved issue behind me.

I calmed down later when I forced myself to research Psalm 30 :11, associated with Rehanghael (39th Shem Ha Mephoresh angel), as part of my daily scriptural study. Although Lenain's description of the angel does not mention this, the Magical Use of Psalms associates Psalm 30 itself with Patience, and Gratitude for blessings. I did not regard it as a coincidence that meditating on this versicle and on this angel helped process the regret I felt over my part in exacerbating my fiancée's reaction this morning, and moved me to both forgive her and seek forgiveness.

When I walked through the door that evening (bearing flowers), I found that Rehanghael had already worked his wonders on my fiancée, as her own mood had improved considerably during the day. By coincidence, a present I had bought for her on Amazon (a copy of Damien Echol's new book) had also arrived. (I briefly leafed through it – it featured material on the Shem Ha Mephoresh angels as well).[161]

We consolidated our reconciliation by practising some "bed-time yoga," i.e., following a video on YouTube. [162] I perceived that pre-conceptions of Freemasonry, which I did not recognise, still upset her, but this time I kept a lid on my thoughts on the matter : so at least I had learnt something from this morning – all thanks to my HGA.

Evening ritual accomplished.

---

[161] ECHOLS (2020)

[162] "Yoga with Adriene" (2019) "Wind Down Yoga - 12 Minute Bedtime Yoga - Yoga with Adriene," https ://www.youtube.com/watch ?v=BiWDsfZ3zbo accessed 2021-06-15

Day 96

17 July 2020

I lay on the floor of my oratory, visualising my astral body as a simulacrum standing next to me. It was 4.30am in the morning. Relaxing completely, I placed my consciousness into my astral vehicle, and performed the Middle Pillar Ritual.

Then, I returned to my physical body, as it were, and began my main ritual.

"*LBRP*.

"*LBRH*.

"*Bornless Ritual*. *Done in astral. This is intense - I can really feel the power flowing into my Body of Light as I do this. Idea of trying to make Sanyama on everything which I invoke is definitely a good idea.*

"*Conjuration*.

"*Confession of Sins*. *Contemplating my inherently sinful nature based on the fact that God is Infinite, I am finite, hence whilst I am not God I inevitably fall short of protection. Nevertheless, I trust in God's grace, and in my HGA's ability to help me improve myself.*

"*Contemplating Christian ROSENKREUTZ which I identified as something I should have done yesterday !*

"*Contemplating* Sanyama *on* samadhi *itself. Profound. Willing that my HGA guide me aright today.*

"*Licence to Depart*.

"*LBRP*.

"*LBRH*.

"*Total time not including preparation : 1 hour 3 minutes.*"

*

I may have asked my Holy Guardian Angel to *guide me aright today,* but this manifested in the form of maintaining my integrity in the face of challenge from my fiancée. When at breakfast she started talking about Qabalistic doctrines of sexual polarity – an advanced BOTA lesson – I became uncomfortable. I thought : "*We already have a sex-life. But if she keeps going on about these sexual teachings, she is implying she doesn't like sex the way it is.*" I suppose I felt insecure. It didn't help that BOTA had some queer notions about not having orgasms (I'm paraphrasing mightily here). I on the other hand thought how much a privilege it felt to have sex at all, and I rather liked my orgasms, thank you very much.

Yet still, I wondered : how can any sex-magick teachers put across their teachings without offending people ? They base their whole teaching method on telling their disciples *"Your sex-life isn't good enough : change it !"* The only people I could imagine who would fall for such a line would have to have such low self-esteem they did not care. I could not help but think of all the nasty cults in history that have tried to maintain slavish obedience in their followers by trying to dictate their sex-lives – although BOTA does not have the organisational set-up to function as a cult *per se.*

When my fiancée finally noticed the look on my face, she asked whether I didn't like the subject. I remained silent, trying to avoid an argument, but she persisted implying that it would not hurt her feelings if I said no. *This proved a flagrant lie.* Foolishly, I said no, and she immediately became upset, wailing about how we could never live as a magical couple.

I immediately took steps to convince her of the opposite. I tried to calm her down by saying that we could practice her sexual polarity teachings this very evening if she wanted to. I tried re-framing the whole matter in my mind as looking upon BOTA's teachings as some sort of kink that one might try out for the sake of novelty – like bondage or sodomy, but with tarot cards. Obviously I did not say that out-loud : instead I managed to reassure her as best I could, and then made my escape from the house to go to work.

During the day : I spent time researching Psalm 88 :15, associated with Ieiazel, the 40th Shem Ha Mephoresh angel. *"This Psalm has marvellous properties,"* Lenain said, *"it serves to deliver prisoners, give consolation and to be delivered from one's enemies."* [163] The Magical Use of Psalms, however, phrased this differently : it helps *"reconcile estranged lovers."*

Although I did not fully appreciate Ieiazel's influence at the time, when I returned home, I had a flash of intuition as to the real reason behind this morning's disagreement. It was not just me who felt insecure : in her own way, my fiancée did as well. She revealed she felt stress about her portal thesis, which she was intent on finishing. Actually she had already done more than enough for her thesis : she stressed herself unnecessarily.

I realised : her early behaviour had been a cry for help in not so many words. I instinctively tried to encourage her : "All you have to do is not worry about the right or wrong answer, but ask yourself : 'Have I written the Truth ?'" I told her. "And if you have, then job done - end of." Despite this, she appeared not wholly convinced : I suppose that even despite being a magician, that level of stress is not something that one can just *conjure away.*

---

[163] LENAIN (2020) p78.

In evening, we watched a film about demons on Netflix, which prompted her to expound forth her views on the subject in general, and the role of God as Creator of the Universe in particular. Apparently her bad experience with Sunday School as a child had queered her appreciation of the Book of Genesis. Which struck me as fair enough : I rather think everyone who comes to the Occult does so seeking a remedy for religion. However, I perceive that within the Occult exist two distinct approaches to *finding* this "remedy" : on the one hand there is one approach says, "don't believe in religion at all" ; whilst on the other, one has something like the Hermetic qabalah, which basically says "take consolation that religion doesn't mean what conventional religionists *think* it means."

So for example : let us imagine that one has an aversion to the Book of Genesis, or any part of the Bible for that matter. The Hermetic Qabalah effectively says : "work with what you hate, but neutralise your feelings by realising its hidden value." In that sense the rationale is similar to that of Shadow-work, or conjuring demons in Ceremonial Magick in general – and *Abramelin* in particular for that matter. *Don't fear demons, learn to work with them responsibly.* Don't fear religion – learn how to *use* it for occult purposes.

However, when I tried to explain my theory that an occultist should treat their fear of religion like a ceremonial magician treats a demon, my fiancée did not immediately appreciate my gist. I perceived she had too much personally invested in her beliefs, so I made my excuses and left the room. After I came back from having got a drink of water in the kitchen, I found her still going on about her point of view, not realising that for the past several minutes I was out of earshot in another part of the house. Actually I think I did well in trying to avoid yet another argument as best I could.

I accomplished my Evening ritual. Later, when I got into bed, Ieiazel's influence had finally kicked in, and we celebrated our reconciliation (by definitely *not* following any BOTA teachings on this occasion).

Day 97

18 July 2020

U p at 4.32am for preparation : mostly deep relaxation, with some contemplation of the Middle Pillar whilst in the astral. Actually the deep relaxation seemed go very well - I made a note to invest more effort in this in the future.

My main ritual of the morning went as follows :

"**LBRP**.

"**LBRH**.

"**Bornless Ritual**. *This time done mostly in physical.*

"**Conjuration**.

"**Confession of Sins**. *Contemplating the Infinity of God in contrast to the Finite Nature of myself. Thanking God and my HGA respectively for the Grace of Salvation and the wherewithal to improve myself as best I can.*

"*Withdrawing from anger is still something I have not yet mastered. Although arguing with my fiancée is the latest manifestation, with insight I see the problem as being more deeper rooted - going back years. I trust that by progressing to a more advanced state I should be able to, quite naturally, slough off old forms of behaviour.*

"*It occurs to me that this Anger is power which can fuel my 'Evil Persona' and hence me. A Thought : what would happen if I visualised 'IAO' at various points up and down my spine (e.g. Chakras) ? Similar to J B Kerning.*

"*Meditating ...*

"**Licence to Depart**.

"**LBRP**.

"**LBRH**.

"*Total time not including preparation : 58 minutes (rushed towards end because of wanting to eliminate).*"

*

During the day, for my scriptural study I investigated Psalm 120 :2, associated with Hahahel (41st Shem Ha Mephoresh angel), only to quickly realise I had already done so some time previously – i.e., when I had previously investigated Pahaliah (the 20th angel). Both the English translation of Ambelain's text and Lenain itself repeated the incongruity. However : Damon Brand had used another versicle in relation to Pahaliah : Psalm 116 :4.[164]

---

[164] BRAND (2016).

Which, if either, was right ? I tried searching through my collection of magical books to see if I had an independent source for the Shem Ha Mephoresh versicles, and realised I had an ebook from the Rose Croix D'Orient, which stated : the 20th versicle (i.e. that of Pahaliah) was indeed Psalm 116 :4, and the 41st was Psalm 120 :2.[165]

I therefore meditated on *two* angels today : i.e. in addition to Hahahel, I went back and thoroughly investigated Psalm 116 :4, and amended Pahaliah's details in my personal Shem Ha Mephoresh grimoire. I wondered : given that Lenain had confused the biblical verse for these two angels, did he confuse anything else he said about them ? On a more positive note, it gave me renewed respect for Brand's book. I had previously considered that he had drawn out the thaumaturgical aspects of the angels, and downplayed the theurgic ones, in order to make his book more commercial. Now however, although my assessment may have had some truth to it, at least he had demonstrated he had done some proper research and not just slavishly followed Lenain, as Ambelain had done.

*

Later, my fiancée expressed concerned about Co-Masonry, i.e. can a woman *really* become a Freemason given that the central myth concerns a man, i.e. Hiram Abiff ? I myself held the opinion that the journey of the candidate through the Craft degrees tells neither a man's story, nor a woman's story, but a *human* story, because it represents a predicament which every human being potentially faces, irrespective of gender.

Take, for example, the ritual of the third degree (Master Mason). For me it narrates how one could interpret the dilemma faced by Hiram Abiff as a metaphor for how each of us would react when facing the most important decision ever in our life. Does one choose bravery and honour – even if it means risking death - or cowardice and betrayal ?

Each individual can then take this metaphor and interpret it in terms which make sense to him- or herself. Hence, a woman (e.g., a mother) could say : "*Well, the most important decision I could ever make in my life would be one regarding my children, so the Third degree is telling me to remain true to my deepest principles no matter what the cost to myself.*"

However, another person could take the same story and interpret it in the way that makes most sense to them. A member of the armed forces might see it as a metaphor for risking one's life for one's country ; a firefighter might think in terms of being brave enough to enter a burning-building ; an artist, in terms of

---

[165] POLYCHRONIS (2008) p237, 239.

maintaining his or her integrity ; or a campaigner for justice attempting to manifest the cause in which he or she believes.

Hence by liberal use of the power of metaphor, one can argue that yes, Freemasonry is for everybody, both men *and* women, because *everybody* is able to make use of its symbolism in ways which are relevant to themselves.

This did not entirely convince my fiancée, as for her the gender of Hiram Abiff proved a stumbling block. I perceived that pressing the point would turn out fruitless : after all, if everybody can interpret the meaning of Freemasonry for themselves, then ironically that meant my fiancée could do so in a way that disagreed with *me*.

As it happened, I fell asleep on the sofa after we had come in from a rare pub visit that evening : I only woke up to prepare for my evening ritual past midnight. Yet nevertheless I completed it : I got to bed about 1 AM.

Day 98

19 July 2020

Up at 4.33am for preparation in a manner similar to yesterday. I had worked out the time of Sunrise as 5.03am : although technically I started my main morning ritual six minutes late, owing to a need to eliminate. I consoled myself that at least, having done so, nothing would disturb my ritual further.

"*LBRP*.

"*LBRH*.

"**Bornless Ritual** - *done in astral. Powerful !*

"**Conjuration**.

"**Confession of Sins**. *The reason I can't get out of arguments easily is that when faced with a situation like this, my instinct is not to avoid arguments but to argue well- which I believe to be a good thing, and hence I find it difficult to change my instinctual behaviour.*

"*There was however one definite no-no I should have avoided - at least one point yesterday I reacted from a place of insecurity / inferiority. I recall to mind what I said a week ago about affirming that I am superior, self-confident and secure.*

"*In attempting to commune with my HGA, I intuitively receive the message : Don't give up whilst there are still steps you are yet to take. Remove obvious obstacles to happiness, e.g. A's thesis. Hence my HGA has come to me like Socrates' Dæmon, turning up to prevent him making a wrong decision.*

"*I meditate on the presence of my HGA - I can feel the stillness. Gratitude.*

"**Licence to Depart**.

"*LBRP*.

"*LBRH*.

"*Total time not including preparation / lateness of starting : 1 hour 16 minutes (probably due to length of meditation during the 'Confession' part)."*

*

After catching some Zzz, I spent the morning investigating Psalm 121 :7, associated with Mikael, the 42nd Shem Ha Mephoresh angel. Interestingly, the word translated in the KJV as "evil" in the phrase "*The Lord shall preserve thee from evil*" actually means "*the Enemy.*" I presume the translator deliberately toned down a potential reference to the Devil. In any case, meditating on Mikael and the corresponding versicle felt good, as if confirming the angel's presence.

However, for the main event of the day we had a ZOOM meeting with the Greatly Honoured Chiefs, and approximately 100 members of the Golden Dawn. By "coincidence," I had manifested a present for her, a "Tree of Life" pendant. It actually consisted of a regular tree-design, although its makers had called it a "Tree of Life" I presume for marketing purposes. Nevertheless she saw the fact that it had arrived on the same day as this Golden Dawn meeting as potent synchronicity, and made a point of wearing it for the first time whilst we sat in on the ZOOM call.

Because we had to accommodate people joining from potentially all the time-zones of continental America *and* Great Britain, it took place at during early to late evening for us, forcing us to bolt down some dinner in front of the computer during a break in proceedings. Nevertheless, I found it very exciting to finally meet a whole load of people many of whom had only previously existed for me as "Facebook Friends." It especially impressed my fiancée, not only to meet the Greatly Honoured Chiefs herself, but also the fact that I knew them as well : so much so, that she behaved in a better than usual mood for intimacy with me after I finally completed my evening ritual at the very end of the day that day.

Day 99

20 July 2020

During the night I dreamt vividly of being with the Adepti of the Golden Dawn. Clearly yesterday's ZOOM meeting had made a great impression on me. Indeed, when I got up to do the Middle Pillar ritual (which I did in the astral), I felt thrilled by the whole encounter. The opportunity to connect and re-connect with so many of my peers had a revivifying effect on me. I wondered : I may have felt excited from yesterday, but would it excite me too much to concentrate ?

In any event, I noted down my morning ritual as follows :

"LBRP.

"LBRH.

"Bornless Ritual.

"Conjuration.

"Confession of Sins. Concentrating on pride, ego inflation, etc. If it be a Qlippah, at its core is a desire to want to do the G.W., to want to achieve KCHGA, to want to help others achieve their spiritual aspirations. Hence, although it is a distraction, it is born from purely worthy motives.

"By meditating on my HGA, I can find a deep sense of stillness - feeling the parts of my being alchemically transmuted. I can console myself that what I thought might be a distraction isn't actually distracting if I do indeed concentrate on KCHGA.

"THOUGHT : Kerning - 'IAO' - etc."

I.e., Johann Baptist Kerning (1774 - 1851), a late-eighteenth and early nineteenth century German Rosicrucian, had proposed a system of letter-meditation consisting of mentally placing letters in or on the body. This had included one exercise in one placed which the letters forming "IAO" in the spine. Clearly Kerning had intuited some equivalent to kundalini yoga, although one of his students blamed the practice for leaving him with a spinal injury ever afterwards. Nevertheless, the notion fascinated me. I had not at that point begun to make a serious study of Kerning's work in detail, but because of the importance of "IAO" in both the LBRH and in the Bornless Ritual, I wondered what the result would be if one tried to draw a correlation between them all.

"Licence to Depart.

"LBRP.

"LBRH.

"Total time not including preparation : 1 hour 2 minutes."

*

During the day, I researched Psalm 88 :14, associated with Veauliah, the 43rd Shem Ha Mephoresh angel, and meditated thereon.

My fiancée felt in the mood to celebrate starting her new job, which she had got with the help of the angel Menadel.[166] We therefore went out to a local restaurant which specialised in sea-food. I chose Bouillabaisse, because Marcel Proust had lionised it so much – and because I thought it a novelty to see it on the menu at all in a British restaurant. Note, I had never read any Proust in my life : I just remembered Bouillabaisse as the only memorable thing people actually said about his books.

When we got home, I performed my evening ritual and went to bed.

---

[166] See : Day 92, *supra*.

Day 100

21 July 2020

I had a troubled sleep – I had to get up several times to go to the toilet. Later, after I had awoken for the day, I had recurring digestive problems, albeit of a non-serious nature, throughout the morning. I suspected the Bouillabaisse I had for dinner yesterday must have had something wrong with it : it had caused me a *Remembrance of Things Past* all through the night and most of the day as well.

Nevertheless, I managed to get some REM-sleep as I recorded at least one dream about a girl I had known from years back. According to a dream dictionary I consulted later, it probably indicated my feelings towards women in general – so, by implication, my fiancée in particular – although I couldn't remember any other details.

I got up at 4.34am for preparation with Middle Pillar Ritual, which I did in the astral. I began my main ritual with the LBRP and LBRH… at which point I had the urge to eliminate, my first indication that I might have an opportunity to make a joke about Marcel Proust. I carefully left the sacred space of the 'oratory' for a comfort-break. I made sure I thanked God and my HGA for enabling me to get rid of an influence that could otherwise have distracted me in my subsequent morning rituals. Upon re-entering the Oratory I took some moments to compose myself and re-attune to the energies I had already invoked.

The rest of the session went as follows :

"***Bornless Ritual***. *Done in the astral. Powerful.*

"***Conjuration***.

"***Confession of Sins***. *Contemplating the contrast between the infinity of God and the finite nature of myself. I am thankful to God and my HGA for the grace of being able to surpass my finite nature in spite of myself.*

"*I can feel the presence of my HGA - deep meditation, powerful. Contemplating sublimating the sins of not just me but all for whom I am responsible.*

"***Licence to Depart***.

"***LBRP***.

"***LBRH***.

"*Total time not including preparation : 1 hour 10 minutes.*"

*

Unwillingly and only out of necessity I fasted during the day, whilst remembering to remain properly hydrated. As part of my scriptural study I investigated Psalm

119 :108, which has to do with Ielahiah, the 44th Shem Ha Mephoresh angel –
whom the texts describe as bringing success in a useful enterprise.

Only by late afternoon or early evening did I feel recovered enough to even
think about food. I nevertheless made a deliberate decision to only eat moderately
that night and get to bed early.

When I performed my Evening ritual that night, I practiced a type of Kriya
Yoga but incorporating IAO into the chakras up the spine : my thoughts about
Kerning the previous day had inspired this. I generated so much power, that when
I ended-up in bed I amazed my fiancée with how much I appeared to buzz : "And
there was much *rejoicing.*"

Day 101

22 July 2020

Contrary to how I felt this time the previous day, everything went well from the get-go, I woke up at 4.34am for preparation with the Middle Pillar Ritual (done physically). It felt noticeably better : not only could I feel the energies I invoked, I appreciated not being disturbed by the state of my physical body.

My main ritual went like this :

"LBRP.

"LBRH.

"Bornless Ritual. Done astrally, as yesterday. Powerful.

"Conjuration.

"Confession of Sins. Again contemplating the infinity of God vs the finite nature of myself. I spend time focussing on Gratitude - for God's grace, for sending me my HGA, for helping me to improve my practice, etc. I contemplate resolving the karma of all my past lives even if I am not consciously aware of it.

"Kerning style Kriya Yoga - good. I make Sanyama *on transforming my etheric body into a fohat-sublimating machine. Also trying to incorporate details from actual Kriya yoga to make it authentic. Good - HGA is present.*

"Licence to Depart.

"LBRP.

"LBRH.

"Total time not including preparation : 1 hour 7 minutes. The decision to eat and drink moderately yesterday and to get a good night's sleep has led to a definite improvement in how I feel this morning."

*

For my scriptural study today I investigated Psalm 94 :18, associated with Sealiah (45th Shem Ha Mephoresh angel). Quite separately, I fitted in reading my latest BOTA lesson, and colouring in Key 20, "Judgement."

The co-masonic obedience to which I belonged had decided that, because they were not beholden to the United Grand Lodge of England, they could get away with decisions that would not fly in men-only Masonry : such as conducting Grand Lodge meetings via ZOOM. They had called one for today, mainly to report on what transpired within the organisation. Now a lot of masonic organisations had held *informal* meetings via ZOOM all along : but my co-

Masonic Grand Lodge made a formal event of it, by getting everyone to be suited-and-booted and dressed in all their regalia, sitting in front of their computer.

I went along with it : ZOOM meetings obviously could not substitute for real meetings, but on the other hand it was not magically important enough to *not* conduct it this way – at least, not this particular meeting. The members all missed the opportunity to dress up in their regalia, so it would prove churlish not to indulge them.

A friend of mine once opined that Freemasonry represents the closest a straight man gets to being a Drag Queen, because the thrill of putting on fancy masonic regalia equals the thrill a transvestite gets from putting on a *fabulous* outfit.

I held a supposedly-important position in this Grand Lodge, so I thought I'd better put my face in. My fiancée, however, refused to attend, and even got angry at me for asking her to join me. The bee she had in her bonnet over the matter completely bemused me. I did not think it worth arguing about, as the matter was largely academic, so I dropped the point.

Evening ritual accomplished.

Day 102

23 July 2020

What with the days now noticeably shortening, I became conscious that by timing my rituals *exactly* in relation to sunrise, I would risk not having enough time to go to work. Besides which, in order to do the Middle Pillar justice, *and* attend to my toilet before the ritual (an ever-present concern), I realised I needed to get up earlier. I therefore kept my alarm on 4.34am instead of adjusting it forward each day. My approach seemed to work as the Middle Pillar went well that morning. Having a better night's sleep last night helped as well.

My morning ritual then went thus :

"LBRP.

"LBRH.

"Bornless Ritual. Done astrally ; still powerful.

"Conjuration.

"Confession of Sins. It was wrong of me to get into an argument yesterday. I should not be imposing my views on my fiancée - not if she is so resistant to it.

"Kriya Yoga type meditation - feeling the presence of my HGA - powerful.

"Licence to Depart.

"LBRP.

"LBRH.

"Total time not including preparation : 1 hour 3 minutes."

I realised as I typed my journal up afterwards that, in mentally reviewing the conversation between us yesterday, I had thought of a flaw in her line of reasoning which I hadn't considered the previous day. But then I realised : I should let this go, as it would only prolong or exacerbate arguments. I would not win the argument, by winning the argument, as it were – I ought to remain silent, for the good of our relationship.

This approach did not wholly work. During the day I kept schtum as she started speaking her mind about a subject which triggered her. She had in effect triggered herself without my intervention. I reflected : *"I really need to learn to forgive myself."*

Apart from this, I investigated Psalm 145 :9, associated with Airiel, the 46th Angel of the Shem Ha Mephoresh – an angel one invokes to have revelations. I was gratified to receive anonymous donation to my JustGiving page.

Evening ritual accomplished.

Day 103

24 July 2020

I got up at the same time as I had yesterday for preparation with the Middle Pillar Ritual. This time, I made a magical ritual out of going to the toilet : I willed that as I cast the eliminants out of my body, so did I expel all crossed conditions from my life. The tension and release which accompanies such a movement is a potent form of Gnosis ! Actually it would not surprise me if the Illuminates of Thanateros had already tried out the idea a long time ago. In any event, I thanked God that at least this wouldn't distract me from my main ritual. This went as follows :

   "LBRP.

   "LBRH.

   "Bornless Ritual. Done in astral - still powerful !

   "Conjuration.

   "Confession of Sins. In amongst all the illogicalities etc, [my fiancée] does have one point - being in a relationship with me she has to put up with more than other people do. I ought to show her more compassion for that reason alone.

   "Kerning type Kriya Yoga. Stillness.

   "Licence to Depart.

   "LBRP.

   "LBRH.

   "Total time not including preparation : 1 hour 3 minutes."

*

Later as part of my scriptural study that day, I investigated Psalm 104 :24, which has to do with Asaliah, the 47th Shem Ha Mephoresh angel, who rules those who raise their spirit to the contemplation of divine things.

Apart from this I must have had a slow day that day, because I somehow had time to have a further go at comparing *"Sacred Magic of the Angels"* to its first edition. I realised I had assessed it completely fairly the first time I had attempted to do so. At that moment my fiancée insisted that we go out for a walk to get some fresh air as well as get some shopping in, so I made no more progress with the book.

Evening ritual accomplished.

Day 104

25 July 2020

I felt pressed for time. I tried setting my alarm so that I would wake up thirty five minutes before I ought to start : but I still ended up five minutes late. The Middle Pillar Ritual proved very good this morning. Actually I could have started on time, except for my need to eliminate beforehand so as not to disturb my ritual.

When I did start it went thus :

"LBRP.

"LBRH.

"Bornless Ritual. Done in astral. I make Samyama on that which I invoke in every direction - adding in the aspiration that the divine presence - samadhi - I feel, is merging or uniting with the actual Divine presence, the real God. As before, the whole thing is very powerful.

"Conjuration.

"Confession of Sins. Contemplating Infinity/Perfection (God) vs Finity / Sinfulness (Me). Allowing thoughts to distract myself is a constant niggle.

"Kerning-Kriya Yoga. The spiralling pattern linking the internal stars indicates a progression of consciousness ...

"Concentrating on my HGA. A thought occurs to me : although a physical body is inherently imperfect compared to God, meaning that it was sinful for an infinite being (ME) to seek incarnation in physical form ... What if : it was only originally *sinful- i.e. Subsequent iterations of me were not failures, but deliberate attempts to spiritually progress by re-entering the physical to improve myself?*

"This in effect is a radical re-imagining of why I re-incarnate. Because I have already taken control of my spiritual evolution and am deliberately using each incarnation to improve - to take a further step forward. As opposed to someone who has not realised their destiny, and re-incarnates willy-nilly because they can't help it.

"In effect, what I try to do to my Evil Persona in this present incarnation is what my Causal Body is doing to me generally over the course of multiple incarnations. By the grace of God, I am already on the path.

"Thoughts on Alchemy - need to be developed ...Perhaps through my fiancée going on about the Great Work something has percolated into me ?"

(These thoughts consisted of some musings on Alchemy's relation to the Qabalah. After I had finished the ritual and had typed up my magical record, I spent some time working them out in detail – see below.)

"Licence to Depart.

"LBRP.
"LBRH.
"Total time not including preparation : 1 hour 13 minutes."

"The Secret of Alchemy"

אהיה - EHEIEH - *relating to Kether, but more specifically the "I AM" consciousness which one experiences in the peak of Nirvikalpa Samadhi.*

יהוה - *YHVH, prosaically "the LORD" but more specifically the fundamental formula by which all existence happens ;*

אדני - *ADONAI - which represents the* א *of Eheieh being linked to the* י *of YHVH.*

Hence through "Adonai" one realises that one's own "I AM" nature is linked or united with the Divine Formula of creation.

In the beginning, God formed the Heavens and the Earth - an alternate translation of Genesis 1 :1 as the word for "creation" has the connotation of "forming." Hence, at the beginning only God existed, the only material He had with which to create the Universe consisted of His own Substance. This he did by differentiating His Substance into separate forms - in the first instance, the Heavens and the Earth.

The creation story thus depicts God performing an Alchemical operation on Himself in order to bring the Universe into being.

The Secret of Alchemy, therefore, consists in realising, via the Qabalah, that one may participate in this Creation. The I AM ness is linked to YHVH, hence the "I AM ness" becomes the "Divine Substance" out of which the Alchemist "creates," following the model established by Genesis.

*

I suppose that my thoughts on the nature of the Tetragrammaton caused me to remember how some time previously I had read about a ceremony called "The Equilibration of YHVH."[167] It purported to evoke YHVH and constrain Him in a Triangle of Art. The creator of the ritual intended to give people, whom their Judaeo-Christian upbringing had traumatised, an opportunity to work out their issues against God and strike a blow against the patriarchy at the same time.

A fundamental Christian would find the idea blasphemous. I, however, thinking like a Ceremonial Magician, found the idea just plain silly. How does one evoke the creative formula of the Universe ? If one tried to *evoke* YHVH,

[167] See : CICERO, CICERO (1995).

then by what power did one call it forth ? "Yod Heh Vav Heh, I conjure you in the name of… um… yourself !" One could only do it if there existed some power greater than the Tetragrammaton, by which to exorcise it. Perhaps if it had conceptualised YHVH as the Demiurge, and called upon the First Mystery as the power by which the exorcist worked, it might have begun to make sense as a Gnostic ritual – but unfortunately it tried to limit itself to the Hermetic Qabalah. The ritual fudged this point, as if to say (like Basil Exposition) : "*I suggest you don't worry about these things and just enjoy yourself.*"

I suppose that I came at it from the perspective of not looking at YHVH as some kind of angry Jehovah. I had fully divorced all thoughts about the nightmare of every fluffy-bunny New Ager, and considered the Tetragrammaton purely as a Qabalistic concept. I had, in fact, overcome the issues to do with an angry and jealous God without having to do anything which could be considered blasphemous. Ironically, though, in taking YHVH as something that I could invoke, meditate on, and use in my ceremonial magic, did I not in fact practise a *greater* blasphemy ?

"*Far more sensible,*" I thought after reading this ritual, "*would be to attempt the 'Equilibration of Satan' instead.*" That, after all would fit in with the whole GD ethos of establishing the proper relationship with one's "Evil Persona." But maybe that added up to the real reason that they didn't publish such a ritual – because it would have been *too* sensible. Instead treating God the same way as one would treat an evocable spirit makes the ritual dark and edgy – as if that's what a Golden Dawn journal really needs.

Anyway – to return from my digression : after I finished my ritual that morning, I returned to bed to catch some Zzz. I had remembered my idea about a ceremony of "The Equilibration of Satan," as I lay in bed… *and then I fell asleep and began to dream lucidly about performing just such a ritual.*

Owing to my familiarity with the Goetia, I visualised the whole scene with myself within a Solomonic circle, evoking the Devil into the Triangle of Art. I just prepared to address my *negotium* to him… when my fiancée chose that moment to wake me up. She had something exciting that she needed to share with me. I pretended to listen intently, but I felt uncomfortable that I had not reached a satisfactory conclusion in the astral : so in my active imagination I did a Licence to Depart to close it down.

I suspected, though, that even if the Devil did not actually exert his influence on me that day, the dream nevertheless portended a bad omen of what would come. During the afternoon, my fiancée and I had a disagreement about whether there are four or five elements – her point being that she did not classify Spirit as a real element. When I trotted out the historical evidence in favour of five elements, she got into an incredibly bad mood.

I retreated to my "oratory" where, for my daily scriptural study that day, I investigated Psalm 98 :2, Mihael, the 48th Shem Ha Mephoresh angel, who reconciles estranged lovers. "*How apt !*" I thought. I petitioned Mihael to help me sort out the position between myself and my fiancée.

Angelic help did not, however, manifest quickly on this occasion. Trivial things set her going : she also seemed intent on taking everything I said as an attack on her. If for example I happened to make a comparison between Golden Dawn and BOTA, she thought I insulted the later, and by implication, *her.* By the evening I gave up on trying to explain myself, and just walked away.

I performed my evening ritual in the sanctuary of my oratory. When I got back to bed, where she lay, another argument started about something else. She went off in a huff. I wondered whether she would spend the night away from me ...

... But she came back a few minutes later, as it happened. Finally, I thought, Mihael had worked his wonders. However, I thought, the fact that it took so long to achieve might indicate that the real problem, despite how it appeared, amounted to something more than Mihael would naturally solve ...

Day 105

26 July 2020

I got up at 4.36am for preparation with Middle Pillar Ritual, which went well that day, and elimination. I recorded my main ritual of the morning thus :

"*LBRP. Prior to doing this I visualise all the troubles I had yesterday as the devil and expel it from my aura. The Pentagrams cause the visualised entity to collapse and disintegrate, as if it is an obsession which I am defeating.*

"*LBRH. I project a beam of Light to the far ends of the Universe when I vibrate 'Ararita.' Outside the boundaries of the fabric of space-time only exists the Unity of God.*

"**Bornless Ritual**. *Done in astral. Again very powerful.*

"*Thought : inspired by a piece about praying before putting on regalia, it occurs to me I should pray also when 'putting on' my astral vehicle. I should, in fact, compose such a prayer, although the only thought that occurs to me at this precise moment is a simple 'Thanks' to God that I am able to enter my body of light and astrally project.*

"**Conjuration**.

"**Confession of Sins**. *Attempts to go argument free have met again with disaster. Do I keep doing something wrong ? In any case, I pray to God and my HGA : if there is any romantic gesture I can make, I will do so ; if there is any way to avoid an argument, I will take it ; opportunities to free my mind from distracting thoughts - I will take them ; any way to heal A - will do so ; etc etc etc.*

"*I concentrate on making Sanyama on my HGA - stillness ...*

"**Licence to Depart**.

"**LBRP**.

"**LBRH**.

"*Total time not including preparation : 1 hour 10 minutes.*"

*

For my scriptural study today, I investigated Psalm 145 :3, and its corresponding angel Vehuel, the 49th Shem Ha Mephoresh angel. In regards to this Angel, the Lenain text says :

"*One should recite the Psalm in its entirety when one is tested by afflictions and when one has a vexed spirit.*"[168]

---

[168] Op. cit. p83.

As it happened, I begun to have something of a reconciliation with my fiancée today, but whichever council looked after the road to recovery had done a bad job keeping it in a good state of repair. I would ask an innocent question and she would react in a way that seemed paranoid. I had had a tension headache beforehand but this exacerbated my state of mind, so I had to go and have a lie down.

Eventually though, she suggested something constructive which made a bridge between us - reading through Paul Foster Case's *Book of Tokens* together. At length she opened up about what had really bothered her : she still felt insecure about completing her Portal thesis, and her subsequent 5=6 advancement. It did not help that she felt left out because I was in the inner order and she was not. So as to alleviate her discomfort, I again stayed away from an inner order ZOOM meeting that month to show solidarity with her : although I repeated that I would willingly discuss actual 5=6 teachings with her, as I had offered the last time this occurred.

Evening ritual accomplished.

Day 106

27 July 2020

Up at 4.39am for preparation with the Middle Pillar Ritual. At least it went without trauma this morning. My ritual went as follows :
    "LBRP.

"LBRH.

"Bornless Ritual. Done in astral. Still powerful !

"Conjuration.

"Confession of Sins. Perhaps I am unconsciously holding my fiancée's future development in the Golden Dawn as a weapon over her ? I interpret her behaviour as hostility, so I respond with some method of trying to assert my authority as a defence (against which she herself takes umbrage).

   "If so, I myself have been exacerbating the predicament in which I find myself. The lessons of SSS* *would indicate that I ought not to engage in this behaviour. I should withdraw, in the hope that it takes two to argue and if I am not arguing it will take the fire out of her as well."*

* When I came to write this up, I realised I had forgotten what "SSS" stood for. My spirit guides told me it meant *Secretissimum Secretum Secretorum*, the most secret Secret of Secrets. It lived up to its name, because I had forgotten what *that* was as well. From its context I presume it to have comprised some kind of moral teaching, kind of like the speech of the Worshipful Master in the Entered Apprentice degree after the Senior Warden first invests the candidate with his "badge." Why I called that "SSS" escapes me.

   "To do this I need to become the Genuinely Humble Man - I keep paying lip service to the idea, and admire it in others, but I have never really been able to do it myself. In this way, I let the Abramelin process genuinely transform me - I keep saying that a genuine student of the mysteries should be open to change, so I ought to put my metaphysical currency where my mouth is, and open myself, as it were.

   "Concentrating on the HGA brings stillness.

"Licence to Depart.

"LBRP.

"LBRH.

"Total time not including preparation : 1 hour 4 minutes."

*

At work I calculated that week 18 - Day 120 – would mark exactly four months since the beginning of my operation : and hence the beginning of the final two months of Abramelin. Only two weeks away ! I made a note to myself of the date to make sure I would have fully prepared before then.

For my scriptural study that day I investigated Psalm 103 :8 which has to do with Daniel, the 50th Shem Ha Mephoresh angel.

I also spent some time on Quora.com answering a question about the identity of the secret chiefs of the Freemasons. Many of the commenters treated it as a joke question : although I pointed out that some co-Masonic traditions, which owe inspiration to Theosophy, believe that Freemasonry has its own Ascended Master, viz., Francis Bacon. Indeed, a cult exists within Freemasonry which appears to worship Bacon, and accredits him with all the achievements of western civilization, despite any historical evidence to the contrary : Freemasonry, Rosicrucianism, Alchemy, authorship of Shakespeare's plays, stuff that other people actually invented, etc.

It strikes me as ironic that the one thing which Bacon *did* invent was Inductive Reasoning, whence comes the origin of the modern Scientific Method. Hence, had he not cheated death and achieved immortality, he would turn in his grave at the amount of *bullshit* spewed out by his followers.

In the evening : my fiancée and I relaxed after dinner by listening to a recording on YouTube of Israel Regardie doing the Middle Pillar Ritual.

Evening ritual accomplished.

Day 107

28 July 2020

Up at 4.36am for preparation with the Middle Pillar Ritual. I tried to incorporate some of the principles I had heard Israel Regardie mentioning in the recording to which I listened the previous evening : they definitely helped. Overall, it left me feeling very positive and full of energy yet at the same time deeply relaxed.

My morning ritual went as follows :

"*LBRP. Feeling powerful - probably because I inherited a lot of good vibes from the Middle Pillar ritual (see above). I am the things I invoke ...*

"*LBRH.*

"*Bornless Ritual. Again done in astral - powerful.*

"*Conjuration.*

"*Confession of Sins. Thanking God and my HGA for all the help they have proffered, especially for guiding spiritual teachers in the past into my orbit so I can learn from them (e.g. Israel Regardie himself).*

"*Contemplating also the Samadhi in the six directions from the Bornless Ritual : but there is yet a* seventh *direction, not outward to any direction of space, but* Inward *- towards the inner planes.*

"*Contemplating my HGA. V still. V powerful.*

"*Licence to Depart.*

"*LBRP.*

"*LBRH.*

"*Total time not including preparation - 55 minutes.*"

*

Later, I contemplated Psalm 104 :31, associated with Hachashiah, the 51ˢᵗ Shem Ha Mephoresh angel, who "serves to raise the soul to the contemplation of divine things and to uncover the mysteries of wisdom," especially when it comes to Alchemy.[169]

During the afternoon, I compiled some notes as to how traditional Qabalists such as Moses Cordovero (1522 – 1570) associated the vowels of the Hebrew language with the Tree of Life, to wit :

---

[169] LENAIN (2020), p84.

Hebrew vowels

Kether	"AH" (hard)
Chokmah	"A" (soft)
Binah	"AI"
Chesed	"EH" (long)
Geburah	"EH" (short) i.e., "ə" or *schwa*.
Tiphereth	"OH"
Netzach	"EE"
Hod	"UH"
Yesod	"OO"
Malkuth	(No vowel)

Hence : the Tetragrammaton in the Ten Sephiroth :

Kether	YAH HAH VAH
Chokmah	YA HA VA HA
Binah	YAI HAI VAI HAI
Chesed	YEH HEH VEH HEH
Geburah	Yə Hə Və Hə
Tiphereth	YOH HOH VOH HOH
Netzach	YEE HEE VEE HEE
Hod	YUH HUH VUH HUH
Yesod	YOO HOO VOO HOO
Malkuth	Yod Heh Vav Heh

Evening Ritual accomplished.

Day 108

29 July 2020

U p at 4.36am for Middle Pillar Ritual - as yesterday. Had to curtail it due to elimination, but it felt powerful, nonetheless.

Sunrise at 5.17pm.

"LBRP.

"LBRH.

"Bornless Ritual. Today I tried doing it in the physical, but seeing if I could incorporate the contemplations I did when in the astral. Fairly powerful - not as much as when completely in the astral, but this is only to be expected when trying to sense vibrations in a denser medium - so impressive as far as it went.

"Conjuration.

"Confession of Sins. Thanking God and my HGA for their assistance. In particular, for inspiring Holy men and women throughout the ages, who in turn inspire me. I.e. God and my HGA speak to me through these people.

"Contemplating resolving the karma of past-lives. It occurs to me that if I am the reincarnation of W L Wilmshurst (an idea which has previously occurred to me) then my destiny is to carry on the work that WLW started but which did not complete. Also the fact that coincidences line up to put me in a position to be able to do so would suggest that higher forces - e.g. My HGA - are at work.

"Concentrating on vibrating the Tetragrammaton with the Hebrew vowels."

I.e., see yesterday. I believe that the original idea for this was that of Moses Cordovero himself.

"It occurs to me that if one vibrated all of the vowels, somewhere in there must be the true pronunciation of the YHVH, so by doing all ten versions one will wind up pronouncing the true version on the 'even a stopped clock tells the correct time twice a day' principle !

"It further occurs to me that the one should visualise oneself in the Cube of Space (here standing in for the Holy of Holies) with the Shekinah, whilst so vibrating, for this was the authentic manner in which the High Priest did so on the day of atonement. For - after all - this part of my Abramelin practice is about confessing my sins to God and my HGA, so the expiation which the High Priest did on Yom Kippur seems appropriate for this."

This proved a fruitful idea which I explored on future days. I should note the prevalence here of BOTA's influence. Formulating the "Cube of Space" in which one imagines the universe as a cube made up of the letters of the Hebrew alphabet forms one of their teachings, introduced in "Tarot Fundamentals." Essentially it derives from the Sepher Yetzirah : its author formulated this cubical arrangement out of memory of the Holy of Holies, which the Bible described as itself cubical. I.e., by contemplating the Cube of Space the Qabalist could enter the mystical equivalent of the Holy of Holies, whose earthly counterpart had long since vanished.

For some reason best known to himself, Paul Foster Case placed the Mother and Double letters on or in *his* Cube in a different arrangement to that of the Sepher Yetzirah, whilst what he did with the finals was unprecedented.

> *"Licence to Depart.*
> *"LBRP.*
> *"LBRH.*
> *"Total time not including preparation : 1 hour 7 minutes."*

*

For my scriptural study that day, I investigated Psalm 7 :18, associated with Aamamiah, the 52nd Shem Ha Mephoresh angel.

Later, whilst surfing the internet, I again went on Quora.com and answered someone's query about a tarot spread. This got me thinking about the Tarot generally. *A propos* of nothing, I eventually formulated a theory : "How to Use Tarot as a key to deriving plots for novels / screenplays." To wit : draw one card to indicate the overall theme of the story, then at least one card to represent each stage of Syd Field's paradigm.[170] Meanwhile, the Court cards can be used to give character ideas.

*

My fiancée and I got into a philosophical discussion – a good natured one, this time – about Morality, and I realised that one could define Morals without reference to either Good or Evil, but *to one's own identity* instead. I didn't know whether anyone else had done so before, but I felt quite clever for doing so. The idea goes like this :

Every individual has a tendency to do what pleases him- or herself, for no other reason than the person likes doing so : the utterly selfish person will do so exclusively.

However, some people – actually mostly everyone except complete solipsists – learn to care for other people, not because it is necessarily a good thing to do, but because they have extended their concept of themselves to include those other

---

[170] See : FIELD (1979).

people as part of their identity. They have gone from thinking in terms of "I" to "We," in other words. One can most easily observable in close family bonds, e.g. a mother caring for her child, or a husband and wife who truly fall in love.

Moreover, many people can extend their identity even further to include "my friends," "my community," "my team," "my tribe," "my country" etc. They extend benevolent relations to them, not because it is good to do so, but because they identify with them, they think that in a way they behave benevolently to themselves.

Conversely, however, every person has a tendency to pay no regard to that with which they don't identify : the stranger, the outsider, the non-family member, etc.

Hence a Moral person has extended his or her identity to the widest circle of people or things, whilst an Immoral person has chosen to limit his or her identity in a purely arbitrary manner.

I had previously identified truly evil people as types of psychopath.[171] In someone like e.g. Hitler's case, he would have identified himself with Germany, but at the same time excluded all those he persecuted from his definition thereof, and indeed could not bring himself to recognise them as human at all.

I believe that most morally questionable acts throughout history have occurred because the perpetrators look out for themselves but see the targets of their actions as outside the limit of people and / or things for whom one should care. A criminal justifies his own crimes, because he acts selfishly towards his victims. Governments justify War, because the Enemy is Not Us, so they don't count. One can explain Racism, homophobia, etc, the same way – loving what you consider part of you or your tribe, whilst not recognising outsiders. One can even class environmental damage as not identifying with the planet as a whole.

Hence in my Identity-Theory of Morality, one can establish morality by whether and to what extent one identifies with other people and things – thus neatly circumventing the need to define "good" and "evil" *per se*, which as concepts always present problems, philosophically speaking.

Evening ritual accomplished.

---

[171] Day 47 – *vide supra.*

Day 109

30 July 2020

U p thirty-nine minutes before sunrise for preparation with the Middle Pillar Ritual and purging my bowels of everything that could distract me from my main session. The Middle Pillar proved very good that morning, thanks to incorporating the Regardie-style visualisations and invocations from that video we had watched on YouTube.

"*LBRP. Powerful - contemplating the divine names in each quarter as divine attributes possessed by YEHESHUAH - who is the Pentagram, after all.*

"*LBRH.*

"*Bornless Ritual. Done in physical. Nevertheless, by concentrating on my astral body whilst performing this physically, I can still sense the power invoked.*

"*Conjuration.*

"*Confession of Sins. Thanking God and my HGA for the grace shown to me already.*

"*Meditating more on my theory of the Cube of Space, the Shekinah, and the permutations of YHVH, upon which I began to ruminate yesterday.*

"*Concentrating on the stillness which the presence of my HGA brings. Very powerful indeed.*

"*Licence to Depart.*

"*LBRP.*

"*LBRH.*

"*Total time taken not including preparation : 1 hour 2 minutes.*"

*

For my scriptural study that day, I investigated Psalm 119 :75, and Nanael, the 53rd Shem Ha Mephoresh angel. As it happened, an unusual synchronicity happened later that day. A friend of mine from the Golden Dawn emailed me a document : seventy-two seals of the Shem Ha Mephoresh, as used by *Eliphas Levi*. I had never seen them before : they appeared quite unique - unlike the ones from Lenain / Ambelain and subsequently used by Damon Brand. This inspired me to seek out the full version of Lenain's text, as up to that point I had only read him second hand through Ambelain.

I also tried out my Tarot Spread for Plot-Lines Idea, and came up with the basis for a story about a woman, represented by the Queen of Swords reversed, whose character develops until by the end she has become in effect the Queen of Swords upright. Nevertheless, I had to park the idea for future reference, as the Abramelin Operation took up so much of my time.

My fiancée continued to stress herself about her portal thesis, as I found out when she invited me to offer constructive criticism on it. More fool me : she had blatantly lied and actually wanted unequivocal praise. My edit-suggestions made her inconsolable : desperate to calm her down and not let this develop into another argument, I came up with the idea of suggesting she seek a second opinion from another adept whose opinion she trusted.

After I had finished my evening ritual accomplished, she appeared in better spirits.

Day 110

31 July 2020

I got up at 4.45am for preparation in a manner similar to previous days. The Middle Pillar ritual again turned out to be good, benefitting from Regardie-style nuances. My main ritual went as follows :

"LBRP.

"LBRH.

"Bornless Ritual. As yesterday, done in the physical whilst yet trying to remain conscious of my astral body. Very good.

"Conjuration.

"Confession of Sins. The fact that I got into a row with A yesterday was a serious mistake. I should have treated her question 'What do you really think about my thesis?' in the way other women ask, 'Does my bum look big in this?' I cannot bring myself to lie, but I don't know how to tell the truth tactfully : or, when I attempt to do so, it doesn't work.

"I have to ask myself : what if someone came along and told me I was doing this Abramelin operation all wrong? How would I feel? On the one hand I imagine I would feel almost as shocked as A purported to be when I didn't give her thesis unequivocal praise. However - on the other hand, the nature of the daily meditations in the Abramelin operation is that one should always be ready to admit one's shortcomings. Therefore, if someone did criticise me in this manner, I would have to examine what they said carefully and if I realised they made a valid point, it become another thing to bring to mind during the daily 'confession of sins.'

"I get an 'in-tuition' (from HGA) that it was correct for me to make sure I removed my ego by recommending A get advice from someone she trusted.

"Formulating the Cube of Space / Shekinah / YHVH etc. Thanking my HGA for its presence.

"Licence to Depart.

"LBRP.

"LBRH.

"Total time not including preparation : 1 hour 1 minute. Later, [my fiancée] appears at first to be in a melancholic temperament, but she brightens up - talking about the Great Work and Concentration i.e. BOTA courses which she said last night she didn't want to do."

*

Investigating Psalm 103 :19, and Nithael, the 54th Shem Ha Mephoresh Angel. Of this Angel Lenain says :

"He serves to obtain the mercy of God, and to obtain long life." [172] (emphasis added).

I recognised this as a clear alchemical reference : the more so because "His throne," as in the versicle's "The Lord has established His Throne..." (etc) in Hebrew equated to "pure gold." Hence this angel's powers correlated to the symbolism of the gematria of the versicle, though not necessarily to correspondence with the Magical Use of the Psalms.

*

Later, I recorded the following in my journal :

"Thought : I keep hearing that Baphomet / Goat of Mendes / etc is really the Astral Light - the 'Great Magical Agent' ..."

I recall Paul Foster Case saying this in one of the BOTA lessons, though he himself had quoted Eliphas Levi.[173]

"... so perhaps that is what I am really evoking when I summon the demons of hell ? On the negative side, it makes the fearful dilletante unwilling to mess with the astral light, but on the positive, it gives the intrepid magus (i.e. Me) a route into making working with Satan etc palatable."

Evening ritual accomplished.

---

[172] LENAIN (2020) p86. Vaughan's translation gives "Nithanael," but the Hebrew spelling is quite clear.

[173] See CASE (2008), p4.

Day 111

01 August 2020

During the night, I experienced dreams of people accusing me of being distant ; also that I didn't have a sense of humour. I thought : "*if I dream of other people saying this about me, does that mean I worry that I am distant / lacking a sense of humour myself ?*"

Then, after a little insomnia, I settled down for a dream in which I became *Lucid* – and started to do the Middle Pillar Ritual. I got as far as vibrating "Eheieh" two times ...

... And then my alarm went off.

I got up for preparation with the Middle Pillar Ritual. I appreciated the irony that had my alarm not gone off I could have completed it : and then I wouldn't have had to do it whilst awake. Nevertheless, it turned out good. Elimination meant I would not be distracted during ritual, but it also meant I started five minutes late.

"*LBRP.*

"*LBRH.*

"*Bornless Ritual. As yesterday.*

"*Conjuration.*

"*Confession of Sins. Thanking God and my HGA for everything. Contemplating resolving the karma of my past lives. Perhaps if my karma is so strong, I can manifest easily whatever I need to resolve it ?*

"*Formulating the Cube of Space etc as yesterday.*

"*Concentrating on the stillness - the presence of my HGA. Making sanyama on mastery of the mental plane - by centring my consciousness in my astral form, and then turning my awareness inwards, on the Mind itself. Good.*

"*Licence to Depart.*

"*LBRP.*

"*LBRH.*

"*Total time not including preparation : 1 hour 7 minutes.*"

*

For my scriptural study today, I investigated Psalm 103 :13, and Mebahiah, the 55th Shem Ha Mephoresh angel, who amongst other things is good for obtaining consolation. Either Mehabiah did work his wonders today, or perhaps because we cycled to the local pub (our first time on bikes together). Perhaps both : but whichever, I noticed relations with my fiancée as happier today than on previous days, which translated into a pleasant night for us both after I had accomplished my evening ritual.

Day 112

02 August 2020

Up at 4.46am for preparation with the Middle Pillar Ritual. Good. Sunrise at 5.23am.

"*LBRP*.

"*LBRH*.

"**Bornless Ritual**. *Done in physical, as on preceding days. Good*.

"**Conjuration**.

"**Confession of Sins**. *I still notice feelings of anger and resentment bubbling up in unguarded moments. I take it this means that it is still there lurking, even when my conscious mind is calmed*.

"*Nevertheless, I meditate on giving thanks to God and my HGA for everything they do for me. I note that yesterday was a better day than previous days - the positive influence from my HGA is having an effect!*

"*Meditating on the Cube of Space, etc.*

"*Concentrating on my HGA - the stillness of mind that comes in deep meditation. Desiring to resolve outstanding issues from previous incarnations, I petition my HGA to be with me when I venture down the Corridor of Many Doors*.

"**Licence to Depart**.

"*LBRP*.

"*LBRH*.

"*Total time not including preparation : 1 hour.*"

*

We tried cycling out to breakfast that day, only for me to realise that in the long period that bike had been out of action, it had developed a puncture. Worse still, the tyre proved unusually tricky to get off the rim for me to change the inner tube : so my re-discovered yen for bicycling lasted all of two days.

For my scriptural study that day, I investigated Psalm 145 :14, and Poiel, the 56th Shem Ha Mephoresh Angel. Given that as the texts describe him as serving "… to obtain what one wants," and "[this] angel rules fame, fortune and philosophy," I petitioned Poiel to see if he could make my previous novel, *Eternal Witch*, a best-seller. Clearly Poiel must have thought my petition an unworthy one, as at the time of writing this has not yet happened.

Evening ritual accomplished.

Day 113

03 August 2020

Up at 4.49am for preparation with the Middle Pillar Ritual. Elimination. Sunrise at 5.24am.

"*LBRP.*

"*LBRH.*

"**Bornless Ritual**. *Done in astral. Good. Reminded of praying for putting on my astral vesture.*

"**Conjuration***.*

"**Confession of Sins**. *The infinity of God vs the 'Finity' of Man (to wit : me) necessarily entails revealing my sinful nature. So too, however, does receiving a new idea on how to improve myself from God. Whilst it is gratifying to discover how to improve oneself, it also means that one is coming from a place of lack or inadequacy. Although there is no shame in coming out of a such a place, it necessarily implies that one was in an imperfect and therefore sinful state the whole time that the one was ignorant of this new revelation.*

"*It so happens that I have had such a revelation, which has led me therefore to confess to my previous ignorant (and hence sinful) condition. It is this : following on from the idea of praying for putting on my astral vesture, I should take this to its logical conclusion and Exorcise and Consecrate all parts of my self - spiritual, mental, psychic, physical, etc. E.g. Using prayers and exorcisms like that used for external objects, but directed inwardly upon myself.*

"*Hence, I would be like the Elus Cohens but directing that power upon me, not just on the objects used in the ceremony. I further have the idea that on this basis I can make a useful start by referring to my copy of* Theurgy *by Mouni Sadhu.[174] The idea behind this all is so curious it is exciting.*"

I should point out that although technically I am a member of the Elus Cohens, I mostly only have theoretical knowledge about them, as the chapter in which I was initiated got off to a very shaky start. I only discovered that members of the seventh degree of "Maître Elu Cohen" had a daily regime of certain rituals prescribed for them after I inherited a lot of Cohen material from a Soror who had been initiated in another order entirely. Nevertheless, what little experience I had of it I enjoyed immensely. The initiation ritual was essentially Ceremonial Magic of the Old School – comparable to the Key of Solomon in the care taken over the preparation of the temple, the items to be used in the ritual – and the Candidate himself.

---

[174] SADHU (1965)

It helped, however, that a particularly meticulous *Réau-Croix* had founded our chapter. He closely studied the original French of the Manuscrit D'Alger[175] to make sure we conducted everything as authentically as possible. It so impressed me that I began to entertain a romantic notion that one ought to conduct all ceremonial magic, and theurgy in particular, in this manner.

For example : the prayers and invocations in the Sadhu book might prompt one to think "is that all there is ?" – if one were not familiar with Theurgy. An Elu Cohen, on the other hand knows that a short half-hour ritual can take *two days* to perform : forty-eight hours beforehand carrying out the "usual abstinences," and then on the day of the ritual, at least a good two hours to prepare everything for the ceremony, by exorcising and consecrating it all, drawing the theurgic circles and so forth. So, by the time the operator actually begins the ceremony, his preparations have keyed him up to an enormous degree – and that, of course, explains the effectiveness of the ceremony.

> *"Contemplating healing my past lives. Contemplating the Cube of Space, etc. Also, my Holy Guardian Angel.*
> ***"Licence to Depart.***
> ***"LBRP.***
> ***"LBRH.***
> *"Total time not including preparation : 1 hour."*

*

As part of my scriptural study today, I investigated Psalm 115 :11, and Nemamiah the 57th angel of the Shem Ha Mephoresh, said to "bring prosperity in all things and to deliver prisoners."

Today marked a big day : my fiancée gave me the finalised version of her thesis, which I sent off for evaluation by the other Adepti. In order to avoid any suggestion of bias, I made it clear to them I would recuse myself from any decision taken. I realised I felt very nervous. I tried to console myself : *"What's the best that could happen ?"* Well, let's see, there's the overwhelming sense of relief I would feel when it gets a warm reception. Or alternatively, the humility of learning I had made a mistake in worrying so much about her.

I reflected : this experience would transform me one way or the other. I just hoped it would transform me for the better. As it happened, initial responses from the other Adepti appeared positive.

*

---

[175] This was not available in English at the time in question, but see now CLELLAND *et al.,* (2021).

That afternoon – directly inspired by my thoughts on Theurgy that morning, I composed a Theurgic ritual, mainly comprising adaptations of Elu Cohen prayers and material from Mouni Sadhu's book. Although I did a good job of translating the Latin, two words eluded me, even after I had recourse to my trusty Cassells dictionary – Google Translate being, of course, useless.

Theurgic Rite for Astral Projection

General Invocation (*3)

+ Our defence is in the Lord's name, Who created heaven and earth. Lord, hear my prayer,
And let my cry ascend to thee !

The General Blessing

O God, in whose light all our actions and even the smallest thoughts are sanctified ! We beseech Thee to extend Thy blessings on this Body of Light, and make me use it with thoughtfulness, according to Thy Will and Thy law, who alone, in Thy goodness can grant it. Through the invocation of Thy most holy name, grant health of body, salvation of soul, and everything necessary for this life, which we beseech with devotion and faith. Through Jesus Christ, our Lord ! Amen.

Blessing of Vestures

(Repeat General Invocation once, then :)

I exorcise you, Astral Garment, here before me, in the name of Him who gave you the purpose to protect and cover human souls as well as for their embellishment.

Be + blessed garment, + pure +, beyond all the power of the demon and his servants, beyond all his traps and witchcraft, no matter what kind they might be. Do not hold any devilish force in you, but Astral Garment, in the + name of the Lord and my Holy Guardian Angel be +pure, +blessed and + sanctified : we implore Thee, O Lord, deign to + purify, to +bless, and to +sanctify this Astral Garment.

That is why I, Thy humble servant, in Thy name and in the name of my Holy Guardian Angel, I + bless, +purify and +sanctify this Astral Garment. Make it so, 0 Lord, that I who will use them will receive Thy grace and an abundance of Thy blessings, and that every demon and his actions will be excluded from I who wear this Robe of Glory, being a weapon against the enemy. In the name + of the Father, of the + Son, and of the Holy Ghost. Amen.

Sprinkle with blessed water.

Elu Cohen Prayers General

Exorciso vos, creaturas omnium rerum que in meo conspectu sunt ad usum laboris mei, ut effugiat ex vobis omnis nequitia et virtus Diaboli et niehi, nec nobis, nec illis noare possint Benedic, Domine+, hos omnes creaturas hic adstantes et sanctifica ut ad meam utilitatem prosint sine imprevimento, et ad majoram gloriam nominis tui sancti. Amen.

I exorcise you, Creatures of all things which are in my sight for the use of my labour, that all iniquity and power of the Devil may flee from you and they may be *(what the hell does "noare" mean ?)* neither to us nor to them. Bless, Oh Lord, these creatures lying here and sanctify them that they may be beneficial to my use without *("imprevimento" caused me problems as well).* And to the greater glory of your holy name, Amen.

On dressing

Per merita angelorum tuorum sanctorum, Domine+, induam vestimenta salutis, ut hoc quod, desidero possim perducere ad effectum ; Per te, sanctissime + cujus regnum permanet in aeternum. Amen.

Through the merits of Your holy angels, oh Lord, I put on the vestments of salvation, that what I desire might be fulfilled ; through You, most holy one, whose kingdom remains in eternity. Amen.

*

That evening, when I performed my final ritual of the day, I passed into a state of deep meditation. Afterwards, when I climbed into bed, my fiancée kept going on about the strange energy she detected from me. We partook of "Sacrament." Afterwards she *still* went on about the strange energy. As much as it gratified me to think that my "Magickal" skills proved so cosmic for her, she talked about it at such length that I feared it would be soon time for me to get up for my morning ritual. I eventually felt relieved when she decided to let me get to sleep for the night.

Day 114

04 August 2020

U p at 4.49am for preparation with the Middle Pillar Ritual. My morning ritual went as follows :

    *"**LBRP**.*

*"**LBRH**.*

*"**Bornless Ritual**. Done in physical.*

*"**Conjuration**.*

*"**Confession of Sins**. Allowing distracting thoughts to enter my mind and interfere with this meditation is sinful. Thinking about morality. In order to love my enemies, I would have to extend my identity - in other words, my concept of 'We' - to include people I don't like. But the only way I can do this is to think long and hard about what I have in common with those people. Uh … We're all human beings ? My problem is that if I think of them as humans it dilutes the concept of 'love,' whereas the only way of which I can think of loving them authentically is to dilute the concept of them as 'human' - e.g. By thinking of them as sub-human, or animals, innocent of the pain which they cause. The latter course of action seems emotionally fraudulent. It offends my own sense of right and wrong that I have to belittle others in order to feel any generosity of sentiment towards them.*

    "I realise that without resolving my feelings towards such people then bringing them to consciousness is putting me in danger of spoiling my meditation. I therefore make an effort to still my mind and concentrate on the influence of my HGA. My Nephesh is transmuted into Nephesh Ha-Messiach. My Ruach becomes the Christ consciousness. My Neshamah, Chiah and Yechidah are directly connected to God. Ah peace."

(I later reflected : one can perhaps find a solution to the dilemma of "I Love Them" by diluting neither the "love" nor the "them" but the "I." The problem does not exist if there is no-one to have a problem.)

    "Thinking about YHVH and Hebrew vowels. Get this : Kether = A (pronounced 'Ah') ; Daath = I (i.e. 'Ai') ; whilst Tiphereth = O. Hence, Daath-Kether-Tiphereth = IAO.

    "IAO thus represents the Middle Pillar of the Tree of Life - as it does in Greek - but in the Hebrew Kabbalah it is shifted up a Sephirah !"

(I found this so inspiring that I posted something about this on social media. It got thirty-four likes, i.e., thirty-four more than I expected for a recondite musing in what itself comprised a niche subject.)

    *"**Licence to Depart**.*

*"**LBRP**.*

"LBRH.

"Total time not including preparation : 1 hour 4 minutes."

*

Over breakfast, a blazing row erupted with my fiancée. I expressed concern when she said that she had received inner order material from another Frater, that this might mean he had broken his obligation. She interpreted this as meaning I felt annoyance towards *her* for receiving material beyond her grade ; but the breaking of an obligation troubled me far more, which concern she did not herself share. It did not help that she resented the whole concept of taking obligations due to some trauma she said she experienced as a teenager, joining a Baptist Church. She did not make clear what the trauma involved exactly, apart from the fact that she did not like the Baptist Church.

On reflection (that is to say - after I had left the house), I wondered : is this *jealousy* ? Over her attempting to gain Ancient Wisdom from another man. *"Insecurity – Bad,"* I thought, mentally cataloguing all the Sins I would have to confess the next time I had an opportunity to do so. But if I told her that of my jealousy in a bid to make her feel guilty, would the wanting to make her feel guilty be itself wrong ?

For my scriptural study that day, I investigated Psalm 6 :4, and Ieialel (58th Shem Ha Mephoresh angel). Ironically, the texts describe him as serving against chagrins, which could have been of enormous help to me right now, except that I still had so much anger and upset that I found it difficult to feel any benefit from meditating on Ieialel.

I tried to calm down, by going on Quora.com and answering some questions about Tarot symbolism and astral projection.

In the evening, a miracle occurred : I effected a reconciliation with my fiancée. So Ieialel came through after all ! I realised that *I* was genuinely at fault in that I misunderstood what exactly the Frater in question had done and when he had done so (no broken obligations after all). She responded positively to the fact that I can feel jealous about her.

Evening ritual accomplished.

Day 115

05 August 2020

I got up at 4.52am for preparation with the Middle Pillar Ritual. Elimination. For some reason existential angst over *fear of death* niggled me that morning. Sunrise at 5.27am.

"*LBRP*. *I precede this by taking a moment to concentrate on my astral body, willing it to be exorcised & consecrated.*

"*LBRH.*

"*Bornless Ritual*. *Done in physical whilst maintaining awareness of the astral.*

"*Conjuration.*

"*Confession of Sins*. *Reflecting on the events of yesterday, I will that the relationship between God, my HGA and me be like a well-oiled spiritual machine, as in the influence comes in automatically without me having to ask or make effort for it. Kind of like the way Socrates' Dæmon showed up at exactly the right time without Socrates having to ask for it to do so. Also, Socrates' Dæmon's habit of saving the Philosopher on the brink of error would be a darned useful thing for my own HGA to do to me ! I.e., I could know to avoid arguments before they happen.*

"*Likewise, the problem of having to love people who do not necessarily love one back. On the basis of taking one's own ego out of the equation, it becomes easy to recognise that distinctions of Time arise because of the illusion of separation as well. Hence, although it is difficult or impossible to love such an antithetical being now, one can recognise that they are separate souls on their own spiritual journey, and there will come a time in the future when such reconciliation is possible.*"

Afterwards, as I typed up my journal, I thought this would make the subject of a funny meme, which I put on social media :

Figure 6 "I don't hate... I just wish people better luck in their next incarnation."

To continue with my contemplations that morning :

"Concentrating on the influence of my HGA transmuting the various parts of my soul into the best possible versions thereof. Soothing, calming stillness. In fact, the whole of this 'confession' has helped me overcome the angst which was bedevilling me earlier (see above).

"THOUGHT : when faced with problems, remember that they are in fact the Great Magical Agent which is actually the source of one's power !

"Licence to Depart.

"LBRP.

"LBRH.

"Total time not including preparation : 1 hour 6 minutes."

*

At breakfast, I tried to do a good job avoiding arguments with my fiancée, despite feeling irked at her going on about Christianity all the time. She herself felt stressed over her thesis, this time over how the other Adepti would treat it. What to do, what to do ...

For my scriptural study today I investigated Psalm 113 :3, and Harachel, the 59th Shem Ha Mephoresh Angel. This angel rules over, *inter alia,* treasures as well as printing and the book trade. When I first invoked Harachel in 2016, I noted in my magical diary that my fortunes improved immediately afterwards, which I interpreted as A Sign...

Later, I read through my latest BOTA tarot lesson concerning Judgement. I came across the following quote :

"The Angel in Key 20 is obviously Gabriel, as he is blowing a trumpet."

Obviously ! I despaired. I could not help but think of the discussion my fiancée and I had on this very point almost three months previously.[176] However, once I looked beyond the dogmatism implicit in the statement, I found that Case did actually write some interesting things about this Key, for example, his description of the Cube of Space.

Evening ritual accomplished. Afterwards, my fiancée repeatedly asked me about whether Abramelin was changing my world microcosmically, or some such. "Well, yes, I should hope so !" I had to reply. This freaked her out : she wanted to talk long into the night about her concerns, but eventually I achieved communication with the spiritual realm in a horizontal position. Zzzz.

---

[176] Day 40, *vide supra.*

Day 116

06 August 2020

Up at 4.46am for preparation with the Middle Pillar Ritual (and Elimination). My morning devotions went as follows :

"LBRP.

"LBRH.

"Bornless Ritual.

"Conjuration.

"Confession of Sins. Thanking God and my HGA for all they do for me.

"Formulating Cube of Space, etc, whilst invoking YHVH with the Hebrew vowels. Willing that not just my karma but that of my past lives be expiated. Reading BOTA lesson last night has proved useful in formulating the Cube. I.e. despite my criticising it, it did turn out to be useful – and relevant.

"Meditating on the presence of my HGA. Good.

"Licence to Depart.

"LBRP.

"LBRH.

"Total time not including preparation : 1 hour 3 minutes."

*

At breakfast, my fiancée continued to seem anxious about the fate of her thesis. Unbeknownst to her, all the Adepti who had responded so far were overwhelmingly positive and approving – including those whom she mistook for her worst enemies. However, when I offered to share the feedback with her in advance of the due time, in the hope that it would calm her down, she refused : thinking that it would contain negative criticism. *Even though I assured her it would calm her down.* I sighed : not only did she beat herself up unnecessarily, but she also did so excessively.

For my scriptural study today, I analysed Psalm 145 :17, and Mitzrael (60th Shem Ha Mephoresh Angel), said to heal spiritual ills and to serve deliverance from those who persecute one. Meditating thereon proved good – an indication of the presence of the Angel itself.

That evening when I had got back, my fiancée seemed better : In fact, she was in such good spirits that we were able to have a good-natured conversation in which I explained my Abramelin-rationale to her.

Evening ritual accomplished.

Day 117

07 August 2020

During the night, I had a dream in which another adept gave me a Fire Talisman as a present. Admittedly, I may have concatenated memory-elements from the previous day.

Up at 4.56am for preparation with the Middle Pillar Ritual. Elimination. Sunrise at 5.31am.

"*LBRP.*

"*LBRH. When I analyse the Key-word, I have an idea of how to modify this - i.e. To prefix contemplation of tetragrammaton and the Hebrew translation of INRI...*"

My inspiration for this came from a paper given at an SRIA High Council meeting in 2019, by a Frater named Sergio Prezioso. The gist ran as follows: "INRI" comprise the initials in Latin for "Jesus of Nazareth, King of the Jews." The Hebrew translation for the same phrase – which would have been written on the superscription at Jesus' Crucifixion below the Latin – would be:

יַהְשׁוּהַ הַנָצְרִי וַמֶלֶךְ הַיְהוּדִים

i.e., "*Yeheshuah Ha-Nazarei Ve-Melekh Ha-Yehudim.*" Note the initials. This would imply that the literal translation of "INRI" into Hebrew is "Yod Heh Vav Heh" – the Tetragrammaton.

This has many implications for both Qabalah and Christian mysticism. Suffice to say that my idea to modify the Analysis of the Key-word went like this:

יהוה	Yod Heh Vav Heh
יהשוה הנצרי ומלך היהודים	Yeheshuah Ha-Nazarai Ve-Melekh Ha-Yehudim
I N R I	
י נ ר י	Yod Nun Resh Yod
י	Virgo, Isis, Mighty Mother
נ	Scorpio, Typhon & Apophis, Destroyer
ר	Sol, Osiris, Slain & Risen
	Isis, Apophis, Osiris

	IAO
	The Sign of Osiris Slain
L	The Sign of the Mourning of Isis
V	The Sign of Typhon and Apophis
X	The Sign of Osiris Risen
	L,V,X - LUX - the Light... Of the Cross.

As I noted in that day's journal entry :

"This is surprisingly powerful, which in turn would mean that SP who gave me the idea is actually a genius – he was certainly onto something."

I continued with my ritual :

"Bornless Ritual. *Performing this in the physical whilst nevertheless attempting to maintain awareness of my astral body. At the highpoint of the ritual -* "Come thou forth and follow me ... " *- I realise my true form as a cube consisting of six inverted pyramids of power - their apices at the centre, their bases or outer limits extending to infinity - the six directions of the Universe, whence I had invoked the various barbarous names. It is almost as if for one moment I forget my physical body altogether... At the very least it puts me in a confident mood for the subsequent parts of this morning's ritual.*

"Conjuration.

"Confession of Sins. *Thanking God and my HGA for all that they have done for me so far.*

"It occurs to me that an idea I had early on in my magical career was that the Absorption process that Dion Fortune described Theodore Moriarty as doing in Psychic Self-Defence was equivalent to Christ dying to take away the sins of the world, albeit on a smaller scale.[177] Now here I am trying to expiate my own Sins, including both the ones I personally have committed and the ones for which I am responsible. Hence, what better way than to follow the example set by Christ, and deployed e.g. By Moriarty ?

"Hence : in a similar manner to yesterday, I formulate the Cube of Space, invoke the Shekinah, and vibrate the Tetragrammaton with the Hebrew Vowels. I then imagine that YHVH is surrounding both my present life and my previous lives in a giant sphere of love and compassion and absorbing all the negativity. Peaceful.

"Meditating on the influence of my HGA in general. Good.

---

[177] *Op. cit.* – see Day 13, *supra*.

> *"Licence to Depart.*
> *"LBRP.*
> *"LBRH.*
> *"Total time not including preparation : 1 hour 5 minutes."*

*

I got through breakfast without arguments this morning, which I interpreted as a good sign.

My scriptural study that day consisted of investigating Psalm 113 :2, and Umabel, the 61st Shem Ha Mephoresh Angel. I realised that the Hebrew phrase "From now until eternity" is equivalent in gematria to "Amen" and אמשת the letters representing the elements !

I had a yen to delve into the Royal Art, so I made a start of reading *Spiritual Alchemy* by Robert Ambelain, one of many ebooks I had downloaded compulsively many years ago, but to which I had not got around to making headway.

A blazing row erupted with my fiancée in the evening. When she started ranting about Christianity, I cut her short abruptly, which made her upset. Never mind that *I* felt upset at her constantly dissing Christianity. Later, however, we made up after she had calmed down.

Evening ritual accomplished.

Day 118

08 August 2020

During night : around half an hour or more before dawn, sacrament. The blood of the red lion mixed with the gluten of the eagle just before my appointed getting up time (4.57am), so as it happened I went into my morning rituals filled with magical energy. Ambelain may or may not intended this as his meaning, but from my subsequent journal entries I seem to have lost interest in his book hereafter.

Preparation with the Middle Pillar Ritual.

I started contemplating my body of light in readiness for my morning devotion a few minutes before the scheduled start time.

"*LBRP*.

"*LBRH* - *with revised analysis of the keyword. Good.*

"*Bornless Ritual*.

"*Conjuration*.

"*Confession of Sins. Thanking God and my HGA for everything they do.*

"*It was a mistake of me to blow up yesterday evening. The problem was that I reacted to what I should have recognised as something obviously provocative. As it happens, A and I reconciled later, but it was still a failing on my part to get into that situation.*

"*Formulating the Cube of Space, invoking the Shekinah, and contemplating YHVH with the Hebrew vowels - which feels powerful as I do so. I contemplate absorbing my karma and all the karma for which I am responsible. Good. Even the exaltation I feel is 'sinful' i.e. Less than perfect compared to the perfection of God - so I absorb that as well. Consequently I pass into a very deep state of meditation indeed.*

"*Thanking God, my HGA, and all spiritual beings who have assisted in getting me to this point.*

"*Licence to Depart*.

"*LBRP*.

"*LBRH*.

"*Total time : 58 minutes. Feeling positive today.*"

*

I attempted to commune with the astral plane in a horizontal position, but my fiancée frustrated my efforts by bounding into the bedroom, insisting that she had a piece of ancient wisdom that she just had to share with me at that particular moment. Somewhat tactlessly on my part, I indicated a lack of appreciation of my otherworldly peregrination being interrupted : which caused her to get upset. Eventually, however, she calmed down when I encouraged her to show me what she meant, and suddenly she became happier again.

I studied Psalm 119 :159, which has to do with Yahahael (the 62nd Shem Ha Mephoresh angel). The meditation thereon proved very good, as if confirming Yahahael's presence.

Later that day, with the end of Phase Two of my operation looming this weekend, I jotted down some notes in my journal as to what I had to do in the Final Third from Monday :

"*The Final Third.*

"*From Day 120 (Monday 10th August) onwards*

"*Additional Prayer*

"*(To be said immediately before the Licence to Depart.)*

"'Oh YHVH, Tzebaoth, Adonai, and my Holy Guardian : I praise you oh God. Accept the ardour of my prayer, and show me Thy mercy. Through Your grace may I have the honour of company with the Holy Angels ; and grant and reveal the hidden Wisdom to reign over the unredeemed spirits and all creatures. AMEN.'

"*Continue to perform morning and evening rituals, adding in this prayer as appropriate.*

"*Add an extra period of prayer (ideally in Oratory) at 12 noon, before Lunch - Conjuration, (meditation), Additonal Prayer, Licence to Depart.*

"*Continue study of Sacred writings as appropriate (idea for what to do after Shem Ha-Mephoresh : first 32 verses of Genesis, analysing them qabalistically and linking them in with the Sepher Yetzirah).*

"*Maintain vegetarian diet, but give up alcohol.*"

Give up alcohol ! For over two months ! So I had better drink it all this weekend ! When I told my fiancée that evening about what I intended, at first she looked at me gape-mouthed in astonishment, but soon she looked mightily impressed. She promised that she would give up alcohol, to support me : and maybe even give up smoking as well.

Evening ritual accomplished, after which I retired and partook with my fiancée of more Alchemical matters.

Day 119

09 August 2020

I got up at 4.59am for elimination and preparation with the Middle Pillar Ritual. My ceremony went as follows :

"**LBRP**.

"**LBRH**.

"**Bornless Ritual**. *As I begin this ritual, I feel uneasy, edgy - as if there is a presence standing behind me. Is it an actual demon ? Or has the fact that I have decided to throw myself into the Final Third triggered another Dweller on the Threshold episode ?*

"**Conjuration**.

"**Confession of Sins**. *Meditating on God and my HGA goes some way to curing the edgy feeling I experienced earlier.*

"*Sins : clearly I handled the argument with A yesterday morning badly at the time. Although I resolved it later, ideally I should have dealt with it before it arose. Prevention is better than cure.*

"*Cube of Space, etc, meditation. Good.*

"*Thanking God and HGA and all spiritual guides and teachers for everything that they do.*

"**Licence to Depart**.

"**LBRP**.

"**LBRH**.

"*Total time : 1 hour 8 minutes.*"

*

This morning, relations with my fiancée went noticeably better than yesterday, given that we had Sacrament before she began talking about her "Ancient wisdom." And she even treated it like a conversation instead of just talking at me (the Ancient Wisdom I mean, not the Sacrament). I reflected that I might have spoken harshly to her yesterday, but I seemed to have left an impression on her - perhaps I had applied just the right amount of Severity after all.

In the afternoon we had a Zoom meeting for our Golden Dawn temple, in which our Imperatrix led us on the Path of Tav and down to the underworld to meet Ereshkigal. Because for once somebody else led the session, I found I could kick-back and enjoy it as a participant. It proved powerful, as I felt myself going into a trance as the meditation progressed.

Later, I investigated Psalm 2 :11, associated with Anauel, the 63rd Shem Ha Mephoresh angel. I noted the meditation as "good."

After downing my last glass of Shiraz after dinner, I performed my Evening ritual, and retired to bed.

PHASE THREE

Day 120

10 August 2020

With the onset of the final battle upon me, I re-formatted my journal so that each entry had three sub-headings : for the morning, midday, and evening rituals. Hence :

Morning Ritual

The first day of Phase Three began in a conventional manner, at 5am, when I got up for preparation with the Middle Pillar Ritual. My first session of the day went as follows :

"LBRP,

"LBRH,

"Bornless Ritual,

"Conjuration,

"Confession of Sins, Contemplating the Infinity of God vs the Finite nature of myself.

"Imagined grievances are distracting thoughts. But why should they arise at all, given that they are fictional ? I think issues arise, and false images crystallise around them. I confess them all the same.

"Nevertheless, I am thankful to God and my HGA that yesterday was a whole lot better than preceding days.

"I formulate the Cube of Space based meditation and imagine that I am 'absorbing' all these imagined grievances and distracting thoughts, and even the ecstasies arising from absorbing these distracting thoughts."

I.e., by "Absorbing" I meant doing to them what Moriarty did to the malignant spirit in the incident mentioned in *Psychic Self-Defence.* The "ecstasies," though pleasant, themselves in their own way constituted distracting thoughts : hence their need for banishment.

"Spending extra time focussing on my HGA to finish it off so that I am in the right frame of mind to go on to ...

*"The **Additional prayer**, which is new for the final third ;[178]*

"Licence to Depart.

"LBRP.

"LBRH.

"Total time not including preparation : 1 hour 7 minutes."

---

[178] *Vide supra* Day 118.

*

Researching Psalm 33 :18, associated with Mechiel (64th Shem Ha Mephoresh Angel). I detected a mistake in Ambelain in that he had also attributed this versicle to Chahaviah whom I investigated on Day 80. Both the RCO and Damon Brand confirmed the Mechiel attribution : Chahaviah had a different versicle albeit similarly worded. Consequently, not only did I investigate Mechiel, I went back and re-did Chahaviah *as well*.[179]

Midday Ritual

I began this just after 12noon and completed it by 12 :28. It consisted of a stripped-down version of the morning ritual, to wit :

Conjuration ;

Confession of Sins ;

The **Additional Prayer** ; and

The **Licence to Depart**.

The "Confession" part today included formulating the Cube of Space, invoking the Shekinah, invoking the Tetragrammaton with the Hebrew vowels, and absorption of all karma - i.e. My own and that for which I hold responsibility. Absorbing all the ecstasy as well, on the basis that even this compared imperfectly to the perfection of God. It felt *very deep* - like an exalted state of meditation. So much so that I prayed the additional prayer in a heightened state of spiritual consciousness. So some magic went on right here : when I made the affirmation in the Additional Prayer – which explicitly deals with aspiring to Knowledge and Conversation of the Holy Guardian Angel – I did so in what Chaos magicians would call a *state of gnosis*. And I expected to do this three times a day for the next sixty days or more.

*

Later, I found time to go through my latest BOTA lesson, which involved colouring in Key 21, "The World."

Having to spend an evening without alcohol turned out not so traumatic after all : I confined myself to water with my meal, but otherwise herbal tea. I had no craving, although I did have the vague apprehension that I missed something. I

---

[179] The mistake was in LENAIN (2020), hence Ambelain only continued it. The RCO and Brand attribute Psalm 33 :18 to Mechiel, and Psalm 147 :11 to Chahaviah.

suppose that my determination to stick to my vow and complete the operation t enforced my willpower and made it bearable.

An argument with my fiancée developed. I disagreed with her about the nature of imagination and visualisation, and "meditating on a point," as in the Neophyte meditation in the Golden Dawn. I felt sure that we had gone over this subject before. The worst of it, though, came when I told her "I'm sure you *do* know how to meditate on a point, you just don't realise it," she thought I meant to attack her : whereas of course I wanted to do the opposite, i.e. to support and encourage her.

Eventually I decided that the best course of action would involve removing myself from the situation to give her a chance to calm down, and to demonstrate that I didn't want to argue just for the sake of doing so.

Evening Ritual

Accomplished - good. When I came to bed, it appeared that calm was restored...

Day 121

11 August 2020

Morning Ritual

I got up that morning at 5am for preparation with the Middle Pillar ritual and some much needed elimination. Despite the necessity of banishing the "qlippoth" from my microcosm, it delayed the start of my main ritual two minutes past the appointed time. I behave like a stickler for accuracy, especially since modern technology made it easy to determine the time of sunrise.

The ritual went as follows :

"LBRP.

"LBRH.

"Bornless Ritual.

"Conjuration.

"Confession of Sins. I examine my conscience regarding last night's argument. The good intention at the heart of my actions was that I genuinely wanted [my fiancée] to feel better about herself than she came across as being. Yet I obviously must have done something wrong otherwise it would not have blown up like that. I pray that my God and my HGA help me avoid doing such in the future.

"The Cube of Space meditation, absorbing all karma. Powerful. <u>So powerful in fact that I feel like I am in an exalted state of consciousness when I subsequently perform the Additional prayer, Licence to Depart, and pentagram / hexagram rituals.</u>

"Additional prayer - see above.

"Licence to Depart - see above.

"LBRP - see above.

"LBRH - see above.

"Total time : 1 hour 3 minutes. Feeling very positive as a result of this ritual..."

... And then breakfast happened. My fiancée ominously warned "You don't want to speak to me at all." I obliged her by keeping silent. Without any sense of irony, she started speaking all the same. It turned out she wanted to have last night's argument all over again. I could see where we differed : she had a set of assumptions, I presume based on what she had read, and I had a *different* set of assumptions because I had read different things. However, if I offered to show her my sources which demonstrated the evidence for my point of view, she did not treat it in a scholarly manner, but thought I meant to attack – leading to me feeling exasperated. Not only could I not argue with her, but trying to make her feel good about herself only seemed to have the opposite effect.

Later, after I had escaped from the house, she texted me to apologise, saying that she had been stressed.

*

Worked proved quiet: both in the sense of a mostly deserted building, as well as me having few tasks to do that day anyway. Hence I had no-one to look over my shoulder : and no-one to see that instead of using my computer to carry out my job, I instead used it productively, i.e., in furtherance of my magical activities.

Hence I found time to research Psalm 90 :13, which has to do with Damabiel (65th Shem Ha Mephoresh angel), and meditate thereon whilst seated at my desk.

I also compiled some notes about this whole Cube of Space type thang which I had recently incorporated into my meditations. I decided that I would thenceforth refer to it as *"The Tea-Pot Meditation"* due to a cunning qabalistic cipher (i.e., the acronym of "True Pronunciation of the Tetragrammaton" is "TPOTT"). Most of this comprised the summation of thoughts I had already journaled from the 28th – 29th July onwards.[180]

The Tea-Pot Meditation

I have based this on an idea I originally had, thinking "what would the grade of Ipsissimus be like if it existed ?" My reasoning went as follows :

I work a Qabalistic system. The 10=1 is the highest grade of that system : hence it must concern itself with the highest possible teachings of the Qabalah. The highest Qabalistic teachings of which I don't actually know but at which I can guess is the True pronunciation of the Tetragrammaton (hereinafter : "TPOTT").

An Ipsissimus therefore would equate to a "Baal Shem Tov."[181] Hence, work out the TPOTT - the true "Unwritten Qabalah" - and *ipso facto* you have the secrets of the grade of Ipsissimus. Ordinarily, one would only ever receive the Unwritten Qabalah from a true "Beshith"[182] from mouth to ear in the manner that masters have transmitted it down the ages. Hence, if a grade ceremony for the 10=1 exists, it must necessarily remain mysterious, as only a true "Beshith" would know how to transmit the Unwritten Qabalah in an appropriate manner.

---

[180] i.e., Days 108, 109 *et seq. Vide supra.*

[181] Literally "Master of the Good Name," with "Good" carrying the additional connotation of divine approbation.

[182] i.e., בשת , the acronym of "Baal Shem Tov."

I, however, have decided to attempt to surmount this intellectual hurdle through the use of inference and unfounded speculation, mainly the latter.

What do I actually know about the TPOTT ? Firstly, and most importantly, the High Priest alone said it, and then only in the Holy of Holies once a year on the day of atonement, for a very specific reason – to expiate the sins of the people. Probably uncoincidentally, known Beshithim *(? Is that a word ?)* studiously avoided pronouncing the Tetragrammaton even when sorely tempted to do so - precisely because they weren't in the Holy of Holies acting as High Priest on the Day of Atonement. The fact that they would rather suffer death or torture than disregard this scruple I find telling.

Secondly : for reasons which probably don't stand up to intellectual scrutiny, I do not believe that the question of the TPOTT consists of how you pronounce it with your mouth, but with your soul - i.e., with one's complete psychic faculties. Now I come to think about this, I think reading Franz Bardon inspired me to adopt this particular prejudice. Hence, the TPOTT essentially involves a metaphysical act of a mystical or theurgic nature.

Thirdly : to the extent that the TPOTT does consist of vocalising, Hebrew only has nine vowels. Hence if one were to vibrate the Tetragrammaton with all the permutations of the Hebrew Vowels, one would unwittingly make the TPOTT by default without realising it, on the "stopped-clock" principle.

Using these postulates, one can propose a guided meditation which attempts to simulate the TPOTT and hence the experience of the grade of Ipsissimus, to wit :

1. Recreate the Holy of Holies of King Solomon's Temple

The Bible describes the Holy of Holies as a Cube. I have long suspected that the Sepher Yetzirah talks about the Cube of Space to enable Qabalists to recreate the Holy of Holies within their own soul. Hence, one should first spend time establishing oneself in the midst of the Cube of Space, by establishing the letters of the Hebrew alphabet in the proper positions.

This being done, one builds upon this setting of place by invoking into the Cube thus established the spiritual equivalent of everything that the original Holy of Holies contained – most importantly, the SHEKINAH. Hence one should spend time invoking the Shekinah, until one can actually feel Her as a real presence in one's consciousness.

2. Pronounce the Tetragrammaton

Acting in tantric union with Lady Shekinah, use the Hebrew Vowel meditation mentioned previously – effectively establishing the Tree of Life whilst doing so.

3. Make propitiation for the sins of the "people."

I imagine this as the Absorption method first mentioned by Dion Fortune in *Psychic Self-Defence.* "People" here presents a difficult concept : for a Christ-like figure, the people would include *all people throughout time and space.* Not pretending to be 100% Christ-like yet, I judge it to be more pragmatic to think of "the people" as myself, and all for whom I am responsible.

Midday Ritual

I found myself in a quandary : being away from oratory, I needed to perform my midday devotions, so what should I do ? As it happened, I began at 12.05pm, following the same structure as yesterday, but with one important difference : I *astrally projected* to my oratory and performed it there, since physically I remained at work.

In effect, I "pulled a Crowley." Crowley himself completed – or purported to complete – the Abramelin Operation on his second attempt, not physically at Boleskine as he had first done so, but whilst he trekked through China. However, all the while he did so, he astrally projected to his oratory at Boleskine – or rather, he brought his Oratory to him, by building it up in his imagination with his psychic awareness – in order to perform his rituals.[183]

Some armchair magicians have argued that Crowley did not complete the Abramelin, at least not in the proper manner, although Crowley himself claimed to do so.[184] I recognise that I may open myself up to the same criticism that Crowley faced : although personally, I began to have a lot more sympathy for his predicament than I had previously.

Nevertheless, the whole discipline of performing the conjuration, Confession of sins - incorporating the "Tea Pot meditation" (see above), Additional prayer and Licence to depart, proved itself a powerful and moving experience. I returned to my body and to normal (albeit exalted) consciousness at 12.20pm.

I made a note to myself to avoid snacking in the morning so that the ritual would be done on as empty a stomach as possible.

*

---

[183] CROWLEY (1929), chapter 58.

[184] Despite this, he only definitively claimed to first behold his HGA when he attempted the Operation a *third* time a year later, at a Hotel in Surrey, England. See CROWLEY (op. cit.), chapter 59.

When I got home that evening, my fiancée had a funny mood, still on edge due to the latest disagreement we had had. However, late at night just before I retired for meditation, we performed the Middle Pillar Ritual together. She had said she had wanted us to do more magic as a couple. She seemed in a noticeably better temperament after the ritual than before, so I presumed she felt it had done her some good.

Evening Ritual

Accomplished - and so to bed.

Day 122

12 August 2020

Morning Ritual

During the night I had a strange dream – one which I had had before over the years. In it I practised Hatha Yoga, performing *asanas* that I could not do in waking-life : e.g., back-bends where I could touch my head with my feet. Now I had practiced Hatha Yoga in waking-life often enough – mostly Iyengar Yoga – and had attained *a* degree of flexibility, but I definitely had a point beyond which I could never go. Hence my only experience of these extreme back-bends came through watching other people perform them (e.g., B K S Iyengar himself).

How then did I manage to dream about them in the first person ? I seriously considered it as evidence of a previous incarnation as a yogi. However, working out *when* this had occurred proved problematic. Although one often hears Hatha Yoga billed as an ancient practice, in reality it had mostly become a forgotten art until the first half of the twentieth century when people like Krishnamacarya (and indeed Iyengar) reponed it, as part of a wider Indian cultural renaissance inspired by Gandhi and the independence movement. Many of the *asanas* most commonly associated with modern Yoga (e.g., the infamous Down-Dog, Warriors one to three, etc) were likely cut from whole cloth right then : as no historicity exists for many of them before then, apart from the seated *asanas,* Corpse pose, and a few others. For example : Pattabhi Jois, the founder of Ashtanga Yoga, claimed that Krishnamacarya worked from an ancient book called *Yoga Koruntha,* although no-one has ever been able to trace the manuscript which he used.

Hence : if I entertained the notion that I had been W L Wilmshurst, then either I would have had to live as a Yogi between 1939 and 1972 ; *or* a tradition like that indicated by the legendary *Yoga Koruntha* did exist after all, confounding the historians.

(This at least I theorised at the time I had this strange dream. With hindsight another explanation might involve alternate timelines and different universes : but for that to work it would prove even more difficult to verify than my reincarnation theory.)

In any event, my alarm recalled me from the astral plane to this portion of the Multiverse at 5am. I got up and prepared with the Middle Pillar Ritual (and elimination as well). My main ritual went thus :

    "LBRP.

    "LBRH.

"Bornless Ritual.

"Conjuration.

"Confession. Thanking God & my HGA for everything they do, and how well the day ended yesterday (eventually). God is Infinite but I am Finite, yet with His grace I can become a little better than I am now. Distracting thoughts are a niggle, so I pray for forgiveness for them. Thanks be to God for despite having difficulties I also had the ability to overcome them.

"The Tea-Pot meditation - absorbing all sins and difficulties identified - all karma including that from past lives."

(i.e., including my putative life as a yogi.)

"Absorbing the ecstasies - absorbing everything. I get the feeling I should be absorbing everything, even when I am not performing this particular meditation. Again, a very exalted state of meditation which leaves me in good spirits for performing the subsequent parts of this morning's ritual.

"Additional Prayer.

"Licence to Depart.

"LBRP.

"LBRH.

"Total time : 1 hour 4 minutes."

*

My fiancée had a broad smile on her face that morning. She later told me excitedly, that she had received an unexpected wind-fall of some sort, so she felt pleased with herself.

Later, at work, I managed to research Psalm 38 :22, associated with Manaqel, the 66th Shem Ha Mephoresh Angel.

Midday Ritual

Beginning at 1.03pm, I followed the same procedure as yesterday : astrally projecting to my oratory to perform my ritual. It took 17 minutes. I again had a feeling of exaltation, though not as impressively as yesterday.

During the afternoon, I read another BOTA lesson, a follow-up to the one on "The World." Typically, BOTA usually issues lessons at the rate of one a week or four a month : despite the fact I did my last one only a few days ago, I wanted to make up for lost time as best I could.

Evening Ritual

Another argument flared up that evening, causing the good mood of the day to evaporate. My fiancée felt threatened by logical argument and found it difficult to entertain the idea that one could have a reasoned debate without intending any malice, which to me proved a sore sticking point, as logical argument and reasoned debate made up the only things with which I felt comfortable. Consequently, I had to force myself to walk away with a lot of sentiments unresolved and seemingly unresolvable.

I completed my evening ritual, conscious that I had a lot of shit to process in doing so.

Day 123

13 August 2020 10 :43

Morning Ritual

I got up at 5am for preparation with the Middle Pillar Ritual. Elimination. I still felt melancholic after last night. In a video on YouTube, Damien Echols had recently talked about "burning out the meridians." I wondered if this might affect me doing this meditation. If so, I would need to recover and take it easy somehow.

I resolved : *"I intend not to dawdle whilst performing my ritual, even though I want to do it as authentically as possible."* It went as follows :

"LBRP - it is the manifestation of Yeheshuah the Repairer."

I.e., the Pentagram, having five points, one for each element, represents the *Pentagrammaton* or יהשוה - Yeheshuah. Martinism does not have the Golden Dawn's pentagram ritual *per se* – although it does have one ceremony which looks suspiciously familiar – but it does attach importance to the Pentagram itself, precisely for its association with Yeheshuah.

It had occurred to me that the great "secret" of the LBRP lies in the fact that in tracing a pentagram in each of the cardinal directions one is effectively *surrounding oneself with Jesus*. Except that no-one hardly ever mentions this because of the many lapsed-Christians in the occult who would prefer not to think about this. However, as this thought popped into my head, I could not help but think of the Martinist influence. In a teaching inherited from the Elus Cohens, Martinism sees Yeheshuah as an emanation from God which actively helps humankind *reintegrate* back into its first estate – that of unity with the divine. I therefore saw the Pentagram ritual as a synthesis with the Martinist doctrine – I didn't just banish the influences for my personal convenience, nor because it was good to do so from a ceremonial magick point of view, but because it formed part of a greater scheme to assist in universal Reintegration.

"LBRH.

"Bornless Ritual - working quickly but still 'absorbing' all ...

"Conjuration.

"Confession of Sins. All the mess that occurred last night. Praying to God and my HGA, I realise : if I am self-actualised and not externally referenced, then I don't need to prove I'm right, hence I don't need to argue. Therefore I ought to be able to remain silent all the time, and most importantly not get a rise out of what I would otherwise see as provocation.

"The Tea-Pot meditation. Even though I am not in the best of moods this morning, it remains a powerful formula.

"Additional Prayer.

"Licence to Depart.

"LBRP.

"LBRH.

"Total time : 1 hour 4 minutes - so much for not dawdling !"

At breakfast, my fiancée appeared to share the same mood as I did, still wanting to get the last word in, but nevertheless a little better than last night.

Midday Ritual

I performed my ritual in the astral as on day 121, this time making sure to do so on an empty stomach. One little refinement : I found a video on YouTube called "Out of Body Music"[185] to help facilitate me projecting to my Oratory (I found it surprisingly effective).

I began at 12 :51 and had just got as far as establishing the single-letters in the Cube of Space, when - horror of horrors ! - one of the few other people in the building interrupted me, and I had to whip instantaneously back into my body (making the Sign of Silence as I did so).

After dealing with the interruption, I settled back into astral projection and began again, starting right over (1310). This time, all went to plan. I got into an exalted state of consciousness during the absorption, much deeper than I had ever yet done doing this particular type of meditation - like *Samadhi* – thus buoying me greatly as I completed the ritual with the Additional prayer and Licence to Depart. Even after I returned to my body & normal consciousness (making, of course, the Sign of Silence) I could still feel my third-eye tingling.

*

That afternoon, I investigated Psalm 37 :4, associated with Eyanghael, the 67th Shem Ha Mephoresh angel, who "serves to receive consolation in adversity and to acquire wisdom." I also spent time compiling data for a future investigation of the first 32 verses of Genesis.

In evening, I detected my fiancée exhibiting behaviour which appeared blatantly argumentative : however, with superhuman effort I resisted (by

---

[185] "Out of Body Music, LEAVE Your BODY Behind with this Music 🎧 Relaxing Music for Astral Projection," https://www.youtube.com/watch ?v=eRKMgzEtqf8 accessed 2020-08-13

"superhuman" I mean I suspected the influence of my Holy Guardian Angel at work).

Evening Ritual

Done. Absorbing all the events of the day ... *Et sic ad lectum.*[186]

---

[186] This is supposed to be "And so to bed," after the manner of Pepys' regular sign-off. However, I *did* rely on Google Translate in coming up with it, so for all I know it might mean any old rubbish.

Day 124

14 August 2020

Morning Ritual

U p at 5am – over forty minutes before sunrise - for preparation with the Middle Pillar ritual, as well as elimination. My morning ceremony went as follows :

"LBRP.

"LBRH.

"Bornless Ritual.

"Conjuration.

"Confession of Sins. Thanking God and my HGA for all they do. I was conscious of not rising to obvious bait last night, a sign I am getting better.

*"The Tea Pot meditation - very powerful - **samadhi** again ! As on previous days when this has happened, I am able to carry forward a positive and optimistic attitude to my subsequent activities (see below).*

"Additional Prayer.

"Licence to Depart.

"LBRP.

"LBRH.

"Total time not including preparation : 1 hour 10 minutes. The good mood caused by the experience of the Tea Pot meditation stays with me for at least several hours."

*

Work, already quiet, now became even more so during the Summer. Everyone used up their remaining annual leave, which they had to do by the end of August, even though they had nowhere to go on holiday. For many people the whole year had proved one giant "staycation." I myself used up my Annual leave by booking every Monday and Friday off, so that the entire Summer became a series of three day weeks and four-day weekends.

Hence today, I could type up my journal at home. The thought occurred to me as I did so : up to now I had devoted myself to resolving *my own* sins, should I eventually move on to being like Christ, and resolving those of others as well ? E.g. The colonial legacy of Britain in India in general, and the influence of Macaulayism there in particular. I cannot help but think, as one interested in Yoga, that the damage done to the Indian education system retarded scholarship of Eastern philosophies by a hundred years or more. On the other hand, if Macaulay hadn't happened, there neither would have Gandhi, as the movement the latter inspired needed something against which to react.

On a different matter altogether, having *samadhi* happen to me this morning inspired me to search on the internet for communities of people in a like situation, but which had remained unaffected by politics, ego-games, or just out-and-out bullshit. My filtering criteria returned me *no results*. The problem lay in the fact that something like a mystical phenomenon, which by its nature is ineffable, indescribable, and intensely personal, cannot provide suitable content which can be shared on social media. If one can't express it, one can't make a meme about it !

More seriously : great minds might discuss ideas, if one believes Eleanor Roosevelt, but no-one can express the Idea, discussion cannot take place, and hence communities which grow around such discussion remain unreified. Hence, one must inevitably have to deal with loneliness when experiencing peak experiences. I thought : "*Where are my fellow Ipsissimi ? ? ?*"

Midday Ritual

1310 - 1330. I performed this physically in my actual oratory, as on day 120. Once again the Tea-Pot meditation felt powerful, although discomfort from sitting in *padmasana* dissatisfied me : I tried not to let this spoil the experience, though.

Later that afternoon, I investigated Psalm 106 :1, associated with Chabuiah (68th Shem Ha Mephoresh Angel). The fact that the Hebrew words for "Thanks" equated in Gematria with "I Am" (i.e. *Eheieh* – the divine name of Kether), both being 21, left me excited – it pointed to the connection between Gratitude and Godliness.

Ironically, whilst surfing the net, I realised I could find that the ultimate BOTA lessons – which my fiancée had not yet received – available on the net – however, due to their bulk, the files proved difficult to download. Nevertheless, I sneaked a peek... Ironically, in its final lessons, BOTA started to touch on what the Golden Dawn taught to relative beginners – such as Elementals, etc. I decided to avoid making anything of this so as to not upset my beloved one.

Evening Ritual

Done. Not only did I perform a review of the day's memories, but I also did the Tea Pot meditation, so that when I eventually finished the ritual, I felt energised.

Day 125

15 August 2020 07 :15

Morning Ritual

I got up at 5.05am for preparation with the Middle Pillar Ritual again, and elimination. The morning ceremony went thus :

"*LBRP.*

"*LBRH.*

"*Bornless Ritual. Thought - TWO HANDS, TWO VOICES. An old Voodoo trick...*"

... Or at least I thought it was : one should, however, read this remark in the light of what transpired on Day 130 – *vide infra.* I described the gist of the practice in my journal thus :

"*I am conscious of both my physical body and its etheric counterpart doing all parts of the ritual simultaneously. The physical body performing on the physical plane, but the etheric reaching out into magical realms. It opens up my senses to the magical forces being invoked, so it is very effective.*

"*Conjuration. Continuing the 2H2V conceit above ...*

"*Confession of Sins. Conscious of jealousy etc which would not arise if I were self-actualised or internally referenced. Obvious thing for which to pray to God and my HGA to help me resolve.*

"*Thinking about sins generally. Many of the so-called sins I have committed may not be actual sins but I feel guilty about them all the same. Perhaps the sin is to wrongfully fetter myself?*

"*Thought : what if I am halfway through or even more than halfway through my spiritual development, i.e. A previous incarnation deliberately willed himself (?) to reincarnate as 'Alex Sumner' to complete his spiritual evolution ?*

"*The Tea-Pot Meditation. Again, powerful.*

"*Additional prayer.*

"*Licence to Depart.*

"*LBRP.*

"*LBRH.*

"*Total time : 1 hour 28 minutes. This strikes me as odd - I didn't realise how long it was - as if I have travelled half an hour into the future.*"

*

More arguments with my fiancée. The actual subject matter under dispute must have been quite trivial, or at least I thought it so, as I did not feel it important to note down afterward. More seriously however, I tried to work out the ultimate cause for why these arguments happen at all.

I certainly failed in keeping silent. What I perceived happening was this : my fiancée asks (what I think is) an innocent question, I try to give an innocent answer - but she does not perceive it as innocent, or thinks that I imply something unpleasant which I don't. Hence an argument develops because instead of shutting up, I try to explain myself, which she interprets as an attack on her. Hence the reason I fail to keep silence is because I get tricked into engaging in what I assume will turn out as a reasonable discussion, only to find out it doesn't and hence I find myself trapped in something which I cannot satisfactorily resolve. Tricky ...

Midday Ritual

I did this from 1235 to 1315 in my oratory, attempting to astrally project. The Tea Pot meditation again proved calming, despite me feeling melancholic from earlier.

That afternoon, I researched Psalm 16 :5, associated with Reahel (69th Shem Ha Mephoresh angel). This Angel appears to influence jurisconsults, magistrates, attorneys, solicitors and notaries : this has nothing to with traditional attributions of this versicle in the Magical Use of Psalms, but it does correspond to the meaning of the Hebrew words with which it shares Gematria. E.g. "Maintaineth" (as in "Thou maintaineth") equates to "House of Justice." The meditation thereon turned out good.

When I emerged from hiding and ventured downstairs, I found my fiancée seeming to suffer very badly because of the arguments earlier : she appeared much put out that I at least could function properly. I tried acting conciliatorily, but I could not help but think that she exacerbated her own problems, so I ended up giving her a pep-talk or two. Eventually her mood ameliorated after watching some television - it enabled her to escape from her mindset.

Evening Ritual

Done : Conjuration, retrospective visualisation of the day's events and Tea-Pot meditation (energising), Additional prayer, Licence to Depart. When I finally got to bed, my fiancée's spirits had completely lifted : she now felt in a sufficiently good mood for "sacrament."

Day 126

16 August 2020 07 :09

Morning Ritual

Up at 5.05am, forty minutes before sunrise, for preparation with the Middle Pillar Ritual. Elimination : I think sitting in *padmasana* stimulates the viscera, and hence expedites the final part of the digestive process. In any case, once ready to start my main ritual, I worked according to the "2H2V" principle I mentioned yesterday.

"LBRP.

"LBRH.

"Bornless Ritual – powerful.

"Conjuration.

"Confession of Sins. Watching TV late at night can cause distracting thoughts in the morning. Bad.

"Tea Pot meditation is again powerful.

"Additional Prayer.

"Licence to Depart.

"LBRP.

"LBRH.

"Total time taken (not including preparation) 1 hour 22 minutes".

This struck me as unusually long. I tried analysing the cause and concluded that it must have been the "2H2V" principle : trying to practice that assiduously prolonged the experience. I speculated that if I integrated the "2H2V" principle so that I did it instinctively, I could streamline the ritual greatly.

Throughout the day, it struck me relations with my fiancée stayed conspicuously free from arguments. In fact they proved downright *pleasant.*

Midday Ritual

I performed this from 12.52 to 13.24 in my oratory, in a similar manner to yesterday, but with the big difference being that I didn't feel melancholic. It went much better today, and I completed the ritual feeling positive and energised.

That afternoon, for my scriptural study, I investigated Genesis 1 :1, associated with Jabamiah, the 70th Shem Ha Mephoresh Angel. The description of the Angel's powers struck me as unusually significant – I will quote at length :

"This angel rules over the generation of beings and phenomena of Nature ; he protects those who desire to regenerate themselves, and to re-establish in themselves that harmony which was broken by the disobedience of Adam,

which they will accomplish by raising themselves before God and purifying those parts which constitute the nature of man through the elements : thus they will regain their rights and their original dignity. They will once more become the masters of nature and will enjoy all the prerogatives which God gave them at their creation."[187]

Immediately I read this I thought : "why, this is nothing but Martinism !" I thought specifically of the central thesis of *Treatise on the Reintegration of Beings,* by Martinez De Pasqually, which interprets Adam's fall as a Gnostic descent – and subsequent imprisonment – of Spirit into matter. The prime difference, however, between that and historical Gnosticism lay in the Fall being cause not by some evil Demiurge, but by Primordial Adam himself, stepping back from his duties as master of that dimension into which God had consigned the spirits who had prevaricated against the Divine plan, or as we would call it, the material Universe.

Hence the ultimate aim of humans consists in Reintegrating back into Divinity. De Pasqually thought this meant that through invoking angelic assistance, and exorcising the recalcitrant demons, a man would Reintegrate by resuming the duties that God had originally intended for primordial Adam.

Although De Pasqually thought of the Elus Cohens as the vehicle for achieving, his most important disciples rejected his methodology, whilst simultaneously retaining his ideology – i.e., the theory of Reintegration. Hence, Louis-Claude de St. Martin taught Reintegration through means of mysticism – i.e., the Way of the Heart ; Willermoz, through reforming Masonic ritual (i.e. the CBCS) ; whilst the Marquis de Chefdebien, an Elu Cohen but a name usually left out of traditional Martinist narratives, favoured a kind of stripped-down theurgy which influenced later orders, such as the Rose-Croix D'Orient.

I have already mentioned my involvement with the Elus Cohens :[188] I had received initiation into them through my involvement with Martinism itself. In this I heeded the advice of the man who introduced me to the Hermetic Order of Martinists. "You'll enjoy the Elus Cohens !" he said, perceiving my aptitude for ceremonial magic. "However, you should become a Martinist first, as that will provide you with the philosophical basis on which the Cohens rest." I therefore received initiation into Martinism and worked my way through it, even to the point of serving a term as Venerable Master of my Martinist lodge.

I should point out that the Elus Cohens and the Martinists form separate orders – no one does not *progress* from one to the other. One theoretically could be an Elu Cohen and not a Martinist, but many practitioners – including my own mentor

---

[187] LENAIN (2020) p96.
[188] Day 113 – *vide supra.*

– think it unwise to do so, whilst a number of orders deliberately make "culmination" in Martinism (i.e., a formal recognition that one has completed the studies of the third degree) a qualification for consideration as a member.

I suppose I read Jabamiah's description through a "Martinist filter," i.e. this particular interpretation would not have occurred to anyone not sharing my background. I knew from personal experience that the rituals and practices of Martinism when worked properly felt powerful, and very moving. I therefore thought it a good idea to petition this Angel to fulfil my Martinist ambitions : after this angelic invocation, I put the matter out of my mind for the time-being.

*

To pass the time I tried working out the precise implications of what would happen if the Cube of Space consisted of a tesseract rather than a 3D cube. It would have to have at least 55 "letters," possibly more, in order to assimilate the Cube of Space into higher dimensions. This might appear as a conceit, but it raises (for me at any rate) an interesting philosophical question, to wit :

Modern science, in its quest to find the theory of everything, posits that the Universe as having eleven dimensions. Therefore assuming that God exists, He would have to have eleven dimensions as well – or possibly more than that, who knows. Why, therefore, does the Qabalah use a *three-dimensional* model to depict an *eleven (or more)-dimensional* God ?

I mentioned Tesseracts earlier : but what if the Cube of Space were not a Tesseract, but a hypercube of even more dimensions, to match those of God and the quantum Universe ? The number of letters needed to populate the edges and faces of such a hypercube would grow exponentially larger with each higher dimension.

We find the twenty-two letters of the Hebrew alphabet sufficient for a Cube of which our puny three-dimensional minds can conceive, assuming God uses Hebrew as His language – but it only makes logical sense from our point of view. Hebrew in the Qabalah really only fulfils the role of a "pidgin" language, created to facilitate communication from the divine to the human realms. The analogy of the Hypercube suggests that God has His own Alphabet, consisting of an infinite number of letters, and He has a language within the divine realm which lies far beyond the possibility of human understanding.

Evening Ritual

Done, as yesterday, trying to extend the 2H2V principle to "two minds" as well - one to consider the regular thoughts, and the second to deal with the magical dimension to them.

Day 127

17 August 2020

Morning Ritual

I got up at 5am for preparation with the Middle Pillar Ritual. For some reason I finished with sixteen minutes to spare before the appointed time for my main ritual, so I started early. I worked as best I could according to the "2H2V" principle.

    "LBRP.

    "LBRH.

    "Bornless Ritual.

    "Conjuration.

    "Confession of Sins. Distracting thoughts again caused by 'late' night TV (actually not that late). I thought I had put a special effort into releasing the memories of the previous evening ...

    "Tea Pot meditation is again powerful.

    "Additional Prayer.

    "Licence to Depart.

    "LBRP.

    "LBRH.

    "Total time taken : 1 hour 13 minutes. Still longer than previously, but today I made an effort to streamline the 2H2V. Need to master the 2H2V principle first before attempting to speed up - it's not the sort of thing for which one can cut corners."

Midday Ritual

I did this in my Oratory : it lasted 31 minutes. The meditation today struck me as very powerful.

In the afternoon, for my scriptural study I investigated Psalm 109 :30, associated with Haiaiel (71st Shem Ha Mephoresh angel).

For some reason I felt anxious : I speculated that it might have something to do with staying in the house all day. To console myself, I dug out my BOTA lessons and read the last instalment in *"Tarot Fundamentals"* which said I had to do a whole month of meditating on the Tarot keys in a particular fashion, before completing an exam which exceeded in length what I had done so far.

This surprised me : the first two courses that BOTA taught, *"Seven Steps in Practical Occultism"* and *"Introduction to Tarot"* end with such easy-peasy exams that anyone ought have the ability to pass them. The third course, however, demanded a potent test of one's mettle. I thought that BOTA had used the first two courses to lull one into a false sense of security before hitting one with the hard work in course number three.

I decided that doing the month of meditations *and* completing the exam would add too much to my Abramelin work, so I decided to postpone any further BOTA studies until after the end of my operation. Nevertheless, it did give me a renewed respect for BOTA, as it implied that when done well it made a proper system of development.

In evening – instead of watching TV, I tried to teach my fiancée horary astrology instead. We did a question about casting a spell to get us to Florida this November – remarkably the Horary figure suggested that it would make a good idea and would prove successful. (With hindsight, though, this proved not otherwise, as the UK went into another lockdown later that year, whilst restrictions in Florida itself remained in place, making international travel at the time doubly impossible. Reviewing the horary chart in light of what happened, it appeared that we could better have interpreted it as saying that we ourselves would have a pleasant time in November, but a potential journey overseas would not – it would have been hit by a combination of factors represented on the figure by a square aspect between Mars on the one hand and Saturn, Pluto, and Jupiter – all grouped in a *Stellium* at the time of the horary figure – on the other.)

Evening Ritual.

Done. Powerful. It felt like my crown chakra opening ... *Et sic ad lectum.*

Day 128

18 August 2020

During the night, I had a particularly vivid dream that Lon Milo Duquette had come to visit, to talk about occult books and stuff. I could not perceive any especial significance of this dream : I enjoyed Duquette's writings, and he had written about things like knowledge and conversation of the holy guardian angel, which obviously held relevance to me at the time. So perhaps it should have surprised me more if I *hadn't* dreamt about him at least once.

Morning Ritual

I got up at 5am for preparation with the Middle Pillar Ritual, and elimination. I again started early. I became conscious that if I literally timed my rituals according to sunrise, they would eat into my day as dawn got later heading into Autumn.

Once again I attempted to use the "2H2V" method which I had mentioned yesterday – it went noticeably smoother than it did the previous day.

"*LBRP.*

"*LBRH.*

"B*ornless Ritual. Powerful. Good.*

"*Conjuration. Good.*

"*Confession of Sins. Thanking God and my HGA for everything they do. Decision to avoid TV last night was definitely a good one.*

"*Tea Pot meditation is powerful again. However, I get to the point of absorbing sins etc, I wonder if I should be ready to take on my responsibilities as one of the Thirty-Six.*"

I.e., I speculated that the ultimate aim of the Qabalah, and hence the grade of Ipsissimus, lay far removed from attaining personal power or glory, or even self-esteem : it really involved performing the ultimate act of service possible for an incarnated being. In my mind, therefore, I linked the 10=1 grade with the Qabalistic legend of the 'Thirty-Six Secret Men of Righteousness' *(Tzadeqim Nistarim),* for the sake of whose prayers God preserves the world from destruction, i.e. that this represented the true vocation of an Ipsissimus.

Actually, I had further speculations about the Thirty-Six, e.g. : because of their Secrecy, not only does no-one know their identity, they probably don't know each other or if they themselves are 'on the list,' as it were. Moreover, *for all we know,* one, some, or all of them might be Women of Righteousness. Besides which, if thirty-six is the minimum needed to keep the world going, they probably number more than that in total, so that if one dies, someone can jump in straightaway from the reserve pool, ready to take his or her place.

I therefore thought that the actions of the High Priest, in entering the *Sanctum Sanctorum* to make propitiation for the sins of the people – i.e., the point of the Sepher Yetzirah in general and my Tea-Pot meditation in particular – equated to the task of the Lamed-Vavniks, since both aimed at preserving humanity through invoking God's favour. I later researched this and found that unfortunately I had *not* come up with an original thought : as apparently one of the derivations of the legend came from a Talmudic saying that in every generation Thirty-Six people exist who "greet the Shekinah every day" (i.e. do service in the Temple).[189]

Hence, the question on my mind that morning that I wanted answering : had doing this meditation, by which I attempted to recreate what the grade of Ipsissimus might resemble, made me ready for the role of *Tzadeq Nistar*, or at least to go on the reserve list ?

"I get an uncomfortable feeling, which thinking rationally probably means 'No.' (Hence the act of wondering about the Thirty-Six is a Distracting Thought, hence a Sin - something to confess next time !)

"Additional Prayer.

"Licence to Depart.

"LBRP.

"LBRH.

"Total time : 1 hour 10 minutes (making the 2H2V practice more efficient seems to be working)."

*

Over breakfast, my fiancée talked about her theories of meditation, with which I did not feel sure that I agreed. But instead of arguing with her, I paused to consider : I based my knowledge of *Dharana*, *Dhyana* and *Samadhi* on what BKS Iyengar wrote.[190] But what if I was *wrong* ? And if so, of what did the states of consciousness I had experienced during peak experiences consist ?

Because my peak experiences seemed to coincide with what BKS Iyengar wrote, I had never seriously doubted his writings – especially as other writers seemed to concur. But did I experience objective reality, or something that conformed to my prejudices ? In short, how could I ever get independent verification for what I went through ?

---

[189] See : https ://www.sefaria.org/Sukkah.45b.6 ?lang=bi&with=all&lang2=en accessed 2021-07-15.

[190] E.g., IYENGAR (1966) ; IYENGAR (1996).

*

For my scriptural study that day I researched Psalm 116 :7, associated with Mumiah, the 72nd and last of the Shem Ha Mephoresh angels. Mumiah presides over bringing things to successful conclusions, so I therefore petitioned this angel to bring my fiancée's quest for adeptship to a successful conclusion, by enabling us to fly to Florida this November for her 5=6. (As it turned out, she certainly qualified for advancement, although opening up international air travel in the face of the renewed pandemic proved outside Mumiah's remit.)

Midday Ritual

I printed out exorcisms, etc, for my body of light as detailed under "Theurgic Rite for Astral Projection."[191] I then performed the ritual by astrally projecting from my place of work to my oratory, whilst "Astral Projection" music was playing via YouTube - in a similar manner to what I did last week. It all struck me as very powerful : it certainly made up for the uncomfortable feeling I had got this morning. The whole thing lasted half an hour from 12 :08 to 12 :38.

Later that day I tried to reading "Qabalistic Doctrines of Rebirth & Immortality," one of the final BOTA courses. I found it heavy going, particularly because the first few lessons didn't exactly give away any secrets or either rebirth or immortality, Qabalistic or otherwise. Clearly I should have to keep this on the backburner for now – ordinarily BOTA members would only get to look at it after fifteen years' study or so.

Instead, to pass the time, I created a sigil - something to visualise whilst doing the "Additional prayer" in my daily meditations. I did this A O Spare style, by taking the wording of the phrase and getting rid of repeating letters, and then making the sigil from those which remained. Actually, I have found that on can do this easily nowadays by typing the phrase into a text editor and then using the "find and replace" feature to systematically get rid of repeating letters : although in reality, it's never the sigil one creates, but always the way in which one empowers it, which makes the difference.

Evening Ritual

I had been feeling anxious through the day, so I deliberately tried to get an early night in case lack of sleep had caused the anxiety. I performed the evening ritual as on previous days, again using the 2H2V principle. Whilst in a deep state of

---

[191] Day 113 – *vide supra*.

meditation, I identified the location of the anxiety and said to it, with the Two Voices, "Be healed."

It went away.

This might have has something to do with the fact that one of the websites I had browsed earlier in the day gave a brief biography of Maître Phillipe De Lyon, who could work healing miracles simply through the power of prayer - and belief. But it may also have indicated that the 2H2V principle had far greater potential than I had first imagined.

Anywho I finished the whole ritual with the Tea-Pot meditation very good, as always ; *et sic ad lectum.*

Day 129

19 August 2020

Morning Ritual

U p at 5am for preparation with the Middle Pillar Ritual. Elimination. I began my main ritual of the morning seventeen minutes before sunrise. Again, I used the "2H2V" principle where possible.

"*LBRP.*

"*LBRH.*

"*Bornless Ritual. Powerful.*

"*Conjuration. Very good.*

"*Confession. Pride, getting full of oneself, lack of humility. All sins, or at least they are sinful thoughts.*

"*The Tea Pot meditation - still powerful after all this time.*

"*Additional Prayer. Visualising the sigil created yesterday whilst in an exalted state of consciousness caused by the Tea Pot meditation.*

"*Licence to Depart.*

"*LBRP.*

"*LBRH.*

"*Total time not including preparation : 1 hour 5 minutes.*"

At breakfast, my fiancée continued to riff on a particular translation of Patanjali's Yoga Sutras which purported to support an interpretation with which I do not agree ("purported" being the operative word – I doubt one could call it truly antithetical). Consequently, a disagreement arose between us : I didn't take a note of the precise sticking-point, so I guess I regarded it as yet another triviality. Nevertheless, she bemused me by claiming to get *stressed* by me sticking to my own point of view. I made a note to myself to remember to keep Silent, as I ought not to have expected her to change her own position based on anything I said.

*

Later that morning, I started my new phase of daily scriptural study, by beginning my analysis of the first thirty-two verses of the book of Genesis. I had decided that I would compile my studies into a Word file which I named "The Heart of the Qabalah" according to yet another cunning Qabalistic cipher : i.e., Hebrew uses the word for *Heart*, Lev (lamed-beth לב) as the way of representing the number Thirty-Two. In other words, with my new project I attempted to discover the mysteries of the *Ma'aseh Bereshith* for myself, instead of just reading about them.

I started at the beginning, with Genesis 1 :1, intending to follow much the same sort of analysis as I had done with previous versicles. I.e., I would go into the versicle in Hebrew, work out the gematria of the individual words, and compare the whole with the corresponding path of the *Sepher Yetzirah.*

In one sense I had a gentle introduction today, as I had already done some analysis of Genesis 1 :1 when I looked at Jabamiah whilst going through the Shem Ha Mephoresh Angels : but I found it intriguing to bring in the extra analysis of the "Admirable or Concealed Intelligence" as well.

Quite apart from this, I also took time to read more about Maître Phillipe. One anecdote mightily amused me, in that he seemed to have "pulled a Plotinus" on Papus when the latter tried to work some black magic on him, i.e., Phillipe had such a virtuous character that the black magic bounced right off him and recoiled onto Papus instead.

Midday Ritual

Done. As yesterday, but this time I did not have access to Astral Projection music due to problems with the internet at work. Not as remarkable as yesterday, although I made sure I did it with complete authenticity.

In the evening, I tried talking about my Abramelin experience with my fiancée, but it seemed clear that she did not have sympathy with the whole concept. Later, things took a turn for the worse when she bewailed having to learn astrology, and said a great many things about the Golden Dawn which upset me because I took them personally. I lost my shit at this point - any good intention I had of trying to remain silent went out of the window. I felt betrayed, and I let her know it, making her almost as upset as me.

Evening Ritual

Ironically, when I did the evening ritual, it proved to be the most powerful experience of its kind so far. When, as a result of the Tea-Pot meditation, I attempted to absorb everything, I experienced *Samadhi*. Energy filled me by the time I finally got to bed.

Despite the harsh words - the harshest I had allowed myself to speak so far – my fiancée embraced the opportunity to cuddle when I woke up at 1.30am. I could not help thinking it was much later - perhaps time had moved so slow so as to give me an opportunity. Sacrament ensued, actually very good.

Day 130

20 August 2020

Morning Ritual

Up at 5am for preparation with the Middle Pillar Ritual (and elimination). I started fifteen minutes early this morning, again working on the "2H2V" principle.

"LBRP.

"LBRH.

"Bornless Ritual. Good.

"Conjuration.

"Confession. Infinite God vs Finite Human implies I am sinful either actually or potentially just by reason of not being God, even if I haven't done anything specifically wrong.

"Wondering about yesterday's harsh words. Was I too harsh? Did I do the right thing? If not, have I made sufficient amends? Questions, questions, questions. The good intention at the heart of my behaviour yesterday was that I wanted what was best for my fiancée, because I love her - despite the fact that she didn't appreciate what she perceived as me forcing her out of her comfort zone.

"Tea-pot meditation is powerful, again.

"Additional prayer.

"Licence to Depart.

"LBRP.

"LBRH.

"Total time : 1 hour 11 minutes."

My fiancée looked and sounded melancholic at breakfast : she felt depressed about divination as a general concept, and also negative about her work. I perceived that she had a tendency to consider herself not good enough when she actually was, and only think about herself in negative, disempowering terms. I sighed : if only she could reframe her situation in positive terms she could empower herself instead.

*

For the past six days I had used what I thought to call the "Two Hands, Two Voices" – abbreviated "2H2V" - technique, to great effect (apparently).

However, I tried researching it in more detail – and found myself plunged into a deep mystery.

As I understood the principle, when drawing a talisman or indeed a *vévé* or sigil, a magician ought to write with "two hands" – i.e., the Physical hand, and the *Magical* Hand. By the " Magical Hand " I mean a simplified way of thinking about all of the subtle bodies, so I suppose that if one were to get all Theosophical and sophisticated, one might call it the Etheric Hand, except that one has concentrated magical power in that part of the Etheric anatomy through willpower and concentration. Hence "writing with two hands" involves remaining conscious of both the Physical and Magical hands simultaneously, so that as one writes with the physical, one maintains awareness of the magical force transmitted by its counterpart.

Similarly, "speaking with two voices" amounts to its equivalent for making a magical invocation. One becomes aware of the existence of a magical or etheric counterpart to the ordinary physical voice : hence when one makes an invocation – even of just one word – one simultaneously experiences the Physical voice vibrating in the air, and the Magical voice vibrating through the subtle planes of existence.

At least : I *thought* I remembered it like that, but today I tried searching on the internet for some scholarly reference which would explain the history of the thing.

I could find nothing !

I racked my brains to see if I could remember where I had read it. I felt sure I first heard it in connection with a post on Voodoo on E A Koetting's website, but I couldn't find anything about it there. Despite the dim reaction that Cool magicians have to Dark Fluff, I have found occasional nuggets of practical worth in it – on the basis that "there is no such thing as a bad idea."

However, searching for " Voodoo" and "two hands" generally on the internet only returned the notion that one who worked with two hands behaved duplicitously – i.e., working for the good of others but also having a darker, more self-serving practice on the side. Despite the fact that I felt sure I had first heard about the idea on the internet, people who responded to me seemed wholly ignorant of the "Two Hands, Two Voices" conception as I had imagined it.

I couldn't have hallucinated it, surely ? Or invented a brand new magical technique by mistake ? Once again it unnerved me to think that I might yet again have travelled "diagonally through time," i.e., the memory I had of reading about "2H2V" belonged to an alternate time-line, from which I had crossed over into this one without realising : in much the same way as I had discovered my first method of invoking my Holy Guardian Angel, or my attempts to pin down references for *Samyama* long after I had read them.

In any event, I only knew that the effort to concentrate on both the ordinary hand or voice, as well as its magical counterpart, had proved an effective way to get me into a psychic state of mind very quickly – immediately in fact. Although I could not now find any reference to the idea in Voodoo or anything else, I felt pretty sure that many years ago Dion Fortune had also said something about using one's etheric body to enchant a talisman or other magical object. Unless of course that had happened in an alternate dimension as well.

Midday Ritual

Done, like yesterday but this time with astral projection music. Very powerful (an improvement on yesterday).

In the afternoon, I investigated Genesis 1 :2, associated with Chokmah and the Illuminating Intelligence. My studies went beyond the *Ma'aseh Berashit*, as I could quite clearly detect Alchemical symbolism in the Gematria, in addition to the purely Qabalistic.

A mishap at work forced me to buy a book from Amazon – i.e. a random demon which I had not banished caused a book I had been looking after for someone else to go for a burton. In order to qualify for free delivery, I added "The Science of the Kabbalah" to the order as well : I had parked it on my wish-list for some time – up to that point I had only relied on Ambelain.

I also took the time to answer a question on Quora.com, "How can a normal person by a psychic ?" (My answer : "The difference between a so-called 'normal' person and a psychic person is that the former is unaware of their psychic ability, whilst the latter *is* aware.")

Evening Ritual

Done. Samadhi-like state again. When I got to bed later, my fiancée had brightened up considerably compared to this morning – sacrament ensued.

Day 131

21 August 2020

Morning Ritual

U p at 5am for preparation with the Middle Pillar Ritual (and Elimination). I started the main ritual 14 minutes before sunrise, again using applying the principles of "2H2V" (or I should say "my principles…" given the results of yesterday's researches).

"*LBRP.*

"*LBRH.*

"*Bornless Ritual. Good.*

"*Conjuration. Also good.*

"*Confession. Thanking God and my HGA for everything they do.*

"*Infinity of God vs Finity of Me is a continuing problem and insuperable as long as I am confined to this human form. It is a constant reminder that I cannot not rely on Grace at least to some extent.*

"*Distracting thoughts - another niggle.*

"*The Tea Pot Meditation continues to be powerful. Not quite as earth-shattering as yesterday but still fairly potent.*

"*Additional prayer.*

"*Licence to Depart.*

"*LBRP.*

"*LBRH.*

"*Total time not including preparation : 1 hour 14 minutes.*"

I found my fiancée in brighter spirits this morning even though she complained of tiredness. As I had a day off today, I took the opportunity to go back to bed for some Zzz. I had had a plan of venturing to London to research some arcane ritual in the Library & Museum of Freemasonry : however, the fact that the United Grand Lodge of England had *gone Dark* during the lockdown stymied me, because most of the facilities at Freemasons Hall remained closed. (As it turned out, I would not get an opportunity to do so until a year later, well after the end of this Operation, but that's another story).

Midday Ritual

Done whilst physically in my oratory, listening to astral projection ("AP") music. It took about 45 minutes. The Tea-pot meditation I noted as " potent."

For my scriptural study today, I researched Genesis 1 :3.

"*Then God said, 'Let there be light' ; and there was light.*

The Gematria of this whole verse in Hebrew adds up to 813, which equates to the notariqon 'ARARITA.' I doubt that one can explain this as a coincidence : rather, Kabbalists deliberately formulated 'Ararita' in order to express the power of Genesis 1 :3 in one convenient word. In any event it adds an intriguing new level of symbolism to the Hexagram ritual. To my mind it would imply that the LVX invoked in the analysis of the key-word corresponds to the Light mentioned in this verse.

Also today I spent time writing a book review of "Meditations for Every Week," primarily because someone I know translated it.

Evening Ritual

After much eating of Pizza for dinner, I performed this as usual. *Et sic ad lectum.*

Day 132

22 August 2020

Morning Ritual

Painfully aware that last night's dinner sat heavier in my digestive tract than it ought to have done, I got up at 5.05am. Hence some welcome elimination, before performing the Middle Pillar Ritual. I then performed my main ritual of the morning as follows.

"*LBRP*.

"*LBRH*.

"*Bornless Ritual. Good.*

"*Conjuration. Good. The 2H2V principle is a welcome improvement to both this and the Bornless Ritual.*

"*Confession. The infinity of God vs the Infinity of Me ; random distracting thoughts, etc ; these are all ongoing issues for which I have to rely on the Grace of God.*

"*Someone wants to interview me for their podcast. Potentially doing this could be a distraction : thinking about it and the attendant publicity certainly is. (Safest thing to do would be to put him off - say I am busy and ask me again after I have finished Abramelin in November).*

"*Thought : assume for one moment that one of my past incarnations was a Yogi - hence the reason that I am able to dream of doing asanas that I don't have the ability to do in waking life. If that is the case, it is possible that I was also a Guru of some kind, with one or more chelas. Hence, I would be responsible for not only my karma but that of my Chelas as well. Perhaps that Yogi deliberately decided to reincarnate as me, because he wanted to reincarnate in a form that would be able to resolve the Karma of those chelas.*

"*It occurs to me that I ought to implore God's mercy not just for my (our) sins, but for my (our) future (i.e. Potential) sins, just in case.*

"*Tea Pot meditation. Starts off well but padmasana is distracting me, so I have to spend extra time meditating just to get a basic sense of meditative stillness.*

"*Additional Prayer*.

"*LBRP*.

"*LBRH*.

"*Total time not including preparation : 1 hour 26 minutes.*"

The latter half of this morning's ritual did not satisfy me as much as the former half. I could think of two possible reasons. (a) I performed the first half standing up, and could get into a deep state of magical consciousness. I performed the second half sitting down in padmasana, and I believe that discomfort in the asana distracted me. Hence one obvious potential solution would involve doing the whole thing standing up, or at least not in a distracting posture. (b) A bodily need to eliminate *again* may have distracted me in the latter half : I did so after finishing. I had eaten heavily last night (strictly vegetarian stuff, of course), but then another obvious potential solution would involve avoiding indulgence (especially when it comes to ordering in Pizza). Ideally, I should try out both potential solutions - I would not probably not order in Pizza for some time, but I could try out the standing stuff later today.

Midday Ritual

Done, incorporating thoughts expressed earlier. In my oratory with AP music playing, I visualised my Body of Light and made the General Blessing and the Blessing of Vestures before assuming it. I then performed the conjuration, confession (+ Tea Pot meditation), additional prayer and licence to depart - all whilst standing up. I definitely noticed an improvement in quality compared to this morning : I felt energised and enthused by doing so. Total time 29 minutes.

Indulging my fiancée in shopping took up all of the afternoon – although I did manage to acquire a Hazel wand for use in the final ritual : the local magick wand shop having all sold out of Almond-ones.

In the evening I made a little study of Genesis 1 :4, although I came up with some insights, nonetheless. It certainly helped to cross reference with the Zohar whilst doing this.

Evening Ritual.

Due to the lateness of the hour when I got round to this - and because I missed the company of my fiancée - I cut this short. I did the Conjuration, and only the very briefest recollection of the day's events before going straight to the additional prayer, and the Licence to Depart. Sacrament, however, with her afterwards proved very good.

Day 133

23 August 2020

Morning Ritual

Up at 5.05am for preparation with the Middle Pillar Ritual (and elimination). Following on from my observations yesterday, this morning I did the whole thing standing up.

"*LBRP.*

"*LBRH.*

"*Bornless Ritual. Only really getting into it towards the end.*

"*Conjuration. Good.*

"*Confession of Sins. Not having any particular sins to bring to mind, I make a general entreaty thanking God and my HGA for everything they do, and asking forgiveness for all sins that I might have committed. I add in prayers for the sins for whom I have taken responsibility as well including past, present and future karma.*

"*The one exception to not having particular sins is that of regretting cutting my evening ritual short yesterday because of the lateness of the hour.*

"*It occurs to me that this really was a grand plan by the Yogi who was one of my previous incarnations. But who was he? He must have lived before the beginning of the twentieth century, possibly more ancient than that by several hundred years. Hatha Yoga was not in its present form back then except amongst a small number of yogis, who would have been familiar with the original Yoga Koruntha (a 'lost' i.e. Mythological book). I should accept that conventional historical techniques will not help me, so I will have to recover actual past life memories.*

"*In quality doing this whole thing standing up is far better than the equivalent yesterday, so that I am able to retain the 2H2V principle throughout. When I do the Tea-Pot meditation, for example, I feel a sense of energy and enthusiasm - free from the distraction caused by sitting in padmasana for an overlong length of time.*

"*Additional Prayer.*

"*Licence to Depart.*

"*LBRP.*

"*LBRH.*

"*Total time not including preparation : 1 hour 21 minutes.*"

Midday Ritual

Done. In astral, though in my oratory, with AP music playing. General Blessing / Blessing of Vestures placing my consciousness in body of light. Conjuration, Confession of Sins, Additional prayer, Licence to Depart. Good.

For my scriptural study today I investigated Genesis 1 :5, associated with Geburah.

> *"God called the light Day, and the darkness He called Night. So the evening and the morning were the first day."*

The words associated with night and darkness equate, by gematria, to various demons. One could read this whole verse as *"And God called the Essence of Glory Beautiful, Satan and the Demons he called Lucifer. There came a great confrontation and battle and dawn came. The first day of transgression."*

Hence, the Fall of the Rebellious Angels happened at this point *here* : which would coincide with Geburah's association with the *Sita Ahra*. The Sepher Yetzirah – the Radical intelligence – on the other hand, points out the *nice* side of Geburah, i.e., by aspiring to Binah one can protect oneself from the sinister aspects here. The Tarot helps in my cogitations, even though this would not have occurred to the authors of *Ma'aseh Berashit*.

Later that day, at my fiancée's request, we did some yoga together. Unlike two nights ago, we dined modestly – we even got round to eating some vegetables we had grown in our own garden.

Evening Ritual

Done, this time properly. Whilst doing the mental review I went back two days, i.e. Doing what I should have done yesterday as well. *& sic ad lectum.*

Day 134

24 August 2020

Morning Ritual

Up at 5am : preparation with the Middle Pillar ritual. In particular, I feel that Kether, the nature of my highest Self, dissolves or destroys everything not itself, thereby making itself perfectly *exclusive*. By contemplating it I exclude all other thoughts and indeed things. It provides a continual source of power and energy which gives meaning to my magical endeavours, for example, by empowering all the 2H2V stuff I do. (Elimination).

I started my main ritual 17 minutes before sunrise.

"General Blessing / Blessing of vestures for Body of Light.

"LBRP.

"LBRH.

"Bornless Ritual. *Good - concentrating on Kether in the manner mentioned above periodically throughout the ritual helps.*

"Conjuration.

"Confession. *I bring to mind and ask forgiveness for sins generally, associated with me being a mere mortal - and responsible for the karma of others generally, standing up. Because I try to keep my mind fixed on Kether when I do so (see above) I find this effective. The chain starts to come off when I sit in padmasana to do the Tea Pot Meditation, as I find I am tensing my muscles without realising.*

"Nevertheless, I do have a profound insight, worthy of further investigation. I see the parallels between the Absorption process, and the exclusionary nature of my Highest self, such that I conflate the two, i.e. Absorption ultimately works by drawing the Absorbee into my aura (i.e. Consciousness) and then dissolving it via the dissolving function of my Highest Self. Will need to meditate on this further (and go back to either standing up or sitting in a chair).

"Additional prayer.

"Licence to Depart.

"L**BRP.**

"LBRH.

"Total time not including preparation : 1 hour 19 minutes."

At breakfast afterwards, I remarked to my fiancée that the length of my ritual had slowly and gradually increased over the course of the operation, and not entirely deliberately. I therefore needed to get up earlier, e.g. 4.30am, so that I could finish with enough time to actually see her in the morning before she went to work.

NB : by doing this and not timing the start of my rituals in relation to sunrise on any given day, I would in one sense depart from the literal wording of The Book. However in another I believed that *my own spirit and my understanding taught me the manner in which I should conduct myself in all points ; because my guardian angel was already about me, though invisible, and conducted and governed my heart, so that I would not err.*[192]

It weighed heavy on my conscience. Note that I recommend strongly against taking liberties with the ritual : *only* a definite indication from one's Holy Guardian Angel could ever justify one doing so, which lies a million miles distant from making a change just because it feels right.

*

For my scriptural study that day, I investigated Genesis 1 :6. I concluded that Tiphereth constituted "Heaven" : for in this verse God establishes for the first time something upon which created beings can fix their attention as the object of their aspirations. However by associating it with the Qabalah in this way, although "Heaven" (Tiphereth) fulfils the aspiration for the common man (or woman), union with God (Kether) as a concept exceeds Heaven itself.

Midday Ritual

Done. In my oratory with AP music playing. Similar structure to yesterday.

As I formulated the Tea-Pot meditation, I visualised the Hebrew letters corresponding to parts of my Body of Light. I had the idea that the Angels of the Shem Ha Mephoresh - and the Spirits of the Goetia – lay *within* those letters. I.e., they all represent the signs of the Zodiac, which contain the said angels and demons (magically speaking), hence I may imagine them as residing within the letters which make up my body of light. Hence further, I may imagine any invocation to one of those spirits as being directed to a part of my Body of Light. I therefore saw the reasoning behind the "*point-chaud*" system, only I saw it as not to do with the degrees of Memphis but the actual letters of the Hebrew alphabet making up my Solar Body. I resolved to get a hold of a copy of the Greenfield book, so I could investigate this further.[193]

---

[192] Paraphrasing MATHERS (1900), book III chapter 11.
[193] GREENFIELD (2014).

Might the same extend to the Abramelin demons – that they too counted as forces within my Body of Light ? After all, I had asked God to reveal unto me the Hidden Wisdom necessary to reign over the unredeemed spirits and all creatures. So ...

*

Reading *"Angels & Archangels"* by Damien Echols. [194] Most of the book consisted of data I already knew, although he did suggest some rituals of his own devising which struck me as interesting. I could have argued with his view of spiritual development, but it might just have amounted to nit-picking.

I could clearly see, however, although Echols did not say so in so many words, that he fancied himself a 9=2 of the A∴A∴ with his own Word to preach to humanity and all that.

Evening Ritual

Done. Managed to do retro-vis and tea-pot meditation in padmasana. Good. Sacrament later.

---

[194] ECHOLS (2020)

Day 135

25 August 2020

Morning Ritual

Up at 5am for preparation with Middle Pillar ritual. Good. I began my main ritual eighteen minutes before sunrise. I aimed to work as quickly as possible, without dawdling. I also did the whole thing standing up, and using "2H2V."

"LBRP.

"LBRH.

"Bornless Ritual.

"Conjuration.

"Confession of Sins. Praying for mercy for my sins and for those of all for whom I have taken responsibility.

"Apologising for incarnating in a mortal i.e. Finite or sinful body at all. Thanking God and my HGA for everything they do.

"Performing the Tea-Pot meditation, giving some contemplation to my thoughts of yesterday, i.e. The spirits being contained within the Hebrew letters which themselves make up my Body of Light. The whole thing is good, makes me feel energised.

"Additional prayer.

"Licence to Depart.

"LBRP.

"LBRH.

"Total time not including preparation : 59 minutes."

Afterwards, I reflected that I had made a mistake with the *"no dawdling"* idea, insofar as it caused me to rush through the ceremony. I ought to have started earlier – e.g., by getting up at 4.30am – as I had indicated yesterday. Nevertheless, the energy of the ritual, particularly the Tea-Pot meditation, had given me a "high" which caused me to leave my oratory in good spirits, greatly encouraged.

*

It proved too good to last – an argument arose with my fiancée over breakfast. Yet again it consisted of something I considered trivial in the great scheme of things, but it blew out of all proportions. She made a factually inaccurate statement, but I made the mistake of – *as mildly as I could* – trying to correct her, by making reference to inner order documents of the Golden Dawn. This set her off, thinking that I meant to put up a barrier between us, because of the difference in our grades. I actually meant that if she wanted to research the matter further, she could find it in inner order documents published in Regardie's *The Golden Dawn.* She had her own copy upstairs, but as far as I could tell, she had barely cracked its spine since first purchasing it. From my point of view, I did not want to raise a barrier, but instead do the opposite – demonstrating how any such barrier could be overcome.

I got sensitive to being accused of bad motives and lost my temper – which in hindsight added up to a further mistake on my part. I escaped from the house, worried : I thought her tendency to overthink, and in doing so mistakenly believe me to act in bad faith, verged on the paranoid. But if it did, how could I deal with the subject without harming our relationship in any way ?

Midday Ritual

I attempted to do this by astrally projecting from my place of work to my oratory, but I suffered *two* interruptions. I restarted after the first interruption, but after the second I went to find some place I knew no-one would disturb me (i.e., because it had a lock on the door). Thus assured, I restarted again, astrally projecting to my Oratory and doing the whole thing, this time without interruption, but also without the benefit of AP music playing. The experience nevertheless proved surprisingly effective : I finished the ritual and walked out, feeling energised and enthused.

I thought : *"Should I cast a spell to arrange my circumstances so I am not disturbed ? It would be doing my True Will, after all !"*

*

That afternoon, I investigated Genesis 1 :7, associated with Netzach and the Occult Intelligence, for my scriptural study. If, in the preceding verse (Tiphereth), God establishes "Heaven," then this verse (Netzach) marked the first time that consciousness turns its attention towards that Heaven. The story of Genesis thus revealed itself not just as an account of the creation of the Universe, but also as a metaphor for the creation of one's self.

I also found time to divert myself on Quora.com by answering a question about wands in the Golden Dawn. Someone had come across a drawing by Steffi Grant of all the different wands used in both the inner and outer orders of the order, and had thrown out a challenge as to whether someone could tell them what they all meant – which I promptly did.

Luckily, my Amazon order came through, enabling me to replace the book which had vanished. I also started to leaf through my new copy of "The Science of the Kabbalah."[195] I already knew that Robert Ambelain had lifted a lot of material wholesale from this book, but I didn't realise, until that moment, that *so had MacGregor Mathers in formulating the knowledge lectures of the Golden Dawn.* It seemed quite clear to me that he had devised the various meditations (Neophyte – a point ; Zelator – from a point to a line to a square to a cube, etc) from Lenain's book. Ironically, given that this new edition translated the book into English for the first time, Mathers must have read Lenain in the original. This did not surprise me : Mathers had proved himself a competent French translator, through his sourcing the Prayers of the Elementals from Lévi – and of course, Abramelin itself.

When I got home, my fiancée still felt concerned about what had upset her earlier, but at least she behaved calmer now - albeit melancholic. I played a lot of comedy on YouTube for her - this seemed to lift her spirits.

Evening Ritual

Done.

---

[195] i.e., LENAIN (2020)

Day 136

26 August 2020

Morning Ritual

U
p at 4.30am for preparation with the Middle Pillar ritual. From now until the Culmination of the operation I would get up at the same time every morning and start my main ritual as soon as I had prepared properly – irrespective of the time of sunrise. The only exceptions to this came at weekends and on days when I had a day off, when I could get up at a more natural hour.

As it happened, preparation with the Middle Pillar ritual this morning took some forty-four minutes : I got so into it that I felt glad I had allowed it plenty of time.

Begin at 5.14am (sunrise at 6.01am). All done standing up.

    "*LBRP*.

    "*LBRH*.

    "*Bornless Ritual. I get more into it as the ritual progresses.*

    "*Conjuration*.

    "*Confession of Sins. Infinity of God vs finity of Man (i.e. Me). Getting angry at my fiancée yesterday. The karma of which I am not consciously aware, including that of people for whom I have taken responsibility. All sins for which I ask forgiveness.*

    "Nevertheless, I thank God and my HGA for grace in general, and e.g. Showing me how to be sympathetic towards A's plight. I pray that I receive such guidance at all times generally.

    "The Tea-Pot meditation. Ok, but not spectacular. Perhaps I need some r&r, in case I am burning out my meridians ?"

I.e., as I had first mentioned on Day 123 *supra*. This meditation had worked powerfully for some time, so an off-day disappointed me particularly. I had not heard of the "burning of the meridians" concept before I saw that YouTube video, as I never normally think in those terms : but I decided to give it a go, just in case.

    "Additional prayer.

    "*Licence to Depart*.

    "*LBRP*.

    "*LBRH*.

    "Total time taken : 1 hour 19 minutes. Getting up at 4.30am definitely a good idea, as the feeling of not having to rush improves quality of the whole thing."

*

For my scriptural study today, I investigated Genesis 1 :8, to do with Hod. This verse along with the preceding two formed a trilogy detailing the establishment of "Heaven" and the personality's natural reaction towards it. Hod may have had its roots in Gedulah, but there also existed a contrast between the two : Chesed struck me as the raw and intuitive side of Water, but Hod as the more phlegmatic.

Midday Ritual

Done - in a similar manner to yesterday, and for similar reasons. I had now resolved to work some kind of Jupiter ritual to get enough money so I could quit my job and finish the rest of my Abramelin procedure in peace. Trying to work out how to go about this, however, caused me to furrow my brow in thought. I could hardly perform magic contrary to the spirit of the Abramelin operation, even facilitating my completion of the very same motivated me. I didn't want harm to come to loved ones, and I had forsworn gambling, including playing the National Lottery, for the time being : hence I would have to earn the money in some manner, but how ?

Evening Ritual

Done - I concentrated on the retro-vis only, giving the Tea-Pot meditation a rest for now.

Day 137

27 August 2020

During the night I had an unusually vivid dream : I meditated, and I remembered managing to maintain *Dharana* successfully. Unfortunately, the alarm went off, hence I would have to leave *Dhyana* and *Samadhi* to another time. Clearly I was out of practice with *Pratyahara* as well, for the alarm clock to catch me out in this manner.

Morning Ritual

I entered the wake-world at 4.30am and prepared for my morning session with the Middle Pillar Ritual (and elimination). I began at 5.10am (sunrise at 6.02am).

"*LBRP*.

"*LBRH*.

"**Bornless Ritual**.

"**Confession**. *Instead of doing the Tea-Pot meditation, I decide to go at least a whole day without it, and instead just meditate plain and simple.*

"*I confess the usual sins (e.g., What I said yesterday). It occurs to me that I have not being paying much attention to my Nephesh recently, whereas before I did : I used to make that a point of the contemplation associated with the Middle pillar ritual. Perhaps this was a sin in itself - i.e. By omitting it I made a mistake ? Concentrating on my Nephesh now, making a point of appreciating it, certainly makes me feel better.*

"*For some reason, music I recall from about 1992 (actually Annie Lennox's Diva album) crops up in my imagination. Perhaps it is a message about something that happened in April 1992 ? This would have been when I was a student in Leeds. Otherwise totally random things are intruding upon my meditation. Also, events which I regret from 2006. I regret what I did, but not the intention behind it. I.e., With the benefit of hindsight I ought to have done something different, but I cannot feel guilty about why I wanted to do so.*

"*Simply concentrating on the presence of my HGA leads to a welcome sense of stillness. I should be meditating like this more often (and incorporating my Nephesh into proceedings).*"

I had previously spoken of the importance of checking in with one's *Nephesh* : I now decided I ought to reinforce this, by deliberately "speaking" to it. I decided to compose a series of affirmations in which I articulated how I envisaged my relationship with my *Nephesh* going. Without realising it, I had anticipated the sentiment of one of the exercises in BOTA's "Developing Supersensory Powers" course, even though I had not yet studied it.

"Additional prayer.
"Licence to Depart.
"LBRP.
"LBRH.
"Total time not including preparation : 1 hour 22 minutes."

*

That morning I investigated Genesis 1 :9 (Yesod, or the Pure Intelligence). More and more alchemical symbolism : i.e., the alchemists based their theories of how transmutation worked on how God created the Universe according to Genesis. (I did not, at the time, consider the alternate possibility, that whichever scribe wrote Genesis, based their theory of Creation on Alchemy.) The appearance of "dry-land" when the waters gather in one place seemed equivalent to the formation of the astral body in the spiritual unfoldment of the self.

I also spent time on the internet answering questions on Quora. How to know if one is purchasing an authentic grimoire ? Answer : check on Joseph H Peterson's excellent site to see if it is featured there.[196] Also : someone wanted to know if anyone had read Poke Runyon's "Book of Solomonic Magick" as they wanted clarification on some of the rituals. When I answered that I had, I heard nothing more on the subject, so I figured that they had lost interest.

Midday Ritual

With AP music playing I did the General Blessing & Blessing of vestures ... Interrupted once, so I started again. Then I projected to my Oratory and did the conjuration, meditation (remembering to thank my Nephesh), additional prayer, and licence to depart. I returned to body and normal consciousness. The quality of my attempt at astral projection encouraged me : by concentrating carefully I could definitely feel myself out of my body. I noted the whole experience today as "good."

In the evening, my fiancée insisted I watch a YouTube video on the chakras with her. It had a short meditation which I found interesting, which I thought could be adapted to the Middle Pillar Ritual. After that, however, it contained a lot of really basic stuff on the chakras, only a little of which I found stimulating : the rest I could just take or leave.

---

[196] www.esotericarchives.com

My fiancée used to feel concerned that her tongue felt "fizzy" for some unknown reason. When the video came on, I joked that perhaps it had to do with her throat chakra : i.e. she felt guilty about talking so much !

She then said "You may joke but there is truth in that ..." Then without irony she started talking non-stop for an hour.

She had some queer notions about Secret Chiefs : but to my mind, the fact of their supposed secrecy means that one can only speculate idly about them, or not at all, as I myself did.

Evening Ritual

Done - as yesterday.

Day 138

28 August 2020

Duzz uring the night : I dreamt of receiving lots of cheques, including one for £1000, from my fiancée. (Unfortunately, this did not literally come to pass : clearly I only dreamed about what I *wanted* to occur).

Morning Ritual.

Up at 4.30am for preparation with the Middle Pillar ritual. I tried to incorporate some of the stuff I saw in the video on chakras last night. I made a point of paying attention to my Nephesh first. Elimination.

I began my main ritual at 5.18am, just over forty-five minutes before sunrise. As before I incorporated my "2H2V" theory into my working : theorising my "second body" as equivalent to the etheric or astral body, throughout the practice I checked in with my Kether-point with the intent of energising and re-energising both itself and what I did.

> *"General blessing & blessing of vestures. I have to try to remember this, or remember the gist, as the sheet on which I had written this all down got ruined in yesterday's rain-storm.*
>
> *"LBRP ;*
> *"LBRH ;*
> *"Bornless Ritual ;*
> *"Conjuration ;*
> *"Confession of Sins ; Anger from how I was mistreated in my childhood flares up. By concentrating on God and my HGA, I expel it from my Self and into my evil persona, willing that my Nephesh is able to regulate it and draw the energy from it when need be.*
> *"Additional prayer ;*
> *"Licence to Depart ;*
> *"LBRP ;*
> *"LBRH.*
> *"Total time not including preparation : 1 hour 19 minutes."*

Midday Ritual

Done, in my actual oratory with AP music playing. I attempted the Tea-Pot meditation as part of my ritual, the first time I had done so since resting it for twenty-four hours.

For my scriptural study today, I investigated Genesis 1 :10.

Bad news later : for some reason my fiancée thought I disapproved of her doing a tarot divination devised by Josephine McCarthy. I *did* make some remark to the effect that she could go right ahead even though I didn't think much of the woman's writings : but to my fiancée that sounded like the severest criticism, and put her off doing the thing, even though I tried to reassure her.

*

Later : with the easing of Covid-19 restrictions which had begun around that time, I had hoped that I could organise the first meeting, since the lockdown began, of the Martinist lodge of which I was Recorder. The lodge usually met on premises owned by the *Societas Rosicruciana In Anglia*. I figured that as long as everyone wore masks, sanitised themselves properly, and otherwise kept socially-distanced, we could just about conduct the ritual we had in mind in an authentic manner. Luckily, I had received assurances from the officers and the candidate that they were ready, willing, and able to participate in the ceremony under these conditions.

Instead, the manager of the venue, the SRIA's "Superintendent-General of Works," emailed me to tell me that the SRIA had banned all meetings taking place there : supposedly because the place had not had a risk assessment done to ensure its Covid-safety. My contact apologised profusely : as the Past Grand-Master of the Martinists, he himself would have wanted the meeting to go ahead if possible. With only a week to go, I found it impossible to find an alternate venue in the time (besides which, we kept all the Lodge's equipment in the very premises that I could not now enter. I felt severely upset that I would have to abandon the meeting, especially as the candidate himself had been looking forward to the ceremony.

I did not realise it at the time, but looking back I suppose that this marked the first indication I received of something seriously wrong with the SRIA – about which more anon.

*

Later still : I got into an argument with my fiancée, but I allowed myself to get angry at her behaving in an irrational or paranoid way, as in, I couldn't explain myself without her taking me the wrong way. I got so upset that I suggested we should split up !

Obviously, I didn't *want* to split up, but then again, I *didn't* want to keep on arguing like this. We effected a sort of reconciliation before the end of the evening, but I felt very disturbed by the whole thing, nonetheless.

Evening Ritual

Done. I felt like a neophyte, having to start again from the beginning. I remembered the relationship problems that others who had done the Abramelin had reported : perhaps I now experienced my version as well. I held on to the idea that they had got over and healed their own relationship difficulties - but I definitely did not want to experience this again.

Day 139

29 August 2020

Morning Ritual

This being the weekend I set my alarm for 5.30am. I prepared with the Middle pillar ritual, which I preceded by communing with my Nephesh. Sunrise today was at 6.05am. Throughout the main ritual I took time to check in with my Kether-point regularly.

"*LBRP.*

"*LBRH. I spend a moment to contemplate the oneness of God, i.e. The underlying meaning of 'Ararita,' in the four quarters, before analysing the key-word.*

"*Bornless Ritual. I imagine that with each barbarous word I am assuming the god-form it represents. I am even assuming the vibration I make of that barbarous word! This proves surprisingly powerful, leaving my energised - something to investigate further.*"

When reading this one should appreciate that I have a peculiar point of view – probably born from long years of meditation. In my mind I look upon Thoughts – even quite abstract ones – as Things, and moreover as *alive* to boot. I first had this realisation as a Theoricus when, following the meditation of that grade, I contemplated the significance of the number "9" : I decided that I could gain mystical insight into its meaning most quickly by evoking it to manifestation and asking it in person. I suppose that this bizarre (even by my standards) way of thinking comes naturally when one removes one's attention from the mundane world to focus on *Yesod,* which I would have done at that point in my magical career. Either that or I had discovered a magical version of Gestalt Therapy – a not unlikely idea, as one of the other things I did whilst in the Theoricus grade consisted of reading and absorb every book on the nature of the unconscious mind on which I could lay my hands.

Hence, although one could easily think of (e.g.) "Ar, Thiao," etc as names of gods whose god-forms could be assumed, my big idea that morning posited that one could reify the actual *vibration* of each name into something which one could assume like a god-form as well. I thus simultaneously became both the Invocation and the Thing Invoked. As I type this now, the power of words to describe functioning or existing at this level fails to satisfy me. On the one hand it seems absurd to assume the god-form of something which does not have "form" in the conventional sense : but on the other, if one insisted on strict rationality, one would wonder at the possibility of assumption of god-forms happening *at all*. To my mind if one would suspend judgement for the sake of experimenting with Magick, one might as well do so for a Big Absurdity as well as for a Little Absurdity.

In that respect this mirrors my approach to Belief – i.e., the first step in achieving anything in Magick, or in the law of attraction, or anything like that, involves Believing in its possibility. I did read one book on the law of attraction which said something along the lines of not starting off attempting to visualise things like mansions or fast cars, but instead attempt to visualise only "realistic" things. But the way I look at it now : why *not* visualise a big mansion ? The idea that one can manifest anything at all through the power of creative visualisation defies rational explanation : hence the distinction between a fantastic and a supposedly realistic goal exists only in one's imagination and quite possibly constitutes a lie with which one disempowers oneself, and puts self-made fetters on one's creativity.

In many respects I therefore believe it better to imagine a Fantastic goal than a realistic one, because the latter might tempt one to stay constrained by old thinking patterns ; but the challenge posed by the former will stimulate creativity. *"I want to live in an expensive mansion. There is a way for me to live in an expensive mansion, all I have to do is discover it. If I already lived in such a mansion, what would I have to have done to achieve that ?"* This kind of thinking will generate more fresh ideas than *"I want to achieve something which is only marginally more improbable than what would happen to me naturally."*

Hence – can one assume something that was never meant to be assumed as a god-form ? Instead of saying "no," attempt to do so and *surprise yourself*. (As can be seen hereafter, this basic idea inspired me so much that I tried it out in various permutations throughout the rest of my rituals today).

"Conjuration.

"Confession of Sins. I feel shitty about yesterday evening. I cannot help but think I must have failed in some respect for things to get that bad. I am an Adept, after all ! Or supposedly. I realise that more than ever I need to rely upon the grace of God.

"On the positive side, however, because there was a way out of it all, which I found, I ought to interpret that as evidence of God and my HGA coming through for me ! Hence, I am thankful for that.

"Additional prayer.

"Licence to Depart.

"LBRP. I have an idea, inspired by my thought during the Bornless Ritual, of when vibrating each divine name in the quarters, to wear the Hebrew letters as a god-form, as well as the vibration thereof - uniting my consciousness with them and rising on the planes to contemplate the most divine or spiritual

versions thereof. I take the opportunity of using the LBRP to expel from my aura all the shittiness which I identified earlier, as if it were an obsession of which I am getting rid.

"LBRH.

"Total time taken not including preparation : 1 hour 15 minutes."

Afterwards, I went back to sleep. I wondered : what if I took an affirmation like 'I am a lucid dreamer,' and 'assumed' *that* as a god-form, as well as 'assuming' the vibration of me chanting this ? As it happened, I *did* have a brief OOBE, although I didn't get round to putting it to magical use before it faded away.

My fiancée, who had been downstairs reading, came up and joined me : she seemed in better spirits this morning, so we shared some intimate moments together.

Midday Ritual

With AP music playing in my oratory, I settled down to : first – checking in with my Nephesh ; secondly the conjuration ; Confession ; Tea-Pot meditation ; asking for forgiveness for my sins and for invoking, amongst other things, prosperity ; the additional prayer ; and licence to depart.

When I did the Conjuration, I had the idea to try out my earlier notion of thinking of the actual Hebrew letters making up the divine names as God-forms one could assume, as well as the vibration of them, uniting my consciousness with them in each case and rising to the highest contemplation thereof. *This proved very powerful.* So, when I did the Tea-Pot meditation, I Assumed each Hebrew letter before assigning it to the Cube of Space. Likewise, the 10-fold invocation of the Tetragrammaton.

All of this blew my mind. I achieved a very deep state of meditation indeed, as if I had discovered a real key here. I continued the idea in general for the rest of the ritual.

Afterwards, for my scriptural study that day, I began to investigate Genesis 1 :11. However I only got as far as translating and transliterating the original Hebrew : I did not attempt any analysis thereof, which I left until tomorrow. Nevertheless, by taking the trouble to incorporate the *niqqudim* into my work, I felt that my knowledge of Hebrew itself as an actual language started to improve.

Evening Ritual

Done. *Et sic ad lectum.*

Day 140

30 August 2020

Morning Ritual

Up at 5.30am for preparation with the Middle Pillar ritual, which I preceded with checking in with my Nephesh. Elimination. Sunrise was at 6.07am – creeping up ever later as Autumn drew nearer, although we would remain on daylight saving time until the last Saturday in October.

"*LBRP. I take the opportunity to expel memories of the film I was watching last night as well as ear-worms going through my head. They trouble me no more thereafter, so in that respect the LBRP works.*

"*LBRH.*

"*Bornless Ritual. Again, powerful.*

"*Conjuration.*

"*Confession. I become aware of sins I committed when I was a teenager. Basically, people acted like assholes towards me, and instead of rising above it like a spiritual person, I reacted with hatred. Even though I was not spiritually aware, I was supposedly over the age of criminal responsibility, supposedly old enough to know better. I regret it, now that I remember it, and I pray for forgiveness for it, i.e. For my reaction : I am still convinced they were assholes, by any objective standard. Ironically it has given me an insight into why there isn't peace in the world : i.e. Only spiritual people can rise above provocation, hatred on the other hand is a normal reaction to someone acting like an asshole, and hatred begets only more assholery and hatred, like a virus. Hence, because there are so few spiritual people relative to normal people, hatred etc continues to survive and grow.*

"*I concentrate on my HGA and will that all this sin gets consigned to my evil persona, safely under the guardianship of my Nephesh.*

"*Additional prayer.*

"*Licence to Depart.*

"*LBRP. Using the opportunity to expel the unpleasant memories I identified during the confession.*

"*LBRH.*

"*Total time not including preparation : 1 hour 18 minutes.*"

After catching some Zzzs, we went out to have breakfast at a nice café around the corner from us. Luckily we got back in time so I could perform my...

Midday Ritual

Done, in a similar manner to yesterday. The conjuration in particular felt intense. I employed the curiously neo-Platonic way of contemplating the divine names and the Hebrew letters which comprised them.

That afternoon I spent more time on Genesis 1 :11, continuing with the more in-depth analysis which I missed out yesterday. Fun fact : Aleph - the Scintillating Intelligence, corresponds to the first appearance of organic life in the book of Genesis, which I at least found interesting.

*

In the evening I got into an argument with my fiancée – I didn't mean to, but things went downhill before I realised. She asked me about my thoughts on the "Dweller on the Threshold." Quite innocently I explained my own interpretation, essentially paraphrasing the theory of which I had previously written, that it all has to do with Karma and the resolution thereof.[197]

At this point everything went wrong : I quickly discovered that my fiancée had a *phobia* about the notion of "Karma," and closed right up to my attempts to use rational explanation. I tried to be conciliatory by saying that I only regarded it as a theory : I didn't want to come over as dogmatic, but it did explain a lot of experiences which I myself had had in the past.

This had the opposite effect to which I intended : she now became horrified by the idea of having to go through this herself, and managed to put a bad spin on everything I said to try and convince her it ought not to turn out as terrible as she imagined.

I tried to defuse the situation with some humour, by making a rude remark about the Josephine McCarthy book she currently read, but this only succeeded in upsetting her more : at this point I decided to remove my ego from the situation and make my escape.

Evening Ritual

Done. By the time I finished, my fiancée seemed to have recovered : when I got into bed she pestered me for sacrament, so I obliged her.

---

[197] Days 6,7,8 – *vide supra.*

Day 141

31 August 2020

Morning Ritual

Up at 5.30am for preparation by first checking in with my Nephesh ; and second, the Middle Pillar Ritual. Sunrise at 6.09am

"*LBRP.*

"*LBRH.*

"*Bornless Ritual. Good.*

"*Conjuration.*

"*Confession. Thinking about last night. 'Telling someone a truth for which they are not ready is as bad as lying to them.' Clearly, this is exactly what happened last night - A was not ready for me telling what I believed to be the truth. In my defence, I was already half-way through telling it when it became apparent that she was not ready for it : but it was a mistake on my part, for which I pray to God for forgiveness, and for guidance in the future as to how to avoid such a thing.*

"*Concentrating on the presence of my HGA ...*

"*Additional Prayer.*

"*Licence to Depart.*

"*LBRP.*

"*LBRH.*

"*Total time not including preparation : 1 hour 15 minutes.*"

Midday Ritual

Done in a similar manner to yesterday, except that instead of doing the Tea-Pot meditation, I just concentrated on the pure presence of my HGA. The conjuration and subsequent meditation proved powerful, nonetheless.

That afternoon, for my scriptural study that day, I investigated Genesis 1 :12. "*And the earth brought forth grass, the herb that yields seed according to its kind, and the tree that yields fruit, whose seed is in itself according to its kind. And God saw that it was good.*" Emphasis added. "L'minehu," i.e. "according to its kind," is equivalent to "Michael" – not just the name of the Archangel, but literally meaning "Like unto God." Hence "According to its kind" is "like unto God" - if one could find one's own true nature one would behold it as God-like.

*

Later my fiancée and I did some Yoga, following a YouTube video. Afterwards, we went out for a meal in a pub – a rare treat. I confined myself to eating vegetarian food and drinking non-alcoholic beer.

Trying to be chatty, she asked me how well my Abramelin went. For some reason I hesitated. Because it had become more intense recently, I suddenly realised that I did not have the confidence I had when I first started. Perhaps that really meant I did not feel cocksure, but in the back of my mind the thought occurred that I ought to have been, although I felt torn between humility and excessive diffidence.

When she sensed my peculiar reaction, I summed up my feelings by saying that I did not want to talk too much about it at that stage in case I spoiled it. Looking back on the incident, I wondered if I didn't go through a very mild "Dweller on the Threshold" incident myself? In which case, I figured that I ought best proceed by following my own advice, and keep on keeping on. I remedied the proximate symptoms of my distress by taking some herbal supplements and tea containing lemon balm when we got back home, which calmed my sense of unease.

Evening Ritual

Done.

Day 142

01 September 2020

Morning Ritual

Up at 4.30am for preparation by first checking in with my Nephesh ; and second, the Middle Pillar Ritual. I began at 5.10am (sunrise was at 6.10am)

"LBRP.

"LBRH.

"Bornless Ritual. Good.

"Conjuration.

"Confession. Thanking God for His grace. It occurs to me : the greatest sins I have committed are against myself - failing to live up to my full potential. Ironically, I committed those 'sins' when I didn't know how important it was not to, i.e. I was not properly spiritually aware. If I had, I would be materially in a better place now, but then, would I have gone down the same spiritual path ? In any case, I pray for forgiveness.

Afterwards, it occurred to me : *"If I am the one against whom I committed the sins, then I need to forgive myself."* To continue :

"Oddly this is empowering ...

"Additional Prayer.

"Licence to Depart.

"LBRP.

"LBRH.

"Total time not including preparation : 1 hour 15 minutes."

*

That morning, for my scriptural study I investigated Genesis 1 :13. I found that knowledge of the Tarot (specifically key two, "The High Priestess,") aided me greatly in interpreting this verse. NB : the title of this card is one of the few true blinds in the Hermetic Qabalah : one should not call it the "High Priestess" but the *Shekinah*, because She is the only feminine presence Whom the High Priest meets within the Holy of Holies. The versicle in question invites one to contemplate Her role when She meets him there, on the day of atonement.

Midday Ritual

At work, with AP music playing, I projected to my Oratory to do the Conjuration, Additional prayer, licence to depart. Despite being brief, the actual effort of astrally projecting and vibrating the divine names, making the prayers, etc, proved powerful. I wondered whether I should use a "personal enn" as part of the meditation, but it occurred to me afterwards it would be better, if I did anything, to invoke my HGA via "the method." That at least would hold more relevance than something from a dæmonalatry source.

Evening Ritual.

Done. Afterwards, my fiancée claimed I had "good energy" - it suddenly made her want to rouse herself from her sleepiness for Sacrament. Very good !

Day 143

02 September 2020

Morning Ritual

Up at 4.30am. I attempted to do the Middle Pillar Ritual, LBRP and LBRH all in the astral. OK, but I had a distraction from a pain in my right shoulder – resulting from either a twenty year-old yoga injury, or perhaps just tension, or maybe a combination of both. It was 5.18am when I started the rest of the ritual.

"**Bornless Ritual**. *Also in astral.*

"**Conjuration**.

"**Confession of Sins.** *I return to body and do this in the physical... Only to astrally project again, and invoke my HGA via The Method,"*

I.e. the one upon which I had hit over twenty years ago.[198]

"*I am not completely immersed in the astral, hence I can only feel a faint glimpse of the power which I first remember. As it happens, M... appears - he tests well."*

By "M..." I refer to the being I identified as my Holy Guardian Angel after having performed The Method to which I referred above. I have redacted his name because I feel reticent about revealing my inner-plane contacts.

"*He tells me to think confidently : to read books on lucid dreaming every day, knuckle down to the nitty gritty of following a lucid dreaming practice in order to get back into lucid dreaming. Also : rewrite daily conjurations, so as to rephrase in terms of someone who has already succeeded in KCHGA.*

"*I am able to concentrate on my HGA ...*

"**Additional prayer**.

"**Licence to Depart**.

"**LBRP**.

"**LBRH**.

"*Total time 1 hour 9 minutes."*

*

At breakfast, my fiancée and I talked about Enochian magic – which terrifies her. She blamed me for coercing her when I stated that it played an important role in GD magic. Honestly ! We had only discussed doing the SIRP, not even talking

---

[198] See Day 15, *supra.*

about Enochian magic *per se* – apart from the fact that the Golden Dawn version thereof incorporates Enochian words of power. An argument ensued, about forcing complete beginners to do "dangerous" magic, i.e. I tried to defend the Golden Dawn position, although my fiancée believed that due to Enochian magic being evil in and of itself, the Golden Dawn's position was indefensible. I escaped from the house, in order to go to work (and extricate myself from the whole mess).

Still, it made me think : if one did want to teach a *complete* beginner Enochian magic, how would one go about doing so ? I thought that if I myself were to devise such a curriculum, I would start with a gentle introduction : first mentioning the subject long before expecting the practitioner to ever attempt any ; and then, they would only start with a little bit at first before delving into it more fully. I realised : *that is exactly what the Golden Dawn does*. It first mentions Enochian in the context of the grade ceremonies of the outer order, before eventually giving the initiate his or her first taste of Enochian in the Supreme Pentagram Ritual, prior to introducing the practice of Enochian magic proper.

Hence, I would not have to invent a curriculum at all, because the GD approach would itself provide the structure for such a teaching course.

Midday Ritual

Being at work, I tried doing this as I had done before, by astrally projecting to my Oratory. I eventually did this after several attempts, being constantly interrupted the first few times. I felt so unsatisfied that I wanted to fit in an extra session later that afternoon just to make up for it – I wondered if that prove permissible in the eyes of my HGA.

*

Whilst I bided my time to when I could concentrate on re-performing my midday ritual, I fitted in some scriptural study, by investigating Genesis 1 :14, getting as far as transliterating the original Hebrew text, though without going into any deeper analysis.

Whilst browsing the internet, someone on Quora asked whether Islam regarded it as *haram* to buy a Tarot deck not for divination, but just because one liked the pictures. All I know about Islam and Tarot is that in some Muslim countries in the Middle East one actually commits a criminal offence by practicing tarot divination or being caught in possession of tarot cards, so whether it will endanger your mortal soul or not is beside the point. As to the theology of the situation, I had to look this up, and this being Google I found conflicting answers. Using playing cards for gambling obviously qualified as a strict no-no : but some sources said that the *fatwa* extended to owning playing cards, whilst others argued that it did not. However, if some Muslims took offence at a pack of ordinary playing cards then a Tarot deck would only prove even *more* outrageous.

I also received a strange email from the Grand Master of the Hermetic Order of Martinists, sounding me out about whether I wanted to be a Grand Officer in the order. NB : grand officers in that order don't actually do much usually, so I interpreted the offer as more of an honorary position than anything else. Still I felt it nice of him to ask me, so I signified my acceptance.

*

As it happened, I fitted in a session at home at 6pm in which I did properly what I should have done for my midday ritual. I tried out for the first time my new way of doing the conjurations, as suggested by M… in which I basically thanked God (and my HGA) for doing what previously I had asked them to do, i.e., as if it were already a done deal : to wit –

"In the names YHVH, Tzebaoth and Adonai, who hath created all Nature and before Whom all Kings bow down and are subject - I thank God that I enjoy Knowledge and Conversation of my Holy Guardian Angel M…, and thereby have power and authority as did Moses, Aaron and Elijah.

"Oh YHVH ! Tzebaoth ! Adonai ! M… ! I thank you that having begged, thou hast heard my plea, and caused my Holy Guardian Angel to always lead me in the True Way, of Wisdom, and Understanding, that the Holy Words will flow into my heart with Wisdom and Understanding the more time I spend studying the Sacred writings.

"In the names YHVH, Tzebaoth and Adonai, and my M…, my Holy Guardian Angel, I conjure all Spirits : I thank you for turning away from evil and for Honouring God ; for serving Him and humanity, and myself in particular ; I thank you for fulfilling all my commands promptly, efficiently, persisting thou therein according to my interest ; I thank you for keeping safe from harm myself, all connected with me and with this place ; I thank you for speaking truthfully to me without murmur or ambiguity in a voice clear and intelligible without equivocation ; I thank you for appearing before me in a fair shape without tortuosity or deformity ; I thank you for remaining constant for so long as I require thee, and only departing hence when I give thee licence.

"In the names YHVH, Tzebaoth and Adonai, and M… my Holy Guardian Angel - AMEN.

"Oh YHVH, Tzebaoth, Adonai, and M… my Holy Guardian : I say : 'Hallelujah.' Thank you for accepting the ardour of my prayer, and for showing me Thy mercy. Thank you for the honour of company with the Holy

Angels ; and for granting and revealing the hidden Wisdom to reign over the unredeemed spirits and all creatures. AMEN.'

It felt empowering, filling me with confidence.

Later, also following up on what M… said, I found a copy of "Exploring the World of Lucid Dreaming" by Stephen LaBerge[199] and started reading it. I felt inspired me to restart my dream journal, the first step in properly (re-)cultivating my lucid dream practice.

Evening Ritual

Done, again with re-worded conjurations.

---

[199] LaBerge, Rheingold (1990)

Day 144

03 September 2020

Duringthe night : I stored a torch and a notepad next to my bed, with the intention of creating a dream journal - I managed to remember two dreams and write them down.

Morning Ritual

Up at 4.30am for preparation with (a) checking in with my Nephesh ; and (b) the Middle Pillar Ritual. Good.

I began at 5.05am

"LBRP.

"LBRH.

"Bornless Ritual.

"Conjuration. I.e., reworded, as mentioned yesterday.

"Confession of Sins. Thinking about getting into an argument with A yesterday. I pray that God and my HGA teach me to avoid doing so in the future.

"Concentrating on the presence of my HGA ...

"Additional prayer. Also reworded along similar lines as the conjuration.

"Licence to Depart.

"LBRP.

"LBRH.

"Total time taken : 1 hour 7 minutes i.e. I finish 1 minute before sunrise which is at 6.13am."

*

The new Grandmaster of HOM had now sent me a formal email, saying he wanted me to become the new "Grand Unknown." I suddenly recognised this as a far bigger deal than I had first imagined. Of all the positions, I would not have wanted to become any other Grand Officer in HOM, as I would have a decent role to play in the Yeheshuah ritual – a Martinist ceremony performed around Christmas time. All the other Grand Officers either didn't do much or just served in an administrative capacity. *It also counted as the third-most important office in the Order :* however, I regarded this as a technicality, as I did not foresee that I would ever exercise any executive power in the role, which in any event neither interested me nor constituted any part of the reason I became a Martinist in the first place.

It was not until much later, that I remembered that on 16th August, eighteen days previously, I had petitioned the angel Jabamiah "to fulfil my Martinist ambitions," and I put two plus two together.[200] Upon realising, I communed with the Angel again to give it belated thanks. Afterwards I publicly praised it on social media (though without explaining why). Technically though, Jabamiah had not completely filled my request, as my ambitions consisted not of attaining high office, but of getting more involved with the spiritual practice – particular in the higher degrees of the CBCS, Elus Cohens, and Rose Croix D'Orient. Nevertheless, I felt sanguine that I had made a step in the right direction

When I came down to breakfast and told my fiancée, however, she did not sound pleased. Although she belonged to a Martinist order herself, HOM remained reserved to male-only Masons and thus excluded her. Hence she first reacted to my good news like a dog-in-a-manger, although I reflected later that she hid the fact that she feared it would force me to spend less time with her.

I did not believe her concerns would amount to anything, but just to play cautiously, I decided that I would not send a formal reply to the Grand Master until I had done some divination on whether I should accept the role. Unfortunately, a Horary figure drawn up for the moment I framed the question proved unhelpful, as the Moon lay right on the cusp of two signs – signifying that the whole thing as inherently ambiguous.

Midday Ritual

I again experienced disruptions like yesterday, although the ritual that I *did* do proved at least better quality than previously.

For my scriptural study that day I continued to investigate Genesis 1 :14, i.e.

*"Let there be **lights** in the firmament of the heavens to divide the day from the night ; and let them be for signs and seasons, and for days and years."* (Emphasis)

I uncovered evidence that the gematria supports an astrological / hermetic point of view – to wit, the "lights" (Hebrew : "Mə-oroth") in the firmament, which essentially comprise the Sun, Moon, and planets, correspond in Gematria to "Elim," i.e. "gods." Subservient to the one true God maybe, but divine beings, nonetheless. In any event, regarding the heavenly bodies as deities forms both the basis for Astrology, as well as a decidedly pagan-point of view – indicating that at one time, the supposedly monotheistic Abrahamic-faiths were *not* so monotheistic after all.

I also fitted in some more reading of LaBerge, which I had begun yesterday.

---

[200] See Day 126, *supra.*

I got back home that evening to find my fiancée poring over the Black Brick[201] : she told me excitedly that she had suddenly realised that it contained all the secrets of the Inner Order, which she had assumed the Adepti had jealously guarded from her all this time. She honestly had not known this, and thought she had put one over on the Inner Order in general and myself in particular by discovering it. Needless to say, I did not remember our relationship in this way, as I could have sworn I had kept telling her for the past two years, and had actively encouraged her to read it, *seeing as she had had it on her shelf all this time.*

Nonetheless, it led to an interesting discussion in which she asked me to explain my views on the work of the adept, as well as the Golden Dawn's method of astral projection. [202] I found it refreshing to revise those particular parts of the GD teachings myself.

Quite apart from all this, my fiancée seemed more open to me becoming the Grand Unknown in HOM, so I decided to email the Grand Master back, signifying my acceptance.

Evening Ritual

Done.

---

[201] REGARDIE (1989)
[202] Ibid. pp106 – 109.

Day 145

04 September 2020

Duringnight : more dream recall, another couple of dreams. LaBerge recommends doing this a dozen or so times before moving on to the next stage, although he does admit that for some people lucid dreaming can come quicker.

Morning Ritual

Up at 4.30am - checking in with Nephesh, and performing the Middle Pillar Ritual. Inspired by what my fiancée had caused me to read yesterday, I tried Astrally Projecting, GD style, to each sephirah, i.e., by projecting a thought-ray to my destination, Willing a sphere of Astral Light to appear there, forming a simulacrum of myself to appear within the sphere and then projecting my consciousness along the thought-ray to the simulacrum : where I would invoke the Divine Name of that Sephirah. In hindsight I thought my attempt proved too busy : I should rather had concentrated on only going to one particular place at a time when APing .

I began my main ritual at 5.13am.

  "*LBRP*.

  "*LBRH*.

  "*Bornless Ritual*.

  "*(Newly-worded) Conjuration*.

  "*Confession. Thinking of the infinity of God vs the finite nature of myself. Also, the problem of distracting thoughts, both during ritual and in everyday life.*

  "*Concentrating on the presence of my HGA, it occurs to me to recall the 'work of the Adept' which I am supposed to be doing and concentrate on raising my lower-will (Tiphereth) to meet my higher-will (Daath) so as to contemplate my Neshamah etc, whilst expelling Qlippothic forces from Nephesh into Evil Persona. It is powerful, like a long-lost friend. I immediately go into a deep state of meditation.*

  "*In the subsequent parts of the ritual hereafter, when I contemplate a divine name in my heart-centre (Tiphereth), I focus on raising that (with Tiphereth) to Daath. Doing this with everything I contemplate - which is essentially the divine names which I vibrate - is potent. Yet it is something I had forgotten but of which I have been reminded. I can thus perceive the influence of my HGA leading me on the right path by causing me to rediscover the tools necessary for completion of the operation - which just so happen to be the GD methodology.*

"*(Newly-worded) Additional prayer.*

"*Licence to Depart.*

"*LBRP.*

"*LBRH.*

"*Total time is 1 hour 7 minutes (sunrise was at 6.15am)."*

The whole idea of uniting the Higher & Lower wills, and hence contemplating the *work of the Adept*[203], clearly amounted to something I had missed heretofore, as it now greatly improved my meditations and rituals. In effect I had translated something presented as dry theory in the GD's original documents into the movement of energy, and of the Sephiroth themselves, within my own subtle body. The lesson I took away from this implied that the structure of the Tree of Life, far from staying a static, rigid pattern, *changes and evolves in relation to one's own spiritual development.* This idea I believe remains unique to the Golden Dawn – other occult schools tend to assume that the Tree of Life is always *the same* Tree of Life no matter whether one is a Neophyte or an Ipsissimus.

My fiancée reminding me yesterday obviously inspired this line of thought – so perhaps my HGA had on this occasion worked through *her.*

Midday Ritual

The "Work of the Adept" or "WOTA" idea I had from this morning proved highly influential thereafter. From my magical diary :

"*This whole thing about the work of the adept is so powerful that, when I perform the Midday ritual applying the WOTA principles thereto, I enter into an ecstatic consciousness which I am able to maintain despite being interrupted. WOTA is also the key to making 'the Method' of invoking my HGA (and by implication, the vibratory formula of the Middle Pillar) effective (i.e. Because this is what I do as part of my midday ritual)."*

Later in the afternoon, for my scriptural study that day I went over Genesis 1 : 15 – the Gematria seemed to indicate the relevance of the stars (i.e. Signs of the zodiac) as well as planets to the Qabalah. In this respect it represented an extension of the principles of yesterday's discovery of a pagan / hermetic cosmological view within Genesis : i.e. not only do the Sun, Moon and planets constitute "Elim," but so too do the stars.

*

---

[203] Hereinafter referred to as "WOTA" or "WOTAP" (i.e., "'Work of the Adept' Principles.")

This being my aged mother's 92nd birthday, the family organised a ZOOM chat in lieu of a party, in which we drank champagne to toast her. Or rather the rest of them did : I pretended to, by sort of holding the flute outside the field of view of the camera. I did not want to mention to my family that I had sworn off alcohol for the time being, as I thought telling them about the fearsome black magick operation with the aim of conjuring and compelling all the demons of hell which I undertook would alarm them unnecessarily.

My mother did not have the faintest understanding of how ZOOM worked, but my brother had set it up for her. Ironically she had moved down to the south-coast to be with my brother's family : but when the pandemic struck – the family had to socially distance themselves from her, as her age placed her in a vulnerable category. I would have thought that ideally she should have become part of a "bubble" with my brother's household, except for the fact that my sister-in-law worked in a school, and hence did not want to risk passing on any infection from her kids to my mother. My mother thus effectively lived on her own, despite the fact that many of her nearest relatives were *immediately next door to her*. My brother alone breached the *cordon sanitaire* to visit her regularly, run errands and perform odd-jobs and so forth. The rest of the family would say hello to her from as near as the front-gate, but no closer.

I was incredibly lucky, I reflected, to live with my fiancée : we had moved in together just as the lock-down began. I doubt I could have spent this much time without social contact of at least some sort.

Evening Ritual

Done - contemplating WOTA whilst I do so - very good.

Day 146

05 September 2020

Morning Ritual

During the night : I noted down one dream. Up at 5.40am for preparation by checking in with my Nephesh, and the Middle Pillar Ritual. Elimination.

Sunrise at 6.17am. Throughout the whole of this morning's rituals I contemplated WOTA principles as I meditated on each thing / vibrated each name, etc. Henceforth, I exclusively used my newly-worded conjurations (unless noted otherwise).

"*LBRP. As mentioned yesterday : I try incorporating WOTA into the Vibratory Formula of the Middle Pillar. Powerful.*

"*LBRH.*

"*Bornless Ritual. V good.*

"*Conjuration. Again, the act of incorporating WOTA into contemplating the divine names in the conjuration, along with the new wording, is empowering.*

"*Confession. Concentrating on the Infinity of God vs the Finite Nature of man. I pray that God help me see off the sin of pride before it happens - i.e. Not let this apparent WOTA success go to my head.*

"*I pray for forgiveness for all my sins, and for all those for which I have taken responsibility. It occurs to me : this would include WLW and the members of his lodge...*"

I.e., W L Wilmshurst, on the supposition that I believed him to be one of my previous incarnations. Whatever the truth of reincarnation in general, or *my* reincarnation in particular, as a matter of logic I could hardly take *credit* for being a historical figure without incurring the *onus* of being that same figure. In this instance I assumed that in forming Lodge of the Living Stones, Wilmshurst had affected the course of the spiritual destiny of the Freemasons who entered within its portals.

"*... Guru ??? And his chelas ; etc...*"

I.e. another previous incarnation, whom I supposed lived as a Yogi from hundreds of years ago, whose name I did not know.

"*... but also the various demons and spirits which I have already evoked (e.g. of the Goetia). Perhaps this means that I must also take responsibility for all the Abramelin spirits and demons as well ? Seeing that theoretically part of the process is evoking them. A sobering thought.*

"Additional prayer.
"Licence to Depart.
"LBRP.
"LBRH.
"Total time : 1 hour 9 minutes. WOTA incorporation is generally good, so I shall incorporate it generally from now on (it is something I ought to be doing as a 5=6 of the GD anyway)."

Afterwards, I returned to bed to catch some Zzzs. My fiancée joined me later, after having spent some time downstairs reading. At first, she remained unusually quiet : I politely asked what she had been up to that morning, but she said she felt reluctant to talk about it.

I said nothing, but waited.

Almost immediately, she found the strain of keeping shtum too much, and talked non-stop for two hours about her ideas on ceremonial magic and the Kabbalah. As usual in such situations I hardly got a word in, except at last to intimate that now might make a good time to have breakfast.

Midday Ritual

Done. Incorporating Tea-pot meditation and WOTA. Very good.

Evening Ritual

Very good, I came out of it full of energy. Sacrament = good.

Day 147

06 September 2020

During the night, a couple of dreams : one of which included me invoking a sephirah by imagining myself standing in it ... Thinking about the Golden Dawn style of astral projection recently probably inspired this, as well as the work I tried doing with the Middle Pillar Ritual two days ago.

Morning Ritual

Up at 5.40am for preparation by checking in with my Nephesh, then the Middle Pillar Ritual. Inspired by my dream, I did not actually imagine myself standing in each sephirah, but instead imagined a mini-tree of life there, which itself carried out WOTAP as I invoked the associated divine name. This proved very good, but the need for elimination caused me to rush the end of it.

Sunrise at 6.18am. Like yesterday, I attempt to apply WOTAP throughout the following.

"*LBRP.*

"*LBRH.*

"*Bornless Ritual.*

"*Conjuration. All good up to here ...*

"*Confession. Contemplating the usual - infinite God vs finite Me, etc. However, my meditation is disturbed by a distracting thought. It eventually occurs to me to ask God not merely to teach me how to still my mind, but to teach my Nephesh to do so - because these distracting thoughts are examples of manifestations of the evil persona which my Nephesh can and does control. Hence by re-affirming my Nephesh connection, the quality of my meditation improves from that point, although I need to work on this more.*

"*Additional Prayer.*

"*Licence to Depart.*

"*LBRP. Expelling distracting thoughts as if they are an obsession to be banished.*

"*LBRH.*

"*Total time : 1 hour 15 minutes.*"

*

For my scriptural study today I analysed Genesis 1 :16. The Greater and Lesser Lights (Sun and Moon) represent the Solar and Lunar senses of interpreting scripture Qabalistically : the former, actively and consciously ; the latter, passively, intuitively, e.g. through meditation and through dreaming. As an alternative interpretation one might speculate that the Solar sense involves the invocation of the Day-Spirits (Angels), whilst the Luna sense involves dealing with those of the Night (demons etc).

Midday Ritual

Done. Meditating on the stillness. Good.

In the afternoon, I helped my fiancée assume the Godform of Thme – i.e., a ritual from the "Golden Dawn Magic" book by the Ciceros.[204] This involved me joining in the Middle Pillar Ritual. She actually performed it very well.

Also for some reason I found a link to a free copy of Donald Michael Kraig's *Modern Magick* on Amazon. Oh well, never look a gift-horse in the proverbial...

Evening Ritual

Done.

[204] CICERO, CICERO (2019).

Day 148

07 September 2020

Morning Ritual

During the night, I managed to record two dreams. Up at 4.30am for preparation with checking in with my Nephesh and the Middle Pillar Ritual.

I begin at 5.13am. WOTAP etc

"*LBRP.*

"*LBRH.*

"*Bornless Ritual.*

"*Conjuration. Concentrating on M... (my Holy Guardian Angel). It occurs to me that perhaps the fact that I was able to download 'Modern Magick' for free from Amazon means that I should look therein for advice on lucid dreaming, astral projection, KCGHA etc.*"

This may or may not have been the case, but later that morning I went and looked the gift-horse in the mouth as I supposedly ought not to have done, and found therein a version so terribly formatted that Amazon should have refused to stock it. I deleted the version from my Kindle and reported it to Amazon : I guess that some rogue must have taken a bad copy and passed it off as a legitimate sale. DMK himself, having taken a hiatus from those spiritual activities which require the use of a physical body, could hardly protest the fraud : although it surprised me that Llewellyn did not, as I would have thought that a publisher controls its authors' Amazon pages.

Ironically, plenty of decent scans of the actual book float about on the internet illegally, but I had looked forward to owning a legitimate copy. Alas ! No such luck for now.

"*Additional prayer.*

"*Licence to Depart.*

"*LBRP.*

"*LBRH.*

"*Total time taken : 1 hour 7 minutes.*"

Over breakfast, I unfortunately got into another argument with my fiancée : this time, she thought the concept of "sex magick" must have something wrong with it, as if this automatically meant sexual sorcery. I tried to avoid exacerbating the situation by asking *"and what's wrong with sexual sorcery ?"* as she appeared to think that one could not use "magick" itself for higher purposes. I must assume that we talked at cross-purposes : one could arguably construe the "Sexual

Polarity" exercises and meditations which BOTA teaches as a type of "sex magick," albeit a very innocent, wholesome version, but I doubt she herself would like referring to them as magick *per se*.

I personally feel ambivalent on the matter : if someone came up to me asking for advice, I would tell them *"Just concentrate on having really great sex. The benefits will be immediate and obvious, and will probably do you more long-term magical good than most of the bullshit that passes for sex magick teaching already out there."*

*

Investigating Genesis 1 :17. In this regard I managed to get hold of an electronic copy of Aryeh Kaplan's translation of the Sepher Yetzirah,[205] which I hoped would prove more illuminating than just trying to rely on Westcott's version. Both had obvious differences in style – for example, Westcott's version says of the seventeenth path :

> *The Seventeenth Path is the **Disposing Intelligence**, which provides Faith to the Righteous, and they are clothed with the Holy Spirit by it, and it is called the Foundation of Excellence in the state of higher things.*

Whilst Kaplan's translation of the same passage reads :

> *17. **Consciousness of the Senses** (Sekhal HaHergesh).[206] This is prepared for the faithful saints so that they should be able to clothe themselves in the spirit of holiness. In the arrangement of the supernal Entities, it is called the Foundation of Beauty (Yesod HaTiferet).*

Westcott translated from a translation, whilst Kaplan translated direct from the original Hebrew. I can sort of see how different people might choose to translate the same Hebrew words in different ways, e.g. "faith to the Righteous" had a sort of similarity to "faithful saints," because in Qabalistic terms, Righteousness constitutes the defining quality of a saint or miracle worker. But who would have thought that "Disposing Intelligence" really meant "Consciousness of the Senses" ?

Midday Ritual

Done. Conjuration. Additional prayer. Licence to depart. All done with WOTAP. Although brief and not in ideal circumstances I nevertheless found it spiritually uplifting.

---

[205] KAPLAN (1997)

[206] שכל חרגש literally "Feeling-mind."

Evening Ritual

Done. *Et sic ad lectum*

Day 149

08 September 2020

During night : my fiancée claimed that astral experiences disturbed her. It did not make her best pleased when I said she could help herself, i.e., by learning how to control her astral experience. I regarded the reality or at least possibility of Lucidity on the astral plane as such a certainty, that I assumed that anyone could achieve it simply through practice ... Unfortunately, she herself believed it proved impossible for her, and (from my point of view) her disempowering belief became a self-fulfilling prophecy.

I, on the other hand, managed to record at least one nocturnal adventure : a pleasant encounter taking lots of photos with someone I remembered from years before (hereinafter referred to as "V"). I could hear music playing all the while : *Sweet Dreams* by the Eurythmics. The irony of the selection only struck me later !

Morning Ritual

Up at 4.30am for preparation - checking in with my Nephesh, Middle Pillar Ritual. WOTAP. I begin at 5.03am.

> "*LBRP.*
>
> "*LBRH.*
>
> "*Bornless Ritual.*
>
> "*Conjuration.*
>
> "*Confession. Thanking God and my HGA for the usual. It occurs to me that perhaps I dreamed about V. because I had the idea that I was meant to be a 'guardian angel' myself for them. In which case I should incorporate V. into those for whom I pray.*
>
> "*Concentrating on my HGA - stillness.*
>
> "*Additional prayer.*
>
> "*Licence to Depart.*
>
> "*LBRP.*
>
> "*LBRH.*
>
> "*Total time 1 hour.*"

*

At breakfast, my fiancée still felt no congruence about coping on the astral. I deduced that the root of her opprobrium lay in her once having what she believed to be an astral experience in which she felt helpless, which had disturbed her. From this she came to believe all astral experiences were *always* disturbing.

I tried to point out that the Astral Plane would not frighten someone if they managed to project onto it with complete control : for example, by carefully planning the astral journey in advance, by taking steps to project with full consciousness, and by making use of techniques to protect oneself both physically and whilst out of the body.

I even made the bold assertion that *no evidence exists that one can die from astrally projecting.* This may run counter to a lot of the horror stories told by bullshit-gatekeepers out there, but my point consisted of this : everything that we know second-hand about the astral plane we owe to people who came back and *lived to tell the tale.* No-one has ever produced empirical evidence that anyone has died as a result of astral projection : the assertion that it might be possible adds up to more than an *a priori* assumption in an untested deductive model.

Of course, the fact that death happens at all would suggest that although no evidence exists that one can die *from* astral projection, it might certainly occur that one can die *whilst* doing so – for example, if something happened to one's physical body during the experience. I personally felt that if that happened, existing in a discorporate state at the time would constitute the *least* of one's worries.

Therefore, I tried to point out to my fiancée that although she had had astral encounters that she did not like, nevertheless she had survived all of them, which provided *prima facie* evidence of her as strong – a survivor – and that the horrors of the astral plane were largely illusory.

However, she refused to accept my line of argument, and refused to think of the astral plane as anything but unpleasant : hence, she felt no motivation to practice controlling her astral projections. And because she did not practice, she would never find out about the true nature of the astral plane, and thought that I and others like me had deserted our senses to even want to try. The very nature of the problem precluded its solution.

Midday Ritual

Done – by astrally projecting to my oratory. Despite its brevity, it felt rewarding in its own way. Certainly no unpleasant astral phenomena for me!

That afternoon, I investigated Genesis 1 :18 for my scriptural study. This proved a tricky verse to fully transliterate, what with trying to incorporate all the niqqudim : so much so that I had to leave it so I could come back to it the following day.

Evening Ritual

Done. *Et sic ad lectum*

Day 150

09 September 2020

During the night, I found it very difficult to remember my dreams : although I seem to recall something about "Hey Ya" by OutKast. The significance of this particular song escaped me, as indeed why my mental jukebox should switch from 80s pop to 00s hip-hop.

Morning Ritual

Up at 4.30am. Preparation with the Middle Pillar Ritual. I began at 5.10 am, trying to go through whole thing quickly for some reason.

    "LBRP.

    "LBRH.

    "Bornless Ritual.

    "Conjuration.

    "Confession.

    "Additional Prayer.

    "Licence to Depart. Hereafter I felt the need for elimination, which I turned into an impromptu banishing ritual itself.

    "LBRP. Calmer now, more measured.

    "LBRH.

    "Total time : 1 hour 11 minutes."

*

Thinking about the "Work of the Adept," and how important to me it had proved, I decided to express myself in the form of a graphic of the Tree of Life, which I created with Photoshop. I made it broadly similar to the well-known Minutum Mundum, but with one important change : I had shifted *Tiphereth* up the Middle Pillar to the position of *Daath*, by which I attempted to signify the uniting of the Lower and Higher Wills.

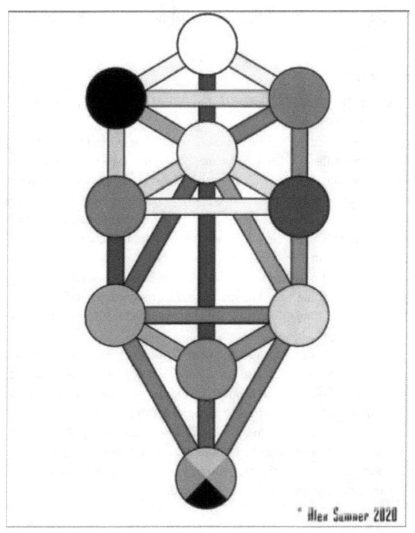

Figure 7 The Work of the Adept, © Alex Sumner 2020 (NB : the original was in colour).

I posted this on social media, with the provocative caption "only a few people will get this." I really wanted to know of anybody out there shared my thoughts and experiences of the "Work of the Adept" : I suppose I had highlighted a particularly recondite detail in the Golden Dawn's already complex system, but that would only make connecting with someone who did appreciate it all the more special.

Alas ! Around sixty people "liked" the picture, which I classed as "a lot," but compared to the typical content shared every day by blue-tick celebrities and Z-list influencers, it pales into nothingness. The most insightful comment was *"Whoa, wait ... what's going on with Tiphereth ?"* : but otherwise everyone noticed the colours, hardly spotting the unusual arrangement of the Sephiroth. *Le sigh.*

Midday ritual.

Done, in a similar manner to yesterday, incorporating invocation of the HGA via "the Method." OK as it went.

As it happened, someone on Quora asked me whether one could astrally project during the day whilst awake. This seemed like a fortunate synchronicity, what with my recent attempts to do just that, and with some success in the process. In brief, I said yes : *however,* the act of astrally projecting naturally caused one to attain an altered state of consciousness – shifting from beta through alpha to theta waves – hence although I did not project whilst asleep, neither could I describe myself as "awake" in the normal sense of the word.

Apart from this I only had time to look briefly at my "Heart of the Qabalah" project. Instead of doing "new" scriptural study, I concentrated on integrating the passages from the Kaplan book which I had acquired into my analyses of the verses from Genesis which I had already done.

Later : I had an idea of what to do about the Equinox meeting of the Golden Dawn – the first time we had had one since lockdown began. Alone out of the order's rituals, a Golden Dawn member should not miss the Equinox Ceremony, as it effectively renews and refreshes the egregore of the order. Consequently, a *force majeure* compelling us to miss it felt particularly galling. Nevertheless, I knew that John Michael Greer had composed a Solo Equinox ceremony,[207] so I thought that I could press this into service. I made a start on transcribing it so I could turn it into a proper ritual at the weekend.

Evening ritual.

Done : good. Checking in with Nephesh also turned out good. "Sacrament" later.

---

[207] GREER (1997).

Day 151

10 September 2020

Morning Ritual

During the night, I made a note of two dreams. Up at 4.30am : I prepared by checking-in with my Nephesh, and the Middle Pillar Ritual. Today I deliberately took things at a calm measured pace so that I could appreciate what I invoked.

I began at 5.03am. (WOTAP applied throughout). From my magical diary :

"LBRP.

"LBRH.

"Bornless Ritual. Very good.

"Conjuration.

"Confession. I perform the Tea-Pot meditation, asking mercy and forgiveness for all sins for which I am responsible. Good.

"Concentrating on the presence of my HGA - on stillness itself - leads to a deep state of meditation.

"Additional prayer.

"Licence to Depart.

"LBRP.

"LBRH.

"Total time : 1 hour 18 minutes. The more careful, calm approach definitely yielded benefits today. Developing a healthy relationship with the Nephesh is definitely a good thing. I felt that I was able to let go and just rely on my Nephesh - this improved the quality of my ritual and meditations generally. WOTAP works when such an attitude is adopted."

*

Someone on Quora.com asked a question wanting to know whether they had had a genuine angelic encounter. It gave me an opportunity to describe something based upon my own experience.

"So to answer your question directly - was what you saw an Angel ? Well, think carefully about how you felt at the exact time it happened. Did you feel excited, exhilarated, surprised, astounded, or anything else that could be described as noumenal *? Or did it just pass you by like something fairly unremarkable ? Ultimately you will know yourself whether your experience was genuine."*

Midday Ritual

Done. Astrally projecting - mostly good although I had one interruption.

More studying of Genesis 1 :18, which I had first begun two days ago. The text for the eighteenth path of the Sepher Yetzirah proved particularly apposite : the psychic sensitivity associated with the sign of Cancer, at its deepest level, becomes the consciousness of the House of Influence (or "Influx" as Kaplan called it) which reveals the secret mystery, etc.

Evening Ritual

Done. Very deep state of meditation – the remarks which I noted in the final paragraph of "Morning Ritual" applied just as well on this occasion – i.e., letting go and relying on my Nephesh improved the quality of my experience.

Day 152

11 September 2020

During the night, I recorded one dream about waterslides : on reflection I thought it might have had to do with the floaty feeling I imagined that letting go and allowing my Nephesh to take control would have.

Morning Ritual

Up at 4.30am for preparation by checking in with my Nephesh and the Middle Pillar Ritual. Elimination. I began at 5.15am. Distracting thoughts plagued me to begin with, but this got better as I completed the Bornless Ritual. From my magical record :

"*LBRP.*

"*LBRH.*

"*Bornless Ritual. Good.*

"*Conjuration.*

"*Confession. Concentrating on my HGA. Willing my higher self to take control of my Nephesh / my Nephesh to invoke my higher self. Very good, very deep - like* Samadhi.

"*Additional prayer.*

"*Licence to Depart.*

"*LBRP.*

"*LBRH.*

"*Total time 1 hour 20 minutes.*"

*

My fiancée greeted me when I came downstairs by cheerfully telling me that whilst reading about Ceremonial Magick, she had mentally analysed the gematria of the Hebrew spelling of "BEELZEBUB" - and then *a fly appeared*. It buzzed in front of her face, as if trying to tell her something (her words).

"Did you banish it ?" I said.

"No, but surely I didn't invoke anything ?" she replied.

"If you thought it was meaningful, then yes you might have," I said.

"Um ... No ... " she said.

"Well did you conjure it ? You know, get it to recognise the holy names of God ?"

"Um ... No ..." she said.

"Did you get rid of it somehow else ? Like by licensing it to depart ?"

"No ! *You're* the Adept ! That's *your* job !"

And with that she skipped off upstairs to have a shower.

Sighing, I invoked M... (my Holy Guardian Angel) via "the Method," and licenced Beelzebub to depart (I could detect no sign of an actual fly, as it happened). Then, imagining my astral body to grow super-tall, I performed the LBRP, visualising that I expelled all contrary influences from the property itself, with the pentagrams and archangels forming a defensive perimeter.

Later my fiancée engaged me in conversation about ceremonial magick generally. She remained blithely unaware of the potential danger she might have caused, and I hadn't the heart to tell her. Still, the idea that one could summon a demon – or any kind of spirit, for that matter – by performing a gematria-based meditation on its name struck me as intriguing : I made a mental note of it for the future.

Midday Ritual

Done. I had to keep it as short as possible, but at least nobody interrupted today.

I spent some time editing my Equinox ceremony. Despite its shortness, I could not finish it all today. I would be able to finish it tomorrow, but then I would not have access to a printer : so I would have to convert it to Kindle format and read it off my smartphone in the middle of the ceremony.

I had little time to do the things I liked because work had suddenly become more busy today : so much so, that I couldn't look at the book of Genesis either. What with the schools having recently come back, the company worked on the assumption that a new spike in COVID-19 cases would soon occur, leading to another lockdown. Hence, they decided they must do an unusually high-volume of work *now,* to leave themselves lockdown-ready at a moment's notice.

Needless to say, this put me under a lot of pressure, potentially interfering with my plans to complete the Abramelin Operation. However, I wondered : *"Was this the fever I had to go through to cure the disease ?"* As in : if another general lockdown *did* occur, this would furnish me with all the time in the world to complete my Abramelin operation in peace. However, for this to happen, first, the mundane world must prepare for such a circumstance - hence my work suddenly becoming a whole lot busier. So I might well have manifested my intention into existence after all !

I put this to my fiancée later, but she did not appreciate the irony or the humour of the situation. (Thought : if one defines a joke as a means of communicating humour, then if only I get it, one cannot call it a joke, because one has not communicated humour. Information Theory applied to comedy !) An argument erupted – I tried to explain a traditional ceremonial magic point of view, but when

I disagreed with her, she took it personally, so I had to spend an inordinate amount of time trying to calm her down and reassure her.

Later however, things had quiesced enough that we could settle down in front of the telly and watch a film on Netflix : for some reason its algorithm suggested *A Beautiful Mind,* so we went with that. It made me wonder : how can magicians deal safely with phenomena that would cause untold misery to a paranoid schizophrenic ? How can I know anything exists in reality ?

I reasoned : I know that magic produces subjective responses within me. I have even had experiences where magic caused *action-at-a-distance* - but if I talked about them widely, people would have me committed - the modern equivalent of being burnt at the stake.

Evening Ritual

Done. *Et sic ad lectum.*

Day 153

12 September 2020

Morning Ritual

I recorded one dream during the night about gospel music. My astral jukebox certainly came up with some diverse choices! I got up at 5.53am for preparation with checking in with my Nephesh and the Middle Pillar Ritual. Elimination. Sunrise occurred at 6.28am, although I began at 6.35am. From my magical record :

"*LBRP.*

"*LBRH. Thought : 'Ararita' is equivalent to 'Va-yomer Elohim "Yehi-aur," ve-yehi aur.' Hence, it is appropriate to use 'Ararita' in the Hexagram Ritual because the 'LVX' invoked in the analysis of the keyword is the same Light that is mentioned in Genesis 1 :3 ! QED*

"*Bornless Ritual. Good. The whole discipline of assuming each barbarous name as a god-form - as well as the vibration thereof - helps calm my mind, leading me into an appropriate magical state. Each time I assume a God-form, I contemplate that the God-form thus assumed is practising WOTAP.*

"*Ironically, I felt bad for not being in a perfect state to start the Bornless Ritual, but the act of doing it caused me to go into that perfect state for performing it during the course of the ritual. Like - each part opens up a new door, takes me to a new level.*

"*Conjuration.*

"*Confession. I am aware of distracting thoughts : rage, repressed anger, holding on to painful memories as if they are luxuries, etc. By praying to God and asking my HGA for help, I perceive that they are born out of a Good desire to defend the integrity of my ego, but they manifest in an unpleasant form. I pray that my Nephesh take control of them and "Archive" them in my Evil Persona (at this rate, if I ever want power for a spell, I will have an unhealthily large reservoir in my EP from which to draw).*

"*Thought : has watching that film last night made me more concerned about my mental state ?*

"*Eventually I get to a semblance of a stilled state.*

"*Additonal prayer.*

"*Licence to Depart.*

"*LBRP.*

"*LBRH. Very good. I incorporate meditating on the connection between Ararita, Genesis 1 :3, and LVX, as well as the idea of assuming the vibration*

of a thing as god-form in its own right. This with WOTAP brings me to a much deeper appreciation of the Hexagram ritual than I had previously experienced.
"Total time not including preparation : 1 hour 19 minutes."

After returning to bed to catch some Zzzs, I spent the morning typing up and finishing tomorrow's Equinox ceremony.

Midday Ritual

Done, in my oratory with AP music playing. Checked in with my Nephesh, then Conjuration ; meditation including Tea-Pot ritual ; additional prayer ; and licence to depart. Very good : my Nephesh led me into a deep state of relaxation ; and when I willed that my Higher Self possess my Nephesh, I entered into a *Samadhi* like state of ecstasy.

For my scriptural study I investigated Genesis 1 :19, to do with Leo. A short verse but rewarding. More especially, it felt good to get back into the swing of Qabalistic analysis.

Later that afternoon, I rehearsed the "Equinox Ceremony for Solitary Use" with my fiancée i.e. although Greer had originally titled it "… for Solitary Use," I had adapted my version for two people – myself as "Hierophant," and my fiancée as "Everyone Else."

Evening Ritual

Done. Good. *Et sic ad lectum.*

Day 154

13 September 2020

During the night, I recorded three dreams. After the first I made a little sigil to give me something to visualise instead of having to repeat "I Am A Lucid Dreamer" all the time.

Morning Ritual.

Up at 5.53am for preparation by checking in with my Nephesh, and the Middle Pillar ritual. Good, as it happens, certainly an improvement on this time yesterday.

I begin at sunrise, i.e. 6.28am. Throughout I was applying "WOTAP," etc. From my magical record :

*"**LBRP**. Very good. I feel as if the Pentagrams are causing Yeheshuah (of whom they are a symbol) the Repairer to manifest in the four quarters."*

I.e. referring to Martinist symbolism : see previously for a fuller explanation.[208]

*"**LBRH**. Goes well : the idea of briefly contemplating Genesis 1 :3 along with vibrating 'Ararita,' is definitely a good one.*

*"**Bornless Ritual**. Very good - feeling magical.*

*"**Conjuration**.*

*"**Confession**. I implore God and my HGA to forgive all my sins and all sins for which I am responsible. I feel my Nephesh leading me into a deep state. I perform the Tea-Pot meditation. Very good. I feel as if I can perceive Karl Popper's 'Third World' - i.e. That of the Objective Content of Thoughts. It's hard to explain but it sort of goes like this :*

"If I perceive an external object, then the said object is 'out there' but the consciousness of the external object is 'in here.' This does not present a big deal for solid, tangible, objectively-verifiable things, HOWEVER : what if I experience something 'in here' which is not linked to something out there ? For example, a thought, a dream, or a spiritual phenomenon ? On the one hand, a die-hard sceptic could argue that they are just figments of my imagination ; however, what if they are connected to external objects, just not ones readily appreciable via the senses ?

"What I learnt today is that I seem to be able to perceive the external causes for internal peak experiences at the intuitive level. I sense that when carried to its logical conclusion it is the basis for evocation and exteriorisation

---

[208] Day 123 – *vide supra.*

phenomena such as Astral projection. In any event I do get the sense of getting down to an even deeper level of meditation than I had previously."

Or in other words, I had previously perceived that *Samadhi* not only evinced the Angel's presence, it was the Angel itself. Linking this idea to Popper's "Third World" (i.e., that of the Objective Content of Thoughts) would therefore provide a philosophical basis for the notion. Incidentally, I never formally studied Philosophy academically : but I had heard Popper's theory mentioned by The Orb in their track "O.O.B.E.," a surprisingly well-researched representation of auditory and other phenomena which occur during an Out of the Body Experience.[209] This, and the fact that I first got into lucid dreaming after reading a Melody-Maker interview with the Aphex Twin would show just how much Ambient House influenced me back in the day.

"Additional prayer.
"Licence to Depart.
"LBRP.
"LBRH.
"Total time taken : 1 hour 22 minutes."

Afterwards I retired to bed to catch up on some Zzz, and managed to record another dream – this time rather more detailed than previously.

Midday Ritual

Feeling jittery – I could tell I had done something profound spiritually because I had gone and set-off a Dweller on the Threshold incident. Outwardly it manifested as stress I felt about my work. Nevertheless, I went into my midday ritual in my oratory with AP music playing. When it came to the Confession, I called upon God and my HGA to empower and enable my Nephesh to manage this "Stress-Monster." I perceived that it had a good intention at its core : my wanting to do the Great Work properly and resenting encroachments on my time and spiritual life had given birth to it. I therefore conjured it, with the authority of my HGA, to devote its legitimate energy to my service but in a manner more harmonious with my conscious-self – and my higher self. This seemed to work : I finished the ritual feeling a lot calmer than when I began it.

On reflection, I would surmise that the deep level of meditation I had experienced in the morning, following my Popper-inspired musing, must have reached deeper than I first realised. I had become so convinced that great spiritual experiences set off "Dweller on the Threshold" incidents that I used the latter as progress markers.

---

[209] From the album *U.F.Orb* (1992) on Big Life.

*

In the afternoon, my fiancée and I had a Golden Dawn meeting via ZOOM where we performed the Equinox ritual together. Technically we could only call it a demonstration of a ritual : done with as much authenticity as we could muster, but we could hardly deem it an official Equinox ritual given that we conducted it in such irregular circumstances. Nevertheless, the Fratres and Sorores decided to join in the spirit of the thing, by sitting in on the ZOOM call in full regalia (even though I had not asked them to). It went well : I felt pleased by how well we did.

In the evening : my fiancée became distraught over losing her purse : she even felt worried that someone might have stolen it and she would have to cancel all her credit cards. However, before she did so, I called on the ever-reliable Andromalius to help me recover it, in a manner similar to how I described previously.[210]

Immediately I got the idea to go out to Aldi, where she had gone shopping earlier. The store had by now closed for the evening. My fiancée expressed doubt that coming here would do any good, but I persisted in trying to attract the attention of the few night-workers there re-stocking the shelves.

Eventually, one of them noticed the strange man waving at them through the window and, instead of calling the police, as my fiancée gloomily feared that they would, decided to come to the front door to ask what I wanted.

When I told the girl of my predicament (leaving out any reference to black magick, obviously), she amazed us by reporting that someone had indeed handed a purse in, but because the manager had gone home for the evening, she could not access the safe where they had stowed it away. Still, it appeared that Andromalius had indeed come through yet again !

I reflected that he had done so several times on behalf of my fiancée, since I had first met her. The first time occurred when someone walked off with her drink at a party : I did a quick conjuration, and told her "Just go up to the bar and tell them the exact truth of what happened." She did : and promptly received a free drink as a replacement. Despite being just a little incident, realising that her new boyfriend was a massively powerful black-magician scandalised her big-time , so I had to spend a lot of the evening thereafter calming her down.

Evening Ritual

Done. & *sic ad lectum*

---

[210] Day 70 : *vide supra.*

Day 155

14 September 2020

Morning Ritual

During the night, I managed to record two dreams. Up at 4.30am for preparation by checking in with my Nephesh and the Middle Pillar Ritual. I began at 5.07am. From my magical diary :

"LBRP.

"LBRH.

"Bornless Ritual.

"Conjuration.

"Confession. Plagued by distracting thoughts re : the SRIA, I call upon God and my HGA to help me consign this energy to my 'Evil Persona' where it can be managed by my Nephesh. Good.

"Willing that my higher self 'possesses' my Nephesh, I again enter a deep state of meditation.

"Additional prayer.

"Licence to Depart.

"LBRP.

"LBRH.

"Total time : 1 hour 18 minutes."

Midday Ritual

Done. Very brief, done at work, but at least this time I had no interruptions.

*

Due to the widely-expected spike in COVID-19 cases around this time, the Government brought in harsher restrictions, including the "Rule of Six," i.e., forbidding indoor meetings of more than six people. This put paid to any early resumption of Golden Dawn temple meetings – the exact opposite of what I had initially hoped would happen around the time of the September Equinox.

The United Grand Lodge of England quickly followed suit by issuing an edict saying that Lodges could only meet if they themselves observed the Rule of Six. Given that one normally needs *seven* officers minimum to run a ceremony, not including any candidates, this effectively meant we would have to postpone resuming Lodge meetings as well.

Most seriously, however, the SRIA – in addition to continuing to suspend its meetings – *banned everyone apart from the SRIA itself from using its headquarters in Hampstead.* Up to now, the SRIA had allowed other organisations, such as my Martinist lodge, and various other orders, to use the space there to conduct meetings and hold rituals. My Golden Dawn temple held its study group there, although we did not use it to conduct rituals due to its lack of size. I also belonged to about four or five other organisations that met there, so it came as a particular blow to me. I could hardly travel into London at all, because of the COVID restrictions, but it meant that I would have nothing to go back to when restrictions *did* end.

More generally, this scandalised a large number of my friends and colleagues, so a slew of messages on Facebook bombarded me, as did emails into which I had been CC'd. In particular one man – the same one who had been the "Superintendent-General of Works" for the SRIA, and hence the custodian of the place at Hampstead (whom I shall henceforth refer to as "CH")[211] – resigned and wrote an open letter of protest to the Supreme Magus, calling this move a prelude to the leadership of the Society selling the property against the wishes of its members. His letter included ominous warnings that this had come about almost immediately after the Supreme Magus *had replaced the senior leadership – and the Society's trustees – with cronies of his from another Masonic order.*

At this stage it proved more of a headache than anything else. The big plan resting at the back of my mind consisted of me completing the Abramelin Operation, writing a book about it, and then going on a lecture tour to promote it, taking in the Metropolitan College Study Group on the way : although right now I didn't feel like remaining a member of the SRIA at all. A large amount of Masonic social climbing had always existed in the organisation, but at least the last Supreme Magus had fitted in some esotericism in between his ambitions for Grand honours. Now the new regime lacked even that saving grace.

At the time : the Secretary-General of the SRIA responded to the accusations (the new Supreme Magus remained distant) by saying that despite the new ruling, they did *not* intend to sell the Hampstead venue outright. However, the plot later thickened...

*

My fiancée recovered her purse when Aldi opened, even as Andromalius told me she would. I posted something on social media publicly thanking him yet again.

---

[211] Day 138 – *vide supra.*

Evening Ritual

Done. I had the clear sensation of my third eye being open. *& sic ad lectum.*

Day 156

15 September 2020

During the night, I recorded one dream, about Krishna, and two eyes merging into one : clearly, what I experienced last night during meditation before going to bed inspired this. Normally I would associate *Shiva* with the Third-Eye, although Hindu iconography often depicts Krishna himself with a *tila*. The precise significance of the symbolism escaped me for the moment, so I parked it.

Morning Ritual

Up at 4.30am for preparation by checking in with my Nephesh and the Middle Pillar Ritual. I begin at 5.10am

"*LBRP. Feeling agitated regarding the SRIA, so I attempt to use this opportunity to Banish it like an obsession. I still feel upset though.*

"*LBRH.*

"*Bornless Ritual. Not really getting into it today, still adversely affected by what I mentioned above.*

"*Conjuration.*

"*Confession. I am able to calm down. I take advice from a BOTA lesson on 'The Devil' - the key to solving the horror represented by the Devil is recognise how absurd it is, i.e., by laughing at it. Laughing at the SRIA and the pettiness of the various members certainly helps relieve the stress I have been feeling. They talk about the Hampstead venue being the SRIA's spiritual home, but its leasehold property, for Christ's sake !*"

I.e., referring to some of the comments in the flurry of emails I experienced yesterday.

"*By its very nature it is transitory ! I could say that I have a lease on my body, which will expire when I do. It is my spiritual residence but only temporary itself. Anyway, at least I am able to end the meditation feeling better than when I started.*

"*Additional prayer.*

"*Licence to Depart.*

"*LBRP.*

"*LBRH. Feeling better than at the beginning.*

"*Total time : 1 hour 7 minutes. Probably so short compared to previous days because I rushed through the Bornless Ritual. I decide to withdraw completely from the SRIA's Facebook group, as this will remove the proximate cause of all my hassle.*"

*

Later : working on Genesis 1 :20 – the first appearance of living creatures in the Bible. I reflected that although I had allowed Qabalistic matters (e.g., the Equinox ceremony of the Golden Dawn) to distract me, I had erred in letting the SRIA do so : it did not deserve my time.

Midday Ritual

Done, at work, attempting to astrally project to my Oratory. I felt rushed.

Later however, in a spare moment, someone on Quora.com asked me "*Is it true that when you try astral projection, you will be able to develop psychic abilities ? Like clairvoyance, etc.*" I found I could write a sympathetic answer ("Yes, but you have to work at it, etc") based upon my own experience.

I also managed to fit in reading more of Stephen LaBerge, where he talked about how the "schemata"[212] we unconsciously adopt mould the type of dreams we have. Cognitive psychology defines a "Schema" as a unit of knowledge which stores information – or in other words, *"A generalized description or a conceptual system for understanding knowledge – how knowledge is represented and how it is used."*[213] However, LaBerge argued that when it comes to dreaming, the Schema largely comprises not "true" knowledge, but an arbitrary set of assumptions, with no objective validity.

E.g., if I believe in the impossibility of walking through walls in dreams, I will never be able to walk through walls in my dreams – that has become part of my Dream-Schema. Yet, looked at objectively, a wall in a dream is only an imaginary object, with no physical substance. We know that dreams don't necessarily correspond to how reality works at all, so no reason exists why the idea *"you cannot walk through walls in dreams"* ought to form a hard and fast rule.

Hence, in order to fully control one's dream life, one has to not only become lucid, but to identify and wilfully modify the schemata which really amount to nothing more than limiting self-beliefs.

Evening Ritual.

Done. *& sic ad lectum.*

---

[212] Singular "schema."

[213] *"Schema Theory"* – https ://www.csus.edu/indiv/g/gipej/teaparty.pdf accessed 2021-08-18

Day 157

16 September 2020

Morning Ritual

During the night I recorded one dream. Up at 4.30am for preparation - checking in with my Nephesh and the Middle Pillar Ritual. Feeling more relaxed and less frantic than yesterday. I begin at 5.07am. From my magical record :

"*LBRP.*

"*LBRH.*

"*Bornless Ritual.*

"*Conjuration.*

"*Confession. Wondering about how to combat distracting thoughts. It occurs to me that what I read in LaBerge yesterday re : Lucid dreams could equally apply to meditation. I.e., The idea that stilling one's mind is difficult is not objectively real, it itself is a kind of Schema which I have adopted. Explode the conditioning, it becomes easy. (I try this, it works)."*

At this point I appear to have passed into a deeper meditative state of consciousness. I would not have described achieving one-pointed concentration as "easy" the very first time I began meditating, but I persisted through daily practice – and, through trial and error, I realised that certain techniques can facilitate the process. For example, performing the Middle Pillar Ritual first helped me calm my mind right down, and hence improved the quality of my subsequent meditation no-end. In other words, I never assumed its impossibility, and I never gave up.

The sentiment which I expressed today would imply that most of the time, a thing – e.g., one-pointed meditation, lucid dreaming, or any other mental or physical discipline – proves difficult not because for any objective reason, but because one *believes* in its difficulty – one has created a barrier in one's mind which causes a self-fulfilling prophecy. Or, to use LaBerge's vocabulary, one has incorporated false information into one's *Schema* regarding the matter.

Logically, one can appreciate that just because an event played out one way one time, does not necessarily mean that it will play out the same way every time : which is why one should not take subjective experience as an infallible guide to future experience – without other evidence to back it up. However, to explode a *Schema* like this effectively means to dissociate the Thought of A Thing, from The Thing Itself, which requires a passing acquaintance with philosophy, or possibly the ingestion of quantities of entheogenic substances (I have always relied on the former method).

"*NB :M... (my Holy Guardian Angel) originally inspired me to read LaBerge, so I have my HGA to thank for this insight !*

"*Another thought, this time inspired by Yoga, i.e. That when one has perfected Ahimsa, other beings become peaceful in one's presence. I.e.*

'*Where non-injury is perfected, all enmity ceases in the presence of him who possesses it.*'[214]

"*On the one hand this could mean being peaceful towards distracting thoughts, but on the other it could mean being peaceful towards the demons* one is attempting to evoke. *Hence, this idea would admirably fit the description of 'the hidden wisdom necessary to reign over the unredeemed spirits and all creatures.'*"

I.e., quoting from the Additional prayer I had added into my conjurations specifically for Phase Three of my Abramelin Operation. I found (and still do find) this a radical notion : the whole idea of being peaceful towards a potentially dangerous demon appears contrary to the idea of dealing with it in a fearful manner, upon which most western Ceremonial Magick bases itself. And yet, when one truly attains Knowledge and Conversation of the Holy Guardian Angel, the experience fills one with that absolute confidence that ought to make this possible.

"*Exciting stuff ! I need to investigate this further. All thanks to God and my HGA for providing me with a breakthrough !*

"*Additional prayer.*

"*Licence to Depart.*

"*LBRP.*

"*LBRH.*

"*Total time taken : 1 hour 21 minutes - longer than yesterday because I was making sure to try and conduct the ritual in a careful manner.*"

*

This morning, whilst at work, I wondered whether asking Andromalius to recover Stanfield Hall (the headquarters of the SRIA), which circumstance had effectively stolen from the orders that meet there, would prove a goer. A Horary figure, however, indicated the question as too close to call : besides taking such an approach would have swings and roundabouts.

---

[214] II.35 – from https ://en.wikisource.org/wiki/Yoga Sutras/Book II accessed 2020-09-16

Upon later investigation, I made an insight which whilst not immediately helpful nevertheless struck me as remarkable. Looking at the Horary figure made me think that every time Mars went Retrograde we (i.e. the Golden Dawn) had venue trouble. I checked back over previous occasions and spotted the connection. Whether it came in the form of having to temporarily move out due to a burst pipe, or to permanently shift premises, Mars Retrograde provided the common factor. I did not find it immediately obvious why this should happen.

Midday Ritual

Done, astrally projecting to my oratory.

For my scriptural study today, I tried to investigate Genesis 1 :21. I got as far as transliterating the Hebrew.

Later, when I got home, I mentioned to my fiancée that I would attend an Inner-Order Zoom meeting at the weekend ... And it "triggered" her. The fact of her being only in the Portal and not having yet taken her 5=6 continued to prove an extremely sore point with her. Trying to discuss it rationally did not help. The more I tried to placate her, the more I seemed to have the opposite effect. Eventually, as on previous occasions, I removed myself physically from the argument, although I should have done so *an hour or two hours previously*. I made a note to myself, not to mention the inner order again. I also realised the irony of what I had written this morning : I had far to go in mastering *ahimsa*.

Evening Ritual

Done. Later, my fiancée seemed in better humour, so sacrament was good ...

Day 158

17 September 2020

Morning Ritual

During the night, I found it difficult to recall my dreams : although I seemed to remember one about a factory, and another about the goddess Niké. I got up at 4.30am, and prepared by checking in with my Nephesh, and the Middle Pillar Ritual. I began at 5.03am. From my magical record :

"LBRP.

"LBRH.

"Bornless Ritual.

"Conjuration.

"Confession. Infinite God vs Finite me. Trying to concentrate on ahimsa, manage to get a reasonably still state of mind.

"Additional prayer.

"Licence to Depart.

"LBRP.

"LBRH.

"Total time : 1 hour 11 minutes."

Afterwards, I went downstairs to say "good morning" to my fiancée, and immediately without me doing anything, last night's argument started up all over again. Thinking about *ahimsa*, I remained silent in the face of provocation. Seeing that she could not get a rise out of me, she became untalkative.

Thinking that she had calmed down, I took a chance on making small-talk by trying to make a polite remark about her current choice of reading. A mistake – she bit my head off : me opening my mouth proved enough to set her off. Feeling sad, I escaped from the house.

While at work, I was able to fit in some scriptural study : I got into investigating the gematria of Genesis 1 :21, the Hebrew of which I had transliterated yesterday. I felt intrigued to find references to Chesed and Gedulah in a verse which the Golden Dawn attributes to the planet Jupiter.

Midday Ritual

Done : it went well, in spite of having a busy day at work.

Apart from this, I had a Zoom meeting of my Masonic Study Circle. Today would have been the day of my regular Lodge meeting : but due to the confounded "rule of six," and the fact that many of our members could not travel in to London to attend anyway, we worked out in advance that we were entitled to abandon the meeting as we could not form a quorum. We went ahead with the Study Circle meeting, however, and found that our virtual attendance far exceeded the usual turn-out for such events, with Brethren from around the globe logging on, grateful for an opportunity to strike a blow against their enforced social isolation and loneliness.

Afterwards, I returned home : my fiancée appeared still upset. She tried hiding it but she did so incredibly badly. However, when I started talking about some of the stuff I done in my investigations into Genesis, she felt inspired to come out of her shell. By the end of the evening she appeared to approach her happy self again.

Evening Ritual

Done. *& sic ad lectum.*

Day 159

18 September 2020

Morning Ritual

During the night I recorded two dreams. I got up at 4.30am for preparation by checking in with my Nephesh and the Middle Pillar ritual. I began at 5.03am – from my magical record :

*"**LBRP**. Unhurried. The Pentagram, being a symbol of Yeheshuah, I briefly contemplate invoking Yeheshuah the Repairer before the ceremony.*

*"**LBRH**. Good - contemplating Genesis 1 :3 continues to prove a good idea. Bornless Ritual. Good.*

*"**Conjuration**.*

*"**Confession**. Thanking God and my HGA for having discovered a way to alleviate problems with my fiancée. It occurs to me that if my problems are my fault, then I need to seek forgiveness for them ; but if they are hers then I have to do so on her behalf, because I have volunteered to take responsibility for her.*

"Concentrating on ahimsa - on my Higher self possessing my Nephesh. Deep state of meditation.

*"**Additional prayer**.*

*"**Licence to Depart**.*

*"**LBRP**.*

*"**LBRH**.*

"Total time 1 hour 20 minutes."

Midday Ritual

The frantic atmosphere of yesterday had vanished : I could do my midday ritual properly whilst astrally projecting to my oratory. I made a decent job of it, or at least I recorded at the time as *"Not bad."*

For my scriptural study today I investigated Genesis 1 :22. This marks first verse which describes God as "blessing" something : as well as speaking to something other than Himself (or more accurately, "His Selves"). Hence, as the Sepher Yetzirah indicates, "blessing" is how *"spiritual virtues are increased"*[215] – i.e. because God told them to be fruitful and multiply.

*

---

[215] The Faithful Intelligence or 22nd path of the Sepher Yetzirah.

Later that evening at home, my fiancée yet again came to me with her woes regarding the Golden Dawn's insistence on a Neophyte having to meditate on a point. We had, of course, had disagreements over this very subject several times before.[216] Today, she went from saying she could not do this, to claiming that she did not *want* to do so, because she thought something horrible would happen.

I tried to explain that, firstly, one-pointed concentration (which is what I believed the "meditate on a point" instruction was aiming for) did not mean *Samadhi :* i.e., according to how I understood Raja Yoga, but rather *Dharana,* a pre-requisite for the same. Hence, one should not imagine that the GD asked the Neophyte to achieve something impossible for a complete beginner. I related my own thoughts about how "difficult" I had found the same experience.[217]

Besides which, I asserted that I had experienced neither one-pointed concentration nor *Samadhi* as horrible. I felt bemused by how she passed judgement on them whilst at the same time claiming she could not experience them. However, I think I uncovered the real reason : she associated ego-dissolution with childhood trauma, and hence had animadversion against any spiritual practice which in anyway suggested its necessity for attaining enlightenment.

I felt sure I had gone through this many times before : my usual approach of trying to reassure her that *Samadhi* wasn't like how she imagined ; that I had had experiences of *Samadhi* which proved quite pleasant ; the supposed "ego-dissolution" differed from what she thought it involved. However, every time I tried to do so she refused to believe me. I think the reassurance she wanted would have required me to agree with her that her fears were justified : but I could not in all conscience bring myself to lie to her by saying so.

Evening Ritual

Done. I feel energised and bounded into bed, excited. My fiancée, however, claimed to be too tired for "sacrament" : although, to my consternation, she was not too tired to keep talking. I cut her off abruptly, so I could get some shut-eye.

---

[216] See, e.g., day 120 – *vide supra.*

[217] Morning ritual, day 157 – *vide supra.*

Day 160

19 September 2020

Morning Ritual

During the night I recorded one dream. Up at 6.04am for preparation with the Middle Pillar Ritual, preceded by checking in with my Nephesh. I began at 6.39am (i.e., actual sunrise). Unhurried, peaceful.

"*LBRP.*

"*LBRH.*

"*Bornless Ritual.*

"*Conjuration.*

"*Confession of Sins. Whilst recalling my sins, I get bad conscience about cutting my fiancée off abruptly last night, so I resolve to go apologise to her ASAP.*

"*Thinking about why I am distracted by angry thoughts. It's as if I think of something, then I imagine how someone might react to it, then I react angrily to how I think they would react - but all the time I am reacting to nothing other than one of my own thoughts. It's as if I am triggering myself! However: perhaps she is a mirror for me, and the advice I tried to dish out to her last night I ought to apply to myself. Hence, I recognise that this anger is not (or at least, ought not to be) connected to any trauma that I experienced in my childhood, therefore there ought not to be any trigger for me!*

"*Thinking about this in this way, a great sense of calm descends on me. It is like I have unlocked a key which releases the hold of these thoughts on my mind, and I am able to attain a new state of calmness. This in turn allows my higher self to take possession of my Nephesh and lead me into a deep state of meditation.*"

This method of being able to look at irrational anger objectively, and hence calm it down, proved helpful in the days to come.

"*Additional prayer.*

"*Licence to Depart.*

"*LBRP.*

"*LBRH.*

"*Total time taken : 1 hour 12 minutes.*"

*

Afterwards, I made a point about apologising to my fiancée, as I had resolved to do : she reassured me that we had reconciled with one another. We then went out to breakfast at a local café which specialised in pancakes and almost nothing else.

It turned out that my fiancée had differing views on the nature of the "higher self" to me. I.e., I characterised the Neshamah – by which I meant the Neshamah, Chiah, and Yechidah collectively as the "higher self" – or at least that is how I interpret Golden Dawn teaching on the subject. She however disagreed with me, thinking that the Higher Self more concerned Tiphereth – to which I only attributed the "Self". I tried to ask her that if she thought of Tiphereth as the higher self, how then did she imagine the Supernal Triad, but she seemed to think that I wanted to argue with her for no good reason, so I left off the subject.

Midday Ritual.

Done in oratory, with Astral Projection music playing. I checked in with my Nephesh, then : Conjuration ; Confession including Tea Pot meditation ; additional prayer and licence to depart. I thought the experience was good, actually.

For my scriptural study, I investigated Genesis 1 :23. Interestingly "Yom Chamishi" (i.e. "the fifth day," or in modern Hebrew, Thursday) is equivalent in Gematria to "living creatures," which is apt as that was when the first living creatures appeared in the creation story.

Evening Ritual

Done.

Day 161

20 September 2020

During the night, I managed to record three dreams including, funnily enough, one in which I tried to work out the best way to invoke Satan on behalf of the SRIA (i.e. Which averse pentagram and such). If I had been lucid, I would have realised that they didn't need my help : they had done a good job all by themselves. But that was by the by.

Morning Ritual

Up at 6.06am for preparation with checking in with my Nephesh and Middle Pillar Ritual. Good, some elimination.

I began at sunrise (6.41am). Relaxed, unhurried.

"LBRP.

"LBRH.

"Bornless Ritual.

"Conjuration.

"Confession. Thanking God and my HGA for everything done so far, asking forgiveness for all my sins, both conscious and unconscious, as well as all those for which I've taken responsibility.

"When I concentrate on my Higher self possessing my Nephesh..."

I.e., my Neshamah, Chiah and Yechidah – the supernal triad of my microcosm.

"... I enter into a deep state of meditation, like Samadhi. Very inspiring - I perform the rest of the ritual in a heightened state of consciousness.

"Additional prayer.

"Licence to Depart.

"LBRP. In such an ecstatic state this morning following the above, that I do this and the subsequent LBRH in the astral. Good.

"LBRH. See above.

"Total time : 1 hour 16 minutes."

*

Later, my fiancée complained about being stuck in the Portal of the Golden Dawn and couldn't wait to start performing the ceremonial magick of the inner order. When I pointed out that much of that ceremonial magick – e.g., Talisman consecration – builds upon Portal work, such as performing the Supreme Pentagram Ritual, she became upset, because she hadn't actually practiced any of that, and did not enjoy doing so. It took some time for her to begin to calm down.

Midday Ritual

Done. Checking in with my Nephesh beforehand : Conjuration ; confession (incorporating Tea-Pot Meditation) ; additional prayer and licence to depart. Again, a very deep state of meditation.

A copy of *The Compleat Rite of Memphis*[218] arrived from Amazon today. I had bought it because I had had it on my Wishlist for some time, and I needed to add something to another order I had made to qualify for free delivery. I felt underwhelmed when I read it : it consisted mainly of material which I had already found on the internet and did not go into sufficient detail about the "*point-chaud*" technique, the only real reason I had bought it.[219] (other books go into the system, but they remain out of print).

A BOTA study-group via ZOOM took place in the afternoon. My previous studies on the book of Genesis assisted me when it came to taking part in the discussion, although I couldn't do new study today. Still, I suppose it could count as revision and consolidation.

Afterwards, my fiancée seemed more her happy self ...

Evening Ritual

Done. *&sic ad lectum.*

---

[218] GREENFIELD (2014)
[219] See Day 134, *supra.*

Day 162

21 September 2020

Morning Ritual

During the night, I managed to record one dream. Up at 4.30am for preparation by checking in with my Nephesh then Middle Pillar Ritual. I begin at 5.05am. From my magical record :

"**LBRP**. *Taking the opportunity to banish thoughts of what I saw on TV last night.*

"**LBRH**.

"**Bornless Ritual**.

"**Conjuration**.

"**Confession**. *Thanking God and my HGA for everything they do and have done so far. I meditate in a similar way to like I did on Saturday,[220] so as to release the grip which angry thoughts have on my mind - thereby attaining something resembling a sense of stillness.*

"**Additional prayer**.

"**Licence to Depart**.

"**LBRH**.

"**LBRH**.

"*Total time taken : 1 hour 11 minutes. Note to self : turn on heating next time - getting into Autumn now !*"

Midday Ritual.

Done, astrally projecting whilst at my desk at work.

That afternoon, the Government announced that far from easing anything up – as I had hoped would happen by September – it would make the restrictions caused by COVID-19 a lot more severe. Quite apart from anything else, this effectively dashed any chance of my fiancée flying to the United States to get her 5=6 in November – the earliest date at which she could have qualified to do so. I reminded her that I had offered to teach her Adeptus Minor stuff to make up for it.[221]

Quite separately, someone off the internet wanted me to get Andromalius on the case for them. I agreed to help, in return for them thanking Andromalius publicly, and making a donation to my fundraiser.

---

[220] I.e., day 160, *supra*.

[221] Day 70 – *vide supra*.

Evening Ritual

Done. *&sic ad lectum.*

Day 163

22 September 2020

Morning Ritual

During the night I recalled a brief fragment of just one dream. I woke up at 4.30am and prepared by checking in with my Nephesh and the Middle pillar ritual. I began at 5.08am :

"*LBRP.*

"*LBRH.*

"*Bornless ritual.*

"*Conjuration.*

"*Confession. Thinking about love and identity. I.e., Love is what happens when you extend your identity to include other people as well as yourself. It therefore occurs to me that a practical way for communing with all these spirits is actually to cultivate love for them i.e. To see them not as evil but having great potential for good.*

"*It strikes me that a lot of people including occultists want to believe that demons and devils are evil. But to entertain the notion that Satan is actually 'the great magical agent' and is not the Devil, or that Lucifer represents a force that can be validly used in 'white' magick, etc, is liable to be met by bemusement by both so-called Satanists and 'white magicians.' Best to keep silent about it all.*"

The central irony of the Abramelin Operation lies in the fact that although I have no doubt about Knowledge and Conversation of the Holy Guardian Angel being "white" magick, one cannot complete the operation without conjuring the four Kings of Hell, the eight Princes, and all their Demon servants. One may therefore call Abramelin in one sense "Luciferian" or "Satanic," in that Lucifer and Satan number among the Kings of Hell thus conjured.

Abramelin does *not,* however, remotely resemble either Luciferianism or Satanism as understood by the general public, the media, or by occultists who identify as followers of the "Left Hand Path." One ought to think of it as neither Black nor White – neither Left nor Right – but a combination of both : using White Magick (the Right Hand) to deal responsibly with the forces of Black Magick (the Left Hand) ; whilst using the latter to actively empower the former.

However, anyone who describes it as "grey" should be taken out and shot. The idea that White and Black Magick can exist together without blurring into an indistinguishable whole ought not to present any problem to the mind of someone familiar with the chessboard, the piano, or who manages not to get killed at the next zebra crossing.

Abramelin will certainly prove unsuitable for anyone with any evil intention, or who has a troubled relationship with their God : the austerity of the Operation has far too much piety for anyone so minded. Unfortunately, most of the people who have turned to the occult whom I know, did so because of their dissatisfaction with the religion of their upbringing. Very few I have encountered swing back to a more mature relationship therewith, although one can never go back to conventional worship.

Satan as "the Great Magical Agent" refers to the concept deriving from Eliphas Lévi, via Paul Foster Case, which I mentioned previously.[222] I suppose that a critic could accuse it of being a kind of "doublethink" – on not only Lévi' and Case's parts, but also on my own - a way to consider what I call "Satan" as not actual Satan, but a positive force. However, I nevertheless experienced the idea as *empowering*, in that I could make use of a great Taboo, something untouchable, and deploy it to great effect. Hence I imagine that those who have strong preconceptions about who or what they think Satan to be – both from the extreme Right- and extreme Left-Hand Path – might well try to "gatekeep" me, each according to their own individual prejudices.

 "Additional prayer.
 "Licence to Depart.
 "LBRP.
 "LBRH.
 "Total time 1 hour 9 minutes. Towards the end I was affected by the need to eliminate so this might have affected my appreciation of the ceremony."

Midday Ritual

Done, in a similar manner to yesterday. Powerful, despite being brief.

I managed to do some scriptural study today, analysing Genesis 1 :24. Fun fact : Air and Water "abounded" with their respective creatures, but God "brought forth" terrestrial animals from the Earth. The former has the implication of propagating like vibrations in their respective media, whereas the latter has the idea of "giving birth" or "wet-nursing."

Evening Ritual

Feeling constipated, but nevertheless did the ritual. Sacrament later (after satisfactorily voiding my bowels) proved good.

---

[222] Day 110 – *vide supra.*

Day 164

23 September 2020

Morning Ritual

During the night, I recalled at least a fragment of a dream, but no more : my recall being not so hot on this occasion. I woke up at 4.30am and prepared in the usual manner (checking in with Nephesh / Middle Pillar Ritual). I began at 5.10am :

"LBRP.

"LBRH.

"Bornless Ritual.

"Conjuration.

"Confession. Thanking God and my HGA for everything they do. Following on from yesterday, I focus on treating Satan etc like the 'Great Magical Agent.' The feeling of rising Kundalini is strong and palpable.

"Additional prayer.

"Licence to Depart.

"LBRP.

"LBRH.

"Total time not including preparation : 1 hour 12 minutes."

*

At breakfast I unfortunately got into another argument with my fiancée, about "magical partnerships" (i.e., in terms of sexual polarity). The way I interpreted what she said, she seemed to think that such a partnership would involve compensating for each other's inadequacies : whereas I held forth to my view that one ought to base such a thing on fullness, not lack. In other words, neither partner ought to accept the role of "inadequate" in any way, but both should act as stars, who take up their respective positions in the partnership because they form part of a team. Sort of like how the Johan Cruyff pioneered the concept of "Total Football" with Ajax and later the Dutch national side in the Seventies, but with Magick instead of Football *per se.*

My fiancée, however, because she belonged to "Ally's Tartan Army," probably did not appreciate this reference to her country's great rivals from that era. Either that or she did not follow Football in general. In any event, she interpreted me as implying that I did not want to partner her magically at all, or that I didn't regard her as an equal. The former I regarded as patently untrue : but as to the latter, I couldn't help but think she kept complaining about things she wrongly believed she could not do. Far from not regarding her as my equal, I constantly tried to reassure her and convince that she was – or even *better than me*. But by not talking positively about herself she became her own worst enemy.

I failed to convince her : she stormed off to work before we could reach a satisfactory (for either of us) resolution. She appeared conciliatory by text message later, however.

Midday Ritual

Done, albeit briefly.

That afternoon, I investigated Genesis 1 :25 (Sagittarius) as part of my daily scriptural study. In this instance I found Westcott's translation of the Sepher Yetzirah more evocative that Kaplan's, because it brought out Qabalistic nuances lacking in the latter.

I also, quite separately, created a fundraiser on Facebook for my birthday in a few weeks' time, to help raise money for my chosen charity.

Later : before I did my evening ritual, I petitioned Andromalius to help the woman who requested assistance from me via the internet. Powerful stuff - kundalini rising.

Evening Ritual

Done.

Day 165

24 September 2020

Morning Ritual

During the night I recorded one dream. I got up at 4.30am, and prepared by checking in with my Nephesh, and the Middle Pillar Ritual. I began at 5.07am. From my magical record :

"LBRP.

"LBRH.

"Bornless Ritual. I am briefly seized by feelings of anger bubbling up, but I concentrate on the ritual and complete it properly. Actually feeling energised.

"Conjuration.

"Confession. Thanking God & HGA for everything they do. Working on conjuring / constraining the anger that I briefly experienced so that I am in control of it, not it of me. Imploring mercy for all my sins, and those for which I'm responsible.

"Am able to really feel my higher self possessing my Nephesh and manifesting thereby.

"Deep meditation - very powerful.

"Additional prayer.

"Licence to Depart.

"LBRP.

"LBRH.

"Total time : 1 hour 22 minutes."

My fiancée later remarked how I always seemed sexually excited after doing these rituals. I personally just regarded it as a natural (and almost unremarkable) consequence of my feelings towards her, combined with the beneficial effects of a course of meditation, but apparently she considered it unusual.

As it happened, I managed to get through the whole of breakfast and escape from the house without a harsh word between us (mainly because I managed to keep my trap shut).

*

During the morning, I spent some time reassuring people on Quora.com. One person felt afraid that they would die that evening just because they had dreamed of Jesus the night before. (Ironically, the original poster never replied to confirm that he or she had survived).

Another poster worried about falling energy levels whilst doing tarot readings. I suggested treating such tarot readings with ritualistic sensibilities, i.e., remembering to close down or banish afterwards. The flip side ? Experiencing depleting energy indicates one's psychic sensitivity, which implies that the Tarot actually *works*.

Midday Ritual

Done, in a manner similar to yesterday, i.e., from my desk at work, I astrally projected to my oratory to perform the ritual. I recorded the whole experience as "good."

For my scriptural study today I investigated Genesis 1 :26 (Capricorn) – the verse in which God decides to create man.

Evening Ritual

Done. Very powerful meditation, as if causing my higher self to manifest. *Samadhi.*

Day 166

25 September 2020

Morning Ritual

During the night : recorded one dream, mostly inspired by the movie we watched last night. I got up at 4.30am and prepared by checking in with my Nephesh, and the Middle Pillar Ritual. I began at 5.09am – from my magical journal :

*"**LBRP**.*

*"**LBRH**.*

*"**Bornless Ritual**.*

*"**Conjuration**.*

*"**Confession**. Thanking God & HGA for everything they do. Working on conjuring / constraining the anger that I briefly experienced so that I am in control of it, not it of me. Imploring mercy for all of my sins, and those for which I'm responsible.*

"Am able to really feel my higher self possessing my Nephesh, and manifesting thereby.

"Deep meditation - very powerful.

*"**Additional prayer**.*

*"**Licence to Depart**.*

*"**LBRP**.*

*"**LBRH**.*

"Total time : 1 hour 22 minutes."

*

At breakfast, I perceived that my fiancée continued to have a bee in her bonnet about magical partnerships : a subject which she broached two days ago *(vide supra)*. She has not shifted from her position, nor I from mine. However, now I perceived a major difference in our respective points-of-view : she believed the *"inner school"* comprised one homogenous experience for everyone, whereas I believed that each person makes their own inner plane contacts. Hence, from my point of view, two magicians accompanying one another on "the path" would each help one another establish their own respective contacts, as opposed to each helping each other establish the same contacts.

In other words, I saw a magical partnership as two partners helping each other become *independent,* not *mutually dependent,* which seems to describe my fiancée's viewpoint. I tried to explain this to her by saying that if I should die, she could carry on without me, although to her credit, she thought the idea of me passing away morbid and horrible.

Nevertheless, I found it intriguing to think that I had always assumed that everyone's self-reliance in this way, without questioning the idea. Perhaps that explained why BOTA apparently taught that only one Holy Guardian Angel existed for all humanity, or one "central Ego." The Golden Dawn had therefore gone up in my estimation, in that it had taught me independence : I earnestly hoped that BOTA and Dion Fortune's lot did not teach the contrary, because it would make them look like personality cults.

Midday Ritual.

Done, whilst astrally projecting from work to my oratory. Like yesterday but this time actually powerful, i.e., more potent than previously.

Apart from this, though, work kept me busy, so that I could hardly do any new scriptural study today. Later, though, I went on Quora, and briefly answered an alleged miracle-worker seeking validation from others : I counselled him to silence, not just for his sake, but for the sake of humanity in general ! In hindsight I wondered whether the advice I gave out on these websites ought to apply equally to myself ?

In the evening, I tried to explain to my fiancée my theory of the necessity for confessing one's sins as part of *Abramelin :* foolishly I did so by using "working out Karma" as a metaphor. I had forgotten that the whole notion of Karma made her seriously uncomfortable, so the conversation became derailed from that point on. When I tried making the point that Karma is not all bad, I had just as much luck as I had last time,[223] so eventually I had to withdraw from the discussion with as much dignity as possible to go do my evening meditations.

Evening Ritual

Done. *&sic ad lectum.*

---

[223] I.e., day 140 – *vide supra.*

Day 167

26 September 2020

Morning Ritual

During the night : owing mainly to the fact that, having reached the weekend, I had the luxury of getting a proper night's sleep I recorded two dreams. I got up at 6.15am for checking in with my Nephesh and the Middle Pillar Ritual. I began at sunrise (6.50am) – from my magical record :

"*LBRP.*

"*LBRH.*

"*Bornless Ritual.*

"*Conjuration.*

"*Confession. Whilst meditating and thanking God for His grace, and thanking Him and my HGA for everything they do, and asking forgiveness for all my various sins etc, I have several insights :*

[Insight #1] "*My fiancée being upset about me talking about Karma which I noted last night : this is a classic example of telling someone a truth which they are not ready to receive which, as MacGregor Mathers said, is as bad as lying to someone - i.e., a MISTAKE.*

[Insight #2] "*'Tzebaoth' can, by a chain of Atziluthic (almost) correspondences, be rendered as 'Righteousness Within the Higher Self And the Universe.' This makes me excited, as if I have reached a new level of understanding of the word.*"

The significance of this arose, of course, because of the role of "Tzebaoth" as one of the only three divine names that The Book said I should use in my conjurations, hence my pre-occupation with it. I may explain the rationale behind this particular idea as follows : in Hebrew its spelling is צבאות , i.e. Tzaddi, Beth, Aleph, Vav, Tav. Hence :

צ	Tzaddi	The initial of *Tzedeq,* i.e., "<u>Righteousness</u>."
ב	Beth	In Hebrew *be* or *b'* literally means "in," as in "berashith" (in the beginning), hence "<u>Within.</u>"
א	Aleph	Because its numeration is one, it is naturally associated with Kether, and hence *Yechidah,* which for present purposes may be colloquially translated as "<u>The Higher Self.</u>"
ו	Vav	*Ve* or *V'* in Hebrew is "<u>And.</u>"

ת Tav　I.e., referring to the tarot key "<u>The Universe</u>." This was a bit
of a cheat, as it was a Yetziratic association rather than an
Atziluthic one. In hindsight, the spelling of the word "tav"
enumerates to 406, equivalent in Gematria to *Atah,* "Thou"
(a divine name), hence the whole phrase could be alternately
rendered "Righteousness within the Higher Self and in Thee
(oh God)."

Back to my magical record of that morning's ritual :

[Insight #3] "*Ironically, the argument about Karma last night has
inspired me. A person is born at a particular time and place because it is
their karma for them to do so. Hence - a person's natal horoscope is in fact
a snapshot of their karma at the time of their birth. This effectively gives a
very simple (now that I think about it) way of resolving one's karma : using
Ceremonial Magick, speak to the spirit of each planet in turn along the
following lines - e.g. Taking the Sun as an example : 'What is the karmic
reason that caused me to be born when the Sun was at such-and-such a
position in my horoscope ?' Then the Solar spirits will reveal the reason,
perhaps in the form of a past-life memory, which reveals the answer to the
question - and by implication, what are the karmic issues which the
individual has to deal with.*

"*In this way, Karma and past-life therapy is linked-in to the Hermetic
tradition and Western Magical tradition, in a quite natural way, without
having to muck about with akashic records or some such - it becomes the
way of dealing with metempsychosis not as some alien dogma rudely
inserted where it doesn't fit, but as Pythagoras and others like him might
have originally envisaged. (If I were creating my own GD order, I could
make this the subject of my 6=5 grade).*

"*Additional prayer.*

"*Licence to Depart.*

"*LBRP.*

"*LBRH.*

"*Total time : 1 hour 23 minutes.*

"*Afterwards I get some shut-eye, in which I have a dream in which I am
briefly lucid, although I don't really do anything magical with it.*"

Midday Ritual

Done. Feeling rushed at first, later I calmed down and reached something of a
semblance of a meditative state.

That afternoon, however, I hosted a meeting of our Golden Dawn study group on ZOOM, in which I re-did a Dion Fortune inspired healing ritual which we had done on a previous occasion.[224] I actually felt the Middle Pillar ritual doing me some good.

Evening Ritual

Done. Very good indeed - *Samadhi*, even. This whole business of inviting my Higher Self to take possession of my Nephesh proved particularly satisfactory.

---

[224] Adapted from FORTUNE (2006)

Day 168

27 September 2020

Morning Ritual

During the night I managed to record one dream. Up at 6.15am for preparation with checking-in with my Nephesh and Middle Pillar Ritual : good. I began at sunrise, i.e., 6.51am. My magical record :

"LBRP.

"LBRH.

"Bornless Ritual.

"Conjuration.

"Confession. Meditation is very powerful. When I ask my Higher Self to take possession of my Nephesh, I attain Samadhi - *very powerful*.

"Additional prayer.

"Licence to Depart.

"LBRP.

"LBRH.

"Total time not including preparation : 1 hour 14 minutes. Overall, very good, the peak state I experienced during the Confession left me with a very positive view of the whole experience. ☺ *"*

I caught some ZZZs afterwards. When I woke up mid-morning, my fiancée joined me in bed and insisted on talking excitedly about Tarot this, tarot that, for almost an hour. I eventually got a word-in to suggest that we get up for breakfast.

Midday Ritual

Done. I decided to give my Nephesh a name – *"Nepheshi "* (which literally means "My Nephesh," so hardly very inventive) and made a sigil for it. Actually, I was able to work it out in my head, as I could visualise where the letters Nun, Peh, Shin, and Yod occurred on the Rose of the Rose-Cross lamen. Also today, I performed the Tea-pot meditation as part of the Confession. All very powerful - very deep meditation.

For my scriptural study today, I made a start of working on Genesis 1 :27 (Mars), mainly transcribing the Hebrew.

However, another ZOOM meeting with the Greatly Honoured Chiefs of the Golden Dawn occupied my time : they had organised it as a follow-up to the first held just over two months ago.[225] Again, approximately a hundred Fratres and

---

[225] I.e., day 98 – *vide supra*.

Sorores from across the globe took part : the meeting lasted most of the afternoon and evening. We didn't get to chat much, as the talks by the GH chiefs dominated the proceedings. However, afterwards, someone did make an offhand remark about some BBC drama serial which had featured Enochian angels, so I made a mental note to check it out.

Evening Ritual

Done. Very powerful. *&sic ad lectum.*

Day 169

28 September 2020

Morning Ritual

During the night I recorded one dream, more vivid than previous nights. I got up at 4.30am for checking in with *Nepheshi* and the Middle Pillar Ritual. I began at 5.05am – from my magical record :

"LBRP.

"LBRH.

"Bornless Ritual.

"Conjuration.

"Confession. Very deep state of meditation. So much so that I perform all the rest of this morning's devotions in the astral.

"Additional prayer.

"Licence to Depart.

"LBRP.

"LBRH.

"Total time not including preparation : 1 hour 11 minutes."

*

This morning, by way of scriptural study today, I finished off working on Genesis 1 :27. When it speaks of God creating Man, it really meant God creating Man *as an intellectual being,* as this would fit in with the Exciting Intelligence, and the fact that Mars as the ruler of Aries governs the head. Hence, my reading of this verse implied a human's capacity for rational thought makes the real "image of God," in which the latter created mankind..

Also, to make up for the fact that I spent little time doing scriptural study yesterday, I worked on Genesis 1 :28. I realised that the verb "to have dominion over" – as in, "…have dominion over the fish of the sea, over the birds of the air, and over every living thing that moves on the earth" – equates in Gematria with "to *conjure,"* which thus gives the Biblical precedent for humans acting as Magicians.

Midday Ritual

Done, astrally projecting from my desk at work. Good, despite the imperfect circumstances of it all.

I thought in general terms about the relationship of the Nephesh to the Ruach, and jotted down the following epithet : *"There's nothing wrong with Monkey-mind, so long as you've got the right Monkey."* I.e., whoever described the unmeditative mind as "the chattering of a thousand monkeys" failed to appreciate that primates have their own animal-cunning and their own predictable patterns of behaviour, and one can even train them (although in a lot of cases the training involves adapting one's own behaviour to that of the monkey as much as the other way round). I decided to sum this up in a meme featuring Rafiki from *The Lion King* on social media.[226]

Evening Ritual

That evening, my fiancée behaved in a funny mood : in which she always seemed to get whenever she chose to wore black for the day. Whether the clothes determined the mood or *vice versa* I didn't know, but I suspected the former. Nevertheless I spent the evening tip-toeing around her.

When I performed my evening ritual, I checked-in with *Nepheshi* and then performed the Lesser Banishing Rituals of the Pentagram and Hexagram in the astral, before doing the actual Evening Ritual. Performing the banishing rituals set me at ease : the meditation arising thereafter turned out to be very good.

Later, my fiancée was feeling better, and suggested we perform the Middle Pillar together. Sacrament ensued.

---

[226] Not reproduced here because I am dubious about the copyright.

Day 170

29 September 2020

Morning Ritual

During the night, I recorded one dream, albeit briefly. Up at 4.30am for checking in with Nepheshi and the Middle Pillar Ritual. I began at 5.05am. From my magical record :

"LBRP.

"LBRH.

"Bornless Ritual.

"Conjuration.

"Confession. Whilst concentrating on my higher self taking possession of Nepheshi, I contemplate how it would feel like to actually conjure the various Demons as in the final ritual. The sensation of hellfire is palpable (but quite welcome on what is a cold morning).

"Additional prayer.

"Licence to Depart.

"LBRP.

"LBRH.

"Total time taken : 1 hour 19 minutes."

*

I tried to briefly answer someone on Quora who asked : *"As a beginner in tarot reading, is it normal to be confused at the results and even feel like the answers don't make sense ?"* I ended up writing a thoughtful piece on what advice I would give to a beginner – i.e., what advice *I* would have liked to receive when I began tarot reading. Treat tarot reading like an Art, like a concert pianist would approach playing the piano. Learn not to rely on the Little White Book ; practice ; read widely ; but most of all *embrace the confusion*, as only by facing challenges one can learn more.

Really I suppose I imposed my own biases on the subject, in order to try and get someone up to the standard that I would expect of myself as a Golden Dawn magician.

Midday Ritual

Done, as yesterday, i.e., whilst astrally projecting from my desk at work.

I did not get round to doing any scriptural study today. In the evening, I spent time on ZOOM listening to CH, who had resigned from office in the SRIA two weeks previously,[227] vent his spleen on his reasons for doing so. In hindsight, I could have used this time itself to devote to scriptural study, as although both he and other participants in the ZOOM call (his friends and supporters) expressed a lot of anger, almost nothing in the way of practical solutions presented itself. Essentially, two things had caused his ire : the treatment of the Hampstead venue ; and the cronyism now rampant in the SRIA. However, I felt that he devoted too much time to the latter and not enough to the former.

On the one hand I chose to take part in the meeting because I retained some loyalty towards CH since his time as Grandmaster of HOM. But really, I had the sense of a slow-motion car-crash happening two times over : although I could predict that CH's time in the SRIA would soon come to an end, I had a certain conviction that the SRIA's own time as a credible force in the esoteric world had expired as well.

I looked round the number of people attending the ZOOM call and sighed : the vast majority of them comprised younger, junior members of the Society who ought to have looked forward to enjoying their membership of it. At the same time, being younger and junior, they would not get to vote on anything important if matters were forced to a head. CH may have spoken to an audience of his friends, but he had addressed the *wrong audience* – the people who had the power to change anything had by and large stayed away. I presume because they thought retaining the favour of the current Supreme Magus actually meant something : ironically reinforcing the very cronyism which had caused the problem in the first place.

Evening Ritual

Done. *&sic ad lectum.*

---

[227] Day 155 – *vide supra.*

Day 171

30 September 2020

Morning Ritual

During the night, I recorded one dream (briefly). I got up at 4.30am and prepared by checking in with Nepheshi, and the Middle Pillar Ritual. I began at 5.12am – from my magical record :

*"**LBRP**. I am conscious that the thought of last night's Zoom conference is distracting me, so I try to expel it from my aura as if it is an obsession, before doing the LBRP.*

*"**LBRH**.*

*"**Bornless Ritual**.*

*"**Conjuration**.*

*"**Confession**. Trying to concentrate on God and my HGA, finding it hard because of the distracting thoughts. Nevertheless, I do calm down a little, so I end the meditation in a better state than when I began.*

*"**Additional prayer**.*

*"**Licence to Depart**.*

*"**LBRP**.*

*"**LBRH**.*

"Total time taken : 1 hour 11 minutes. Need to eliminate soon after, so perhaps my digestion was disturbing my mental state ? Feeling better afterwards."

Midday Ritual

Done. I managed to lock myself in the archive room and perform my meditation, attempting also to Astrally Project and invoke my Holy Guardian Angel via "The Method." Feeling nervous.

Later : I completed the eBay-sale of something which I manifested from the Universe, and consequently donated £150 to my JustGiving page. I noted : *"Total money from all sources is now approximately 5.16% of my stated target."*

Again, due to being busy at work, I could not do any Scriptural Study today. I had to wonder though : I would soon run out of verses of Genesis, I would still have time before the end of my Operation, so what would I do then ?

Evening Ritual

Done, with meditative music playing via YouTube.

Day 172

01 October 2020

Morning Ritual

During the night I recorded two dreams. I got up at 4.30am for checking in with Nepheshi, and the Middle Pillar Ritual. I began at 5.08am : not as distracted as I felt this time yesterday, but more relaxed and unhurried.

"*LBRP.*

"*LBRH.*

"*Bornless Ritual. Good. Feeling powerful.*

"*Conjuration.*

"*Confession. Random thoughts appear when I try meditating, but instead of becoming I agitated, I wonder : perhaps my subconscious is sending me a message ? Some ideas about what to do with mundane life. Eventually I get a semblance of mental stillness.*

"*Additional prayer.*

"*Licence to Depart.*

"*LBRP.*

"*LBRH.*

"*Total time taken : 1 hour 20 minutes.*"

Midday Ritual

Done, at work. I managed to lock myself away elsewhere so at least nothing disturbed me.

I managed to do some proper Scriptural Study today : I worked on Genesis 1 :29. An interesting fact : although this verse seems to prescribe a vegetarian diet for mankind, the word "for food" is equivalent in Gematria to "Elohim" – denoting God as the true source of sustenance.

I also found time to answer the query of someone who wrote "*I'm a 15-year-old Capricorn and I just found out that the devil tarot card is connected to my zodiac sign. Am I going to hell because of it ? I'm scared.*" I had to point out that if all Capricorns were going to hell, then so would Jesus and one-twelfth of the human race. Honestly ! This person would have already realised this if they had had a proper education, or watched *Monty Python's Life of Brian*, or both.

Evening Ritual

Done, in a manner similar to yesterday.

Day 173

02 October 2020

Morning Ritual

During the night : I had trouble at first recalling my dreams, but on waking at 4.30am, I curled up into the foetal position and tried to do some "free association" – on the basis that one can access the unconscious this way. Thankfully, the impromptu bit of psychoanalysis caused one of my dreams to pop back into memory.

I prepared by checking in with Nepheshi – and on this occasion meditating only briefly on the Middle Pillar. I began at 5.10am – from my magical record :

"LBRP.

"LBRH.

"Bornless Ritual. Powerful.

"Conjuration.

"Confession. Meditation upon God and my HGA, asking for forgiveness etc. I come up with a theory of 10-Dimensional Reality."

This refers to a rather recondite (even by my standards) theory which asserts that one can conceive of, and meditate upon higher, non-Euclidean dimensions. I think the germ of it came from me first thinking about Tesseracts and Hypercubes over six weeks ago.[228] The gist of my new theory ran thus :

One cannot literally experience higher dimensions – e.g., those upon which M Theory, Superstrings, etc rely – but one can experience a *simulation* of those higher dimensions by finding a way to represent them within the dimensions with which we have familiarity.

It so happens that one way of representing four-dimensions in two – e.g., the graph of a function performed on a Complex number, such as the Mandelbrot set – consists of creating a colour-coded diagram, i.e. one determines the RGB value of the colour of any given point by performing a Complex function on the co-ordinates of that point.

Hence, one can represent four-dimensions on a two-dimensional surface, by adding *layers of Meaning* to that surface. Therefore : "Meaning" constitutes the way in general of representing higher dimensions to our ordinary consciousness.

We can turn this round by saying that although one can use a four-dimensional object [229] invested with extra layers of meaning to represent an actual

---

[228] Day 126, midday ritual – *vide supra.*

[229] i.e., having the conventional physical dimensions of height, width and depth, plus duration in Time.

hyperdimensional object, e.g. a component of M-theory, so the converse can happen – one can take four-dimensional phenomena, together with the layers of meaning both objective and subjective with which we ascribe them, as *imaginary* hyperdimensional objects. One can even *meditate* upon hyperdimensional phenomena, by taking :

- the object of meditation itself ;
- the layers of objective meaning one ascribes to the object of meditation ; and
- the layers of *subjective* meaning further attached thereto ;

each as a representation of a dimension. The number of dimensions which one can represent in this way is potentially infinite, although in my meditation this morning I counted Ten : the four dimensions of Space-Time ; an extra dimension which I called "Existence" ; and then layers of subjective meaning each attributed to the former five.

I conceived of the dimension of "Existence" thus : if a thing exists within space-time – such as a thought or dream – but cannot be measured in terms of height, width, depth, or time, then its magnitude must be expressed by a fifth dimension independent of the first four. (This of course assumes that thoughts and dreams have both magnitude and direction, i.e. are *Vectors*, which I appreciate some would see as a big-ask, but from my own subjective experience of them I would say so.)

After the end of my ritual, as I typed up my magical journal, I added a note : "*Probably should be Eleven Dimensions- the extra dimension accounts for the Witness.*" I.e. that the fact that the Mind can witness these dimensions must mean it stands outside them – in its own Dimension.

In any event : my account of that morning's ritual continued.

"*Also very deep meditation when letting my higher self take control of my nephesh - momentary* Samadhi.

"*Additional prayer*.
"*Licence to Depart*.
"*LBRP*.
"*LBRH*.
"*Total time : 1 hour 23 minutes.*"

*

This morning I tried reading "*Shadows of Ecstasy*" by Charles Williams, on the grounds that not only did he hang around with JRR Tolkien and CS Lewis, but he had a background as an occultist as well (at least nominally, if belonging to

Waite's FRC counts). I had seen the novel billed as the story of an adept who had prolonged his life through Sinister means (i.e., literally the "left-hand" path).

I didn't think it was very good ! It failed at being a thriller, it failed at discussing the occult principles involved, and it had a bunch of unsympathetic characters as the protagonists. It didn't help that its colonial mindset dated it terribly. To be quite honest, I can see why he remained not so well-known as either Tolkien or Lewis. Despite not being a relation, he was, in effect, the *"Michelle Williams"* of the Inklings.

Midday Ritual

Done, at my desk at work. At least I nothing disturbed me. Feeling sleepy : I didn't do any scriptural study today, as I had a masochistic determination to finish off that damned book, to see if it would redeem itself if I got right through to the end (it didn't).

Evening Ritual

Done, in a similar manner as previous days. A very deep state of meditation ensued – directing that energy inwards gave positive results. Ironically therefore I managed to make better use of the principles outlined in Charles Williams' book than Charles Williams did ! *&sic ad lectum.*

Day 174

03 October 2020

Morning Ritual

During the night, I managed to record one dream in detail, plus fragments of another dream. I got up at 6.27am for checking in with Nepheshi and the Middle Pillar ritual. I began at 7.02am (sunrise) – from my magical journal :

> "*LBRP.*
>
> "*LBRH.*
>
> "*Bornless Ritual. Powerful, again.*
>
> "*Conjuration.*
>
> "*Confession. Whilst meditating I attain a deep state, like* Samadhi. *The 11-Dimensional model helps in organising my thoughts (into stillness).*
>
> "*Additional prayer.*
>
> "*Licence to Depart.*
>
> "*LBRP.*
>
> "*LBRH.*
>
> "*Total time not including preparation : 1 hour 16 minutes.*"

Afterwards, I couldn't go back to bed, as I had agreed to go with my fiancée to a particularly ghastly town in Essex, where her son works (ironically in a shop which sells new age and magical stuff, even though he himself does not believe in any of it). I personally considered the journey as a fruitless one which ate up most of the day : although I later discovered that my fiancée had an ulterior motive for doing so *(vide infra)*.

In any event, she had an opportunity to go shopping, so she had not wasted any time from her own point of view. She insisted on talking about "The Sun" tarot card, although I thought BOTA had some strange teachings on the subject.

Midday Ritual

We got home by the middle of the day, so I managed to do my ritual in my oratory properly, with astral projection music playing on YouTube. Very good - a deep state of meditation again.

That afternoon I spent time working on Genesis 1 :30 for my scriptural study. Ironically this corresponds with Resh and *the Sun* in both astrology and the tarot (I did not notice the synchronicity with what my fiancée had talked about until much later). Given that astrology mainly concerns its path – the path of the ecliptic – through the zodiac, one can easily see why the Sun goes nicely with the

Collecting Intelligence (the thirtieth path of the Sepher Yetzirah), i.e., *"because Astrologers deduce from it the judgment of the Stars."*[230] However, because it all fits pat, it adds practically nothing to what one already knows about either the Sun or the Collecting Intelligence, so it hardly does a good job of enlightening anyone.

Evening Ritual

Done. I willed that my higher self, when it took possession of *Nepheshi*, to not just manifest within me, but as a thing which to raise up my *sushumna*. I had an intense *Kundalini* experience. *Samadhi*.

---

[230] WESTCOTT (1887).

Day 175

04 October 2020

Morning Ritual

During the night I managed to record one dream. Up at 6.28am for checking in with Nepheshi, and the Middle Pillar ritual. I began at 7.03am (sunrise). From my magical journal, it appears that I went through the whole of the morning ritual as normal, without making any additional observations of note. On the plus side, however, I didn't record anything bad about it. The whole time it took not including preparation was 1 hour 24 minutes.

Afterwards I retired to bed and recorded another dream. *"Thought : what if there were a pagan version of* Sister Act *? i.e. A comedy which does for Paganism or occultism what Sister Act does for Catholicism ? Hmm."*

My fiancée and I had watched the said film on Now TV the previous : hence the inspiration. I often get plot-ideas from dreams – and nightmares too, which provide the best horror stories. In fact, because I derive so much inspiration from nightmares, far from them disturbing or terrifying me, I *enjoy* experiencing them.

(At time of writing I have not yet developed this into a new literary or dramatic work, so I want everyone to know that the idea is © copyright Alex Sumner 2022.)

*

I responded to a couple of questions on Quora, as I saw that I could use them to provide help and encouragement to young people starting out in magick. I started off answering someone who asked me about my first astral projection. I thought back, to over a quarter of a century ago. "It was odd, though not unpleasant," I wrote.

"I had actually been trying to lucid dream at the time, when by chance I had picked up a book entitled 'The Art & Practice of Astral Projection' *by Ophiel.[231] Then, late one evening I lay on my bed, and suddenly found myself having an out of the body experience. I know it was an OOBE because (a) I felt myself spinning out of my body and then standing upright ; (b) I felt lucid ; but strangest of all (c) I was aware that my physical body could still hear noises from elsewhere in the flat in which I was living at the time (i.e. my flat-mates talking), so my physical body could not have been asleep in the ordinary sense of the word.*

---

[231] Op. cit.

"I did not really do anything deeply significant with this OOBE, so after wandering around for a bit, I decided to return to my physical body, get back in and go to sleep. Nevertheless, it did have one important significance for me : it gave me a realistic idea of the kind of thing I should be trying to achieve when astrally projecting properly, and inspired me to keep up the practice."

The second question came from a beginner to witchcraft who had doubts about it all, because her attempts to do protection magick seemed not to work. I responded by suggesting thinking of it in terms of problem-solving : identify the underlying problem, e.g., through divination such as astrology or tarot ; then devise a magic ritual to zero-in on that issue. Alternatively, one could try out alternative protection rituals to find the best one for oneself, e.g., the pentagram and hexagram rituals, the Rose-Cross ritual, etc. The querent responded in amazement, saying she did not realise that protection magick consisted of anything other than a one-size-fits-all approach. Hopefully I had inspired her enough to delve back into the subject and learn more.

Midday Ritual

With Astral Projection music playing via YouTube, I performed my midday ritual. Checking in with Nepheshi, then : conjuration ; confession (incorporating Tea-Pot Meditation) ; additional prayer, licence to depart. After the Tea-Pot meditation I again had an intense Kundalini experience.

During the afternoon, I joined my fiancée in practising yoga with her. She revealed she had an early birthday present for me : a Harry Potter scarf she had knitted – in the colours of Gryffindor (naturally).

Evening Ritual

Done. Again, very intense kundalini as I concentrate on my higher self taking possession of Nepheshi. *&sic ad lectum*

Day 176

05 October 2020

Morning Ritual

During the night I managed to record one dream. Up at 4.30am for preparation with checking in with Nepheshi, and the Middle Pillar ritual. I began at 5am. From my magical journal that day :

"LBRP.

"LBRH.

"Bornless Ritual.

"Conjuration. Praying for forgiveness on account of all the people I have offended. Could I ever bring myself to forgive the people who have offended me ? I am reminded that I really cannot do anything except rely on the grace of God and be wary of spiritual pride.

"Thought : perhaps these downer attitudes are in fact the DoTT ? I have after all been experiencing 'illuminating' states over the past few days, so perhaps it is a natural consequence.

"Nevertheless, I do manage to achieve a deep state of meditation and experience Kundalini rising as I imagine drawing my higher self up my spine (in a manner similar to yesterday).

"Confession.

"Additional prayer.

"Licence to Depart.

"LBRP.

"LBRH.

"Total time taken (not including preparation) : 1 hour 13 minutes."

Midday Ritual

Done, at my desk at work. I made a remark in my magical journal *"thought : honesty is the best policy !"* However, in retrospect I can't honestly remember what the hell this referred to. I presume it must mean that my HGA stirred my conscience regarding some matter.

I can hardly think it would mean that the best way of performing my ritual would involve saying to my work colleagues *"Would you excuse me for about half an hour, whilst I do some astral projection as part of an operation to invoke my Holy Guardian Angel and summon and bind all the demons of Hell ?"* It would be out of character for me.

*

That evening, my fiancée and I watched 'Requiem' on Netflix – the same BBC drama which a Frater on the Zoom call with the GH Chiefs mentioned, which supposedly involves Enochian angels.[232] We had not seen any evidence of Enochian angels on screen by episode 3, but Enochian magic continued to terrify my fiancée : she would not listen to my attempts to reason with her. Needless to say, a blazing row developed. I withdrew, conscious that whatever I tried to say would ultimately do no good.

Evening Ritual

This actually went well. I appeared to have processed the emotions which I had felt earlier this evening, so I had an immensely powerful Kundalini experience. *& sic ad lectum.*

---

[232] Day 168 – *vide supra.*

Day 177

06 October 2020

Morning Ritual

During the night I managed to record one dream. Up at 4.30am for preparation with checking in with Nepheshi and the Middle Pillar ritual. I began at 5.05 am. From my magical journal that morning :

"LBRP.

"LBRH.

"Bornless Ritual.

"Conjuration. Reflecting on the events of yesterday evening (the argument, not the Kundalini). It is obvious now that I fell into the trap of telling a truth for which my fiancée was not ready (i.e., The nature of Enochian magic as I believed it to be), which of course is as bad as lying to someone. I pray to God that my HGA warns me when this is happening so that I can avoid it (in the past I did not avoid it until too late).

"When I will my higher self to take possession of Nepheshi, my consciousness is flooded with images from the past. Perhaps this is the Dweller on the Threshold manifesting ? After all, I did have a particularly powerful Kundalini-experience last night. The otherwise distracting thoughts are all memories of the late 1970s and 1980s, which if I'm right would mean that a karmic lesson for me is bound up with my childhood / teenage years.

"A thought : perhaps I should find a bible verse on which to meditate, in case my mind is assailed by distracting thoughts in such a manner in the future ?"

As it happened, I followed this up later that afternoon with some extra scriptural study. Using *The Power of the Psalms* to help me find an appropriate versicle, I came up with this, from Psalm 29 :11 :

$$\text{יְהוָה--עֹז ,לְעַמּוֹ יִתֵּן ; יְהוָה ,יְבָרֵךְ אֶת-מוֹ בַשָּׁלוֹםע.}$$

Yəhvah oz l'aamo yeeten, Yəhvah yəbarekh et-amo bashalom ("The LORD will give strength, the LORD will bless His people with peace.")

"How ironic," I thought. Qabalists had vexed themselves with the true pronunciation of the Tetragrammaton for years : yet it had lain right there in the Hebrew Bible all this time, plain to see. The Tetragrammaton with the vowel-pointing inserted : "Yəhvah" – a *schwa* followed by a *kamatz*. I felt rather

disappointed : out of cognitive dissonance made fully conscious, or in other words, bloody-mindedness, I decided I would continue to pronounce the Tetragrammaton as "Yod Heh Vav Heh" by default. I would stick to my previous, exotic theories, such as the Tea-Pot Meditation, and all the rest of the Qabalah for that matter because they gave me so much more fun in which to indulge.

To continue with my magical record :

"Confession.

"Additional prayer.

"Licence to Depart.

"LBRP.

"LBRH.

"Total time taken (not including preparation) : 1 hour 21 minutes."

Another blazing row occurred over breakfast, regarding the supposed evils of Enochian magic, and why the GD acted dangerously by exposing unsuspecting fratres and sorores to it. Actually, my fiancée did the blazing : I tried remaining silent as best I could. In effect she wanted to have last night's argument all over again – when I tried to withdraw from it, she still had plenty to say, and she had saved it up all night. It appeared that even though I had processed the events of last night, she had not.

Now that I reflected on the gist of what she said, I could see the problem. She had become obsessed with reading articles on the internet which say that Enochian magic is terrible. She had never once Googled an article which argued the contrary point of view : that Enochian magic acted as a positive, edifying force, when used in a responsible manner. This gave me a plan : before I left for work that morning, I promised I would find her something to read which would make her see the subject in a different light.

*

This morning I managed to get in some scriptural study, by working on Genesis 1 :31.

I emailed my fiancée a link to an article on Enochian Magic which *I* had written : specifically "EHNB," in which I described my adventures skrying into the four letters of this entity's name individually, and then evoking it as a whole.[233] If she wanted to read a lot of rubbish about Enochian magick, the least she could do is read one I wrote which says the opposite.

---

[233] SUMNER (2003)

Midday Ritual

Done, in a manner similar to yesterday, i.e., by astrally projecting to my oratory from my desk at work.

When I got home, my fiancée had changed completely. She told me she read my article after I emailed her, and sheepishly admitted that had she read that first, she would have formed an entirely different opinion on Enochian magic - i.e., a favourable one. I wrote that article in 2003. The irony that she had to go to my website to get it instead of just asking me did not escape her.

That evening I started compiling notes on what the rituals for the final seven days of the Operation would entail.

Whilst in the middle of doing something else, I realised to my annoyance that I had lost my copy of *Golden Dawn Enochian Skrying Tarot* (i.e., the book not the deck). I decided to dig out my trusty Pendulum, which told me that I still had it *somewhere*. I should have thought so ! I could hardly imagine idly mislaying it the last time I moved house). I mused : *"Perhaps Andromalius can help ? Although normally his forte is stolen goods."*

Evening Ritual

Done in a manner similar to yesterday evening. Kundalini. Profound.

Day 178

07 October 2020

Morning Ritual

During the night, I had difficulty recalling any dreams. I got up at 4.30am for preparation by checking in with Nepheshi, and the Middle Pillar ritual. I began at 5.10 am. From my magical journal :

"LBRP.

"LBRH.

"Bornless Ritual.

"Conjuration.

"Confession. Praying for forgiveness ... Thinking about the events of this time yesterday morning, I can remember falling into evil when in an evil situation when I was a teenager (by 'evil' I mean thoughts of which I would be ashamed now - I didn't actually do anything). It occurs to me that the kernel of goodness was that I was trying to protect myself. I could have chosen not to but then I wouldn't have been protecting myself. It reminds me of the dilemma of evil in this world, i.e., that not everyone can live up to the standard of Christ and willingly accept crucifixion in the face of evil - instead of resorting to self-defence.

"In any case, I will that the part of me that resorted to evil devote its energy to protecting me (its original intention) but in a way that is in accordance with my higher self.

"Willing the higher self to take possession of the Nephesh. Kundalini - profound.

"Additional prayer.

"Licence to Depart.

"LBRP.

"LBRH.

"Total time taken (not including preparation) : 1 hour 13 minutes."

Afterwards, at breakfast, my fiancée was in noticeably better spirits compared to the same time yesterday.

*

This morning I worked on Genesis 2 :1, for my scriptural study : the final verse of this particular project. Analysing in regard to the Sepher Yetzirah proved particularly problematical. Westcott's version calls this path the "Administrative

Intelligence," but Kaplan's calls it the "Worshipped Consciousness," "because it is prepared so as to *destroy* all who engage in the worship of the seven planets," as opposed to "directing and associating the planets even in their due courses."

Sekhel Ne'evad as far as I can make out means "destroying consciousness," which would give sense to the second half of Kaplan's sentence, but it poses the questions : why did Rittangelius (whom Westcott translated) have this as "Administrative" ; why did Kaplan translate "destroying" as "worshipped" : and what the hell does it all mean anyway ? It didn't help that Kaplan did not provide any notes or commentary to this particular part of his translation.

Midday Ritual

Done, similar to yesterday, but instead of astrally projecting from my desk I managed to lock myself away somewhere so that no-one would disturb me.

Evening ritual.

Done : powerful stuff. In order to avoid the embarrassment of not recalling any dreams in the night, I resorted to, immediately before going to bed, taking my dream diary and writing in capitals at the top of the page : "I WILL REMEMBER MY DREAMS."

Day 179

08 October 2020

Morning Ritual

I woke up at 4.30am : I did actually remember at least one dream. So, resorting to an old piece of advice I once heard about dream recall did in fact work. I prepared for my morning session by checking in with Nepheshi, and the Middle Pillar Ritual. I began at 5.03am :

"LBRP.

"LBRH.

"Bornless Ritual.

"Conjuration.

"Confession. Whilst concentrating on asking mercy for my sins, I think about the August Order of Light, of which I was briefly a member. On the one hand there were several things wrong with them, but was I too harsh on them ?

"Some meditation.

"Additional prayer.

"Licence to Depart.

"LBRP.

"LBRH.

"Total time (not including preparation) : 1 hour 19 minutes."

Midday Ritual.

Done, in a similar manner to yesterday. Today was a very hectic day, with not much time to do anything but work.

*

When I got home, my copy of *The Golden Dawn Enochian Skrying Tarot* turned up. So Andromalius came through - and due to where I had found it, the pendulum divination proved correct as well. I shared some stuff on social media in appreciation. By chance I found a post referring to Wynn Westcott's paper "The Divining Rod," which I first heard at the same Dowsing day-out which inspired me to take up the pendulum in the first place.

Evening Ritual

Done, in a manner similar to how I did it this time yesterday. I felt pain in my knees, so I gave *padmasana* a break. Sacrament later.

Day 180

09 October 2020

Morning Ritual

During the night I recalled one dream. Up at 4.30am for checking in with Nepheshi and Middle Pillar Ritual. During the latter I took the opportunity to direct healing energy at myself, as I felt I might be developing a cold (hopefully nothing worse than that). I began at 5.03am :

"LBRP.

"LBRH.

"Bornless Ritual.

"Conjuration.

"Confession. As I ask for mercy for my various sins, I am reminded of the need to forgive others especially if I have already accepted responsibility for them.

"Also thinking about the importance of sublimating anger etc.

"A thought occurs - perhaps my HGA is synthesising the contents of my recent memories into new ideas ? Anywho - watching a series on Netflix very loosely about Enochian magic last night (and by loosely I mean not at all) ... I.e., the series *Requiem,* mentioned previously.

"... it occurs to me that instead of having The Magus or any of my other books adapted into a film, why not as a TV series instead ? Or a Netflix series. Hmmm ...

"I am able to reach a reasonably deep state of meditation in which I contemplate the Kundalini rising up my sushumna.

"Additional prayer.

"Licence to Depart.

"LBRP.

"LBRH.

"Total time not including preparation : 1 hour 11 minutes."

Midday Ritual

From my magical journal :

"I check in with Nepheshi, then attempt to AP using the GD method to my oratory - i.e., first I establish sphere in that part of Nepheshi corresponding to my oratory ; then I formulate a simulacrum there ; then I will that the TOLPIAS be established, and the fourfold dragon formulae pour in their coruscations of energy."

I.e., TOLPIAS is my acronym for the "Tree Of Life Projected In A Sphere," a Theoricus Adeptus Minor teaching of the Golden Dawn. Establishing this involved contemplating *all* the Sephiroth with their respective divine names, and then placing all the Minor Arcana and the trumps corresponding to the signs of the Zodiac around the sphere. NB : TOLPIAS has *two* pillars of Mercy and Severity, and *four* reflections of the Middle Pillar on the sphere's surface. As however Kether and Malkuth, the poles, only occur once, one ends up establishing twenty-four sephiroth. The fourfold dragon formulae comprise part of the same teaching.[234]

This may sound complicated, but I had made it straightforward to learn by breaking it down into chunks. Nevertheless, the concentration required to establish this astral model helped me get into as deep an immersive state as I did.

> *"Then I transfer my consciousness to the simulacrum thus established and perform : Conjuration ; invoking HGA via 'The Method' ; additional prayer ; and licence to depart. I return to my body (at my desk at work) and normal consciousness - Sign of Silence.*
>
> *"I was noticeably in a trance when I did this, meditative - when I come back, I feel light and full of energy."*

*

Regarding the idea that I had during the morning ritual, I calculated that I could indeed adapt *The Magus* into a six-part serial...

Ironically though, the last episode of *Requiem,* which had inspired that train of thought (which we finally watched that evening), didn't prove up to much. It left too many unanswered questions and didn't resolve the storylines satisfactorily. The plot resembled *The Wicker Man,* without the sex or a charismatic villain, but with a *"Deus Ex Machina"* ending for getting the central character out of the clutches of the cultists, who came across not so much as sinister but as a bunch of *rank amateurs.* This probably annoyed me the most out of that wretched episode – the realisation that *I could have done a better job* of calling forth an Enochian entity by myself than the supposed-villains.

The lack of resolution had clearly meant to set-up a sequel, although I later found out that the BBC had mercy-killed it after its first series.

Evening Ritual.

Done, in a similar manner to yesterday evening - *&sic ad lectum.*

---

[234] Regardie (1989) pp594-691.

Day 181

10 October 2020

Morning Ritual

During the night I managed to record two dreams. It probably had something to do with getting a good night's sleep. Up at 6.38am for preparation with checking in with Nepheshi and Middle Pillar Ritual. I began at sunrise : 7.13am.

"*LBRP.*

"*LBRH.*

"*Bornless Ritual.*

"*Conjuration.*

"*Confession. Distracting thoughts - a constant niggle. If I have taken responsibility for the sins of others, then I should be actively forgiving even as I want forgiveness for my own sins.*

"*At length I am able to quieten my mind sufficiently enough to achieve a satisfactory meditative state.*

"*Additional prayer.*

"*Licence to Depart.*

"*LBRP.*

"*LBRH.*

"*Total time taken (not including preparation) : 1 hour 16 minutes.*"

*

Today I had my birthday. After I finished my morning ritual, I got a chance for some shut-eye, after which my fiancée joined me for Sacrament. She then revealed that she had got me as a birthday present a proper altar, i.e., a little witchy-table.

As it happened, several weeks previously I had given some thought to what to do for an altar for my oratory : I had imagined some sort of smallish low-table, low enough that I could sit before it. And lo ! I found just such a table – an old piece of garden furniture – which someone had left out in the street, hoping someone would take it away – which I did. My feat of cosmic ordering impressed me greatly : I thought that just a wipe-down and perhaps a coat of paint would make it ready for business.

My fiancée, however, took one look at it and declared it far too scruffy – and evidently decided to get me an actual witch-altar from an occult gift-shop instead.

I had to admit that it certainly looked smarter and more *à propos* than the one I had manifested myself.

Midday Ritual

From my magical journal :

> "*In my oratory at home, with Astral Projection music playing via YouTube, I first check in with* Nepheshi *and then : conjuration ; confession ; additional prayer ; licence to depart. Whilst meditating as part of the confession, I will that my Higher Self possess* Nepheshi *; I then perform the Tea-Pot Meditation. Good, so far ... But then I will that I am raising the whole Tea-Pot meditation - the whole Holy of Holies thus established - up the spine, up the sushumna / Middle Pillar to Kether / Sahasrara ...* SAMADHI - *a more powerful Kundalini experience than I can remember experiencing. SO powerful, that I immediately express gratitude to God and pray that the subsequent Dweller on the Threshold experience won't be too severe (or that I will be able to deal with it properly).*"

*

To further celebrate my birthday, my fiancée took me to the only Vegan restaurant in town. Neither of us had visited it before : we had only thought of going there because of the vegetarian diet I followed at the time. It also gave me an opportunity to wear some brand new Killstar clothes which she had got me as an extra birthday present.

To say that the merits of Veganism, as opposed to simple vegetarianism, had left me "*not convinced*" , would understate my sentiment greatly. Vegan Cheese *offends* me. Eurgh ! I find it so bad that I believe that trying to evince moral arguments as to why Vegan food is better for you amounts to emotional abuse.

Ah well, I could not blame my fiancée. Neither of us were to know : it was a novelty for her as well as for me. We both agreed not to go back there in the future.

Evening Ritual

Done, in a manner similar to yesterday evening. After reviewing the events of the day, I meditated on drawing the experience of *Samadhi* itself up the spine - I achieved a very deep state of meditation, comparable to what I had experienced in the middle of the day, though this time it did not take me by surprise.

Later, when I climbed into bed that evening, my fiancée said I had "good energy ... Like a sun."

Day 182

11 October 2020

Morning Ritual

During the night I managed to record one dream. I got up at 6.40am for preparation with checking in with Nepheshi, then Middle Pillar Ritual. Elimination. I began at 7.15am, i.e., sunrise. From my magical journal :

"LBRP.

"LBRH.

"Bornless Ritual.

"Conjuration.

"Confession. Whilst meditating, my thoughts are drawn to the 1980s - my teenage years. What did I do that was sinful ? I remember that, like King Lear, during that time I was 'more sinned against than sinning.' But then it occurs to me - perhaps I was sinning against myself by not standing up for myself. Perhaps - I am sinning against myself now from the point of view of my future self! How should I know if I am ? I will that God and my HGA send me guidance.

"Am able to get something like a proper meditative state, but I get the feeling that I need to eliminate again, so I bring the session to an end as best I can.

"Additional prayer.

"Licence to Depart.

"LBRP.

"LBRH.

"Total time taken : 1 hour 17 minutes. I think it was the Vegan cheese that did it : I didn't particularly like it when I was eating it. Not sure I could ever become properly Vegan if I was forced to eat that ever again. Claiming to be Vegan is unnecessary virtue signalling."

Midday Ritual

Done, in a manner similar to yesterday. I got into a deep state, but it proved a milder experience than that of yesterday. I prayed that I would not spoil this with any pride or vanity.

*

Afterwards, I conducted a Golden Dawn Zoom meeting in which I presented "*Ritual Meditation on the Throne of the Stolistes*" by Chic & Tabatha Cicero[235] : preceded by some last-minute preparations to put together a suitable slide show to go with it.

Talking with my fiancée later, I tried to reassure her yet again regarding astral projection and skrying and stuff. As I thought more about it, I did not think she had actually experienced the astral plane, in which she had had such a negative reaction, but I could not convince her otherwise.

Evening Ritual

Done. *&sic ad lectum.*

---

[235] See : CICERO, CICERO (2000).

Day 183

12 October 2020

Duٌring the night : I managed to record a brief fragment of one dream, but only after doing some free-associating upon waking up. I also found I had won an eBay auction for a .925 silver dog-tag, which I intended to use as the "plate of silver" in the final ritual. I had been willing to go up to £15, but luckily, I got it for slightly less than £9.

Morning Ritual

I got up at 4.30am - elimination, brief middle pillar ritual and checking in with Nepheshi. I began at 5.08am. From my magical journal :

> *"LBRP.*
>
> *"LBRH.*
>
> *"Bornless Ritual.*
>
> *"Conjuration.*
>
> *"Confession. Whilst meditating I am able to devote more time to concentrating on my higher-self taking possession of Nepheshi and raising the experience up my spine like Kundalini. Deep.*
>
> *"Additional prayer.*
>
> *"Licence to Depart.*
>
> *"LBRP.*
>
> *"LBRH.*
>
> *"Total time taken : 1 hour 18 minutes."*

*

This morning, whilst at work, I found time to compile the conjurations for days 2 to 4 of the final seven days - the Convocation of the Good Spirits.

Midday Ritual

Done at my desk, astrally projecting to my oratory. Despite its brevity it gave me an idea - to pull the exaltation I felt when I vibrated the divine names up my spine like Kundalini. This proved surprisingly powerful.

Evening Ritual

I had a relatively early night : I performed the evening ritual in a manner similar to preceding days, but this time incorporating the idea I had at lunchtime today. Powerful !

Day 184

13 October 2020

Morning Ritual

During the night I recalled one dream, mostly inspired by thoughts about what I saw last night on TV. I got up at 4.30am, and prepared by checking in with *Nepheshi*, and the Middle Pillar ritual. I began at 5.05am. Following an idea I had yesterday, I attempted to raise every feeling of exaltation I had on vibrating a divine name up my sushumna. This had the effect of getting me into a meditative state when performing the **LBRP**, **LBRH**, and **Bornless Ritual** : but it also meant that it took me longer than usual to do them – not necessarily a bad thing.

I continued with :

*"**Conjuration**.*

*"**Confession**. Distracting thoughts are a constant niggle. I notice that the random images which do crop up all seem to be memories of things I experienced during the 1980s, when I was a child / teenager. Are these sins ? Am I repressing some trauma from that time ? I experienced traumatic things, but I don't think I'm repressing any of it.*

"Eventually, however, after willing my Higher self to take possession of Nepheshi, *and partly inspired by memory of reading about 'Samyama' in my fiancée's copy of Patanjali, I am able to calm my mind down and achieve a meditative state.*

*"**Additional prayer**.*

*"**Licence to Depart**.*

*"**LBRP**.*

*"**LBRH**.*

"Total time not including preparation : 1 hour 29 minutes (cf : 'it took me longer than usual')."

*

At breakfast yet another blazing argument occurred with my fiancée. Well, it became blazing anyway - I did not even feel angry, just mystified. She started off by pointing to where the authors of the GD Enochian Skrying book said they didn't use Eastern tattvas, but I described this as a "modernist" fancy : the original GD set great store by the Eastern tattvas and even developed (or would have developed) advanced teachings regarding them.

I failed to appreciate, however, that she had apparently invested her self-esteem in the "rightness" of the modern version, and the "wrongness" of the Eastern tattvas : hence, she thought by referring to the history of the situation I had made a personal attack on *her*. What bemused me, though, was that I had not actually wanted to raise the subject : she had insisted on talking about it herself. I thought : "*Perhaps she deliberately does this to get an excuse to be demotivated from attempting to practice magic !*"

Midday Ritual

Done, in a manner similar to yesterday. Good, despite the shortcomings of my situation.

Later, when I had got back home, my fiancée appeared to have calmed down.

Evening Ritual

Done in a manner similar manner to yesterday. It didn't feel as satisfactory as preceding days, however, as I felt bloated from eating too much earlier in the evening.

Day 185

14 October 2020

Morning Ritual

During the night I recalled a fragment of at least one dream. I got up at 4.30am : checking in with Nepheshi, Middle Pillar ritual. Elimination. I began at 5.07 am. From my magical diary :

"LBRP.

"LBRH.

"Bornless Ritual. In two minds about drawing the energy up the spine. I think it is possible to treat this too slowly.

"Conjuration.

"Confession. Distracting thoughts are a constant niggle. I am aware of repressed anger : on the one hand I have a desire to protect myself, protect my ego : on the other it has attached itself to an unhealthy form of expression. I will that the desire to protect my ego be sublimated so that the energy involved still protects me, but this time in a more agreeable manner.

"Although am able to get a semblance of a meditative state, I feel distracted by my digestive system (see below). Thought : does my digestion cause the distraction, or does it just interfere with my efforts not to be distracted ? Hmm ...

"Additional prayer.

"Licence to Depart.

"LBRP.

"LBRH.

"Total time taken not including preparation : 1 hour 15 minutes. I have to eliminate almost immediately after, which is probably why I felt the morning ritual was unsatisfactory. I also have to eliminate a further two times at least later in the morning - last night's food was definitely excessive !"

*

By way of scriptural study that morning, I went through "The Heart of the Qabalah" : finishing off Genesis 2 :1 and going over Kaplan's translations for Gen 1 :2-16.

My fiancée texted me to say she wanted me to do a spell for her to win £10K in a prize draw. I immediately thought I should not agree to this, as I had given up gambling during the Abramelin period ...

Midday Ritual

Done, astrally projecting from my desk at work.

Clarification : she didn't enter the prize draw after all, so the issue of me casting a spell which broke my obligations never came up.

Later though, when I got home, she kept going on about how much she didn't like astral projection. She had riffed on this repeatedly since I had known her : she never took my advice, nor did she feel inclined to alter her viewpoint. I felt worried that she preferred to have a belief which disempowered her, because the cognitive dissonance of admitting to being wrong all this time would prove too much for her.

Evening Ritual

Done in a manner similar to yesterday but feeling better due to not having eaten so much this evening.

Day 186

15 October 2020

Morning Ritual

During night, I briefly recalled one dream. I got up at 4.30am for preparation by checking in with Nepheshi, and the Middle Pillar ritual. I began at 5.05am. From my magical journal :

"LBRP.

"LBRH.

"Bornless Ritual.

"Conjuration.

"Confession. Thinking about loving my past lives. Able to concentrate on my higher self taking possession of Nepheshi. Remembering the importance of Samyama *is key to quietening my mind.*

"Additional prayer.

"Licence to Depart.

"LBRP.

"LBRH.

"Total time : 1 hour 25 minutes."

Midday Ritual

Done, in a like manner to yesterday.

Someone on Quora asked : "Is there any novel about summoning a demon ?" It amused me to fit in a gratuitous plug for *"The Magus."*[236] Ironically, though, I made the description of the evocation ritual during the first pinch far more Luciferian than ever I would attempt in real-life. If I were working with the *Goetia*, I would use conventional Qabalistic, Hebrew divine names : but I needed to make that part more controversial for dramatic purposes.

I had based the Succubus-incident, however, on something which did happen to me, although I made sure the villain in my novel avoided the mistakes I had made the first time I had encountered such a spirit.

Evening Ritual

Done. Much better than previous days, a very deep state of meditation resulted. *&sic ad lectum.*

---

[236] SUMNER (2009).

Day 187

16 October 2020

Morning Ritual

During the night : one rather vivid dream, in which the current Supreme Magus of the SRIA called me to do *great things*. thinking about the SRIA yesterday evening probably inspired by me : as might also a nagging thought that I needed on with "great things." I doubted it meant anything prophetic *per se*. (NB : looking back with hindsight I must conclude that the figure in my dream represented my unconscious' way of symbolising Authority, or perhaps *how I wanted the SRIA to be*. It certainly didn't prove to represent either the SRIA or its Supreme Magus as they were at the time).

I got up at 4.30am. I actually had a ritual shower first : then checked in with *Nepheshi* and did the Middle Pillar ritual.

I began at 5.05am, trying where possible to incorporate thoughts on *Samyama* into my practice.

    "*LBRP*.

    "*LBRH*.

    "*Bornless Ritual. Good.*

    "*Conjuration. Good.*

    "*Confession. Very deep state of meditation here - applying principles of* Samyama *definitely helps.*

    "*I contemplate my ideas of 11-dimensional Spirituality - this further helps me still my mind. It occurs to me that if a Tesseract is a 4D Hypercube, one might be able to visualise even higher dimensions in terms of Tesseracts within Tesseracts. One might even go so far as to conceive of Astral Projection as a kind of 'hyperspace travel,' i.e. To conceive of the starting point and destination of an astral journey, whilst being infinitely apart in the three-dimensional universe, as being no more than a short distance in a hyperdimensional universe.*"

I find this concept difficult to explain. I believe it can only properly make sense if one has already immersed oneself in a hyperdimensional state of consciousness.[237] Nevertheless, I felt so inspired by it that I later tried reaching out to my fellow hyperdimensional beings via social media (my post got a mere two likes, so the world was not yet ready to receive these particular higher teachings).

---

[237] See day 173 – *vide supra*.

"But what, then, are the keys to accessing higher dimensions ? ? ?
"Additional prayer.
"Licence to Depart.
"LBRP.
"LBRH.
"Total time taken (not including preparation): 1 hour 25 minutes. Generally good, especially incorporating 11-dimensional thinking, Samyama - also Ritual Shower."

Midday Ritual

Done. Deep, despite being short in duration.

*

I had not paid much attention to the current stars and planets in the past few days, but I happened to remember that Mercury had just turned Retrograde (it had done so three days ago). It would not station direct until after I had finished the Operation. For one moment I felt uneasy that this had to happen now : would I have begun my Operation if I had realised ? But then I dismissed the thought. Given that it occurs three or four times a year, one inevitably cannot perform the Abramelin Operation without it turning Retrograde once during that time. Perhaps I had done well not to pay too much attention to the astrology of the situation, as otherwise I might have let superstitious dread cause me to miss this opportunity.

A lot of people fear this time of year, but as I discovered once after a supermarket cashier forgot to ring up a bottle of whisky in my shopping, Mercury Retrograde holds no terrors so long as all the unlucky stuff happens to other people. A sort of *Schadenfreude* view of the phenomenon. Besides which, I interpreted the message of Hermeticism to mean that ultimately one ought to develop oneself spiritually so that one can learn to stand apart from the influence of the planets, instead of remaining passively affected by them. This, I supposed, formed the whole rationale of the planetary magick of the Golden Dawn. Adverse astrological conditions might disquieten the great unwashed, but they should merely present a challenge to an Adept worth his or her salt.

I reflected on my current situation. I felt equipoised, but the curse of the Adept is that even if one can rise above the influence of the stars and planets, one still has to deal with people who cannot, e.g. one of the managers at my place work seemed to have a bee in his bonnet about some misunderstanding, so I had to exercise seemingly infinite patience in dealing with him.

I wondered if retrograde Mercury affected my fiancée ? That evening an argument about Karma arose. Once again she was all "woe is me," but I in my turn continued to counter with "it's not as bad as you think," yet I got blamed for it. My attempts to reassure her proved to no avail, so I resolved never to talk to her about Karma again.

(NB : in hindsight this proved a difficult resolution to keep, as Karma seemed one of my fiancée's favourite subjects about which to talk, even if the concept horrified her).

Evening Ritual

Done. Events earlier distracted me, made me upset, so I meditated as best I could even though I found it difficult to do so.

Day 188

17 October 2020

Morning Ritual

During the night, I recalled one vivid dream ... I got up at 6.50am for ritual shower and checking in with *Nepheshi*. Actually, I only recited the versicle *Asperges me* etc after finishing the shower. I started six minutes after sunrise at 7.31am. Incorporating ideas on *Samyama* into the various parts of the ritual.

"*LBRP*.

"*LBRH*.

"*Bornless Ritual*. *V good*.

"*Conjuration*. *Also good*.

"*Confession*. *Reflecting on last night's argument, it occurs to me that I erred in giving my fiancée the wrong impression about karma. Specifically, she might have thought I was trying to interfere or poke my nose into* her *karma. Given that everyone follows their own Dharma, that would imply that it is up to each person to resolve their own karma in the way which is most appropriate to them. If one were to start pontificating about someone else's karma, one would be setting oneself up as a Guru. I had no intention of claiming that this was the case in regard to me, but she may nevertheless have misunderstood me : so I ought to reassure her.*

"*Thinking in terms of higher dimensions. Achieve a very deep state of meditation indeed.*

"*Additional prayer*.

"*Licence to Depart*.

"*LBRP*. *Feeling so ecstatic after the meditation, I do this ritual in the astral. Perhaps - attempting the* Samyama *type of meditation whilst out of the body needs to be investigated further ?*

"*LBRH*.

"*Total time : 1 hour 19 minutes.*"

Afterwards, my fiancée seemed to be in a funny mood. I tried reassuring her regarding last night, but she still seemed off. I thought : "Perhaps it *is* because of Mercury Retrograde ?"

The silver dog-tags which I intended to use in my ritual arrived. However, I had tried to order an Almond Wand *via* eBay instead of the Hazel one I had purchased locally.[238] I realised I had ordered it a month ago, but I had seen no sign of it. When I checked the tracking information, I found it had languished in some depot *en route* for all this time. Covid must have seriously disrupted courier services in the United States. If someone had simply taken the package and carried it *by foot* the thousand miles to the next way-station, from where it would ship, it would actually have got there by now.

Midday Ritual

Done – Astral Projection music playing in my oratory. I checked in with Nepheshi, then did Conjuration ; Confession including Tea-pot meditation ; additional prayer ; and licence to depart. I experienced the tea-pot meditation as powerful (again I incorporated *Samyama* principles into the meditation when I did so).

My fiancée still seemed in a funny mood - negative. She had the impression that I needed some kind of silver mirror (until I explained to her that the silver dog-tags would suffice for me). Nevertheless, we went to a local crystal shop where I bought her a tarot bag and myself a copy of the "Millennium Thoth" tarot.

Later I found that I had lost the signet ring that she had given me. I panicked… But after a brief petition to Andromalius, it turned up again in a shopping bag. Either it fell off my finger as carried the bag or, as was "more" likely, Andromalius caused a hole in the time/space continuum to open up and transport it from where I had dropped it to the bottom of the said bag. Lucky ! I had almost bought a replacement ring as well.

Evening Ritual

Done, in a manner similar to yesterday. Deep meditation - good.

---

[238] Day 132 – *vide supra.*

Day 189

18 October 2020

Morning Ritual

During the night, I recorded one dream in which I spoke about the importance of the Body of Light and Spiritual Alchemy and stuff. I talked to people not in the Golden Dawn but who wanted me as their Secret Chief! Ha.

I got up at 6.50 for preparation with checking in with Nepheshi and Middle Pillar ritual. I began the ritual at 7.27am (i.e., actual sunrise).

   "*LBRP.*

   "*LBRH.*

   "*Bornless Ritual. Have been trying to incorporate* Samyama *principles into my rituals. It feels difficult to do so at first, gradually getting easier, until partway through the Bornless Ritual it sort of clicks into place. It occurs precisely at the time I vibrate* IAO *for the first time. It ends feeling powerful.*

   "*Conjuration. Good.*

   "*Confession. Meditating. Good. Very deep - ecstatic.*

   "*Additional prayer.*

   "*Licence to Depart.*

   "*LBRP. Like yesterday, I am still in an ecstatic state when I get to this point that I do the LBRP in the astral.*

   "*LBRH.*

   "*Total time taken not including preparation : 1 hour 19 minutes.*"

*

Later : my fiancée had turned up the Wheel of Fortune as her tarot card of the day – she claimed genuine surprise at finding that the Romans had worshipped Fortuna as an actual goddess, who had as her symbol nothing other than the *Rota Fortunae* - the same as depicted on the Visconti deck.

This aside, over breakfast we settled down to watch *The Blue Planet 2* on BBC iPlayer, as we were often wont to do on a Sunday morning. St David of Attenborough casually mentioned that some types of Coral were over four thousand years old. This excited me greatly, so I afterwards I went to record my thoughts in my magical journal :

"Coral ! A substance which some sources allege to be the Philosophers' Stone ![239] *It occurs to me that there is a great lesson here. The Coral gets to be so old - i.e., to enjoy the longevity conferred by the* Elixir Vitae *- by becoming not just a being on its own but an ecosystem in which other creatures thrive and survive. It's the other beings who live in the Coral who contribute to the Coral's longevity, whilst the Coral itself provides for them.*

"Hence : one should attain immortality by becoming like the Coral - making of oneself an ecosystem in which others can thrive and survive. It would be the ultimate act of service to humanity - to become a source of healing and prosperity etc for others. In this sense, far from trying to exist apart from humanity, one would achieve immortality only by fully integrating into it - the complete opposite of selfishness.

"In this sense Christ (e.g.) really is immortal, because he has enabled an Ecosystem of people to thrive in Him. Not just the conventional church, but all people who owe their existence to him, such as artists, musicians, and even heterodox thinkers. However, atheists and secularists are doing to the spiritual heritage of mankind what polluters are doing to the physical Coral reefs - gradually destroying them, making us the poorer for it."

Midday Ritual

Done, in a manner similar to yesterday.

In the evening : I helped my fiancée do a tarot divination (she was studying *The Oracle* as part of her BOTA studies).

Evening Ritual

Done. Very deep state of meditation. *&sic ad lectum*

---

[239] Cf : "The Stone of the Philosophers is likened to these, and especially to Corall," *et passim.* MAIER (1617), Emblem XXXII.

Day 190

19 October 2020

Morning Ritual

During night I manage to record one dream (about the Golden Dawn, as it happens). Up at 4.30am for ritual shower (which I did properly this time); checking in with *Nepheshi*; and the Middle Pillar ritual. I began at 5.11am.

"*LBRP.*

"*LBRH.*

"*Bornless Ritual.*

"*Conjuration.*

"*Confession. Whilst contemplating what sins I need to atone for, a list of concerns of everyday life flood into my head. On the one hand, these could be seen as 'distracting thoughts,' but on the other, they could be seen as the answer for which I was in fact looking. I.e., things like finishing off preparations for the Abramelin ritual, and the equipment needed - also things like doing something for TORC.[240] These are all things I need to finish off this week so that they do not disturb me next week.*

"*Additional prayer.*

"*Licence to Depart.*

"*LBRP.*

"*LBRH.*

"*Total time taken: 1 hour 12 minutes. Feeling the need to eliminate immediately afterwards caused the last parts of this morning's ritual to feel rushed, also why I did not reach as deep a state of meditation as I might have done.*"

*

Afterwards at breakfast: when my fiancée claimed that she had nothing to do Golden Dawn wise, I "indelicately" pointed out she could actually do the suggested exercises in the Portal papers, such as the Supreme Ritual of the Pentagram. I say "indelicately"" - what I mean is that the fact that I mentioned it at all proved indelicate. Cue another rant against the whole notion of the Golden

---

[240] I.e., the "True Order of the Rosy Cross," a Rosicrucian Order with which I am involved.

Dawn asking its members to invoke supposedly unsafe things, or indeed anything at all. This upset me : I escaped from the house to go to work.

Midday Ritual

Done, at my desk at work. Feeling nervous, mainly because ...

... I had been working on finishing off the typing of the Conjurations for the Final Seven days. By the end of the day I had done and dusted this. I now felt some of the relief that I imagined I would feel when I finished the ritual itself.

My fiancée had calmed down by that evening when I got home.

Evening Ritual

Done in a manner similar to yesterday. *&sic ad lectum.*

Day 191

20 October 2020

Morning Ritual

During the night, I had difficulty recalling my dreams, although I think one of them had imagery related to *The Da Vinci Code*, seeing as we had watched that last night on Netflix. I'm glad I never saw it at the cinema. I would have felt tempted to shout out the answers to all the puzzles, because of "Robert Langdon" (i.e., Tom Hanks)'s painful slowness at solving them. Obviously one could not blame Hanks : in this respect the script merely followed Dan Brown's original story.

Incidentally, *The Da Vinci Code,* no less, originally inspired me to become a novelist : I was like, *"Surely I can write a better book than this ?"*

Anyway, diversion aside : I got up at 4.30am for ritual shower, checking in with *Nepheshi,* and the Middle Pillar Ritual. I began at 5.13am.

> *"LBRP.*
>
> *"LBRH.*
>
> *"Bornless Ritual. Trying to apply* Samyama *principles, only starts to work part way through the ceremony, roughly kicking in at the* IAO *stage, as before.*
>
> *"Conjuration.*
>
> *"Confession. NB remember the importance of sublimating the energy which fuels the distracting thoughts.*
>
> *"The problem which caused the argument yesterday - where I now see that I erred - was that I told the truth, but in an inappropriate manner, i.e., tactless. By being more subtle and circumspect I could have accomplished my aim, that of encouraging and motivating my fiancée. I was all stick and no carrot - hence : cognitive dissonance on her part, and the barriers went up. I will that I avoid this crass error in the future.*
>
> *"Additional prayer.*
>
> *"Licence to Depart.*
>
> *"LBRP.*
>
> *"LBRH.*
>
> *"Total time taken : 1 hour 19 minutes. Feeling the need to eliminate afterwards. I wonder if this is a problem. Might I try Senokot tablets just in case ?"*

*

A shitty day (no pun intended, given my concerns about my bowels earlier) at work today – I felt the effect of the Mercury Retrograde. *"For shame,"* I thought. *"I should be better than this !"*

Still, following up on yesterday's notion of doing stuff for TORC, I started putting together a resource of downloadable books for members on Google drive. Many of the members had come brand new to Rosicrucianism, and did not feel quite sure of what it consisted, so I gathered together various basic resources, such as the manifestos, and various historical documents now in the public domain.

Midday Ritual

Done, astrally projecting to my oratory from my desk at work, as yesterday.

In the afternoon I printed out a list of the demon names for the day 6 ritual (the Conjuration of the Eight Princes) in the Final Seven days.

In the evening, I found that my fiancée had done some magic without me. I missed it ! (Ironically, the remark which I had made yesterday which caused an argument, and which I regretted during my confession that morning, had spurred her to action after all.)

I found a practical use for the old table I had manifested which I had intended to use as an altar, before my fiancée decided to get me a proper one for my birthday. I discarded the table-legs and painted the top to create a Triangle of Art, to serve as the "terrace" where the spirits would appear : by lucky chance it proved just the right size to fit in the oriel of the oratory.

Evening Ritual

Done, as yesterday. Quite a deep state of meditation at the end.

Day 192

21 October 2020

Morning Ritual

During the night I managed to recall one dream - better than yesterday. I did try taking a Senokot tablet last night, but it had no discernible effect – perhaps it doesn't work if one does not have constipation *per se*.

I got up at 4.30am for ritual shower, checking in with *Nepheshi*, and the Middle Pillar Ritual. I began at 5.15.

   "LBRP.

   "LBRH.

   "Bornless Ritual.

   "Conjuration.

   "Confession. The events of yesterday when I complained about how shitty my day was, was due to carelessness on my part, i.e., a sin !

   "Thinking about how 'Meaning' is the way of representing higher-dimensions (as in the 11D model of spirituality). So, for example if I experience the purely physical manifestations of (e.g.) samadhi, in attaching a meaning to it I am attempting to perceive a higher dimension. This helps calm my thoughts right down.

   "Additional prayer.

   "Licence to Depart.

   "LBRP.

   "LBRH.

   "Total time taken : 1 hour 15 minutes."

*

Later that morning : work continued awfully and threatened to spoil my day. Despite me being fastidiously careful, people tried to blame me for things which went wrong anyway. In other words, *I* had managed to transcend the effects of the Mercury Retrograde today, but my managers and co-workers had not, so I had to deal with their bullshit, nonetheless. In effect, I suffered from *Mercury Retrograde by Proxy.*

   I made a note to myself : *"Wishing ill on a senior manager is probably a sin which I should not be doing."*

Midday Ritual

Done at my desk at work.

In the evening, when I got home, my fiancée expressed an interest in a book about the OTO, which I thought naughty of her. I didn't make a note of which book, so it can't have been terribly important.

Evening Ritual

Done, in a manner similar to yesterday evening. Very deep indeed. Meditating on higher dimensions certainly helped.

Day 193

22 October 2020

Morning Ritual

During the night, I recorded two dreams. Up at 4.30am for ritual shower, checking in with *Nepheshi*, and the Middle Pillar Ritual. I began at 5.09am. From my magical journal :

"*LBRP.*

"*LBRH.*

"*Bornless Ritual.*

"*Conjuration.*

"*Confession. Distracting thoughts. I feel that I need to learn to meditate in spite of my body. Perhaps I should be doing Yoga early in the morning, or getting up half an hour earlier ???*

"*As it happens, I conjure up an impromptu servitor to protect me from people and or things who might upset me today.*

"*Additional prayer.*

"*Licence to Depart.*

"*LBRP.*

"*LBRH.*

"*Total time taken : 1 hour 17 minutes.*

*

I spent the morning editing my notes on the final seven days into a form in which they could be printed. I thought : *"Funny to think that this will soon be over."*

Midday Ritual

Today I checked in with *Nepheshi* and made a point of Astrally Projecting in the Golden Dawn manner to my Oratory to perform the ritual. It felt incredibly good actually, full of energy.

Later, when I got home, I found my fiancée in a funny mood, wanting to be alone yet clearly equivocating on the subject.

Evening Ritual

Done. Very deep state of meditation. *&sic ad lectum*

Day 194

23 October 2020

Morning Ritual

During the night : I recorded one dream quite vividly. Indeed, I got to the point of becoming lucid as I noticed a singer not using a microphone. I didn't do anything magical with it, though.

Up at 4.30am. Had been worried about my bowels / digestion, specifically, whether I had any danger of constipation, but I thought : *"Perhaps I have been too worried?"* Anyway : brief Ritual ablution, followed by checking in with *Nepheshi* and full-length Middle Pillar Ritual – directing healing energy inwardly upon myself. I began at 5.10am. From my magical journal :

> *"LBRP.*
>
> *"LBRH."*

Here I broke off to go for elimination. I thought : *"Better to do so now, so as not to disturb the rest of the ceremony. Nice to know my worries mentioned above were unfounded. Hey ! Perhaps this is the result of the Banishing ceremonies ?"*

Having finished celebrating the *Crapitious Mysteries*, as Kenneth Grant would call them, I returned to the Oratory :

> *"I resume, applying* Samyama *principles as I do so. THOUGHT : what if the God-forms etc invoked here themselves practice* Samyama *???*
>
> *"Bornless Ritual. Powerful.*
>
> *"Conjuration. Very good.*
>
> *"Confession. Imagining I have a 'Samadhi Self' - a higher self which is practising Samyama. The result is profound, a very deep state of meditation which leaves me full of energy afterwards.*
>
> *"Additional Prayer.*
>
> *"Licence to Depart.*
>
> *"LBRP.*
>
> *"LBRH.*
>
> *"Total time taken : 1 hour 27 minutes."*

The unusually large surge of energy I experienced during the meditation meant that I felt the last four parts of the ritual as especially powerful, e.g. That I put extra pizzazz into my pentagrams and hexagrams, that the Archangels really stood about me. I felt quite satisfied with today's ritual, and also the preparation (I had had two senakot tablets last night just in case). I think I had made the right decision by giving myself permission to eliminate, especially as I did it in such a way as to not disrupt the flow of the ceremony.

Thus pleased with myself I bounded downstairs ... And into yet another blazing argument with my fiancée. I tried to make the point that a Golden Dawn ritual should concern itself solely with the God-forms, not necessarily the personalities of the people performing it ("should" of course being the operative word). Unfortunately, I *won* the argument, causing her to storm out of the house very upset. (One does not win kudos for correctness, in situations like this).

Midday Ritual

Done, like yesterday, but with the addition of Astral Projection music playing. Good, at least I could feel my third-eye opening.

When I got back home, my fiancée seemed to have calmed down. I reflected : I experienced a state of nervous excitement, not dissimilar to how I felt immediately before I got the 5=6 over ten years ago. I felt as if this Abramelin thing meant "going up a grade" – in terms of the feeling of anticipation one experiences before an advancement ritual – though I would be utterly pretentious to say going up *to what*.

My fiancée felt uneasy about the idea of my personality "disappearing" in *Samadhi*, even though I tried to reassure her by reminding her that all the yogis describe it as *Ananda,* i.e., "bliss."

*

A remark by my fiancée reminded me that a girl with whom I once went out, some twenty years ago, effectively *cheated on her boyfriend* by going out with me. I couldn't remember if she told me about this before or after – I hardly think I would have countenanced doing so if she told me before, I certainly bore no ill-will to the fellow (I never met him). As it happened, the relationship with this girl did not come to anything ... For me, that was. The other fellow, however, died a short while later whilst doing a parachute jump for charity : in the girl's mind she had an obvious question as to whether he accidentally on purpose forgot to pull the rip-cord and whether he felt depressed over breaking up with her. On reflection, though, I thought that surely charity parachute jumps didn't work like that – they all worked on a static line - i.e., his parachute would have opened automatically - or else he would have jumped strapped to an instructor, who would have ensured the chute opened. Yet he died, nevertheless. Perhaps he had just had incredible bad luck.

Question : irrespective of whether this was an accident or suicide, should this bloke's death have been on *my* conscience ? I felt as if it was, all the same. Arguably I indirectly caused it, or helped caused it, but I had had no idea that this would prove the case. His ex-girlfriend has more proximity than I – after all she knew she cheated on him, whereas I did not. Or she might have said, "it's over between us" referring to this bloke, and I didn't know otherwise.

The possibility that it might have been an accident provided little consolation. It struck me that part of the Great Work involves recognising that we all ultimately bear responsibility for one another, whether we bear any fault or not.

Evening Ritual.

In advance of tomorrow, I cleared a lot of superfluous things out of my oratory and made sure I had all the equipment there. Part of the superfluous equipment included my laptop ; hence I performed my evening ritual without usual AP music playing. Feeling jittery ...

THE FINAL SEVEN DAYS

Day 195 : The Consecration of the Implements

24 October 2020

Morning Ritual – the Consecration itself

I managed to record details of one dream during the night. I got up at 7am, for a brief ritual lustration, followed by checking in with Nepheshi, and Middle Pillar ritual. Elimination.

During the last seven days, I fasted completely from the time I got up until Sunset, although I did have a light collation (strictly vegetarian, of course) in the evening.

I began at 7.37am i.e., Sunrise. I followed the ritual for the consecration ritual, which I composed on the 6th of October, for all my implements, i.e. :

"Take all implements and garments from place and place on the Altar."

NB: the Almond Wand had not turned up – so I used the Hazel Wand I had got a couple of months ago.[241]

"Light lamp and charcoal.

***"LBRP* ;**

"LBRH

"Holding oil in left hand, place incense on charcoal.

"Kneel and pray :

'O Lord God of mercy ; God, patient, most benign and liberal ; who grantest thy grace in a thousand ways, and unto a thousand generations ; who forgettest the iniquities, the sins, and the transgressions of men ; in whose presence none is found innocent ; who visitest the transgressions of the father upon the children and nephews unto the third and fourth generation ; I know my wretchedness, and that I am not worthy to appear before thy divine majesty, nor even to implore and beseech thy goodness and mercy for the least grace. But, O Lord of Lords, the source of thy bounty is so great, that of itself it calleth those who are ashamed by reason of their sins and dare not approach, and inviteth them to drink of thy grace. Wherefore, O Lord my God, have pity upon me, and take away from me all iniquity and malice ; cleanse my soul from all the uncleanness of sin ; renew within me my spirit, and comfort it, so that it may become strong and able to comprehend the mystery of thy grace, and the treasures of thy divine wisdom. Sanctify me also with the oil of thy sanctification, wherewith thou hast sanctified all thy prophets ; and

---

[241] I.e., on Day 132, *supra*.

purify in me therewith all that appertaineth unto me, so that I may become worthy of the conversation of thy holy angels and of thy divine wisdom, and grant unto me the power which thou hast given unto thy prophets over all the evil spirits. Amen. Amen.'

"*Anoint : forehead, four corners of altar, all implements and garments with oil.*

"*Trace with oil around the altar :*

בְּכָל־הַמָּקוֹם אֲשֶׁר אַזְכִּיר אֶת־שְׁמִי אָבוֹא אֵלֶיךָ

וּבֵרַכְתִּיךָ׃

i.e., Bekal-hamaqom asher azakoir et-shamoi aboa eleik ve-berakathoik. (Everywhere my name is mentioned I shall come to you and bless you.) "[242]

NB : As it happened, I just traced the Hebrew letters themselves : I omitted the *Niqqudim* (the pointing), although it came in useful for figuring out the correct pronunciation when it came to chanting this versicle, which I did for good measure.

"*Put away all implements and carry on with -*

"***Bornless Ritual.***

"***Conjuration.***

"***Confession.***

"***Additional Prayer.***

"***Licence to Depart.***

"***LBRP***

"***LBRH.***"

As I recorded in my magical journal :

"*Feeling nervous ... This ritual is not so different from all the rituals that have gone before, yet for the first time I am getting an idea of how important this really is. I am so keyed up it is difficult to feel warm fuzzy feelings I normally associate with meditation ... But maybe that's the point, i.e., the ritual is working in exactly the way it's supposed to at the moment.*

"*After meditating for a long while, I finish in the normal manner.*

"*Total time : 1 hour 33 minutes.*"

*

---

[242] Excerpted from *Exodus* 20 :24, which describes how God instructed Moses to build the altar of sacrifice, appropriately enough.

My fiancée spent the morning wittering on about the tarot card "The Lovers." Later she revealed she had avoided *Sacrament* this week because she had thought I that I needed to conserve my Odic force ! This naffed me off to say the least : I tried to convince her, "No, no, I'm like a *Matador*, you know what I'm saying ?" This did not sway her.

Midday Ritual

"Midday and Dusk rituals to follow a similar pattern to those of the final phase." (My notes)

Although I had stowed my computer downstairs, it occurred to me that I could always just use my smartphone to get the Astral Projection music. With this in mind, I performed my midday ritual, in my oratory, with AP music playing. Checking in with *Nepheshi* ; conjuration ; confession - including the Tea-pot meditation ; additional prayer ; licence to depart. During the confession I prayed for the soul of that bloke who died on a parachute jump. I experienced the Tea-Pot meditation as soothing, recalling some of the energy I had previously felt when performing it in the past. I interpreted this as a good sign.

In the afternoon, a Golden Dawn study group meeting on ZOOM about the history of the Western mystery tradition.

Evening Ritual

At 17.44 – i.e., Sunset - I went to my oratory and performed the evening ritual, which follow the exact the same format as the ritual I had on previous days performed just before going to bed. Meditating on my "Samadhi Self" itself practising Samyama, I pulled it up my sushumna like kundalini and attained *SAMADHI*. Very powerful, filled with energy. I thought : *"Augurs well !"*

Afterwards I broke my fast with an apple. Spent the evening with my fiancée watching *Quadrophenia* on NowTV.

Day 196 : The first day of the Convocation of the Good Spirits

25 October 2020

I recorded one dream during the night, which I think watching *Quadrophenia* the previous evening inspired. I may have made a mistake in doing that, as I didn't want the distracting thoughts.

In addition to my practice of fasting, during the next six days until the end of the last ritual I made sure I observed complete silence during the day as well – except when for when I performed the various rituals in the Oratory.

Ritual

Up at 6am (GMT)[243] for preparation with checking in with *Nepheshi* and Middle Pillar Ritual. Elimination. Encountering the same sort of nervousness that I had experienced this time yesterday.

Sunrise occurred at 6.39am but I only started with the ritual proper five minutes later at 6.44am. I used the following ritual for the first day of the convocation of the good spirits, which I had typed up myself after making notes from The Book :

"DAWN : Go to the Oratory : wear BLACK robe and anoint head with ashes from the censer from yesterday.

"There should be ready : altar with censer, incense + lit charcoal ; 'lamp' ; wand ; silver plate ; also a pen and paper."

(As it happened, I had also stowed away several bottles of mineral water, to maintain hydration.)

"Light lamp ; open window ; prostrate before the altar, and with a pure heart place incense on the charcoal.

"Prostrate yourself before the altar again. Say :

'In the names YHVH, Tzebaoth and Adonai ; I humiliate myself before you Oh Lord, and your celestial court.'

"Then, morning ritual as normal, but when getting to the Conjuration add :

'In the names YHVH, Tzebaoth and Adonai, may my Holy Guardian Angel be pleased to sign this silver plate upon the altar.'

"Meditate as usual, until there is some evidence that the Holy Guardian Angel has manifested (Samadhi). If necessary, take a suitable break, and then repeat the ritual."

The first time I tried meditating, I felt agitated ... So I tried doing the Tea-pot meditation. I didn't manage to reach what I would have called a satisfactory state

---

[243] NB : daylight saving time had ended during the night, today being the last Sunday in October.

of meditation, so I paused for a while, before meditating again. This proved not much better – I worried that even the little amount of potatoes I had eaten last night proved too many. So I ended the ritual for the time being.

After some brief rest, I had a ritual shower, and repeated the whole ritual from the beginning. I noted that the Bornless Ritual went very well this time, like I had entered a heightened state of consciousness. More meditation – then a pause – then more meditation.

"When the HGA has definitively manifested it will have left a spirit-signature on the silver plate : observe this and make a note with the pen and paper. Also, note down any specific counsel received from the HGA." (From my ritual notes.)

I thought : *"It must surely be the case that my HGA is already here, it's just that my senses are too dull to appreciate the fact !"* Given that the *raison d'être* of today's ritual consisted of the HGA showing some evidence of being present at all, and more particularly, of leaving a spirit-signature on the silver plate on the altar, I had an idea : to skry into the silver plate, as if going on a tattva journey.

So there I was, going through a shadowy door-way in my mind (the negative of the image of the silver plate) and I vibrated M..., the name of my Holy Guardian Angel which I had received on a previous occasion. M... answered and tested well. I asked : "What is the sign which should appear on the silver-plate ?"

M... answered : *"It should be the word* Samyama *written in Sanskrit - to signify the fact that Samyama was and is the key to attaining the consciousness associated with Knowledge and Conversation of the Holy Guardian Angel."*

I thanked M... as appropriate and left. Back in my oratory (i.e., back to normal consciousness), I adjourned the proceedings and went to lie down for some rest, and to look up exactly how *Samyama* appears when written *(see below)*.

After catching some ZZZs (apparently, I slept for one and a half hours), I got up and went back to the Oratory, and resumed. I meditated again, this time incorporating what M... had said whilst I had skryed. This time it went better : I attained something like an altered state of consciousness, with my third-eye definitely feeling as if it had opened.

"This being done, close the ritual for the day, leave the lamp and incense to burn themselves out, whilst leaving the Oratory for the rest of the day.

Remain silent at all times. Rest, and 'eat soberly' after sunset." (My ritual notes.)

I closed the ritual again with the additional prayer, licence to depart, and LBRP and LBRH. It was now about 2pm – I had been at it on and off with breaks for approximately eight hours. I later noted that my ordeal was not dissimilar to that of Jacob, who wrestled with the Angel all through the night and would not let go until the Angel had blessed him. Perhaps Jacob himself went through an experience like the Abramelin Operation at the time.

After resting, I got up and dressed, and pottered about (remaining silent) with my fiancée for a while until I broke my fast at sunset with another apple, and a light collation later that evening.

I felt uneasy about the results of today's ritual. Compared to the peak states of previous days, today struck me as Spiritual Dryness by comparison. As I noted in my magical journal :

> *"In short, I did* not *experience mind-blowing ecstasy as I did during the evening ritual last night. On reflection, however, perhaps that was not actually the point of today's ritual ? In any event I have lots of HGA rituals to perform over the next two days."*

Day 197 : The second day of the Convocation of the Good Spirits

26 October 2020

Morning ritual.

During the night I managed to record one dream partly inspired by *The Secret Garden* on TV last night. I got up at 6am for Ritual shower (elimination – a good sign, as I had not looked forward to either constipation on the one hand or being distracted during the middle of the main ritual on the other) ; and a brief Middle Pillar Ritual.

I began at 6.44am with the morning ritual for the second day of the convocation of the good spirits which I had compiled. From my ritual notes :

"Go to the Oratory : wear BLACK robe and anoint head with ashes from the censer from yesterday.

"There should be ready : altar with censer, incense + lit charcoal ; 'lamp' ; wand ; silver plate ; also a pen and paper.

"Light lamp ; open window ; prostrate before the altar, and with a pure heart place incense on the charcoal.

"Prostrate yourself before the altar again. Say :

'In the names YHVH, Tzebaoth and Adonai ; I humiliate myself before you Oh Lord, and your celestial court.'

"Then, morning ritual as normal, but when getting to the Conjuration add :

'In the names YHVH, Tzebaoth, and Adonai, I humbly pray unto and supplicate you oh Lord that you may have pity on me, and that deign to fulfil my prayer ; grant unto me the vision of Your holy angels, and that the elect spirits may deign to grant unto me their familiar converse.'

"Meditate as appropriate, spending at least two hours on the whole morning ritual."

Feeling more relaxed this morning. When I got to the meditation, I applied the principles of Samyama. I got an insight : to meditate on my "Samadhi-Self" practicing Samyama, whilst my Higher Self itself did so as well. This had a curiously powerful effect, focussing my meditation more effectively.

I also got a second insight : instead of *passively* waiting for M… to appear by himself, I ought to deliberately visualise the form of the Angel before me and pro-*actively* summon M… to take possession of it. This too seemed to make my meditation more effective (it resembled how I imagined magicians like PB

Randolph had described "evocation" : hence theoretically it could be used for other spirits as well).[244]

"Close for the time being and rest." (My ritual notes.)

I meditated three times : once, then rehydration break ; second time, then another rehydration break ; then third time before finishing with the additional prayer, licence to depart and LBRP / LBRH. Using these insights in the second and third sessions proved encouraging.

"After finishing, leave oratory, allowing lamp and incense to burn themselves out." (My ritual notes.)

I finished at around 8am, and then quit the oratory to go lie down for a few hours.

Midday Ritual

"Follow a similar procedure to the morning ritual ; though this time spending an hour." (My ritual notes.)

At 12noon I returned to the Oratory and performed the Midday ritual - essentially the same as the morning one, except that The Book said to only spend an hour on the whole thing. I did, however, perform this ritual with one important difference : right from the outset I contemplated the first insight which I had had this morning, regarding Samyama. This made the rituals such as the LBRP, LBRH, and the Bornless Ritual especially far more powerful. Meditation felt good, consequently, though distracted my bowels distracted me (had to eliminate soon after – I thought : *"how much shit is there in there ?"*). Otherwise, good. Finished at 1.15pm, so slightly more than an hour as it happened.

Afterwards I typed up my magical diary and had another lie down.

Evening Ritual

"Follow a similar procedure to the previous ritual. WASH thoroughly before retiring for the evening." (My ritual notes).

I re-entered the oratory for a 4.44pm start (i.e., Sunset). As at midday I applied Samyama type principles. Bornless ritual proved powerful. Meditation ... I seemed to be able to maintain a waking-trance type of consciousness. Weird, as if I could sense the presence of my HGA, although it didn't feel as earth-shattering as on previous days. I finished just after 6pm (again, slightly more than the prescribed hour). Washed thoroughly afterwards as my ritual said.

Later : I broke my fast ... My fiancée had bought me another birthday present : it had arrived only now as it had been on order. It turned out to be the new edition

---

[244] Cf RANDOLPH (1988), Chapter VII, "Tirauclairism" p27 *et seq.*

of "*Enochian Vision Magick*"[245] - so could have a go at that after I had finished this Abramelin business.

---

[245] DUQUETTE (2019)

Day 198 : The third day of the Convocation of the Good Spirits

27 October 2020

In my dream during the night, my fiancée talked about how sexy I am (i.e., in waking life) : but she also refused sacrament, saying that I had to conserve my Odic force ! Where does she get these notions from ???

Morning Ritual

Up at 6am for elimination, then ritual shower. I thought : "*So I can't be constipated, as I have had two regular movements without having to take Senokot. Hallelujah.*"

Then : the Middle pillar ritual.

I began at sunrise (6.44am), this time playing Astral Projection music on my smartphone. I followed the ritual for the third day of the convocation of the good spirits which I had compiled, to wit :

"*Enter into the oratory, but with naked feet.*"

"*Place the fire and the perfumes in the censer and light the lamp.*"

"*Put on the WHITE vestment.*"

"*Ritual as normal...*"

(Incorporating Samyama principles – Bornless ritual turned out good.)

"*... but when one gets to conjuration, KNEEL before the altar and pray thus :*

'*In the names YHVH, Tzebaoth, and Adonai, I thank you God for all your benefits, and firstly for having granted unto me a treasure so great and so precious.*

'*In the names YHVH, Tzebaoth, and Adonai, I give thanks also for the holy guardian angels, and I pray that henceforward they will have me in their care for the whole period of my life.*

'*In the names YHVH, Tzebaoth, and Adonai, I pray that [my special and particular guardian angel] will never abandon me, but will lead you in the way of the Lord, and that he will watch carefully over me to assist me, and consent unto the present operation of the Sacred Magic, so that I shall have such force and virtue that I may be able to constrain the spirits accursed of God, unto the honour of my creator, and for my own good and that of my neighbour.*

'*Oh ... my Holy Guardian Angel ! Appear before me in unequalled beauty ! Be pleased to converse with me in words so full of affection, goodness and sweetness that no human tongue could express the same. Animate me in the fear of God.*

'Make me mindful of the Blessings I have received, that I may be thankful for them.

'Bring unto me remembrance of the sins by which I have offended God during the whole period of my life : and instruct me and give unto me the manner in which I shall be able to appease God by a pure, devout, and regulated life, and by honest and meritorious actions, and such things as God shall ordain unto me.

'Show me the true wisdom and the Holy Magic ! Show me how I have erred in my operation, and how henceforward I should proceed in order to overcome the evil spirits, and finally arrive at my desired ends.

'Promise never to abandon me, but instead defend and assist me during the whole period of my life : in token of which I promise to obey your commands and not voluntarily offend my creator.

'In the names YHVH, Tzebaoth, and Adonai – AMEN.'

"*Remain in familiar conversation with Holy Guardian Angel (i.e., Meditate) for the whole morning, making a note of any information received.*"

When it came to receiving guidance from my HGA, I meditated for a long while, summoning the visible image of M… before me. In answer to the question "how do I command the obedience of the Kings of Hell ?" M… gave me this mantra :

"*The God by Whose grace my sins are forgiven, the same God now Commands you.*"

I meditated for some time on this mantra, repeating it, trying to get inside it, visualising it as words in front of me, trying to translate it into Latin, etc. Then I noticed it had 15 words - 15, the number of YAH, coincidentally, but also as a number divisible by five, I could, in theory, fit it onto the five sephiroth of the Middle Pillar of the Tree of Life.

I got a confirmation from M… that I should incorporate it into the *Middle Pillar Ritual itself*, i.e., first perform the ritual to invoke the Sephiroth generally, then concentrate on placing the words of the mantra into the appropriate places :

Kether	The God by
Daath	Whose grace my
Tiphereth	Sins are forgiven,
Yesod	The same God
Malkuth	Now commands you

By now, my legs were aching from sitting in padmasana so much, so I spent a while recovering in Savasana, before trying this out. I performed the Middle Pillar

Ritual and then focussed on the mantra. It had a calming, relaxing effect, a buzz of a higher state of consciousness - reassuring given these past few days.

I then closed with the additional prayer and licence to depart, although without the LBRP and LBRH on this occasion. I then quit the oratory for a lie down – the time had reached 11am.

I saw my fiancée outside. I put my finger to my lips because of my commitment to remain silent. She thought that I meant that *she* should remain silent. I then wrote down a note which I showed to her saying, "*I have taken a vow of silence until sunset. You can talk all you like, however!*" Thus assured she proceeded to pour forth all her news about the Tarot card she had studied today.

Eventually however, with the time fast approaching 12noon, I managed to pause her and by the power of mime indicated that I needed to go back to the oratory for another ritual. She looked confused at first, thinking that I meant to play charades ("Is it a film? How many letters?") It went better than the corresponding scene in *Young Frankenstein,* and less dangerous too.

Midday Ritual

Following the afternoon ritual I had compiled, like in the morning. Not having banished at the end of the last ritual, I went straight into the Bornless ritual, and then the conjuration. As I wrote down in my own notes:

"*Ritual as normal but for conjuration, pray:*

'In the names YHVH, Tzebaoth, and Adonai, I thank you God for all your benefits, and firstly for having granted unto me a treasure so great and so precious.

'In the names YHVH, Tzebaoth, and Adonai, I give thanks also for the holy guardian angels, and I pray that henceforward they will have me in their care for the whole period of my life.

'In the names YHVH, Tzebaoth, and Adonai, I pray that [my special and particular guardian angel] will never abandon me, but will lead me in the way of the Lord, and that he will watch carefully over me to assist me, and consent unto the present operation of the Sacred Magic, so that I shall have such force and virtue that I may be able to constrain the spirits accursed of God, unto the honour of my creator, and for my own good and that of my neighbour.

'Oh ... my Holy Guardian Angel! Appear before me in unequalled beauty! Be pleased to converse with me in words so full of affection, goodness and sweetness that no human tongue could express the same. Animate me in the fear of God.

'Make me mindful of the Blessings I have received, that I may be thankful for them.

'Bring unto me remembrance of the sins by which I have offended God during the whole period of my life : and instruct me and give unto me the manner in which I shall be able to appease God by a pure, devout, and regulated life, and by honest and meritorious actions, and such things as God shall ordain unto me.

'Show me the true wisdom and the Holy Magic ! Show me how I have erred in my operation, and how henceforward I should proceed in order to overcome the evil spirits, and finally arrive at my desired ends.

'Promise never to abandon me, but instead defend and assist me during the whole period of my life : in token of which I promise to obey your commands and not voluntarily offend my creator.

'Oh ... my Holy Guardian Angel ! Grant unto me distinct and ample information regarding the evil spirits and the manner of bringing them into submission.'

"Here pause a while to discern whatever the Holy Guardian Angel has to say on the matter. Carefully write down and take note of the answers. Check whether it is necessary to evoke each King separately, or whether one has to do it one at a time."

This time, I looked into the incense smoke rising from the brazier, and skryed into it. I spoke to M… about the ritual tomorrow. He said :

"Perform the Middle Pillar Ritual with the Mantra I have given you immediately before the main conjuration, to ensure that you are able to compel the spirits.

"Do not do the four Kings all at once. Instead, have one opening, and one closing, but in between have a separate conjuration for each one. This is not so long as you have feared.

"In the future, you may use the Enns, but only after first invoking me, M…."

M… then gave some notes on how to address the four Kings :

LUCIFER – "great being of Light" ;

SATAN – "great magical agent" ;

LEVIATHAN – "monstrous force of the sea" ;

BELIAL – "guardian and gatekeeper of the north."

M… also added :

"Remove Demon Detective stories mentioning Belial, so as not to cause offence."

As it happened, I did this after I completed the Operation. As I had published them all published online as Ebooks, I simply removed the files, and uploaded new versions referring to a completely fictional demon instead. I came up with this new Demon's name by using an online "Random Demon Name Generator" (apparently, such things do exist on the internet).

"Regarding Z ... Z ... N ... Z ... Do not use this unless you know the closing formula as well."

M... here referred to the well-known formula which Crowley used to "open the gates of Hell" during his conjuration of Choronzon. Ironically, although Crowley revealed that the opening formula from the old times, he didn't reveal any wording to *close* the gates of Hell as well. In his own Choronzon ceremony, Neuberg ended it by writing "Babalon."

"Research the sigils."

(See below.)

After this I closed the ceremony by saying *"In the names YHVH, Tzebaoth, and Adonai – AMEN,"* (again, no banishing rituals), and quit the oratory.

*

Afterwards, following the guidance I received, I made some notes as to what I believed the sigils of the four Kings should be :

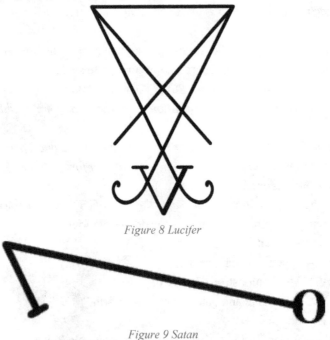

Figure 8 Lucifer

Figure 9 Satan

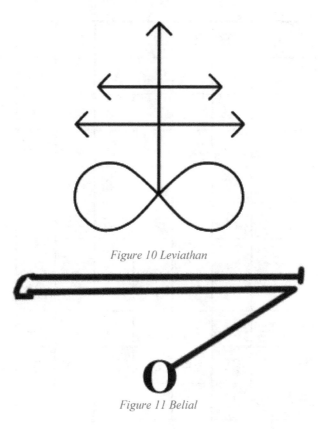

Figure 10 Leviathan

Figure 11 Belial

The sigils of Lucifer and Leviathan here come from old grimoires. However, because I could not easily Google Sigils for Satan and Belial – that is to say, not ones with which I was satisfied, I created sigils for these myself. I derived them from the Hebrew spellings thereof, put on an 11 *11 Magic Square.

56	117	46	107	36	97	26	87	16	77	6
7	57	118	47	108	37	98	27	88	17	67
68	8	58	119	48	109	38	99	28	78	18
19	69	9	59	120	49	110	39	89	29	79
80	20	70	10	60	121	50	100	40	90	30
31	81	21	71	11	61	111	51	101	41	91
92	32	82	22	72	1	62	112	52	102	42
43	93	33	83	12	73	2	63	113	53	103
104	44	94	23	84	13	74	3	64	114	54
55	105	34	95	24	85	14	75	4	65	115
116	45	106	35	96	25	86	15	76	5	66

Figure 12 An 11 by 11 Magic Square

I tried Googling "Z... Z... N.... S..." but the only references I discovered led back to Crowley himself: I could find no independent evidence of its historicity. Hence, I could hardly work out the closing formula, assuming that one existed.

Evening Ritual

"As at the morning. Close in the appropriate manner. Leave oratory, leaving lamp and incense to burn themselves out. Eat soberly then get an early night." (My notes).

I re-entered the Oratory at Sunset and performed the evening ritual – rather like the Morning ritual, but again, because I did not banish at the end of the last one, I omitted the LBRP and LBRH this time as well.

Before commencing the Bornless Ritual, I briefly contemplated M..., the sigil of and principles of *Samyama*, and the way in which the mantra I received earlier related to the Middle Pillar of the Tree of Life, with the energy circulating around. The combined effect of doing so led me into an exalted state of consciousness by itself.

I performed the Bornless Ritual (good) and the conjuration of the day. I then settled down to meditate, again on the mantra / Tree of Life. I remember something I read in a quote by Jung which my fiancée had sent me - about "laddering back" (as part of achieving the active imagination).

I went into a very deep state of meditation indeed – even *Samadhi*. So deep in fact, *that I was led to believe I really had attained Knowledge & Conversation of my Holy Guardian Angel.*

I also realised that the Jung quote provided the key to enabling one to perceive the physical and the astral at the same time. As it proved such a vital component of my experience on this, the third day which I had set aside for attaining KCHGA, I shall reproduce it here in full, as I received it. However, when I later tried to track down the source of this quote, I discovered that the original idea did not derive from Jung at all : he had instead commented on *Edward Maitland*, whose work with Anna Kingsford most proximately inspired the Hermetic Order of the Golden Dawn. Jung wrote :

"The reflecting on an idea, related ideas became visible, so to speak, in a long series apparently reaching back to their source, which to him was the divine spirit. By concentrating on this series, he tried to penetrate to their origin. He *[i.e. Maitland]* writes :

'I was absolutely without knowledge or expectation when I yielded to the impulse to make the attempt. I simply experimented on a faculty ... being seated at my writing-table the while in order to record the results as they came, and resolved to retain my hold on my outer and circumferential consciousness, no matter how far towards my inner and central consciousness I might go. For I knew not whether I should be able to regain the former if I once quitted my hold of it, or to recollect the facts of the experience. At length I achieved my object, though only by a strong effort, the tension occasioned by the endeavour to keep both extremes of the consciousness in view at once being very great.

'Once well started on my quest. I found myself traversing a succession of spheres or belts ... the impression produced being that of mounting a vast ladder stretching from the circumference towards the centre of a system, which was at once my own system, the solar system, the universal system, the three systems being at once diverse and identical. .... Presently, by a supreme, and what I felt must be a final effort ... I succeeded in polarizing the whole of the convergent rays of my consciousness into the desired focus. And at the same instant. as if through the sudden ignition of the rays thus fused into a unity, I found myself confronted with a glory of unspeakable whiteness and brightness, and of a lustre so intense as wellnigh to beat me back .... But though feeling that I had to explore further, I resolved to make assurance doubly sure by piercing if I could the almost blinding lustre, and seeing what it enshrined. With a great effort I succeeded, and the glance revealed to me that which I had felt must be there .... It was the dual form of the Son ... the unmanifest made manifest, the unformulate formulate, the unindividuate individuate, God as the Lord, proving through His duality that God is Substance as well as Force, Love as well as Will, Feminine as well as Masculine, Mother as well as Father.'"[246]

On reflection (and with the benefit of hindsight), I came to appreciate the true meaning of "the Dark Night of the Soul." Many people have confused this with Spiritual Dryness : but when St John of the Cross originally coined the phrase, he really meant that if one likens the coming of the full knowledge of God to the light of a new day at sunrise, then the seed of that enlightenment must have been planted during the Dark Night which preceded it. Hence, far from marking a time of spiritual anguish, the Dark Night of the Soul constitutes a time of growth, and hope in the future.

Hence, I now realised that the dissatisfaction I had experienced on the first day of the Convocation of the Good Angels, instead of just spiritual dryness, had marked the start of my own Dark Night where – unappreciated by me at the time – the seed of full Knowledge & Conversation resolutely germinated : whilst this evening's experience represented the full flowering of the Holy Guardian Angel, and the new Dawn of spiritual consciousness.

St John of the Cross' book, incidentally, represents the Christian counterpart to *The Song of Songs*, in its imagery and intensity.[247]

I finished with the Additional Prayer, Licence to Depart, and this time the Banishing Rituals. I left the oratory feeling exalted, confident that I now had achieved the wherewithal necessary to complete the final three days of the Operation.

---

[246] JUNG (1967) p 26 – quoting MAITLAND (1896), pp129-130
[247] See (e.g.) https://en.wikisource.org/wiki/The_Dark_Night_of_the_Soul_(Peers_translation) accessed 2022-01-24

Day 199 : The Conjuration of the Four Kings of Hell

28 October 2020

Ritual

"Ritual shower. Elimination. Vitally important that I remain undisturbed by bodily functions throughout the whole day." (My ritual notes.)

I managed to record one dream during the night. I got up at 6am for a ritual shower, checking in with *Nepheshi*, and a brief Middle Pillar ritual – incorporating the mantra I had received yesterday. Good.

I entered the Oratory. I had put up net curtains around the Oriel window : so that I could keep the ordinary curtains fully open, without worrying about the neighbours from across the road seeing in and being disturbed by me summoning all the demons from Hell.

"Wear white robe, with wand and silver lamen. Altar ready, triangle of art with tray of river sand in the east, outside the oratory."

Before beginning it occurred to me that M... had said I should write his name in the triangle as well. I did so, using a piece of charcoal : I made a mental note to do it with something better for tomorrow's ceremony.

I began at 6.44am (Sunrise), with the Ritual I had compiled for the first day of the Convocation of the Evil Spirits. Throughout today's ritual I made sure I incorporated all the principles I had learnt from yesterday.

"LBRP.

"LBRH.

"Bornless Ritual.

The Bornless Ritual turned out well. Before the first conjuration (that of Lucifer), I did the full Middle Pillar Ritual + Mantra, and meditated on laddering back : as a result, I managed to satisfactorily recall some of the state of consciousness that I attained yesterday evening.

"Conjuration of Lucifer :

'In the names YHVH, Tzebaoth and Adonai, who hath created all Nature and before Whom all Kings bow down and are subject - may I always practice Knowledge and Conversation of my Holy Guardian Angel, that I may have power and authority as did Moses, Aaron and Elijah. AMEN

'Oh YHVH ! Tzebaoth ! Adonai ! I entreat you to deign to command your Holy Angels to lead me in the True Way, and Wisdom, and

Knowledge, by studying the which assiduously in the Sacred Writings there will arise more and more Wisdom in my heart. AMEN.

'Oh YHVH, Tzebaoth, Adonai, and my Holy Guardian: HALLELUJAH. Accept the ardour of my prayer, and show me Thy mercy. Through Your grace may I have the honour of company with the Holy Angels; and grant and reveal the hidden Wisdom to reign over the unredeemed spirits and all creatures. AMEN.

'In the names YHVH, Tzebaoth and Adonai, and [my Holy Guardian Angel], I conjure LUCIFER: turn away from evil and Honour God; serve Him and humanity, and myself in particular; keep safe from harm myself, all connected with me and with this place; fulfil all my commands promptly, efficiently, and according to my interest; speak truthfully to me without murmur or ambiguity in a voice clear and intelligible without equivocation; appear before me in a fair shape without tortuosity or deformity; and remain until I give thee licence.

'In the names YHVH, Tzebaoth and Adonai, and my Holy Guardian Angel - AMEN.'"

Lucifer's conjuration went according to plan. I seemed to perceive a glow of energy in the Triangle of Art, and Lucifer's sigil hanging in mid-air there: I interpreted this as a sign that he had manifested and so I carried on with the ritual as intended.

'Welcome thou most noble King LUCIFER, Great Being of Light! I say you are welcome unto me because I called you through him who created both heaven & Earth & Hell and all that is contained therein and you have obeyed also. By the same power that I called you forth I bind you that you remain affably and visibly hear before this oratory in this triangle so constant and so long as I have occasion for you and not to depart without my licence until you have faithfully and truly performed my will without any falsity.

'By the power of YHVH, Tzebaoth, Adonai and [my Holy Guardian Angel] have I called you forth. Give unto me a true answer:

'Firstly - do you agree that you recognise the virtue, power and authority of YHVH, Tzebaoth, Adonai and [my Holy Guardian Angel], that has made you subject to all His creatures, and which has brought you here to my feet?

'Secondly: do you recognise that my object is not at all a malign curiosity, but one tending unto the honour and glory of God, and to my own good and that of all the human race. That further, every time that I shall summon you, by whatever sign or word, and in whatever time and place, and for whatever occasion and service, you shall appear

immediately without any delay, and obey my commands. And that in case you shall have some legitimate hindrance hereto, you are to send unto you some other spirits assigning then and there such as shall be capable and potent to accomplish and obey my will and my demand in your place. And you shall promise and swear to observe this by the most rigorous judgment of God, and by the most severe punishment and chastisement of the holy angels, inflicted upon you. And that you will consent to obey, and name unto me the eight sub-princes, whom you will send in your place to take the oath as I have already said, to appear at once on the following morning when I command ; and that you will duly send the eight sub-princes ?

    'Then you will signify your assent be swearing upon this wand.'

I perceived the "glow" in the Triangle give an affirmative signal to both of my questions, and reach up to embrace my wand as I held it out in front of me. Taking this as successful, I licenced Lucifer to depart.

I then did the conjuration of Satan : the wording of this, and indeed all the subsequent conjurations this day, remained the same as the one for Lucifer but with the name of the Demon King changed as appropriate. I recited the Enn, though I left out the last *"Ave Satanas"* because I thought this too much resembled *worshipping* Satan. Besides which, it did not strike me as grammatically correct Latin.

Halfway through the conjuration I remembered missing out calling him "Great Magical Agent" as M… said to do yesterday : *hence I repeated the whole thing from the beginning.*

Nevertheless, I did perceive a *downward pointing pentagram* hanging in the air in the Triangle of Art, so I took that as a sign that he had manifested, and that in future I should use this as Satan's sigil instead of the one I had made up yesterday. I carried on with the conjuration, to a similar result as I had had with Lucifer previously. On finishing I licenced Satan to depart.

The conjuration of Leviathan proved straightforward : I perceived Leviathan's sigil hanging in the air as a sign that he had manifested. Again, on finishing I licenced Leviathan to depart.

I paused here to relight charcoal and add more incense : then I continued with the conjuration of Belial. Belial appeared as a sort of column of light in the Triangle. On finishing this I licenced Belial *and all other spirits trapped by this ceremony* to depart.

I then closed the whole thing down with the LBRP and LBRH, and quit the oratory.

During the ceremony, I perceived pertinent images appearing in the air in the Triangle : for example, when asking the questions of the spirits, I thought I saw the word "YES" appearing when I demanded whether the Spirits agreed or not. I suppose that I must have experienced this through clairvoyance, or something like "Auric-vision." The whole thing took approximately 2 hours and 10 minutes.

Afterwards I went to have a lie down for a time.

Day 200 : Conjuration of the Eight Princes

29 October 2020

Ritual

During the night I half remembered one dream, very badly but at least more than nothing. Up at 6am for ritual shower, checking in with *Nepheshi*, and brief Middle Pillar Ritual. I began at 6.47am (i.e., Sunrise). Astral Projection music playing. I followed the ritual I had compiled for the second day of the convocation of the Evil Spirits :

"Prepare in a manner similar to yesterday but place a list of all the names of the Servient Spirits in the Triangle of Art."

Feeling nervous : but concentrating as I did at the beginning of yesterday's ritual calmed me down.

"LBRP.

"LBRH.

"Bornless Ritual.

The Bornless Ritual again went well. I then did the Middle Pillar ritual combined with the mantra I had received, which again encouraged me.

I performed the conjuration :

'In the names YHVH, Tzebaoth and Adonai, who hath created all Nature and before Whom all Kings bow down and are subject - may I always practice Knowledge and Conversation of my Holy Guardian Angel, that I may have power and authority as did Moses, Aaron and Elijah. AMEN

'Oh YHVH ! Tzebaoth ! Adonai ! [My Holy Guardian Angel] ! I entreat you to deign to command your Holy Angels to lead me in the True Way, and Wisdom, and Knowledge, by studying the which assiduously in the Sacred Writings there will arise more and more Wisdom in my heart. AMEN.

'Oh YHVH, Tzebaoth, Adonai, and [my Holy Guardian Angel]: HALLELUJAH. Accept the ardour of my prayer, and show me Thy mercy. Through Your grace may I have the honour of company with the Holy Angels ; and grant and reveal the hidden Wisdom to reign over the unredeemed spirits and all creatures. AMEN.

'In the names YHVH, Tzebaoth, Adonai, and [my Holy Guardian Angel], I conjure LUCIFER - SATAN - LEVIATHAN - and BELIAL : remember your promises and oaths made yesterday and send unto me the

eight Princes : ASTAROTH, MAGOTH, ASMODEUS, BEELZEBUTH ;
ORIENS, PAIMON, ARITON, and AMAYMON.

'*In the names YHVH, Tzebaoth, Adonai, and [my Holy Guardian*
Angel], I conjure and command all spirits : turn away from evil and
Honour God ; serve Him and humanity, and myself in particular ; keep
safe from harm myself, all connected with me and with this place ; fulfil
all my commands promptly, efficiently, and according to my interest ;
speak truthfully to me without murmur or ambiguity in a voice clear and
intelligible without equivocation ; appear before me in a fair shape
without tortuosity or deformity ; and remain until I give thee licence.

'*In the names YHVH, Tzebaoth, Adonai, and [my Holy Guardian*
Angel] - AMEN.'

I imagined seeing the eight princes of Hell appear as eight flames encircling
the dish of sand in the Triangle of Art. I got the impression that if I were to attempt
to skry into one of these flames I would get to know more closely the Prince of
Hell that it represented.

I continued :

'*Welcome, most noble Kings LUCIFER - SATAN - LEVIATHAN -*
BELIAL, and ye Princes ASTAROTH, MAGOTH, ASMODEUS,
BEELZEBUTH ; ORIENS, PAIMON, ARITON, and AMAYMON. I say
you are welcome unto me because I called you through him who created
both heaven & Earth & Hell and all that is contained therein and you
have obeyed also. By the same power that I called you forth I bind you
that you remain affably and visibly hear before this oratory in this
triangle so constant and so long as I have occasion for you and not to
depart without my licence until you have faithfully and truly performed
my will without any falsity.

'*By the power of YHVH, Tzebaoth, Adonai, and [my Holy Guardian*
Angel] have I called you forth. Give unto me a true answer :

'*Firstly - do you agree that you recognise the virtue, power and*
authority of YHVH, Tzebaoth, Adonai, and [my Holy Guardian Angel],
that has made you subject to all His creatures, and which has brought
you here to my feet ?

'*Secondly : do you recognise that my object is not at all a malign*
curiosity, but one tending unto the honour and glory of God, and to my
own good and that of all the human race. That further, every time that I
shall summon you, by whatever sign or word, and in whatever time and
place, and for whatever occasion and service, you shall appear
immediately without any delay, and obey my commands. And that in case
you shall have some legitimate hindrance hereto, you are to send unto

you some other spirits assigning then and there such as shall be capable and potent to accomplish and obey my will and my demand in your place. And you shall promise and swear to observe this by the most rigorous judgment of God, and by the most severe punishment and chastisement of the holy angels, inflicted upon you. And that you will consent to obey, and compel to appear tomorrow morning when I command the spirits named in this document now lying in the Triangle of Art, and take the oath as I have already said ?

'Thirdly : do you, oh spirits Oriens, Paimon, Ariton, and Amaimon, each of you assign and consign unto me my familiar spirit, which from the day of your birth you are compelled to give unto me ; and that you will compel these familiar spirits to appear before more tomorrow morning when I command to take the oath ?

'Then you will signify your assent be swearing upon this wand.'

I "saw" each flame affirming "yes" to the demands which I made of them, likewise of Oriens, Paymon, Ariton and Amaimon agreeing to send me a familiar. I "saw" them all touching the tip of my wand in confirmation.

I then closed with the Licence to Depart, LBRP and LBRH. This ceremony lasted 1 hour 25 minutes in total. I then quit the Oratory for the day.

*

As on previous days I remained silent and withdrawn until sunset. Come the evening, when the bridle on my tongue and the seal on my lips had been lifted for the day, I narrowly avoided an argument with my fiancée. She believed that true "Adepts" can dissolve and reconstitute matter – including their own bodies – at will. Hence, anyone who could not do this *literally* could not call themselves a true Adept. Apparently, this added up to a big deal with her, because she regarded it as one of BOTA's core teachings. I refrained from voicing my own opinion on the subject, as I thought it of the utmost importance to remain calm and have a clear mind, now more than anytime else. (I later realised that Paul Foster Case had got this from the "Powers of the Magus" described by Eliphas Levi.[248])

Later, I recorded in my journal :

"Am worried that I may have consumed too many carbohydrates recently, as I have a more than usual urge to pass water. I hope I am not going diabetic ! NB : on the bright side I have experienced this in the past (once) and once the level of carbohydrates in my body returned to normal levels, the urge to pass water did as well."

---

[248] LEVI (1896), pp13-14.

Before going to bed, I spent a lot of time extracting all the magic squares from the lever-arch file in which I kept them, and carefully arranging them in the order I would require them in tomorrow's ritual, so that I would not have to faff about on the day.

Day 201 : Conjuration of the Servitor Spirits

30 October 2020

Ritual

During the night : I had difficulty recording any dreams. Nevertheless, I got up at 6am for my ritual shower ; checking in with Nepheshi ; and a brief Middle Pillar Ritual (incorporating mantra).

I began at sunrise (6.48am), first contemplating M…, *Samyama*, and the said mantra etc, to get me in the mood. I used the ritual of the third day of the convocation of the evil spirits which I had compiled :

"Prepare in a manner similar to yesterday but have ready the various Squares to place in the Triangle of Art.

"LBRP.

"LBRH.

"Bornless Ritual.

The whole active imagination / laddering back idea helped ensure that the Bornless Ritual went particularly powerfully. Before proceeding further, I settled down to meditate on the full Middle Pillar Ritual again, with the Mantra, and concentrated on laddering back whilst maintaining awareness of both the outer/peripheral consciousness and inner/central consciousness. I attained a state of meditation similar to what I experienced in the evening of the third day of the convocation of the Good spirits – which I interpreted as an augur of success for today's ritual.

"Conjuration *:*

'In the names YHVH, Tzebaoth and Adonai, who hath created all Nature and before Whom all Kings bow down and are subject - may I always practice Knowledge and Conversation of my Holy Guardian Angel, that I may have power and authority as did Moses, Aaron and Elijah. AMEN

'Oh YHVH ! Tzebaoth ! Adonai ! [My Holy Guardian Angel]! I entreat you to deign to command your Holy Angels to lead me in the True Way, and Wisdom, and Knowledge, by studying the which assiduously in the Sacred Writings there will arise more and more Wisdom in my heart. AMEN.

'Oh YHVH, Tzebaoth, Adonai, and [my Holy Guardian Angel]: HALLELUJAH. Accept the ardour of my prayer, and show me Thy mercy. Through Your grace may I have the honour of company with the

Holy Angels ; and grant and reveal the hidden Wisdom to reign over the unredeemed spirits and all creatures. AM EN.

'In the names YHVH, Tzebaoth, Adonai, and [my Holy Guardian Angel], I conjure ye Kings LUCIFER, SATAN, LEVIATHAN, and BELIAL ; and ye Princes ASTAROTH, MAGOTH, ASMODEUS, BEELZEBUTH ; ORIENS, PAIMON, ARITON, and AMAYMON : remember your promises and oaths made yesterday.

'In the names YHVH, Tzebaoth, Adonai, and my [Holy Guardian Angel], I conjure and command all spirits : turn away from evil and Honour God ; serve Him and humanity, and myself in particular ; keep safe from harm myself, all connected with me and with this place ; fulfil all my commands promptly, efficiently, and according to my interest ; speak truthfully to me without murmur or ambiguity in a voice clear and intelligible without equivocation ; appear before me in a fair shape without tortuosity or deformity ; and remain until I give thee licence.

'In the names YHVH, Tzebaoth, Adonai, and [my Holy Guardian Angel] - AMEN.'

I went through the invocations, feeling confident. I imagined I could see the sigils of the various demon Kings appearing, whilst the Princes again appeared as flames. Interpreting this as success (so far), I continued :

'Welcome, most noble Kings LUCIFER - SATAN - LEVIATHAN - BELIAL, and ye Princes ASTAROTH, MAGOTH, ASMODEUS, BEELZEBUTH ; ORIENS, PAIMON, ARITON, and AMAYMON. I say you are welcome unto me because I called you through him who created both heaven & Earth & Hell and all that is contained therein and you have obeyed also. By the same power that I called you forth I bind you that you remain affably and visibly hear before this oratory in this triangle so constant and so long as I have occasion for you and not to depart without my licence until you have faithfully and truly performed my will without any falsity.

'By the power of YHVH, Tzebaoth, Adonai, and [my Holy Guardian Angel] have I called you forth. Give unto me a true answer :

'Firstly - do you agree that you recognise the virtue, power and authority of YHVH, Tzebaoth, Adonai, and [my Holy Guardian Angel], that has made you subject to all His creatures, and which has brought you here to my feet ?

'Secondly : do you swear that every time that I shall call one of you by your name, that you shall at once appear in such form and place as shall please me, and that you shall punctually execute that which shall have commanded you ?

'Signify your assent be swearing upon this wand.'

I got the psychic impression that the Kings and Princes did indeed agree to the conjuration, and swore upon my wand.

I then proceeded to conjure each set of Servitors, specifically through conjuring the Prince immediately superior to them. The first set were under the presidency of **Astaroth.** I placed the word squares of the chapters 8 and 23, in the Triangle of Art, and made the following conjuration :

> *'In the names YHVH, Tzebaoth, Adonai, and [my Holy Guardian Angel], I conjure thee oh Prince ASTAROTH, and all the Spirits subject unto thee, that in cases when it may not seem fit unto me to command you verbally, that as soon as I shall take one of these signs in my hand and move it from its place that the spirit marked in the sign shall do and execute that which the sign beareth, and that which my intimation joined thereto shall indicate ; also that in the case that in the sign none of you shall be specially named, that all in general shall be obliged promptly and readily to perform the operation commanded ; and that if also in the time to come, other signs or symbols be made by me which be not here included, that then also you shall be equally bound to observe and execute them also.*
>
> *'I conjure thee, ASTAROTH, for your own sake and in the name of all the rest, to signify your acceptance of this Conjuration by touching this Wand.' (Done)*

Upon receiving the impression that the Prince and the spirits over which he held responsibility had indeed accepted the pact, I removed the word squares relevant to Astaroth and replaced them with those of the next Prince, and performed the next conjuration. I did this for each set of Servitor spirits, only changing the name of the relevant Prince or Princes on each occasion and taking care to remove the previous word-squares and replace with the correct ones. Hence, the subsequent conjurations went as follows :

Prince or Princes	Word squares from chapters...
Magot	10, 11, 14, 21, 30
Asmodeus	12
Beelzbuth	9,20,22
Astaroth and Asmodeus jointly	6,7,16
Asmodeus and Magot jointly	15
Oriens, Paymon, Ariton and Amaimon jointly	1,2,3,4,5,13,17,27,29
Oriens	28
Paymon	25

Ariton and Amaimon jointly	26
Ariton	24
Amaymon	18

I added one last-minute innovation from the ritual I had originally written : when it came to each separate invocation (including that of Astaroth), I chanted the names of *all the servient spirits* related to the Prince or Princes whom I addressed at that particular part of the ritual. This obviously lengthened the ceremony, but it also got me into a sort of altered state of consciousness.

Fortunately, at the end of each invocation, I got the impression that they all consented to me conjuring them in this manner, and touched the tip of my wand accordingly.

I then arrived at the Conjuration of the Familiar Spirits. I removed all the previous word squares and placed the word squares of the chapter 15 in the Triangle of Art, and received an intuition : the *spiritus familiares* would all come from amongst the list of the common servitors of Oriens, Paymon, Ariton, and Amaimon (this at least would make sense from the context of the ritual). I therefore decided that I should do have the list of these spirits in front of me when I did the conjuration, so the Demon Prince only had to say, "that one."

In this way I managed to pick the names of the spirits by first getting an indication from the Demon Prince I address at that particular moment as to where on the list I should look, then actually consulting the list itself, and then finally checking back with the Demon Prince that I had identified the right spirit.

I therefore conjured first Oriens, saying :

> *'In the names YHVH, Tzebaoth, Adonai, and [my Holy Guardian Angel], I conjure thee oh Prince ORIENS to grant unto me the use of a Familiar Spirit, telling me its name, and the time during which it shall be obliged to serve me.'*

Then, using the method of which I had thought, I came up with a first name from among the common spirits of those four Princes. I repeated a similar process for each of Paymon, Ariton, and Amaimon.

Hence, I derived my own particular familiar spirits thus :

Oriens	NOGAH	From dawn until midday;[249]
Paymon	EREMITES	From midday until dusk;
Ariton	RAGARAS	From dusk until midnight;
Amaimon	YPARCHAS	From midnight until dawn.

I then conjured these four spirits -

---

[249] the times here mentioned are all actual times not clock times, so for example during summer it would be 1pm BST or whenever the Sun was actually on the midheaven, likewise midnight would be whenever the Sun was actually on the *Imum Coeli*.

'In the names YHVH, Tzebaoth, Adonai, and [my Holy Guardian Angel], I conjure ye spirits Nogah, Eremites, Ragaras, and Yparchas, that ye swear not only upon these symbols collectively, but also each one separately, that from this time forward you will observe duly and with diligence the six hours destined; and that you promise to serve me with fidelity, performing all which you are obliged to do whenever I command your services; and that you shall not in the slightest degree be false and lying as regardeth me; also, that if by chance I should assign over one of you unto another person, that you shall act as faithfully by him or her as by myself; and, lastly, that you are to fulfil, perform, and execute, that which God for their chastisement hath destined unto them for sentence of judgment.

'Signify your assent to this Conjuration by touching this Wand.'

These spirits too signified their assent to being conjured.

Finally, I licenced all the spirits to depart, and finished off with the LBRP and LBRH. Feeling relieved and happy. The time was 09 :15 - the entire ritual has taken approximately two and a half hours.

Later, after tidying away the magic squares I come downstairs to have a proper breakfast for the first time in a week. My fiancée was pleased to see me and gave me a little present (a bottle of malt whisky). In fact, she felt so excited that she talked almost non-stop for another two hours. Needless to say, I hardly got a word in edgeways, being too polite.

*

I spent the afternoon typing up my journal for the last time. I realised that the Physical problems which I reported the previous evening, which had made me worried about diabetes, had vanished to my great relief.

I compiled a list of things to do now that I had finished the Abramelin Operation. The most obvious was that although I had vowed to raise £10,000 for charity as part of my oath, as of today my JustGiving page had only come up with £621. I therefore considered, as a matter of honour, that I ought to continue to raise the other £9739 anyway. I reflected that this would be a good opportunity to make use of the Abramelin magick for a specific purpose.

Aside from this I realised I had numerous things to do, spells to cast, rituals to learn, and work to perform for the various orders of which I was a member : principally BOTA, the Golden Dawn, and the Martinists. I even jotted down ideas for new books which I could write.

In the evening, my fiancée took me out for a celebratory meal at a local restaurant, during the course of which I broke the abstinences I had been observing for the past two months straightaway. Although she expressed amazement that I had completed the Abramelin operation, being impressed that I had done so, ironically she knew so little about it that she found it difficult to articulate what sort of questions to ask me about it, so we muddled through the conversation.

*

In the evening, instead of a formal Abramelin ritual to do, I nevertheless did some retro-vis meditation before bed : in doing so I practiced this outer/inner thing which at the time I still thought as "Jungian."

I attained *Samadhi*. Powerful did not describe it. Perhaps the result of completing the Abramelin operation involved unexpected benefits ? It would certainly make sense that if it proved a door opening to new things.

THE AFTERMATH

What others have written about Abramelin

Had I done the Operation correctly, or had I made a serious blunder ? This question, the answer to which I feared to discover, occupied my mind as I now researched into other people's accounts of Abramelin. I had waited until now, in case anything I did read might spoil my appreciation of the Operation whilst I had it still in progress.

Very few full accounts actually exist of someone doing an Abramelin Operation. As far as I am aware, William Bloom, Ramsey Dukes, and Marcus Katz have made the only other full-length descriptions. A number of other occultists have published summaries of their experience (e.g., Crowley), or have mentioned that they undertook the operation without going into details – at least publicly. Some have dropped various hints, including, bizarrely enough, the late comedian Michael Bentine.[250]

(Katz mentioned that he had read "The Abra-Melin Experience," the account of a gentleman in Australia named "Ishariyah,"[251] but later clarified to me that it had been privately printed, and hence not widely available.[252])

"Club Abramelin" hence has rather an exclusive membership, although I do know that the number of people who have gone through it exceeds those who publicly mention the fact (I number some of these alumni amongst my personal acquaintances). However, this dwindles completely, compared to the number of people, both internet-trolls *and* serious occultists, who have not gone through Abramelin but nevertheless seem to think they have some kind of entitlement to comment about it anyway.

Nevertheless :

William Bloom

Bloom described his experiences in the book *The Sacred Magician*, which became the first and for a long time only full account of an Abramelin operation. He performed the Operation whilst living in Morocco in 1973, and published the results of his adventures three years later.[253]

I now settled down to reading the 1992 revised edition of his book. I found it full of purple prose, Alice Bailey inspired sentiment, and purple prose consisting of Alice Bailey inspired sentiment. I suppose that for Bloom, reading Bailey's works constituted making a daily study of the "sacred writings." *Chacun à son*

---

[250] BENTINE (1991).

[251] KATZ (2020)

[252] In private correspondence with the author (2021).

[253] BLOOM (1976, 1992).

gout : I did not care much for her myself, so this left me with the continual urge to keep skipping forward where possible.

Things turned exciting, however, when Bloom got to the final seven days. As I read, I could not help but think how much his experience had mirrored my own. Both he and I reacted with dismay when hit by Spiritual Dryness on the first day of the Convocation of the Good Spirits. Likewise, both he and I only finally experienced something to which we could confidently point and say, "Yes, that really *is* Knowledge and Conversation of the Holy Guardian Angel" on the evening of the third day.

I could discern, however, one major difference between Bloom and myself in our reactions to when the Dryness hit. I tried to keep going as phlegmatically as possible, willing that the process would yield results so long as I didn't give up.

Bloom, however, came across like a complete drama queen, ripping pages from his magical diary over how the awfulness of his predicament, so that when the Angel finally did appear, it seemed all the more miraculous.

I also felt disappointed that he appeared to end his diary rather suddenly after the end of the operation, as it doesn't really go into detail about how much use Bloom made of the Sacred Magic, or his life as a Sacred Magician. From the little details he wrote, he got ill immediately after, and *didn't* actually use the Sacred Magic either much or at all. I wondered : did he just get-it-and-forget-it ? In his 1992 epilogue he explained that despite not using the Abramelin system *per se*, the experience did inspire him in the spiritual direction his life took thereafter.

Nevertheless, precisely because his account accorded so closely with my own, I believe quite willingly in William Bloom's sincerity : and that he really did attain KCHGA as a result of his efforts.

Ramsey Dukes

I had read the first few pages of Duke's book before beginning, just so that I knew on what terms to frame my Oath at the outset of the Operation. I now completed the rest of the book to see what happened.

The book left me, to say the least, "bemused." Like both Bloom and I, Dukes appeared to hit some Spiritual Dryness on the first day of the Convocation of the Good Spirits. His reaction, however, differed yet again. Whereas Bloom had perceived himself plunged into deep existential anguish, and I had soldiered-on as best I could, Dukes at that point decided to up-sticks and *go with some friends for a two-week holiday to Brighton.*

I would have found it more interesting had the book has a twist ending – i.e., that his Holy Guardian Angel had turned up unexpectedly in the middle of him having a gay old time in the party capital of the south coast, and that he had completed the Operation after all. Alas, no such luck ! His previous efforts appeared to go unresolved, and the story concluded unsatisfactorily. At least his diary had the merit of brutal honesty.

Marcus Katz

Katz completed the Operation in 2004 : he published his account of it in 2011.[254] The first thing that struck me when reading his book was how different it seemed to complete the Operation in a time when an international Pandemic had not gripped the world. When Katz did his Abramelin, he could travel freely about the countryside. Consequently, he would often go on long walks and find himself struck by spiritual thoughts which seemed apposite whilst he visited areas of outstanding natural beauty.

I, on the other hand, found myself stuck in the middle of a town due to the extreme nature of the lockdown conditions then in force. The nearest place which came close to being an "Area of Outstanding Natural Beauty"[255] lay about three miles away : a short drive, in normal circumstances, but impossible at a time when venturing outside one's house for anything more than was strictly necessary led to Society treating one lower than Judas Iscariot, or even danger of arrest by the police.

Katz appeared to have structured his Abramelin Operation differently to the manner in which I did. He did scriptural study in the first third ; whilst moving on to calling for the angels in the second third. I however focussed on confession of sins in the first part, then scriptural study, then calling for the angels. *Katz almost entirely misses out mention of confessing one's sins, except a passing reference without details that it happened.* (Also, I didn't drop the scriptural study when moving on to the next phase). Ironically, Katz commented that his Holy Guardian Angel inspired him to subsequently change his career to Counselling, which required him to take part himself in undergoing regular counselling sessions as a professional requirement. What one doesn't do during the Abramelin Operation, one ends up doing anyway.

Quite clearly, in Neurolinguistic Programming terms, Katz' prime Modality is *Visual* (with *Auditory* coming in second). Hence, Katz continually described what he *saw* happening around him, the beauty of the *appearance* of the places he visited : he even talked about how he used drawing to articulate his thoughts and help him perform the convocation of the evil spirits. (I mention *Auditory* as

---

[254] KATZ (2011).

[255] NB in Britain, the Government must officially designate an AONB as such for it to qualify for that description, which did not apply in this instance. See https ://www.gov.uk/guidance/areas-of-outstanding-natural-beauty-aonbs-designation-and-management accessed 2021-10-27

second preference because he faithfully noted the music to which he listened throughout his Operation which inspired him at the time).

More tellingly, Katz judged success in attaining KCHGA in terms of *seeing* an Angel appear. I'm quite willing to believe in Katz' genuineness on this point : however, my own experience differed. I suppose if I analysed myself in NLP terms, I would describe my prime Modality as *Kinaesthetic,* with *Visual* coming in second. I.e., when I perceived what I believed to be definitive evidence of KCHGA, the physical sensations it produced within my body more concerned me than did what it looked like : because, from my experience, this *felt* like a more reliable indicator.

I do believe that visual phenomena of a præternatural origin can and do occur. I myself have seen such things, although I continually surprise myself when I do so. For me, *clairsentience* comes more quickly than *clairvoyance*. Katz however seems to believe that the *vision* of the Angel is all-important, and does not appear to give consideration to other modalities.

One remark of Katz intrigued me : he imagined the culmination of the operation as a "conception" – he noticed major changes in his life as a result of attaining Knowledge & Conversation of the Holy Guardian Angel some nine months thereafter. This immediately got me thinking : what was *I* doing nine months after my own Operation ?

Checking through my magical journal, I recognised that as the exact time I found myself dealing with the consequences of leaving the SRIA. During the course of 2021, the doom-laden prophecies of CH came to pass just as he had predicted.[256] For his efforts of "whistleblowing," the leadership of the SRIA treated him in a manner specifically like that which anti-whistleblowing legislation supposedly outlawed.[257] The Society *did* sell the Hampstead venue, the decision being taken just over a month after the then Supreme Magus in his annual report stated that he had no intention of doing so. At that point I resigned : the messages of support I received immediately afterwards convinced me that I had made a further advancement in Rosicrucianism in one day by *leaving* the Society, than I had in twelve years of remaining a member.

Nevertheless, I still had to deal with the practical problem of removing property belonging to the various orders to which I belonged which used to meet there, in advance of the finalisation of the sale. Hence, some nine-months to the day after finishing my Operation, I found myself back at Hampstead with a

---

[256] Day 177 – *vide supra.*

[257] Anti-whistleblowing legislation applies only to one's employment, not to one's membership in a private members' club, or so it would seem.

colleague, boxing up a large quantity of books and removing them, with the aid of a man and van, to storage in a safe location.

Whilst there, I took possession of a suitcase full of Martinist paraphernalia. At the same time, an old friend from the SRIA donated me something from out of the cupboards which they were clearing out – a ninth degree robe – so he must have had the impression that I would one day re-join the Society.

Looking back now, quite clearly I received a message from my Holy Guardian Angel that I should pursue my interests in both Rosicrucianism and Martinism independently of the SRIA. A number of events happening at that time in my life re-enforced the message, by making sure that I would be disqualified from re-joining the Society even if I wanted to. Ironically, I sensed the presence of "dark forces" at work, steering the society in the direction it found itself going : whilst pushing me onto my new trajectory from behind just as much as my Angel pulled me from the front. As another friend told me not long thereafter, "*Sometimes it takes the Devil to do the Lord's work.*"

In short, Katz' account is worth reading because he writes sympathetically from the point of view of a magician in general, and a practitioner of *Abramelin* in particular. More recently he has also described how, unlike Bloom for example, he does make practical use of the magical word-squares from time to time.[258]

---

[258] KATZ (2020).

Using the Word Squares

The temptation might exist in the mind of someone who didn't know any better, that given that the last part of the Book comprises word-squares promising fabulous magical powers, one ought to expect to immediately become a terrible sorcerer manifesting wealth, power, fame etc with just a swish of one's magic wand. The reality for me, however, turned out far removed : I deliberately took a conservative approach to utilising my thaumaturgic abilities. It didn't help that many of the word-squares only spoke to the mindset of half-a-millennium ago.

The Book *did* have, however, three word-squares which appealed to me as relevant to my current situation : to do with healing, finding lost books, and Alchemy.

Alchemy

My thoughts turned to Alchemy almost immediately after completing the Operation. In its immediate aftermath, I spent a lot of time researching the history of the concept of the "Holy Guardian Angel," in the course of which I also researched the etymology of a term bandied about by contemporary occultists, the *Augoeides.*

Crowley implicitly used this as a synonym for "obtaining Knowledge and Conversation of the Holy Guardian Angel."[259] However, taken literally, the word *Augoeides* does not refer to an angel or dæmon at all – it means "dawn-like image" or "shining body." Hence, *Augoeides* should more properly refer to the Resurrection- or Solar-Body, which is the Philosophical Gold.

Or to put it more simply, if one imagines Divine Union as a destination, the *Augoeides* becomes the car which takes one there, whilst the Holy Guardian Angel adopts the role of the driving instructor who teaches one how to drive it in the first place.

I thought : could I use *Abramelin*-magick itself to help me realise my *Augoeides* ? The Book describes the function of the third word square of part IV, chapter 7 as "*to learn all sorts of Alchemical arts from the spirits.*"[260] Perhaps this really meant *Internal Alchemy* ? If so, then in amongst all the word-squares which promised rather worldly, low-magick attainments, I had found one which could provide me with practical help as a Hermetic magician.

---

[259] "The Master Therion" (1929), chapter II, "The Formulae of The Elemental Weapons."
[260] Dehn (2006), p152.

I intended to go about using the Word Square by constructing a ritual based around scrying into the square to verify I had the correct version : i.e., following my own advice on the subject.[261] I planned it for the following weekend, when I would have enough time without having to worry about work. However, a strange thing happened : from the time I first gazed upon the Word Square and formed my intention to use it to discover the secrets of Internal Alchemy, an uncommon motivation seized me, that I should read all I could on the subject : from the writings of Paul Foster Case, and Golden Dawn papers to which I had previously paid scant attention, to the writings of people like Isaac Newton, Michael Sendivogius, Schweighart, Paracelsus – and of course, *The Emerald Tablet of Hermes Trismegistos.* Hence by the time I got round to performing the ritual, I brimmed full of ideas so much that I thought I might have already discovered the answers for which I had sought.

When it came to the actual ritual itself, I recorded it in my journal as follows :

"Up early (6.16am) for ritual shower, checking in with Nepheshi, and brief Middle Pillar - elimination. With Astral Projection music playing (on my phone, not computer) I begin my Abramelin ritual at 7.16am (i.e., Sunrise).

"I contemplate the notion of inner/outer consciousness (taken from the Jung quote), and perform the LBRP and LBRH, and then the Bornless Ritual. All good, I achieve a very deep meditative state of consciousness."

I.e., I did not at that stage realise I should more properly call it "the Maitland quote."

"I then perform a full Middle Pillar ritual, also contemplating M..., *'Samyama,' and the mantra I received. I am momentarily deluged by potentially distracting thoughts, but I manage to control them eventually.*

"Going into the Conjuration proper feels much better, as I regain a lot of the confidence that I felt during the Bornless Ritual. Specifically, I conjure **Ashtoreth, Asmodeus** *and* **Nogah** *…"*

I.e., because the Book said that Ashtoreth, Asmodeus, and the servant spirits controlled the workings of Chapter 7, Nogah being my own particular servant spirit for the time the ritual took place.

"… enjoining them to remember the oaths they have already sworn on my magic wand, as well as the usual. I brandish the third Word-Square of chapter 7 of book IV of 'Dehn,' To learn all sorts of Alchemical arts from the spirits, and tell them I want to realise my Augoeides or Resurrection Body so that I can accomplish the Great Work, and that for this purpose I will discover all information, be put in touch with all the right teachers ; and that they will explain the precise lettering of this word-square.

---

[261] *Vide supra :* Day 53 – "Abramelin Musings : Square Dancing."

"The Spirits respond firstly that I should develop the Inner Alchemy method I mentioned yesterday, as I was on the right track already : my discovery was inspired by my desire to use this square to discover the secrets of alchemy earlier this week."

I.e., I had come up with a theory that the planetary metals were the "Interior Stars," and that "Vitriol" represented the power of meditation and contemplation – of *Samyama,* even. Therefore, I should "pour Vitriol" on each "metal" and draw up the vapour arising therefrom, making it ascend from the earth to the heaven and letting it again descend to the earth, thus receiving the force of things superior and inferior. I thus look upon it as a westernised, Hermeticised form of laya yoga, but beefed-up by directing the full force of planetary ceremonial magick not outward towards the Macrocosm, but inward towards oneself.

"As to the word-square, the spirits confirm that - as I suspected – 'NAMALON' rules this particular square and his name should replace the sixth line thereof..."

Dehn had given this word square as "*IPOMANO, PAMERAM, ONALOMI, MELACAH, ARORAMI, NANAMON, OMIHINI.*" Now it so happens that according to the Book, in the guidance for the third day of Convoking the Dæmons – the day on which one conjures them specifically to empower the word-squares or "signs" as to which they are referred – it is implied that the signs may contain the name(s) of the spirits which rule them. "Aha !" I thought. "Surely if this square contains the name of a spirit, it would be one of those listed as being the servants of Ashtoreth and Asmodi ?"

Consulting this list drew a blank – at least at first. However, I did notice that one of the spirits serving Ashtoreth and Asmodi was "*NAMALON.*" Thus the spirits now confirmed my theory that the name of this spirit should stand in place of "Nanamon."

"... hence :

I	P	O	M	A	N	O
P	A	M	E	R	A	M
O	N	A	L	O	M	I
M	E	L	A	C	A	H
A	R	O	R	A	M	I
N	A	M	A	L	O	N
O	M	I	H	I	N	I

Figure 13 Third word square of book IV, chapter 7 : with the sixth line altered following my magic ritual.

"I then conjure Namalon in particular : visualising this new word-square as a door in front of me, I walk through, and summon Namalon to appearance. He tests well by names (i.e., M..., Ashtoreth, Asmodeus). He explains the significance of the fact why Alchemy is supposedly in the domain of 'demons.' The true Adept, having attained KCHGA and thus integrated the demons into a balanced world view, is able to sublimate the alchemical art, realising its full spiritual potential as a means of achieving the high goals of Hermeticism. The puffer, however, meets only the Demon without being guided by his HGA, and thus does not recognise the spiritual goals of the Art - he thus becomes seduced by materialism, and is only interested in making gold.

"Namalon agrees that I should publish this revised word-square by way of showing gratitude to him. I thank him and leave. (This I do by blogging about the subject).

"I finish the session with the Licence to Depart, and then the LBRP and LBRH again. The whole thing has taken me approximately one and three-quarter hours."

The aftermath of this magical ceremony found me filled with motivation to continue my alchemical research. I meditated regularly on the "interior stars" and came away each time refreshed and filled with energy. I personally experienced the Kundalini as the Secret Fire, as had other alchemists before me. As I did a lot of this Alchemical meditation last thing at night, I would often bound into bed with a great deal of vigour with which my fiancée tried valiantly to keep up.

Moreover, I came to the conclusion that the real First Matter must be the Divine Spark within oneself. This being the case, I theorised that one could discern the three principles by considering the nature of consciousness itself. E.g.,

- "Salt" was equivalent to Thought (any thought) ;
- "Sulphur" was the Consciousness *containing* that Thought ; and
- "Mercury" was the Light which shines through that Consciousness.

Hence the whole business of "Solve Et Coagula" really consisted of the ability to deconstruct the nature of Thought and Consciousness – which has a Spiritual dimension not readily appreciated by the Psychologists - and putting it back together again whilst in a state of deep meditation.

I wondered : perhaps by attaining Knowledge & Conversation of the Holy Guardian Angel – which after all had its own associated sates of deep mystical awareness – I had already found the First Matter ?

Healing

Because the Covid-19 Pandemic still gripped the world at the time, I wondered whether I could leverage my Abramelin Magick into helping end it ? I first seriously started considering the idea in late November 2020, some three weeks after finishing the Operation.

As I generally spent at least one day a week (Sunday) communing with my HGA, I would often get new ideas at this time as to what direction to go with my current magickal work. Hence one such session gave me the idea to use the DEBHER square specifically (i.e., Book IV, chapter 18, square 3), whose function the Book describes as "to heal Plague" : this being the closest thing, the more so because the name COVID-19 didn't exist in the fifteenth century.

My research whilst drawing up my book of word squares during the Operation had convinced me that the square given by Dehn, which corresponded to the versions in both the Dresden and Leipzig manuscripts, seemed the most plausible, i.e. :

D	E	B	H	E	R
E	R	A	O	S	E
B	A	R	I	O	H
H	O	I	R	A	B
E	S	O	A	R	E
R	E	H	B	E	D

Figure 14 Book IV, chapter 18, square 3 : "to heal Plague."

The word "Debher" phonetically renders the Hebrew דבר meaning a "plague, murrain or pestilence." Hence it made much more sense than "Bebher" (sic), the equivalent in Mathers' Bibliothèque de l'Arsenal manuscript.

(My fiancée practised Tarot divination at the time. I asked her to divine whether I ought to go ahead with my proposed healing ritual : her cards reported favourably.)

As I prepared my ritual I speculated as to who ruled this square, given that word squares supposedly incorporate the names of various spirits in them. Amaymon presides over the Squares of this chapter in general – however : this particular square does not contain the name of either Amaymon himself or any of his servant spirits. The third line, BARIOH, however, is one letter away from the name *Bariol* – who *is* one of Amaimon's servants. At least according to Dehn, Dresden and Leipzig – Mathers' version gave this spirit as "Buriol," just to confuse matters. Hence, might "Bariol" indeed govern this square, and if so, was it lettered correctly ?

I finally managed to find time to work a full ceremony on Saturday 5th December, now some two weeks after the inception of the idea. I recorded the results in my journal :

"Up at 6.46am for elimination and ritual shower. LL Ritual : good. At 7.46am I begin an Abramelin working - LBRP ; LBRH ; Bornless Ritual.

Concentrating on my inner consciousness whilst holding onto the periphery greatly enhances the efficacy of all of these - am much encouraged.

"I then do the conjuration, specifically speaking to Amaymon and his servant spirits. I sense that I am in contact with Amaymon and that he acknowledges my HGA and the Oath he had previously sworn to me. Talking specifically about square 4 of Chapter 18, Book 4 of Abramelin, we establish that the square is (as suspected) under the presidency of BARIOL, who is one of Amaimon's servant spirits.

"I then called upon Bariol himself, who himself acknowledged my HGA and the oath sworn by Amaymon. Bariol explained that although the word in the third line is inspired by his own name, the spelling of the square itself should be left as is. Instead, the square should be re-drawn to include the name 'Bariol' in an outer circumference - this addition suffices to link his energies to that of the square more properly.

"Mentally formulating the new version of this square, I go through it and astrally formulate it being laid upon the Earth itself. I conjure Bariol to make sure the vaccine for Covid 19 is distributed freely across the Earth, and in particular the state in Florida clears up to such an extent that my fiancée and I will be able to go there in February next year .... Although conjure Bariol to harm neither me, anyone connected with me, etc etc.

"I leave and thank Bariol and Amaymon as appropriate and licence them to depart. Close with the LBRP and LBRH."

Afterwards I drew the new version of the square :

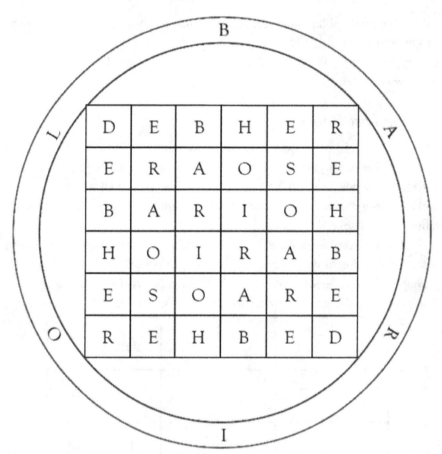

Figure 15 Book IV, chapter 18, square 3 - author's version.

On the basis that according to The Book, one ought to use these Word Squares by laying them over the afflicted part, I created a graphic of my new version of the square being superimposed upon the whole planet, and published it on social media. Not only did I hope this would bring about the desired world healing, but it also provided an opportunity to publicly thank Bariol whilst doing so. I noted that I felt spiritual the whole day : meditation in the evening proved very good - very deep.

Ironically, however, when I looked in the news, in the short time between me planning this magical operation and me getting around to actually carrying it out, I noted that a vaccine had now been approved for use, although at the time it had not been yet widely distributed. Intriguingly the same phenomenon had happened with the Alchemical word-square : the magic seemed to happen after forming the Intent and looking upon the square, not by deploying the square in the manner which I had expected.

By February the following year, mass vaccinations had begun in my country, but the political situation had not yet caught up to allow international travel. I ruefully noted that this new word-square would probably only become relevant for the *next* pandemic...

Finding Lost Books.

Whilst editing this very book, it occurred to me : in order to track down the references that had so far defied my attempts to find them, could I not use my Abramelin magick itself to help me ? I therefore attempted another magical working during the summer (hence the reason I got up so early, i.e., to be ready in time for sunrise).

"Up at 3.42am : ritual shower, then Middle Pillar ritual, after first having focussed on Nepheshi. It occurs to me that Abramelin square 2 of book IV, chapter 11, is all about obtaining lost Magical books. Perhaps this could be used to track down the reference which I have been seeking ?"

L	A	C	H	A	L
A	R	A	I	B	A
C	A	L	A	I	H
H	I	A	L	A	C
A	B	I	A	R	A
L	A	H	C	A	L

Figure 16 Square 2 of Book IV, chapter 11 : "To obtain lost magical books."

"Consequently, for my morning ritual, I perform it in the usual manner, but this time make the conjuration about conjuring Magoth in particular."

I.e., all of the squares of chapter 11, which are about obtaining lost books generally, are given by the Holy Guardian Angel and are under the presidency of Prince Magoth.

"*Incidentally, I try to incorporate my ideas of Samyama into my performance of the LBRP, LBRH, and Bornless ritual : it turns out to be very powerful indeed, as if I can feel all the divine and angelic forces which I have invoked.*

"*I perceive that both* M... [my Holy Guardian Angel] *and Magoth manifest and consent to work with me. Accompanied by them, I project into the square itself : I sense that I am in a library of old books. The librarian is a spirit who claims to be HYRYS (one of the servants of Magoth) who tests well when I vibrate 'M...' and 'Magoth.' Hyrys agrees to help me find the book in question - I tell him to get to work immediately. I also get him to agree to help me find magical books in general in the future.*

"*There is a great sense of power as I perform this ritual, as if I really am in the presence of Magoth and Hyrys.*

"*Afterwards I thank Hyrys and take my leave. Additional prayer, licence to depart, LBRP and LBRH. The total time taken was just over one hour. Feeling full of energy, I return to bed for several hours' worth of Zzz, during which I have some vivid dreams, including imagining Hyrys as a female figure going about searching for the book in question.*

"*When I wake up, I go round the house and manage to find all the books it could have been, including some which my fiancée had left down the sides of some chairs and had forgotten about. I did manage to get material which was closer to what I had remembered but still not exactly as I thought I recalled it. I assume that Hyrys did as best as she could in the circumstances.*"

Conclusion

At time of writing, I have spent just over a year editing this memoir for publication: consequently, I shall have to revisit in the future how completing the Operation ultimately affects me. However, if I were to draw some preliminary conclusions from the preceding twelve months, I would say that making use of the word-squares for the purposes of Thaumaturgy comes a distant third in the list of things for which I use Knowledge and Conversation of the Holy Guardian Angel.

Instead, on a day-to-day basis, I prefer calling upon my Familiar Spirits. I use this as a way of performing miscellaneous magical tasks which I consider important at a particular time, but which do not merit going through the rigmarole of finding or researching a magic square or performing a full-scale evocation.

I first became aware of the possibilities of working with my Familiar Spirits when I tried to do some black magick – helping my fiancée to get a refund on something which she was afraid she wouldn't get. At first, the idea of working a sigil in a Chaos Magick style tempted me, but then I thought: instead of attempting to "raise gnosis," why don't I just address a petition to the Familiar Spirit who presided over this part of the day? I took a moment to concentrate, mentally calling upon the Spirit, and imagining that I gave it the sigil I had already drawn up. I thanked the Spirit and sent it on its mission. Then, confidently walking out to the place which issued refunds, we just asked and got it no bother.

A sceptic might naysay this, but I have experienced dozens of instances which would seem trivial to anyone else but have been enough to convince me. I have therefore begun to develop a theory, that attaining Knowledge & Conversation of the Holy Guardian Angel and completing the Abramelin Operation constitutes *an alternative to Chaos Magick.* I.e., that instead of having to expend effort to "raise gnosis" every time one wants to execute a Sigil, for the cost of six months out of one's life spent in intense magical activity one can acquire the facility to manifest results through the aid of the Familiar Spirits.

But by far the most use I make of my experience comes through regularly communing with my Holy Guardian Angel. One hears the platitude of ideally being led by one's angel: but I rationalise that I can do this best by dedicating time to specifically opening myself up to its guidance. The alternative would be that if one did not force oneself to spend time with one's angel, one might run the risk of spending *no* time at all. Hence, I interpret the instruction in The Book to spend "the Sabbath" (actually in my case, Sunday) with my HGA as the opportunity to guarantee I will always have time in the week to work on maintaining consciousness of my Angel, when neither the cares of the mundane world, nor other magick, distracts me. Such a practice has the long-term aim, of course, of using repetition to turn such consciousness into a habit.

In my case my Sunday devotions mainly consist of recreating the kind of ritual I did every day during the course of the Operation. So I would get up an hour before dawn for a ritual shower, and preparation with the Middle Pillar ritual. Then I would perform the Lesser banishing rituals of the Pentagram and Hexagram ; the Bornless Ritual ; and the conjuration. I have added lines to the form into which it evolved during the last third of the operation, to give my especial thanks to my Familiar Spirits, and to remind the spirits generally of their continued allegiance to the Oaths which they have sworn upon my magic wand.

Then : a period of meditation, followed by the additional prayer from the same last third ; followed by the licence to depart, and the pentagram and hexagram rituals.

These sessions have the main advantage of inspiring me to develop my personal practice generally. I go into them with a blank mind : but I come out of them bursting with ideas of where to go with my magical career : most proximately, what I should do over the next seven days or so. "Alex, you should do this and that," "Alex, you should meditate on such and such," etc. Often, I receive intuitions as to what I ought to do as my next major magical project. At other times, I may only receive something small by way of practical advice, like altering one detail about how I vibrate a divine name – and yet it makes a big difference, nonetheless. Advice on refining the details of my daily magical exercises comes in small packages, but each brick gradually builds up a larger edifice.

On at least one occasion, communing with my HGA became a sort of Divination, a substitute for Tarot or astrology or the like : i.e., my HGA helped clarify my thinking on a spell I had planned, telling me the advantages and disadvantages of the idea, and what I should do to improve its chances of success. I believe that this indicates the true nature of Knowledge & Conversation of the Holy Guardian Angel, that the insights one receives have a far *better* quality than what one could gain through more common forms of divination, and in fact ultimately supersede them. Instead of reading the language of Nature, one can access the Thought behind that language.

But mostly though, the experience of having conscious awareness of the Holy Guardian Angel *is* the point of having Knowledge & Conversation thereof. It has a naturally healing and restorative effect, and I'm sure it does a lot of good for me at an unconscious level. However : in the moment of actually communing with the Angel, I put this out of mind and concentrate purely on the act of communion itself. On *being*, indeed.

Knowledge and Conversation is only a beginning : after all, when Jacob wrestled with *his* Angel, that merely marked start of his life as "Israel." However, for the purpose of attainment – "pure Will delivered of the lust of result" – it nevertheless constitutes in itself an end.

Bibliography

Abramelin Manuscripts :[262]

The Leipzig Manuscript

"Cabala mystica Aegyptiorum et Patriarcharum, das ist das Buch der wahren alten und göttlichen Magia geschrieben von Abraham den Sohn Simonis an seinen jüngern Sohn Lamech - Cod.mag.15," https ://histbest.ub.uni-leipzig.de/receive/UBLHistBestCBU_cbu_00000038 accessed 2021-03-03

The Dresden Manuscript

"Magia Abraham oder Underricht von der Heiligen Cabala - Mscr.Dresd.N.111," https ://digital.slub-dresden.de/werkansicht/dlf/65720/1/ *et seq.* accessed 2021-03-03

The Bibliothèque de l'Arsenal Manuscript

Ms-2351. « La sacrée magie que Dieu donna à Moyse Aaron, David, Salomon, et à d'autres saints patriarches et prophètes, qui enseigne la vraie sapience divine, laissée par Abraham à Lamech son fils, traduite de l'hébreu. 1458 » https ://gallica.bnf.fr/ark :/12148/btv1b52508378q accessed 2021-03-03

The Hammer Edition

VON WORMS, A (1725) *"Die egyptischen großen Offenbarungen, in sich begreifend die aufgefundenen Geheimnißbücher Mosis..."* Peter Hammer, Cologne, https ://www.digi-hub.de/viewer/image/BV045865348/7/ *et seq.* accessed 2021-03-03

Other

AGRIPPA, H C, "J F" (translator) (1651) *"Three Books of Occult Philosophy : Book one – natural magic,"* http://esotericarchives.com/agrippa/op1.htm accessed 2021-04-21

AMBELAIN, R (1951) *"La Kabbale Pratique,"* https ://archive.org/details/la-kabbale-pratique-robert-ambelain/page/n1/mode/2up accessed 2021-06-01/

---

[262] Other Abramelin manuscripts do exist, but during my Abramelin Operation and the subsequent typing of this book, I was only able to consult those that have been digitised and put online.

BARDON, F, Radspieler, A (translator) (1971) *"Initiation into Hermetics : A Course of Instruction of Magic Theory & Practice,"* Dieter Ruggeberg, Wuppertal, West Germany.

BARTLETT, R A, Cotnoir, B (preface), Hauck, D W (foreword) (2009) *"Real Alchemy – a primer of practical alchemy,"* 3rd edition, Ibis Press, Lake Worth, FL, USA.

BENNETT, A, CROWLEY, A, Rons, I (editor) (2003*) "Sepher Sephiroth (Revised),"* https ://www.magicgatebg.com/Books/liber_d.pdf accessed 2021-05-06.

BENTINE, M (1991) *"Open Your Mind,"* Corgi, London, UK.

BETZ, H D (editor), (1992), *"The Greek Magical Papyri in translation, including the Demotic Spells,"* 2nd ed., The University of Chicago Press, Chicago (USA) & London (UK).

BLOOM, W (1976, 1992) *"The Sacred Magician, a ceremonial diary,"* Gothic Image Publications, Glastonbury, UK.

BRAND, D (2014*) "Magickal Cashbook : Attract Money Fast with Ancient Secrets And Modern Wealth Magick,"* The Gallery of Magick.

- (2016) *"The 72 Angels of Magick : Instant Access to the Angels of Power,"* The Gallery of Magick.

CAMPBELL, J, MOYERS, W (1988) *"The Power of Myth,"* Doubleday, New York NY, USA.

CASE, P F (2006) *"Esoteric Keys of Alchemy,"* Ishtar Publishing, Burnaby, BC, Canada.

- (2008) *"Occult Fundamentals and Spiritual Unfoldment, volume 1 : the early writings,"* Fraternity of the Hidden Light.

CICERO, C (ed.), CICERO, S T (ed.) (1995) *"The Golden Dawn Journal, book II – Qabalah : Theory and Magic,"* Llewellyn Publications, St Paul, Minnesota, USA

- (2000) *"Ritual Use of Magical Tools,"* Llewellyn Publications, St Paul, Minnesota, USA

- (2012) *"The Golden Dawn Magical Tarot,"* Llewellyn Publications, St Paul, Minnesota, USA

- (2019) *"Golden Dawn Magic : A Complete Guide to the High Magical Arts,"* Llewellyn Publications, St Paul, Minnesota, USA.

CLELLAND, S, Wages, J, Adams, S (illustrator) (2021) *"The Green Book of the Elus Coëns,"* Lewis Masonic, Shepperton, UK

CROWLEY, A, *et al.,*(1909 – 1913) *"The Equinox,"* volume I, http ://the-equinox.org/vol1/index.html accessed 2021-12-19

CROWLEY, A, 1909, *"777,"* published in "The Qabalah of Aleister Crowley," 1973, Weiser, New York, USA.

- Symonds, J (ed.), Grant, K (ed.) (1929) *"The Spirit of Solitude, An Autohagiography, Subsequently Re-Antichristened The Confessions Of Aleister Crowley,"* Penguin, London, UK.

- (writing as the Master Therion) (1929) *"Magick in Theory And Practice : Part III of Book Four,"* Castle Books, New York, USA.

- (1954) *"Magick Without Tears,"* Ordo Templi Orientis, New York NY, USA.

DE MONTFAUCON DE VILLARS, N (1913) *"Comte De Gabalis,"* The Brothers, London, UK.

DUKES, R (2018) *"The Abramelin Diaries : The Nice Man Cometh,"* Aeon Books, London, UK.

DUQUETTE, L M (1997) *"Angels, Demons & Gods of the New Millennium,"* Weiser, York Beach, Maine, USA.

- (1999) *"My Life with The Spirits,"* Weiser, York Beach, Maine, USA.

- (2019) *"Enochian Vision Magick, a practical guide to the Magick of Dr. John Dee and Edward Kelley,"* Weiser Books, Newburyport, MA, USA.

ECHOLS, D (2018) *"High Magick : A Guide to the Spiritual Practices That Saved My Life on Death Row,"* Sounds True, Boulder, Colorado, USA.

- (2020) *"Angels & Archangels, a magician's guide,"* Sounds True, Boulder, Colorado, USA.

FIELD, S (1979) *"Screenplay : The foundations of screenwriting,"* Dell Publishing Company, New York, USA.

FORTUNE, D (1930) *"Psychic Self-Defence : A Study in Occult Pathology and Criminality,"* The Aquarian Press, Wellingborough, UK.

- (1935) *"The Mystical Qabalah,"* The Aquarian Press, London, UK.

- (2006) *"Principles of Esoteric Healing,"* Thoth Publications, Leicester, UK.

GODDARD, D (1996) *"The Sacred Magic of the Angels,"* 1st ed., Weiser, York Beach, Maine, USA.

- (2019) *"The Sacred Magic of the Angels,"* Revised & expanded edition, Rising Phoenix Foundation, London, UK.

GODWIN, D (1992) *"Light in Extension : Greek Magic from Homer to Modern Times (Llewellyn's Western Magick Historical Series),"* Llewellyn Publications, St Paul, Minnesota, USA

GREENFIELD, A H (2014) *"The Compleat Rite of Memphis – 21st Century Edition,"* Free Illuminist Press.

GREER, J M, (1997) *"Circles of Power : Ritual Magic in the Western Tradition,"* Llewellyn, Minnesota, USA.

IAMBLICHUS, Wilder, A (translator), (1911) *"Theurgia or The Egyptian Mysteries,"* http ://www.esotericarchives.com/oracle/iambl_th.htm accessed 2021-12-16.

IYENGAR, B K S (1977) "Light on Yoga," HarperCollins, London, UK.

- (1996) *"Light on the Yoga Sutras of Patanjali,"* Thorsons, London, UK.

JACKSON, K B (2012*) "Beyond the Craft,"* 6th ed., Lewis Masonic, Shepperton, UK.

JUNG, C G, Hull, R F C (translator) (1967) *"Alchemical Studies,"* the Collected Works of C G Jung volume 13, Princeton University Press, Princeton, NJ, USA.

KAPLAN, A (1997) *"Sepher Yetzirah : the book of creation in theory and practice,"* 2nd revised edition, Weiser, York Beach, Maine, USA.

KATZ, M, Duquette, L M (Introduction) (2011) *"After the Angel,"* Forge Press.

KATZ, M (2020) *"Book Six : The Magick of Abramelin the Mage,"* Llewellyn's Complete Book of Ceremonial Magick, Llewellyn Publications, Woodbury MN, USA.

KRAIG, D M (1996) *"Modern Magick – Eleven lessons in the High Magickal Arts,"* 2nd ed., Llewelyn Publications, St Paul, Minnesota, USA.

KRIYANANDA, GOSWAMI (1992) *"The Spiritual Science of Kriya Yoga,"* 4th ed., The Temple of Kriya Yoga, Chicago IL, USA.

LABERGE, S, RHEINGOLD, H (1990) *"Exploring the world of Lucid Dreaming,"* Ballantine, New York NY, USA.

LEITCH, A (2012) *"Abramelin – Be Afraid !?"* https ://aaronleitch.wordpress.com/2012/07/17/abramelin-be-afraid/ accessed 2021-01-25

- (2020) *"How to derail every conversation about Abramelin,"* https ://aaronleitch.wordpress.com/2020/09/26/how-to-derail-every-conversation-about-abramelin/ accessed 2021-02-11

LENAIN, L, Vaughan, P A (translator) (2020) *"The Science of the Kabbalah,"* Rose Circle Publications, Bayonne NJ, USA.

LEVI, E, Waite, A E (translator) (1896) *"Transcendental Magic – Its Doctrine and Ritual,"* Rider & Co., London, UK.

MATHERS, S L M (translator) (1900) *"The Book of the Sacred Magic of Abramelin the Mage,"* Watkins, London, UK.

MATHERS, S L M (translator), Crowley, A (editor) (1995) *"The Goetia – The Lesser Key of Solomon the King – Clavicula Salomonis Regis,"* 2nd edition, Samuel Weiser, York Beach, Maine, USA.

MAIER, M (1617) *"Atalanta Fugiens,"* https ://www.alchemywebsite.com/atalanta.html accessed 2021-10-13.

MAITLAND, E (1896) *"Anna Kingsford, her life, letters, diary and work,"* Volume one, 2nd edition, George Redway, London, UK.

MEAD, G R S (1906) *"Thrice-Greatest Hermes : Studies in Hellenistic Theosophy and Gnosis,"* Volume 2 – Sermons, The Theosophical Publishing Company, London (UK) and Benares (India).

- (1919) *"The Doctrine of the Subtle Body in Western Tradition,"* J M Watkins, London, UK.

NEWCOMB, J A (2002) *"21st Century Mage : Bring the Divine Down to Earth,"* Weiser, York Beach, Maine, USA.

NIMIS, E (2018) *"Kriya Yoga : synthesis of a personal experience,"* http ://www.kriyayogainfo.net/Eng_Downloads1.html accessed 2021-05-13.

"OPHIEL" (PEACH, E C) (1974) *"The Art and Practice of Astral Projection,"* Weiser, York Beach, Maine, USA.

PLOTINUS, Porphyry (introduction), MacKenna, S (translator), Page, B S (translator) (250AD / translated into English 1930) *"Plotinus : The Enneads,"* https ://www.sacred-texts.com/cla/plotenn/enn000.htm accessed 2021-02-02

POLYCHRONIS, D G (2008) *"An Anthology of Theurgic Operations of the Rose + Croix of the Orient,"* 2nd edition, Athens, Greece.

RANDOLPH, P B, North, R (translator, editor) (1988) *"Sexual Magic,"* Magickal Childe Publishing, Inc., New York NY, USA.

RANKINE, D (2009) *"The Book of Treasure Spirits,"* Avalonia, Glastonbury, UK.

REGARDIE, I (1989) *"The Golden Dawn,"* 6th edition, Llewelyn Publications, St Paul, Minnesota, USA

- (2001) *"The Tree of Life : an illustrated study of magic,"* 3rd edition, Llewelyn Publications, St Paul, Minnesota, USA

- Cicero, C (editor), Cicero, S T (editor) (2002) *"A Garden of Pomegranates – Skrying on the Tree of Life,"* 3rd edition, Llewelyn Publications, St Paul, Minnesota, USA.

SAVIN, O (translator) (2001) *"The Way of a Pilgrim and The Pilgrim Continues His Way,"* Shambhala, Boston & London.

SADHU, M (1965) *"Theurgy, the art of effective worship,"* George Allen & Unwin Ltd, London, UK.

STEINBRECHER, E (1988) *"The Inner Guide Meditation : A spiritual technology for the 21st Century,"* 5th edition, Weiser, York Beach, Maine, USA.

SUMNER, A (2003) *"EHNB,"* https ://solascendans.com/articles/ehnb/ accessed 2021-09-15

- (2004) *"The Bornless Ritual,"* Journal of the Western Mystery Tradition, vol 1 no. 7, http ://www.jwmt.org/v1n7/bornless.html accessed 2021-02-25

- (2009) *"The Magus,"* Bihutys Books, London, UK.

- (2012) *"Reincarnation : A Hermetic approach,"*
https ://solascendans.com/2012/04/07/reincarnation-a-hermetic-approach/
accessed 2021-01-27

- (2013) *"Taromancer,"* Bihutys Books, London, UK.

- (2019) *"Skrying in Theory and Practice,"* The Light Extended, a journal of
the Golden Dawn, volume one, Kerubim Press, Dublin, Ireland, pp210-217.

- (2020) *"Abramelin Musings : Square Dancing,"*
https ://solascendans.com/2020/06/04/abramelin-musings-square-dancing/
accessed 2021-01-25

SYMONDS, J (1951) *"The Great Beast : The Life of Aleister Crowley,"* Rider
& Co., London, UK.

"THREE INITIATES," (1908) *"The Kybalion,"* Yogi Publication Society,
Chicago, Illinois, USA.

VON ECKARTSHAUSEN, K, de Steiger, I (translator) (1909) *"The Cloud Upon
the Sanctuary,"* William Rider & Son Ltd, London, UK.

VON ECKARTSHAUSEN, K, Hanswille, G (translator), Brumlich, D (translator)
(1989) *"Magic: the Principles of Higher Knowledge,"* Merkur Publishing
Company Limited, Wisdom of the Occident, Canada.

VON WORMS, A, Dehn, G (editor), Guth, S (translator) (2006) *"The Book of
Abramelin,"* Ibis Press, Lake Worth FL, USA.

WAITE, A E (1911, 2006) *"The Book of Black Magic and Ceremonial
Magic,"* The Book Tree, San Diego, CA, USA.

WESTCOTT, W W (translator) (1887) *"Sepher Yetzirah,"* 3rd edition,
https ://hermeticgoldendawn.org/sepher-yetzirah/ accessed 2021-09-08

WILBER, K (2000) *"One Taste : Daily Reflections on Integral Spirituality,"*
Shambhala, Boulder CO, USA.

WILSON, C (1987) *"Aleister Crowley, The Nature of the Beast,"* The
Aquarian Press, Wellingborough, UK.

YOGANANDA, PARAMHANSA (1946) *"Autobiography of a Yogi,"*
https ://www.ananda.org/autobiography/ accessed 2021-05-13

About the Author

Alex Sumner (born 1972) is a novelist and writer on the occult. He has written non-fiction articles for *"The Journal of the Western Mystery Tradition,"* *"The Hermetic Tablet"* and *"The Light Extended."* He has also written six occult fiction novels, beginning with *The Magus* in 2009. He is also a ceremonial magician, astrologer and tarot reader. He lives with his fiancée in Essex, England.

To contact the author:

Sol Ascendans – the website of Alex Sumner

www.solascendans.com

Alex Sumner on Facebook

www.facebook.com/alexsumnerauthor

Alex Sumner on Twitter

www.twitter.com/alexsumner

Other books by Alex Sumner

"The Magus Trilogy"

The Magus
Opus Secunda
License to Depart
(Republished in an omnibus volume, "The Magus Trilogy," 2021).

Other novels

Taromancer
A Fairy Story by Any Other Name
Eternal Witch.

Other Titles from Thoth Publications

THE GOLDEN DAWN COMPANION
By R.A. Gilbert

The Hermetic Order of the Golden Dawn epitomized the paradox of an intellectual elite who rejected orthodox religion and yet remained within the social establishment of its day. The colourful story of these would-be magicians is well known to students of nineteenth-century social history, but the private archives on which the definitive history of the Order (Ellic Howe's *The Magicians of the Golden Dawn*) was based have only recently become accessible for study by scholars.

In this new edition of *The Golden Dawn Companion* the texts of both official and unofficial documents are made available for all. Here are the full texts of the Order's Constitution, Rules and Regulations, the Obligations of candidates for both the Outer and Inner Orders, the 'General Orders' of the R.R. er A.C., and the complete membership Lists from the official Address Book, the Order Rolls and other lists compiled within the various branches of the Order up to 1914. There are also detailed descriptions of the Temples, the Grade rituals, and the manuscript collections that comprise the archives.

In addition, the original texts of the various theories of origin of the Golden Dawn are brought together, and there is a comprehensive, updated and annotated bibliography of printed material relating to the Order.

ISBN Soft cover: 978 1870450591

ISBN Hardcover: 978 1913660123

SECRETS OF A GOLDEN DAWN TEMPLE
By Chic Cicero and Sandra Tabatha Cicero

The act of constructing a wand or other ritual object is an act of magic. The magician spends an extraordinary amount of time creating ritual objects, not because it is only through these objects that magic can rightly be performed but because the act of creating is a magical process of growth, one which initiates the development of the will in accordance with the divine intent or purpose. This in turn contributes to the success of the ritual.

The construction of a ritual object should be treated like any other magical operation. It should focus all parts of the magician's mind (intellect, creativity, imagination, spiritual self) onto one purpose – to manifest an object which will be a receptacle for higher forces, in order that the magician too can become a worthy receptacle of that which is divine.

With this book, clear instructions are finally available on how to fabricate the wands and implements of the Golden Dawn, some of the most significant, profound and beautiful of all the ritual tools that have ever been produced in the Western Magical Tradition. The various tools presented here each have a very specific symbology attached to them. With the materials and tools available to the modern magician, these instruments can be recreated with stunning accuracy and magnificence.

"Here is a superb do-it-yourself book that tells you every step to take in the construction of any GD wand, implement, or temple furnishing, complete with rituals. Constructing such implements from scratch is a spiritual path of its own." David Godwin, author of *Godwin's Cabalistic Encyclopedia.*

Soft cover ISBN: 978-1870450645
Hardcover ISBN: 978-1913660055

AN INTRODUCTION TO RITUAL MAGIC
By Dion Fortune & Gareth Knight

Teachings on the theory and practice of ritual or ceremonial magic.

This is something of a unique event in esoteric publishing - a new book by the legendary occultist Dion Fortune. Well there are to be several, of which this is the first. Especially with its teachings on the theory and practice of ritual or ceremonial magic, by one who, like the heroine of two of her novels, was undoubtedly "a Mistress of that Art". In a work that has hitherto appeared only in fragmented form in rare journal articles, she deals in successive chapters with types of mind working; mind training; the use of ritual; psychic perception; ritual initiation; the reality of the subtle planes; focusing the magic mirror; channelling the forces; the form of the ceremony and the purpose of magic - with appendices on talisman magic and astral forms. Each chapter is supplemented and expanded by a companion chapter on the same subject by Gareth Knight. In Dion Fortune's day the conventions of occult secrecy prevented her from being too explicit on the practical details of magic, except in works of fiction. These veils of secrecy having now been rolled back, Gareth Knight has taken the opportunity to fill in much practical information that Dion Fortune might well have included had she been writing today. In short, in this unique collaboration of two magical practitioners and teachers we are presented with a valuable and up-to-date text on the practice of ritual or ceremonial magic "as it is". That is to say, as a practical, spiritual and psychic discipline, far removed from the lurid superstition and speculation that are the hallmark of its treatment in sensational journalism and channels of popular entertainment.

Soft Cover ISBN: 978-1870450263
Hardcover ISBN: 978-1870450317

DION FORTUNE & THE INNER LIGHT
By Gareth Knight

Dion Fortune & the Inner Light is enthusiastically recommended to anyone interested in the western esoteric tradition and in the colourful individuals who contributed to it over the last 100 years. Dion Fortune played a significant role in modern esotericism, and we are indebted to Gareth Knight for this intriguing biography. Knight was inducted into the Fraternity in 1953, seven years after Fortune's death. Despite the fact that they never met, he is often regarded as her protégé. His *Guide to Practical Qabalistic Symbolism* (1965) formed a continuation of *The Mystical Qabalah*. In 1998 he returned to the Fraternity, after many years, to edit and republish several of her other books and to conduct research in its archives.

'The biography is an important product of that research. *Dion Fortune & the Inner Light* is enthusiastically recommended to anyone interested in the western esoteric tradition and in the colourful individuals who contributed to it over the last 100 years.' John Nash, *Esoteric Quarterly Review* 2009

Soft Cover ISBN: 978-1870450454
Hardback ISBN: 978-1913660109

EXLORING ENOCHIAN WORLDS
By Robin E.Cousins

This is the Angel Nalvage describing the Thirty Æthyrs surrounding the Four
Watchtowers of the terrestrial world of the four elements to John Dee and
Edward Kelley during the reception of the Enochian system of Angel Magic
in 1584. There is no record of Dee or Kelley exploring these angelic worlds –
a journey which can offer a path to spiritual enlightenment. Over 300 years
later, Aleister Crowley was the first. He recorded his scrying of the Thirty
Æthyrs in *The Vision and the Voice* (1911). Other Thelemic practitioners
such as Lon Milo Duquette and David Shoemaker have subsequently
published their experiences.

Now join Robin E. Cousins and friends scrying through the Watchtowers
and the Æthyrs in both solo and group workings and read their visionary
revelations. They preferred to employ the original system of Dee and Kelley
rather than the over-elaborate revision devised by the Hermetic Order of
the Golden Dawn (Neo-Enochiana) and favoured by Crowley and his
followers.

To obtain ones's Enochian bearings an overview of the Angelic Universe is
provided detailing the Watchtowers and the Æthyrs, plus the rituals,
invocations and calls required to cross the threshold into these magical and
mysterious realms.

Included are many diagrams, original and historic photographs, a detailed
itinerary of Crowley's Algerian odyssey through the Æthyrs, and an
exposition of the differences between the original and the Golden Dawn
Enochian systems (Aleister Crowley and Enochian Magic).

Soft cover ISBN: 9781870450911
Hardback ISBN: 9781913660215

WESTERN MYSTERY TRADITION

By Christine Hartley

A re-issue of a classic work by a formidable priestess, pupil of Dion Fortune and working partner of Charles Seymour, F.P.D., *The Forgotten Mage*. Working at a time when many were turning to Eastern spirituality, Christine Hartley believed that Britain had its own mystery tradition, hidden in myth and legend and in the land itself. She had known Merlin on the inner planes, journeying with him to the Celtic Underworld and she was more than happy to show us the entrance to this realm. Drawing on folk lore and song, the legacy of Druidic culture is brought alive, providing practical guidelines for modern students of the ancient mysteries. *Western Mystery Tradition* is the basis of the Western religious feeling, the foundation of our spiritual life, the matrix of religious formulae, whether we are aware of it or not. To it we owe the inspiration and force of our spiritual life. Very much reflecting the current return to paganism in our search for the spiritual, Christine Hartley reminds us that 'The corn is still green and the ears are ripening for the harvest.'

ISBN: 9781870450249

PRACTICAL ATLANTEAN MAGIC

By Murry Hope

This book will take you on a journey through the mystical, psychological and psychic evidence of the existence of Atlantis and all that it has stood for within the Collective Consciousness of human culture through the ages. Subjects covered include: the Atlantean basis of Western magic, the peoples and the priesthood of Atlantis, Stellar and Solar magic, lessons, exercises, prayers and rites.

ISBN: 9781870450577

Printed in the USA
CPSIA information can be obtained
at www.ICGtesting.com
LVHW090949151023
761044LV00009B/12